Middle English Debate Poetry

MIDDLE ENGLISH DEBATE POETRY

A Critical Anthology

Edited by

John W. Conlee

EAST LANSING
COLLEAGUES PRESS
1991

ISBN 0-937191-18-3
ISBN 0-937191-23-X paper
Library of Congress Catalog Card Number 90-86173
British Library Cataloguing in Publication Data available
Copyright © 1991 John W. Conlee

Published by Colleagues Press Inc.
Post Office Box 4007
East Lansing, MI 48826

Distribution outside North America
Boydell and Brewer Ltd.
Post Office Box 9
Woodbridge, Suffolk IP12 3DF
England

Contents

Acknowledgments

This volume has benefitted from the suggestions and assistance of many people. Special gratitude is owed to Derek Pearsall, Karen Stern, and the late Elizabeth Salter for their generous and invaluable help in the volume's earlier stages of preparation. Many of their suggestions have been incorporated in the headnotes and in the critical commentary on the texts. A great many individuals have contributed to the preparation of the glossary; special thanks are due to Ellen Arnold, Jill Cowan, Nancy McCleskey, Laura McCord, Jennie McMillion, and John Wing. For helping me come to terms, finally, with personal computers and the mysteries of word-processing, I am much indebted to Bonnie Chandler, David Morrill, and Cristen Kimball, who patiently tutored me and frequently (but not always) rescued me from disaster. I am also grateful to Roy Underhill, the woodwright at the Colonial Williamsburg foundation, for sharing with me his knowledge of early tools, which enhanced the annotations for the *Debate of the Carpenter's Tools*. Finally, I wish to express my gratitude to John Alford of Colleagues Press for his expertise and his patience.

This volume has also benefitted from the generous support and kind assistance of a large number of institutions. I am grateful to the Committee on Faculty Research of the College of William and Mary, which has supported the work on this volume by means of summer research stipends and a semester research assignment. I am also extremely grateful to The British Library, The National Library of Wales, The National Library of Scotland, The Bodleian Library, The Cambridge University Library, and The College of Arms for their kind permission to publish these texts.

Preface

This anthology of Middle English debate poetry was originally designed for the Second Series of the York Medieval Texts, a series recently discontinued. It reflects the principles developed for that series by its general editors: the presentation of major works or major fields of writing as a whole, to allow scholars and students specializing in medieval literature the opportunity to experience a major work or a major literary genre in its entirety, an experience "which is necessary for the fullest understanding of a literary period and its writings." Thus the poems collected in this volume have been chosen to reflect the considerable variety of debate poems produced by Middle English writers. These poems have been selected as much for their representative qualities as for their literary qualities, and it will be apparent that they differ significantly in a great many respects, not the least of which is artistic merit.

Many of the most highly regarded debate poems from Middle English literature *have* been included here—the best of the Body and Soul debates, all three of the Middle English alliterative debates, most of the poems in the sequence of Middle English bird debates. Yet a few very notable poems are absent. The great comic debate poems the *Owl and the Nightingale* and William Dunbar's *Tretis of the Twa Mariit Wemen and the Wedo*, for example, have been excluded for reasons of economy of space (the *Owl and the Nightingale* would have required a short volume all to itself), and because reliable modern editions of these poems are fairly readily available. Chaucer's *Parliament of Fowls* has been excluded for similar reasons. The omission of these few well-known (and lengthy) poems makes it possible to include a number of works that are not so well-known or that are not so easy to obtain.

Of particular importance to the matter of text selection for this volume is the fundamental concept of "debate poem." As is true for most of the major genres of medieval literature, the defining characteristics of the debate poem are not at all precise. Let it suffice to say here that only works written in verse which are verbal contentions between relatively evenly matched opponents have been included. Certainly there are other varieties of dialogues with clear affinities to the debate genre — the dialogues between Christ and Mary, Christ and the Cross, and Christ and Man, for example — which might have been represented. The particular Middle English debate poems which have been included fall naturally into certain categories: poems relating to the body and soul tradition; poems in the bird-debate tradition; alliterative debates; and lovers' dialogues. The one essentially miscellaneous category is the one labeled "didactic and satiric debates," but even within this category several of the poems form certain logical associations or groupings. The overall intention has been to achieve a balanced selection of poems, balanced in regard to representativeness, literary importance, and our familiarity or lack of familiarity with them.

The *Introduction* is intended to provide broad historical and literary contexts for the study of these poems. The headnotes and explanatory notes are intended to supply the reader with factual and descriptive information of a kind pertinent to the individual poems. No attempt is made to provide full bibliographical references to scholarly and critical studies of these poems, although occasional references are made in the notes and in the headnotes to studies that relate to specific questions of interpretation. The *Glossary* is designed only as an aid to the reading of the texts of these particular poems and not as a philological or lexicographical tool.

Introduction

Dichotomies have always appealed to the human mind. A polar opposition can order the widest possible spectrum of otherwise chaotic phenomena. To have the idea of freedom versus necessity is to have a handle for organizing *all* behavior. Up versus down takes care of almost everything. Aristotle made generation from contraries the cornerstone of his philosophy, and he was following a tradition from the preSocratics. A preoccupation with the interaction of opposites characterizes the basic thinking of many cultures. . . .

(Peter Elbow, *Oppositions in Chaucer*, 14–5)

A preoccupation with the interaction of opposites is perhaps nowhere more evident than during the Middle Ages, when it became a fundamental habit of mind. A concern with dualities, polarities, and dichotomies is reflected in nearly every variety of writing by writers who perceived that virtually any thing, concrete or conceptual, animate or inanimate, could be seen to have a natural or logical counterpart which it often rivaled but also complemented. A great many of these complementary pairs sprang readily from divisions suggested by the "Book of Scriptures"—the Old and New Testaments, the Old Dispensation and the New Dispensation, *Ecclesia* and *Synagoge, caritas* and *cupiditas*, the vices and virtues, the sins of the spirit and the sins of the flesh, the body and the soul, redemption and damnation; equally as many were observable in the "Book of Nature"—night and day, spring and winter, sun and moon, sea and land, plant and animal, male and female, youth and old age. But although this medieval propensity for observing contrasts and dualities was reflected in most of the varie-

ties of writings produced during this era, it is in one particular genre—
medieval debate poetry—where this habit of mind became the generating
principle underlying the entire literary enterprise.

Medieval debate poetry, like most medieval literary genres, resists sim-
ple definition, and the various works which are traditionally assigned to
this genre are quite heterogeneous in form, style, tone, subject matter, and
authorial intentions. It is clear, nonetheless, that fundamental to all debate
poems is the depiction of a verbal confrontation between a pair of natural
opponents. Medieval debate poems invariably depict two (and occasional-
ly more than two) rather equally-matched disputants who engage each other
in an emotionally charged contest of words. The presence of strong emo-
tion—often stemming from the mutual antipathies of the participants—is
central to these poems, as is reflected by the Latin terms *conflictus, altercatio,
contentio,* and *disputatio,* which were common designations for them. It is ap-
propriate, therefore, to distinguish these debates from the larger body of
medieval dialogue literature to which they generally belong by viewing them
as "conflict-dialogues" or "contention-poems"—as examples of the *Streitgedicht,*
the poetic category posited by Hans Walther in his standard study of Latin
debate poetry, *Das Streitgedicht in der lateinischen Literatur des Mittelalters* (Munich,
1920). Thus, although these poems exhibit considerable variety and ingenuity
in regard to such matters as the creatures they depict in debate, the issues
disputed, the situations and circumstances used to generate the debates,
and the matter of any final resolution to the debate, all of them consist of
a series of verbal exchanges spoken by fairly evenly matched and natural
rivals, exchanges which reveal both the contrasting values and personali-
ties of the speakers and their fundamentally antagonistic natures.

It is also appropriate to observe that debate poetry, in contrast to many
of the literary genres which were popular during the Middle Ages, is primar-
ily a medieval literary phenomenon. It came into being during the Carolin-
gian Revival; it grew in popularity among the Latin writings of European
churchmen between the ninth and twelfth centuries; and it flourished sub-
sequently between 1200 and 1500 in most of the European vernacular liter-
atures. But as the Middle Ages waned, so did the popularity of this genre,
and only a few of the handful of debate poems written during the Renais-
sance possess any particular literary interest.

Debate poetry made its initial appearance in English literature around
the year 1200 in the *Owl and the Nightingale,* a debut which was followed later
in the thirteenth century by the earliest Middle English *Body and Soul* de-
bates and by the *Thrush and the Nightingale,* the first of the *Owl and the Nightin-*

gale's several successors in the Middle English bird-debate tradition. The debate poem enjoyed even greater popularity in England during the fourteenth century with the Middle English alliterative debates (*Winner and Waster, The Parliament of the Three Ages,* and *Death and Life*), several poems in the bird-debate and body-and-soul traditions, and a variety of didactic and satiric disputations. The fifteenth century witnessed the final stages in the bird-debate and body-and-soul traditions, as well as the writing of several debates in a more overtly comic vein, poems such as the Middle Scots *pastourelles* and William Dunbar's colorful *Tretis of the Twa Mariit Wemen and the Wedo.* But by the end of the fifteenth century the debate poem had more or less exhausted its potential as a distinctive literary genre.

Historical Antecedents

The debate poems that began to be written in English and the other European vernacular languages late in the twelfth or early in the thirteenth century reflect both social and literary influences. Social influences include the schools and universities, where exercises in disputation between young clerks or between student and master became customary, and the legal profession, where new stress was being placed on the artful conduct of litigious argument. Both scholastic and legal argumentation are parodied or alluded to in a number of Latin and vernacular debate poems. Two literary influences that may be singled out are the animal fable and the allegorical conflict of the vices and virtues (beginning with the *Psychomachia* of Prudentius). The earliest extant example of a debate poem, and the work usually identified as the probable point of origin of medieval debate poetry, is the late eighth-century poem *Conflictus Veris et Hiemis* (the *Contention of Spring and Winter*). Often attributed to Alcuin, the *Conflictus* is a pastoral poem in which two shepherds, young Daphnis and old Palemon, preside over a debate between the personified figures of Winter and Spring. At issue is whether the cuckoo, the bird whose song marks the arrival of spring, should be allowed to come. Winter, relishing the repose, good cheer, and warmth of his hearthside life, speaks against the cuckoo's arrival. Spring urges that the cuckoo be permitted to come and accuses Winter of being self-indulgent, slothful, and sterile. The shepherds find in favor of Spring, and the poem ends with the shepherds singing a song of invitation to the cuckoo.

Much in the same vein is the *Rosae Liliique Certamen* (the *Contest between the Lily and the Rose*) of Sedulius Scottus, possibly the second medieval debate poem, written around the middle of the ninth century. Here the verbal strife occurs between two rival spring-time flowers, each of whom boasts of her own flowerly attributes and attacks those of her competitor. When the debate becomes heated the personified figure of Spring intervenes, reminds the two that they are both sisters of the earth, and interjects a religious note by observing that both flowers possess sacred meanings — the rose symbolizing martyrdom, the lily virginity. These early debate poems seem to have established the initial pattern for the medieval debate poem: they are essentially light-hearted but also somewhat learned; their surrounding frames are minimal; the exchanges between the debaters are few, brief, and carefully balanced; the element of personal animus, while distinctly present, is somewhat muted; and they achieve a resolution.

It is clear that early Latin debate poems such as the *Conflictus Veris et Hiemis* and the *Rosae Liliique Certamen*, and others such as the lengthy *Conflictus Ovis et Lini* (the *Contention between the Sheep and the Flax Plant*), reveal their authors' familiarity with the pastoral eclogue of classical literature, an important general source for the medieval debate poem. Virgil's eclogues — in particular the third and seventh — and the eclogues of the later Roman poets Calpurnius Siculus and Nemesianus are likely precursors of the early Latin debate poems. Another literary model for the medieval debate poem may be found in Ovid's *Amores* (3.1). Here the poet, wandering in the woods and contemplating his literary future, encounters the personified figures of Elegy and Tragedy, who proceed to debate each other in an attempt to win the poet's favor. This inset piece, even more than any of the eclogues, possesses the general characteristics associated with the medieval debate poem. However, the individual poem from classical literature which most closely approximates the true medieval debate poem is the third-century *Iudicium Coci et Pistoris* (the *Contest of the Cook and the Baker*), by the otherwise unknown poet Vespa. This poem is also notable as a forerunner of the numerous medieval debates between members of rival professions, even though there is no real evidence that this poem was actually known by later writers.

Although Latin debate poems began rather simply and modestly, they underwent a substantial evolution as subsequent poets freely adapted materials according to their own purposes and imaginative impulses. Among the important earlier innovations was the introduction of a first-person narrator, who served as the auditor and reporter of the debate that he had overheard. This innovation, which was probably introduced during the eleventh century, was accompanied by a tendency to elaborate the framing materials used to surround the debate component of the poem. The result of these two developments was greater structural complexity and a more extensive narrative element. Yet another significant development among the later Latin poems was the introduction of the dream-vision. Used first in poems of serious didactic import such as the *Visio Fulberti*, an important Latin prototype for the vernacular Body and Soul debates, the dream-vision soon became the vehicle for goliardic whimsy in poems such as the *Goliae Dialogus in Aquam et Vinum* (*Golias' Debate between Water and Wine*). By the twelfth century it was common for Latin debate poems to have well-developed narrative contexts and for the actual debate exchanges to be unrestrained in several senses, including the matters they touched upon, which were sometimes comically risque. Thus there are wide divergences between many of the complex and ornate poems written later on in the Latin debate tradition and the simple, relatively sedate poems with which the genre had begun.

By the thirteenth century vernacular debates had begun to appear alongside the Latin disputations, and the Latin and vernacular poems of this period share a set of conventions which suggest that debate poetry had come to be accepted, however tacitly, as a discrete literary genre. For example, it appears that poets recognized that their debaters should be selected from objects belonging to the same general class or the same level of abstraction. In fact, the great majority of paired debaters were drawn from four large categories: 1) personified abstractions such as Justice and Mercy, Faith and Reason; 2) inanimate objects such as the Sun and Moon, Water and Wine; 3) living things such as the Violet and the Rose, the Chicken and the Pigeon; and 4) rival aspects or parts of a single entity such as the Body and the Soul, the Heart and the Eye. Some recent commentators have made a distinction between "horizonal" debates in which the disputants are of equal status and "vertical" debates in which they are not; vertical debates might involve men disputing with devils or with abstract beings such as Reason or Philosophy (see, for example, S. Gilman, *The Art of La Celestina* [Madison, 1956], p. 159). These so-called "vertical debates," however, as interesting as they are, do not reflect the conventions of the *Streitgedicht* and are not usually germane to a consideration of the true contention-poem. (But see the debate between *Jesus and the Masters*, printed in this collection.)

As medieval debate tradition developed, several topics came to enjoy widespread popularity. The *Conflictus Veris et Hiemis*, for example, was the first of several debates between personified seasons, and the *Certamen Rosae et Liliae* initiated a tradition of debates between rival flowers. Despite their popularity, however, neither of these topics is the primary concern in any of the debate poems recorded in Middle English. The *Altercatio Ecclesiae et Synagoge* was among the earliest poems to depict the conflict between Christianity and Judaism, a theme at least partially reflected also in the Latin debate between *A Christian, a Jew, and a Mohammedan*. This topic does occur among the Middle English debates, most notably in *A Disputation between a Christian and a Jew* and *Child Jesus and the Masters of the Laws of the Jews*. As mentioned already, the *Visio Fulberti* was one of the first debates to depict the schism between Body and Soul, and the *Goliae Dialogus in Aquam et Vinum*, along with the Latin debate *Denudata Veritate (Truth laid Bare)*, initiated a tradition of water and wine debates. Body and Soul debates appear throughout the European vernacular literatures, with some of the most dramatic poems of this kind occurring in English. The Wine and Water theme also appears in numerous variations, particularly in French literature, where disputes involving specific pairs of wines, wine parliaments (e.g. *La Desputoison du Vin et l'Iaue*), and wine and beer (*Altercatio Vini et Cervisiae*) are extant. The intent of these amusing debates, in most instances, was simply to celebrate the joys of wine-drinking. There are no Middle English debates devoted exclusively to this theme, though *Winner and Waster* probably reflects its influence.

Debate poems also depicted the strife between the Ages of Man, as in the Middle English *Parliament of the Three Ages* but particularly between Youth and Old Age. A great many debates took place between members of rival professions or occupations. *Mede and moche thank*, in which a courtier and a soldier confront each other, is an example of such a debate in Middle English. An early Latin poem which merges the youth-age rivalry with the rivalry between professions is the fragmentary ninth-century dialogue between *Terence and the Delusor*, in which a youthful Mime (the *delusor*) confronts an aged writer of tales — a poem which apparently ended with the older man fleeing from the threatened fisticuffs of the younger man. Another early and also fragmentary debate in this general category is the poem *De Navigo et Agricultura* (the *Sailor and the Farmer*). Later debate poems commonly treated the rivalry between clerks and farmers, as exemplified by the *Altercatio Rusticorum et Clericorum* and the Middle English *Dialogue between a Clerk and a Husbandman* (*Index* 344). Debates also frequently took place between members of rival religious orders or persuasions — a Cistercian and a Benedictine, an abbot and a prior, a priest and a logician.

The subject of love, in one fashion or another, became the concern of a great many debate poems. The Latin poem *Amor et Numor*, which presents the age-old conflict between "love" and "money," is an early example. Another Latin poem in this tradition is the *Iudicium Parisis*, based on the classical episode in which Juno, Minera, and Venus attempt to win Paris' approbation. Perhaps the most notorious poem in this vein is the *De Ganymede et Helena*, described by F. J. E. Raby as a "shameless contest" (*Secular Latin Poetry* 2:290); it compares the joys of loving women with the joys of loving boys, with Helen (and women) winning out. An entire sub-category of "love debates" depicted pairs of female disputants engaged in discussing their preferences in lovers, for example, the *Altercatio Phyllidis et Florae*, in which Phyllis extols the amorous virtues of her knightly lover, Flora the virtues of her clerkly lover. The arguments of this pair are clever, amusing, and colored by the poet's sense of irony and satire. Flora describes her cleric as rich, well-fed, and a polished courtier — all things he shouldn't be — and Phyllis further undercuts Flora's portrayal of him by noting that he frequently turns up at morning mass with a hang-over. Phyllis' knight, though poor, is said to be brave, handsome, and the author of inspired poetry. In order to get their dispute settled, the poet transports these ladies from the world of reality into a world of myth and enchantment, where the god of love himself reviews their claims. Cupid resolves the debate in favor of Flora and her cleric, but as W. T. H. Jackson has observed, "It is hard to escape the feeling that the verdict is given tongue in cheek" (*The Literature of the Middle Ages*, p. 239).

Phyllis and Flora, written in the twelfth century, spawned several imitations, most notably *Florence et Blancheflor*, *Hueline et Aiglantine*, and *Melior et Ydoine*. It is generally the case in these poems, as in *Phyllis and Flora*, that gentlewomen engage in comparing the virtues and amorous capabilities of their particularly preferred groups of lovers, usually knights or clerks. (In the *Love-Council of Remiremont* the satire is carried yet a stage further as the nuns of the convent themselves participate in a kind of lovers parliament.) The fact that the comparisons in these poems tended, on the whole, to work to the detriment of knights and the advantage of clerks shouldn't be surprising, considering the likely authorship. This tradition of debate poems in which women compare the merits of their male lovers — which may be reflected in a sense in the *Wife of Bath's Prologue*, though with a twist — is again encountered near the end of the Middle Ages in William Dunbar's *Tretis of the Twa Mariit Wemen and the Wido*, a comic inversion in which the speakers attempt to surpass each other in describing their lovers' deficiencies rather than their virtues; here the satiric exposé is clearly double-edged. Written along similar lines but greatly inferior is the obscene poem "The Gossips' Meeting" (*R-C* 1852), which Furnivall titled "A Talk of Ten Wives" (*Jyl of Breyntford's Testament and Other Poems*, London, 1871). The topic of women and the value and danger of loving them also became a primary concern in several of the Middle English debate poems, particularly the bird debates, as will be discussed below.

From their beginnings Latin debate poems had been imbued with a playful spirit. Although they were clearly the work of learned writers, many of the earlier Latin debates were intended to amuse as much as they were intended to instruct. By the end of the twelfth century it had become common for the writers of the Latin and vernacular debates to make liberal use of irony, parody, and comic bawdiness. There is surely much truth in J. H. Hanford's observation that these clever, entertaining poems "represent the reaction from, often the parody of, the sober pursuits of the school room, and are the work of monks and pedagogues on a crabbed literary holiday . . ." (*Romanic Review* 2 [1911], 138). One source of the amusement in these poems stems from the rapid deterioration of neat and tidy exchanges into rancorous, no-holds-barred contests for supremacy. Often a disputant's over-riding desire to achieve victory, by fair means or foul, leads to dissembling, intimidation, and the shameless hurling of abuse. (Later on this hurling of abuse became the chief element in the Middle Scots *flytings*, poems which represent a curious off-shoot from the mainstream of medieval debate tradition.) In many cases the egos and senses of self-worth of the debating parties are of greater importance to them than their ostensible beliefs, and thus some of these later poems are marked by highly personal attacks, attempts to humiliate a rival by exposing his or her most private habits and foibles. Thus it is not surprising that debaters sometimes threaten each other with violence, although actual combat never takes place.

Various kinds of comic, ironic, and satiric elements regularly appear among the debate poems extant from the Middle Ages, even in poems with serious didactic intentions. Humor may stem from the rowdy, rancorous conduct of the disputing parties, or it may arise from the choice of creatures who are placed in opposition to one another. In rare instances comedy might inhere in the ludicrousness of a particular pairing—such as a crab debating with a rainbow. More common is the opposing of particular character types, such as a pompous and self-righteous prude and a frivolous and self-indulgent sensualist. Variations on this pair of characters turn up in the Water and Wine debates, the debates between the seasons, and the conflicts between the ages (especially in the characters of Youth and Middle Age). Versions of this stock pair are also seen in the *Owl and the Nightingale* and *Winner and Waster*. Another important source of humor is created by the debaters' argumentative ingenuity. The spouting of learned lore—especially proverbial lore and allegedly pertinent passages of scripture (again recalling the Wife of Bath's *Prologue*) — is quite common. During the earlier phases of debate tradition, to be sure, the citing of scriptural references was not done facetiously or for comic effect. In the long-winded and sententious Latin debate between a sheep and a flax plant (the *Conflictus Ovis et Lini*), probably an eleventh-century poem, the rivals amass biblical evidence as they dispute their relative usefulness to man (a fairly common debate concern), and in the *Altercatio Ecclesiae et Synagoge* one debater adduces support from the New Testament, the other from the Old Testament. But after the twelfth century the probability is that such references, though usually offered in all seriousness by their speakers, are intended by the poets to be seen as highly dubious attempts at self-justification. In the *Goliae Dialogue inter Aquam et Vinum*, in the *Owl and the Nightingale*, and in *Winner and Waster*, the comic manipulation and application of scriptural support provides a means of characterizing the speakers and of revealing their argumentative disingenuousness.

There is really no consistent pattern among either the Latin or vernacular debate poems in regard to a final resolution; some poems offer nothing at all in the way of a resolution, some contain implied resolutions, and some are resolved absolutely, with a winner clearly specified or with a loser freely offering his own capitulation. In some of these last cases, the dice have been loaded from the outset — the Jew is *not* likely to best the Christian in the Middle English *Disputation between a Christian and a Jew*, even though for a time it looks as though he might. In those cases where a resolution is sought, it may or may not involve the intervention and possible adjudication of a third party. In the *Conflictus Veris et Hiemis*, the earliest recorded medieval debate, judges are present and a victor is declared. In many of the earlier Latin poems, however, poems which are little more than school exercises, no definite conclusions are reached. The point of such exercises, in all probability, was for beginning students in dialectic to determine the truth on their own. Many later debates are similarly unresolved, forcing their hearers or readers to judge the efficacy of the opposing arguments for themselves. Even in poems where a judge is introduced there may be no explicit judgment. In the *Violet and the Rose*, Philip de Greve's debate between the *Heart and the Eye*, and the Middle English *Winner and Waster*, the judge-figure attempts to reconcile the speakers to each other, or points out the worthy qualities of each, or simply attempts to keep them at arm's length. In the Middle English *Parliament of the Three Ages* the figure of Old Age — who gives the appearance of sitting in judgment on Youth and Middle Age — denounces them both, and yet the views which he himself advances may be equally suspect. Certainly, there is always a possibility of irony when a specific judgment is rendered. There is even a possibility of irony in the choice of a judge. Is Nicholas of Guildford really the exemplary figure the Owl and the Nightingale make him out to be? He *probably* is, but we don't know for sure, and there is always the possibility that he isn't.

The purposes for which medieval debate poems were written are extremely varied. As Raby observes in regard to Latin debate tradition, the conflict-dialogue "could be used with immense effect for satire, for buffoonery, or for poetical trifling; or again it might be used to put before the reader important moral or spiritual issues" (*A History of Secular Latin Poetry in the Middle Ages*, p. 308). In all probability, though, poems of the latter sort are in the distinct minority, and even when debate poems do raise serious issues, they are not always seriously explored. While a general intent to edify underlies most forms of dialogue and debate poetry—underlies, in fact, most varieties of medieval literature—edification is frequently subordinated to broader satiric and comic purposes. Often the clash of personalities becomes more prominent than the clash of ideas. Because the characters in many debate poems have little real interest in ascertaining "truth," what often emerges is a more general commentary on human nature, on man's pretensions and inflated sense of self-importance, on his pettiness, peevishness, and his blindness to what he really is.

Middle English Debate Poetry

The debate poems written during the Middle English period constitute a literary genre of considerable diversity. The many poems which are indisputably "Middle English debate poems" reflect widely differing styles, structures, tones, and intentions, and they cut across many of the traditional designations and poetic traditions. Middle English debate poems appear among the works of the Alliterative Revival, among the poems associated with the court of Richard II, among didactic poems of the most serious kind, and among light-hearted entertainments and satiric works. Some debate poems have a close association with the animal fable tradition, some reflect an association with romance, a few have firm ties with the fabliau, several intersect with dream-vision poetry, and others—especially the *pastourelle*-like lovers' debates—are closely allied with lyric tradition.

Many of the greatest English poets of the Middle Ages contributed works to the genre of debate poetry, and others reveal the influence of the debate in their work. The authors of the *Owl and Nightingale* and the *Debate Between*

the Body and Soul (*Als I lay on a winteris nyt*) are among the finest English poets
of the early Middle English period. The authors of *Winner and Waster* and
the *Parliament of the Three Ages* rank high among fourteenth-century poets.
Langland's *Piers Plowman* reflects the influence of the debate in various ways
(and specifically the influence of *Winner and Waster*), and Chaucer's *Parlia-
ment of Fowls*, even if it cannot be characterized as being principally a de-
bate poem, possesses a substantial debate element. Lydgate, Henryson, and
Dunbar, three of the chief British poets of the fifteenth century, composed
debate poems in addition to drawing upon debate tradition more generally
in their poetry. Nearly all of the very great Middle English poetic miscel-
lanies — manuscripts such as Harley 2253 and the Auchinleck manuscript —
contain at least a few debate poems, and in some manuscripts debate poems
seem to be featured prominently, as for example in Digby 86 from the thir-
teenth century, the Vernon manuscript from the fourteenth century, and
BL MS Addit. 37049 from the fifteenth century.

Debate poetry begins in Middle English literature with the *Owl and the
Nightingale*, the longest and most complex, the most controversial and yet
most highly esteemed of all Middle English debate poems. Composed in
the south of England in the late twelfth or early thirteenth century by an
author whose identity is still disputed, the *Owl and the Nightingale* is regarded
as the greatest comic poem in English before Chaucer and one of the true
masterworks of early Middle English literature. Such a lofty assessment rests
on an appreciation of the poet's skillful control of form and structure, his
use of vivid and realistic detail, his sophisticated sense of comedy, and his
creation of a pair of contentious creatures of striking vitality. The poem
is all the more remarkable, in the view of many critics, for having been
written in English rather than in Anglo-Norman French probably no more
than a century and a half after the Norman Conquest. But although the
Owl and Nightingale is an English poem, it appears to grow out of the sophisti-
cated Anglo-Norman literary culture of the twelfth century. The poem is
written in the octo-syllabic couplet, the primary metrical form of narrative
poems written at this time in French, and it reflects the writer's familiarity
with contemporary works of proverbial lore, natural history, fables, and lays.
The poet's temperament and personality, suggested in part by the colloqui-
al style and comic tone of the poem, distinguishes his work from the other
English writings of the time. Not until the second half of the fourteenth
century do other imaginative works in English exhibit similar qualities of
erudition, animation, and comedy.

The *Owl and the Nightingale* appears to have exerted little influence on subsequent works. With the possible exception of the author of the *Thrush and the Nightingale*, it is unlikely that later debate poets had any first-hand knowledge of this remarkable predecessor — certainly, there are no clear references or allusions to it among the later works. Thus in many ways the *Owl and the Nightingale* stands alone as an unprecedented and anomalous poem. And even though it has received greater scholarly attention than any other debate poem in Middle English, it continues to be one of the most enigmatic poems of the period.

Middle English Bird Debates

Drawing their inspiration as well as their authority from such diverse sources as the nature histories of Pliny and Alexander Neckham, bestiary lore, classical and early medieval fable literature, passages in certain influential works such as Ovid's *Metamorphoses*, and various passages from the scriptures (e.g. Ecclesiastes 10:20), medieval poets found many valuable uses for talking birds. In the early courtly poetry of France, talking birds became a device for expressing a variety of human attitudes toward love and for commenting on them (for a discussion of the thirteenth and fourteenth century poems that gave rise to the bird parliament, see the appendix to D. S. Brewer's edition of Chaucer's *Parliament of Fowls*). In Chaucer's poetry loquacious birds play prominent roles not only in the *Parliament of Fowls* and the *House of Fame* but also in the *Complaint of Mars* and in the tales of the Nun's Priest, Squire, and Manciple. The use of talking birds as counselors or as foils to foolish or despondent human beings occurs frequently in later Middle English, in dialogues such as the *Mavis and Lover* (R-C 1214.5), the *Quatrefoil of Love* (*Index* 1453), and the *Poet and the Bird* (*Index* 2018). Talking birds also play central roles in works such as Lydgate's *The Churl and the Bird*, Holland's *Buke of the Howlat* (Book of the Owlet), and Henryson's fable of the *Cock and Fox* in which Chanteclere's three hen-mistresses voice their distinctive attitudes toward their abducted lover. It is not surprising, then, in view of this frequent anthropomorphism, that talking birds should have become the *dramatis personae* in debate and parliament poems. Extant in Middle English are four debates between pairs of rival birds, several dialogues in which one of the speakers is a bird, and several bird parliaments. The bird debates are the *Owl and the Nightingale* (written late in the twelfth or early in the thirteenth century), the *Thrush and the Nightingale* (written late in the thirteenth century), the *Cuckoo and the Nightingale* or the *Book of Cupid* (probably from late in the fourteenth century), and William Dunbar's the *Merle and the Nightingale* (from the end of the fifteenth century). A fifth poem, the *Clerk and the Nightingale I* and *II* (actually two fragments of what seems to be a single work), is here considered along with the others because of its general relationship to them and its special relationship to the *Thrush and the Nightingale*.

The Middle English bird debates are linked by several important characteristics of form and content. In each there is a narrative frame that describes a spring or summer setting and usually introduces a first-person narrator who reports the debate which he has overheard; more importantly, in each poem there is a pair of contending birds, one of which is a nightingale, the other one of the nightingale's traditional rivals. Four of the five poems (the *Owl and the Nightingale* is the exception) focus on the nature and value of woman's love and particularly on the question of woman's fidelity in love; and thus the bird debates clearly belong to the larger body of medieval literature preoccupied with the "woman question." Several other characteristics are shared by two or more of the five poems. In the *Thrush and Nightingale*, *Cuckoo and Nightingale*, and *Clerk and Nightingale* the conflict occurs between the same character types — a disillusioned cynic and a romantic idealist. In the *Thrush and Nightingale* and *Cuckoo and Nightingale* a female nightingale defends women and their love from the onslaught of a male bird, suggesting an actual battle of the sexes. In the *Clerk and Nightingale* and *Merle and Nightingale* a reversal of roles occurs and the nightingale becomes the misogynist. In the *Cuckoo and Nightingale* and the *Clerk and Nightingale*, dream-visions are incorporated into the narrative frames of the poems. In the *Thrush and Nightingale* and the *Merle and Nightingale* the debates are concluded on a serious religious note.

The authors selected their debaters with a careful consideration of their symbolic qualities. The nightingale, the owl, and the cuckoo, in particular, possessed reputations firmly rooted in literary tradition. Frequently the nightingale was thought of as the herald of spring, the bird that "clepeth forth the grene leves newe," as she is described in Chaucer's *Parliament of Fowls* (352). She has that role to some extent in the *Owl and the Nightingale, Thrush and Nightingale*, and *Cuckoo and Nightingale*. Even more frequently she was considered to be the inspirer of romantic love or sexual desire, as her song stirred man's emotions and turned his thoughts to love. Sometimes, however, the nightingale was portrayed as a singer in praise of divine love, as in Lydgate's *A Saying of the Nightingale* and Dunbar's *Merle and the Nightingale*. Like the nightingale, the owl evoked contradictory associations, largely stemming from biblical references to the *bubo* and *nyticorax* (e.g. Leviticus 11:16–7 and Psalms 101:6–8). Most often the owl was presented in an unfavorable light;

its mournful cry portended ill-fortune, often death, as in the *Parliament of Fowls* (343); it was a creature of filthy habits that fouled its own nest; and it preferred the darkness to the light. But the owl could also signify the devout Christian desirous of helping those who dwell in the darkness, a meaning the Owl imputes to herself in the *Owl and the Nightingale*. Resulting from its association with Athena, the owl could also be viewed as a symbol of wisdom, as is still the case. The cuckoo was associated with the coming of spring, as in the Middle English lyric "The Cuckoo Song." In fact, as noted earlier, it is the impending arrival of the cuckoo that ignites what is probably the earliest medieval debate poem, the *Conflictus Veris et Hiemis*. In the later Middle Ages, however, the cuckoo came to be viewed with disfavor. In the *Parliament of Fowls* it is referred to as a bird *ever unkynde* (358), as an unnatural bird that lays its eggs in other birds' nests, and one whose greedy offspring bring about the deaths of their foster siblings. Ultimately the cuckoo came to be the emblem of deceitful, adulterous love, the embodiment of cuckoldry. The remaining bird debaters, the thrush and the merle, lack the abundant symbolic associations of the other three, but each was well-known for its spring-time singing. The thrush was often portrayed as a cantankerous and complaining bird, and the author of the *Thrush and the Nightingale* appears to be drawing upon this reputation. The merle (the European blackbird) makes few appearances in medieval literature, but there is some evidence that it, like the nightingale, was reputed to elicit romantic feelings in those who listened to its singing.

Middle English Body and Soul Debates

Perhaps no theme occurs so widely or with so much vitality in medieval debate tradition as the conflict between the body and the soul, a theme which appears in several manifestations in the literatures of the European Middle Ages. Although the concept of a contentious relationship between man's physical and spiritual natures is not unique to Christianity, it seems to have held particular fascination for early Christians, who found this rivalry adumbrated in various New Testament scriptures. Galatians 5:16–7 provides its most explicit expression —". . . the flesh lusteth against the Spirit, the Spirit against the flesh: and these are contrary one to the other . . ."; less explicit corroboration of this conflict is found in Romans 8:13, I Corinthians 9:27, and John 5:28–9, and in passages of scripture pertaining to the reunion of the body and soul on the Day of Judgment, such as I Cor. 15:51–6 and Rev. 11:18. Poems depicting the conflict between the body and the soul occur in English literature as early as the Anglo-Saxon period and as late as the poetry of Andrew Marvell in the mid-seventeenth century. But it was during the Middle English period that body and soul poetry was especially in vogue.

The earliest poems in the body and soul tradition tend to be rather brief monologues in which the soul addresses its body soon after death. The first examples in Old English are found in the Vercelli and Exeter Books (for example, Riddle 43). Early Middle English literature also preserves several monologues in which the soul addresses its body. The curious and starkly powerful poem known as "The Grave" (included in this volume) may possibly be an example of such an address, but the Middle English lyric "Nou is mon hol and soint" (also included in this volume) and the lyric "Nu þou unseli bodi up-on bere list" (*Index* 2369) provide more characteristic examples. The emphasis in these poems is on the soul's castigation of the body for having failed to live a moral life and on the soul's scornful depiction of the body's impending corruption in the grave. The handling of this theme becomes more complicated and sophisticated in a series of poetic fragments known as the *Worcester Fragments*, a rich repository of images and ideas that appear and reappear in Middle English poems concerned with death. Contained in the *Worcester Fragments*, for example, are descriptions of the signs of death's approach, the humiliating and insensitive treatment the body receives prior to burial, the paltriness of the grave which will be the body's future "house," the *ubi sunt* formula, the body's dissolution in the grave, and the greed and faithlessness of the body's heirs — all of which become commonplaces in the body and soul dialogues and debate poems.

In the early monologue stage in body and soul poetry the soul's stinging imprecations went entirely unchallenged. In the next stage in this evolving tradition the body was re-animated to the extent that it could raise its head from the bier and respond to the soul's diatribe. In this second stage the personified body and soul actually engage each other in a dialogue, yet their verbal exchanges fall short of constituting a full-fledged debate. In general the body's remarks tend to be relatively mild and may even serve to underscore the ostensible truth of the soul's contentions. The body does not attempt to deflect or rebut the soul's allegations or to mount a counter-attack on the soul, but rather emphasizes the remorse it feels for having failed to live a moral life and for having placed the two of them in eternal jeopardy. At this stage the body does not raise the possibility that the soul may have failed to discharge *its* moral responsibilities. The poem *In a þestri stude I stod* (included in this volume) provides the best illustration from Middle

English literature of this intermediate phase in the evolving body and soul tradition. In this poem there is a large number of brief exchanges, with the body becoming progressively more irritated by the soul's relentless chiding; towards the end of their dialogue the body urges the soul to go away and leave it alone, for "me is woe enough."

The full potential of the body and soul theme was finally achieved in poems such as the Middle English *Als I lay on a winteris nyt*, in which the body responds to the soul's initial diatribe by mounting its own vituperative counter-attack. In this poem the body poses a serious challenge to the soul in regard to the question of moral responsibility quite possibly reflecting the Thomistic view that sin occurs when the rational faculty of the soul (*ratio* or reason) fails to exercise proper control over the body. *Als I lay on a winteris nyt* places the body and soul debate within a dream-vision, a convention seen in the *Visio Philberti*. Variously ascribed to such notable figures as St. Bernard, Walter Mapes, Robert Grosseteste, and Philip de Greve (though unlikely to have been the work of any of them), the *Visio Philberti* exerted considerable influence on the vernacular body and soul debates, an influence especially marked in the French poem *Une samedi par nuit*. The Middle English body and soul debates, however, are actually closer in conception to the Latin *altercatio* between *anima* and *corpus* preserved in British Library MS Royal 7 A iii (beginning *Nuper huiusce modi*) which concludes, like *Als I lay*, with a description of demons carting off the terrified soul to hell (see E. K. Heningham, *An Early Latin Debate of the Body and Soul* [New York, 1939]).

The figure of the dead man whose body and soul contend in these debates was typically that of a proud and wealthy knight whose entire life had been devoted to his own selfish pursuits, at the expense of his obligations to the church, his fellowman, and his own spirituality. By giving the dead man wealth commensurate with his aristocratic status, wealth which is lost to him at death, the poets underscored the foolishness of accumulating temporal goods. Like wealth, physical prowess and sexual attractiveness are fleeting; and the soul often remarks, sardonically, that once the body of this nobleman is in the grave, he will be harder pressed to find willing bed-companions. The emphasis on the decay of physical strength and beauty becomes more poignant in the death poems which describe a beautiful aristocratic lady rather than a knight, such as "Whan the turf is thy tour" (*Index* 4044) and the *Disputation between the Body and the Worms* (in this volume), one of the final adaptations of the body and soul theme in Middle English literature. Whereas in poems such as *Als I lay* emphasis is placed on the torments which will be meted out to the damned soul in hell, in the *Body and Worms* the emphasis is on the impending corruption of the body in the grave, as the woman's body is beset by a host of "suitors" which include toads, snakes, spiders, and maggots.

The Alliterative Debates

For a period of about one hundred years, from the middle of the fourteenth century to the middle of the fifteenth, English literature witnessed the remarkable phenomenon now generally referred to as the Alliterative Revival, in which a large number of narrative poems were written in a similar form of unrhymed alliterative verse. Apparently originating in the West Midlands and then moving on to the North of England, this literary development represents a dramatic revitalization of native poetic tradition. The poems that make up this movement share many distinctive characteristics — similar stylistic traits, a rich and rather archaic alliterative vocabulary, and the tendency to enrich their narratives with detailed descriptive passages, to cite only some of the most obvious ones. The majority of these alliterative works fall into one of two major groups. The first group consists of poems primarily concerned with social and didactic matters such as *Piers Plowman, Richard the Redeles, Pierce the Ploughman's Creed, Mum and the Sothsegger, The Crowned King*, and a few other poems. The second group, composed primarily of secular romances and historical epics, includes the alliterative *Morte Arthure, Sir Gawain and the Green Knight*, the Alexander poems, *The Destruction of Troy*, and *The Siege of Jerusalem*. A few important alliterative poems, for instance *Cleanness* and *St. Erkenwald*, possess the chief characteristics of both groups. This is also the case for the three debate poems of the Alliterative Revival, *Winner and Waster, The Parliament of the Three Ages*, and *Death and Life*, didactic poems with a substantial infusion of romance elements.

Winner and Waster, written in the 1350s, is among the earliest poems of the Alliterative Revival. Its only text, which is incomplete, is preserved in British Library MS Additional 31042 (one of the two "Thornton MSS"). *Winner and Waster* is preceded in the Thornton manuscript by the only full text of the *Parliament of the Three Ages*, a poem probably composed during the final quarter of the fourteenth century. The date of *Death and Life*, the third of the alliterative debates, is less certain, though the first decade of the fifteenth century seems a reasonable guess; the sole text of this debate was recorded much later, around the middle of the seventeenth century, in the famous Percy Folio. These three Middle English alliterative debate poems have a good deal in common, in addition to having been written in the alliterative long line: they are poems of middle length (a little less or a little more than 500 verses); they exhibit strong similarities in their overall designs; and in each of them an elaborate narrative frame encloses a dream vision in which the central feature is a debate between allegorical opponents. It seems likely that *Winner and Waster* established a general pattern that was consciously imitated by the authors of the two later poems. Another common link between the three poems is found in their close relationships with *Piers Plowman*. *Winner and Waster* exerted a certain amount of influence on Langland's poem. The *Parliament of the Three Ages* and *Death and Life*, both written after *Piers Plowman*, reflect its influence to various degrees. *Death and Life*, in fact, probably owes its central conception of an allegorical confrontation between Lady Death and Lady Life to *Piers Plowman*.

Despite their important similarities and their interconnectedness, the three Middle English alliterative debates also exhibit distinctive qualities. *Winner and Waster* is primarily an exploration of the economic instability of the times. It is essentially a satirical exposé, and it reflects the poet's deep emotional involvement in contemporary social and economic concerns. Like most of the poems in the Alliterative Revival *Winner and Waster* includes many vivid descriptive passages, yet the poet's most distinctive literary attributes are his flashes of comic wit and his biting satire, characteristics largely absent from the other two alliterative debates. The *Parliament of the Three Ages* focuses on the necessity for man to be spiritually prepared for death. Here the poet evinces little concern with current social matters. It is curious, though, that while the *Parliament of the Three Ages* is a denunciation of man's pursuit of the worldly things which undermine his spirituality, the poem also reveals its author's intimate knowledge of medieval romance literature and his familiarity with and apparent love of hunting and hawking, things which are decidedly worldly. The *Parliament* also contains striking descriptions, and the introductory account depicting the activities of the solitary deer-hunter is especially memorable. When the *Parliament* is considered as a whole, it must be observed that it lacks the meticulous attention to structural proportioning that characterizes the other two alliterative debates. *Death and Life*, like the *Parliament of the Three Ages*, is a poetic homily, but the poet's intention is to assuage man's fear of death by providing hope and consolation. The poem offers a warm and loving portrait of human society, one which is not permeated by the social ills depicted in *Winner and Waster* nor filled with the kinds of self-indulgent pursuits which characterize man's successive stages in life in the *Parliament of the Three Ages*. Although *Death and Life* is in some ways the most derivative of the three alliterative debates, it possesses several highly effective descriptive passages, and it reflects its author's scrupulous attention to structural balance and symmetry.

The three Middle English alliterative debates may be seen to represent successive stages in a progression, from *Winner and Waster's* initial concerns with the state of contemporary society and the immediate realities of living, to the *Parliament's* emphasis on the importance of man's spiritual preparation for his imminent death, to *Death and Life's* consoling message of life's ultimate victory over death. The opposing values represented by the allegorical figures of Winner and Waster are shown to be narrow and self-serving but nonetheless forces that are essential to the economic health and general well-being of society. The values of Winner and Waster are mirrored by the preoccupations of Youth and Middle Age in the *Parliament of the Three Ages*, but these values are then explicitly condemned by Old Age who argues that the inevitability of death renders them, and all other varieties of human accomplishments, essentially worthless. *Death and Life* provides an optimistic antidote to the more pessimistic implications of the two earlier poems. In this final alliterative debate poem the value of man's temporal existence is reaffirmed. The joys which he may experience through human companionship and his happy, fruitful existence in a naturally beautiful world are not negated by death, for when man moves beyond the temporal realm into the eternal realm, death itself is vanquished.

The Middle English Dream Debates

". . . whate I seghe in my saule the sothe I schall telle"
                              (*Parliament of the Three Ages*, 103)

By the twelfth century it was not uncommon for Latin debate poems to be set within dream-visions. The fusion of dream-vision and debate became even more commonplace in vernacular poetry of the later Middle Ages. In the earlier debate poems with dream-vision settings the dream tended to serve only as a narrative convenience, providing a degree of plausibility to the often-astonishing events which the narrator described; usually no attempt was made to integrate the frame into the poem thematically. In some of the later debates, however, the dream-visions began to contribute to the poems' larger thematic concerns. In *Als I lay on a winteris nyt*, for example, the winter's-night setting seems to carry pertinent symbolic implications and also a suggestion about the narrator's state of mind as he enters his dream. Thus a tension is established between the narrator's own psycho-logical state and the anguish of the personified soul and body who debate within his dream. Attempts to integrate the framing narrative into the poem's larger thematic design culminate in a small group of Middle English poems which may be termed "dream debates," poems in which the dream is not just an expedient mechanism but a structural and thematic unit of central significance. This is the case in Chaucer's *Parliament of Fowls*, Clanvowe's *The Cuckoo and the Nightingale*, the three Middle English alliterative debates, and the fifteenth-century *Disputation between the Body and the Worms*.

The structural design of these Middle English dream-debates is quite complex. Each poem consists of two major structural elements—a central disputation section and an elaborate surrounding dream-vision framework which may approach or even surpass the disputation in its total number of verses. The relationship between the dream-vision frame and the enclosed debate is never explicitly stated and may even appear to be somewhat puz-zling, yet as the poems develop, the frame and the debate can be seen to be complementary and mutually dependent elements. It is through the *persona* of the narrator that the basic human problem or concern of the poem is initiated, for in the introductory frame the narrator manifests fears or anxi-eties which have led him to a precarious emotional condition. His troubled state of mind may stem from his uncertainties about love, or from his fears concerning death and its aftermath, or from other causes, but regardless of the specific cause, he falls asleep with an uneasy mind. Once his vision-ary experience has begun, the narrator often finds himself in a beautiful or wondrous land which absorbs his attention. This transitional section be-tween the outer frame and the inner disputation sets the stage for the im-pending debate but also helps to calm the narrator's mind, perhaps contributing to his greater receptivity to what is to come. In the debate which follows, the specific matters which have created the narrator's anxie-ties are examined more specifically and concretely. From his on-looker's per-spective the narrator witnesses the confrontation of debaters who provide a kind of objective correlative to his own clashing emotions. Thus the nar-rator is able to view his dilemma from outside, dispassionately and with greater objectivity.

It should be observed that these Middle English dream-debates have much in common with other Middle English dream-visions such as the *Pearl* and Chaucer's *Book of the Duchess*, poems which also address fundamental human anxieties. And yet they differ in some important respects. In *Pearl* the nar-rator becomes an active participant in his own vision, engaging directly in the "vertical dialogue" (that is, one in which the participants are on differing planes of enlightenment and authority) which constitutes the central, instructional section of the poem. But in the dream debates the debate is horizontal in nature (the disputants are on an essentially even footing), and the narrator remains primarily an uninvolved observer who learns indirectly, if he learns at all. Whether or not the narrator succeeds in gaining a clearer understanding of his emotional dilemma, (and in some of the dream debates he may not), at least an opportunity to achieve greater insight has been presented to him through the debate he has witnessed.

Death and Life and the *Disputation between the Body and the Worms* adhere most closely to this general dream-debate pattern. In both, the basic concern is with man's fear of death and its consequences. At the outset in both poems the narrators' concern with death, and quite likely their considerable fear of it, is implied. In the visionary experiences which follow, both narrators reveal their love of life in this world and their dismay at its fleeting and mutable nature. But as the visions unfold, their anxieties are dispelled and a sense of consolation is effected, as the narrators are assured that their initial anxieties were not well-founded. The *Parliament of the Three Ages* is more complicated. The introductory section of this poem seems to reveal a narrator who is completely absorbed in his pursuits of the moment, to the neglect of his spiritual welfare. His dream-vision seems to serve an admonitory function, suggesting that his disregard of his spiritual needs has placed him in considerable jeopardy, since the moment of death's arrival is always imminent. Perhaps there is a suggestion in the *Parliament of the Three Ages* that the narrator does have at least a subconscious awareness of his moral danger, and it is this awareness which provokes his homiletic dream. Although the concluding verses of the poem are ambiguous, it appears that when the narrator awakens from his dream, he immediately acts upon his new awareness of his mortality. In Chaucer's *Parliament of Fowls* and Clanvowe's *Cuckoo and the Nightingale*, the narrators' anxieties are generated by romantic love. Their fears and desires subsequently take shape in the conflicting attitudes toward love expressed by the birds who confront each other in their dreams. Although the dilemmas of these two very similar narrators are not resolved, their dreams appear to contain insights which could be of value to them. *Winner and Waster* stands somewhat apart. Here the narrator's turmoil and consternation result from the chaotic state into which contemporary society has fallen. His dream-vision provides him with a concrete visualization and analysis of the forces which have been allowed to produce the current state of affairs. His dream may also provide him with a knowledge of how these forces could be brought under control through the exercise of kingly authority; but it seems to have been the king's own irresponsible actions which have led to the present disorder. Because the concluding verses to *Winner and Waster* are lost, we do not know if the poem ended on a more positive note than the one on which it began.

In the Middle English dream-debates the dream-vision framework assumes much greater prominence and thematic importance than it does in the various other debate poems which also employ a framing device. In the dream-debates the conflicting fears and desires that create the narrator's emotional turmoil become externalized in the form of the personified debaters in his dream, allowing him and the reader to examine more clearly the forces which create these common human anxieties. Thus the debate provides the dreamer with a chance to understand his situation better and to come to terms with his emotions.

The Parliamentary Debate

The parliamentary debate is a specialized variety of debate poem in which several participants, each of whom is delegated to speak for the membership of a larger group, express their views on a particular issue. Although parliamentary debates never rivaled the more conventional forms of medieval debate poetry in popularity, they are encountered nonetheless throughout the length and breadth of medieval debate tradition. Poems such as the early religious debate in Latin between *A Christian, a Mohammedan, and a Jew*, with its overtly didactic intentions, and Dunbar's late secular debate *Tretis of the Twa Mariit Wemen and the Wedo*, with its comic and satiric intentions, represent the extreme possibilities that were realized within the parliamentary mode. Philip the Chancellor's *Disputatio Membrorum* provides another example of a relatively early (thirteenth century) parliamentary debate in Latin, one which is related in concept to the more conventional two-party debate between the *Heart and the Eye*.

The chief interest in parliamentary poems probably resided in the opportunity afforded the poet to introduce a colorful array of individual speakers who could express diverse opinions on a question. Because of the multiplicity of speakers and viewpoints, parliamentary poems usually assume a quite distinctive character. In contrast to the more conventional one-on-one debates, which have the character of verbal sparring matches or jousts, parliaments often have the character of verbal melees. The free-for-all atmosphere in some of the French parliament poems involving several wines (e.g. *La*

Desputoison du Vin et de l'Iaue) is a unique and colorful feature. Yet a major limitation of the parliamentary poem in which there is a large number of participants is their restricted opportunities to express their views, usually reduced to no more than one or two brief speeches. Whereas in the one-on-one debate the lively and numerous exchanges of charge, rebuttal, and counter-charge allow the debaters to reveal a good deal about themselves, in the parliament such self-characterization is usually not feasible, and as a result characterization generally suffers.

The parliamentary debate did not come into vogue in Middle English literature until the later part of the fourteenth century. The *Parliament of the Three Ages*, which was written during the final quarter of the century, is among the earlier examples (but is only marginally a true parliamentary poem, as will be explained below), and Chaucer's *Parliament of Fowls* was written at about this same time. Both of these poems exerted some influence on later works, especially Chaucer's *Parliament*, which provided the major inspiration for several bird and animal parliaments in Middle English and Middle Scots during the fifteenth century. Chaucer's poem itself reflects a tradition already well-established in French courtly poetry in which birds function as commentators on matters involving love. In the Old French *Florence et Blancheflor*, for example, the god of love convenes a parliament of his barons—who are birds—to weigh the arguments of the lovers. Much closer to Chaucer's poem in both date and content is Oton de Graunson's *Le Songe Saint Valentine*, a poem with definite affinities to Chaucer's *Parliament* (in fact, it is not certain which poem influenced which). The brilliant Chaucerian imitation *The Cuckoo and the Nightingale*, although not a parliamentary poem, sets up the possibility of convening a parliament in order to settle the birds' dispute, and an informal parliament does take place in the highly lyrical Chaucerian imitation *The Parliament of Birds*.

Many of the later poems in the parliamentary debate tradition—Lydgate's *Debate of the Horse, Goose, and Sheep*, Henryson's "Parliament of the Four-footed Beasts" and "Cock and Fox" from the *Morall Fabillis*, and Richard Holland's *Buke of the Howlat*—are as much in the animal fable tradition as they are in the debate tradition. Dunbar's *Tretis*, which owes a great deal to Chaucer, provides a comic debunking of many aspects of the debate tradition, probably parodying the early debates in the tradition of *Phyllis and Flora*, in which women compare the virtues of their lovers, and possibly even parodying the *Tretis'* alliterative forerunner the *Parliament of the Three Ages*. Aside from the bird and animal parliaments, another late development with some characteristics in common with the parliament are poems in which there are assemblies of the gods. Precedent for such gatherings is of course found in classical literature, but Boccaccio's poems and Chaucer's *Knight's Tale* seem to have provided the immediate models for Henryson (in the *Testament of Cresseid*) and for *The Assembly of the Gods*, formerly attributed to Lydgate. The lively fifteenth-century poem known as *The Devils' Parliament* may be related to this group too, though it is in fact a verse sermon.

The Pastourelle

Medieval literature offers several varieties of lovers' dialogues, but only a few of them possess the character of the debate or contention-poem. Chief among these few is the *pastourelle*, a poem which depicts a young courtier's attempted seduction of a rural maiden. Although the *pastourelle's* rustic setting suggests its association with the pastoral mode of classical literature, the *pastourelle* actually originated during the twelfth century amidst the courtly literature of southern France. Like several of the new poetic types that first appeared during this time in the south of France, the *pastourelle* experienced considerable popularity, so that by the end of the thirteenth century *pastourelles* could be found in all of the major vernacular literatures of Western Europe. In Provençal literature the number of surviving poems is not very great, roughly about twenty-five, but they include some of the most celebrated examples — such as Marcabru's *L'autrier jost'una sebissa* ("The other day along a hedgerow") and Gui d'Ussel's *L'autrier cavalcava* ("The other day I was out riding"). Italian literature also produced several striking examples, such as Guido Cavalcanti's *In un boschetto* ("In a little wood I found"). The *pastourelle* appears to have enjoyed its greatest vogue in the literature of northern France, where close to 200 poems are extant. Although the group of *pastourelles* extant in Middle English and Middle Scots is quite small — perhaps no more than a dozen poems altogether — it is a varied and intriguing group that reflects an interesting evolution. As a distinct literary type the *pastourelle* went out of fashion during the sixteenth century, yet the "pastourelle theme" continued to appear in the ballads, folksongs, and nursery rhymes of later centuries.

As it was originally conceived, the *pastourelle* was essentially a young man's romantic fantasy in which he imagined himself encountering an attractive "pastourelle," a young shepherdess, in a secluded rural setting. Spontaneous encounters between young men of high birth and pretty young women of lower social status undoubtedly occurred in real life, but the *pastourelle* provided an opportunity to exploit the imaginative possibilities offered by

such encounters. Although there is no single, clearly-defined narrative out-
line, *pastourelles* typically begin on a spring morning as a youthful narrator
wanders into the country and happens upon a pretty maiden involved in
her chores. He attempts to woo her but meets with stern resistance. He
speaks words of flattery and offers gifts, but she spurns his offers. Within
a fairly short time, however, their battle of wits achieves a resolution. Some-
times the maiden holds out to the end, forcing her disconsolate wooer to
depart; sometimes she extracts the young man's promise of marriage be-
fore agreeing to submit to him. Quite often, however, she suddenly capitu-
lates, agreeing to fulfill his desires there and then. The implication of her
surprising *volte face* seems to be that her earlier protestations had been sim-
ply for the sake of appearances.

The *pastourelles* recorded in Middle English fall into two distinct groups,
an early group composed near the end of the thirteenth century and a later
group composed near the end of the fifteenth century. Three poems sur-
vive from the earlier period — the well-known "Now Springs the Spray," "The
Meeting in the Wood" from MS Harley 2253, and the less well-known "As
I Stood on a Day," poems closely tied to the European *pastourelles* of the twelfth
and thirteenth centuries. "Now Springs the Spray" is actually a partial ren-
dering of a longer Old French *pastourelle* from which the ending, where the
maiden's final actions are made quite explicit, has been omitted — possibly
by accident, possibly by design. The other early Middle English *pastourelles*
may also be modeled on French originals. In any case, like many of the
thirteenth-century European *pastourelles*, they are characterized by formal
and metrical complexity, by a fairly serious tone, and by lyric qualities —
characteristics which are generally absent from the later group of Middle
English *pastourelles*. This later group includes three poems from MS Rawlinson
Poetry C 813, several Middle Scots poems, and the *pastourelle*-like songs of
the early Tudor period. While preserving the basic features of the earlier
poems, these late *pastourelles* also draw some of their features from the
ballad, and they often are very light and comic in tone and intention,
in a fashion reminiscent of the goliardic *pastourelles* found in the *Carmina
Burana*.

The Middle English *pastourelles* differ in certain respects from their French,
Italian, and Latin counterparts. For example, whereas the European poets
often emphasize their descriptions of the rural setting and the attractive
features of the maiden, the English poets tend to place a greater emphasis
on the psychological and verbal struggle, with the result that the English
poems sacrifice some of the *pastourelle's* lyric potential in order to fulfill its

dramatic potential. The English poets also tend to make much less of the social distinction between the lovers, perhaps providing only subtle indications that such a distinction exists, or perhaps ignoring it altogether. It has been observed that the English *pastourelles* on the whole exhibit a more puritanical attitude toward these sexual encounters than do French *pastourelles* (the alterations in the Middle English version of *Now Springs the Spray* certainly offer some support to the observation), but the English poems are by no means straight-laced, and the indecency imputed to the Old French *pastourelles* may be somewhat exaggerated.

Two other varieties of lovers' dialogues are frequently discussed in conjunction with the *pastourelle*: the *aube* (or *aubade* or *alba*), the dawn song of parting lovers, and the "dialogue of the night-visit," in which a young man woos his lady-love from beneath her window. Actually, only the latter has much in common with the *pastourelle* for example, the verbal contest between lovers in which they match wits and wiles. These night-visit dialogues differ from the *pastourelle*, though, in regard to the time and place of the lovers' meeting, and they depict lovers who are previously acquainted and who are usually on a more equal social footing. *De clerico et puella*, the well-known dialogue from Harley 2253, is the finest example of a "night-visit" dialogue in Middle English, and William Dunbar's *In Secreit Place this hyndir nycht* offers an astonishing parody of works in this vein. Robert Henryson's delightful poem *Robin and Makyn*, which fuses together elements from both the *pastourelle* and the night-visit dialogue, makes effective use of comic inversions, a frequent technique among the debates, flytings, and *pastourelles* of the Middle Scots poets.

A Note on the Texts

The texts of the poems in this volume were newly transcribed from the manuscripts containing them. In most instances the manuscripts were examined at first hand, although in a few cases microfilm copies were used. Textual readings which differ from those of previous editions are mentioned in the notes only when the discrepancies are significant.

A majority of the poems printed here are extant in only a single manuscript text; where a choice of texts existed, in almost every case the oldest text was selected as the copy text. An exception was made for the *Cuckoo and the Nightingale*, because the most authoritative text of that poem (contained in MS Fairfax 16 of the Bodleian Library) is available in a recent edition, while the one used here (from MS Tanner 346, also of the Bodleian Library), though not as authoritative, possesses considerable interest in its own right but is not available in a modern edition. Also somewhat unorthodox has been the practice followed here for the body and soul debate *Als I lay on a winteris nyt*; in this instance the text has been taken principally from Bodleian Library MS Laud 109, but with a lengthy section supplied from the Auchinleck manuscript of the National Library of Scotland in order to fill a gap.

Aside from these two exceptions, the editorial practices followed have been largely traditional and conservative. Emendations and readings from other manuscripts have been introduced sparingly. Deviations from the copy text have been recorded in the textual notes, and readings from other texts are placed in square brackets in the text. Obvious errors in the copy text have been corrected silently, with the actual manuscript reading recorded in the textual notes. The textual notes do not provide an *apparatus criticus* for the text, and they do not include variant readings from the other manuscripts unless an important point of interpretation is involved.

Manuscript abbreviations and contractions have been expanded silently, in accordance with conventional practice, and modern punctuation and capitalization have been used. However, the archaic letters of the alphabet used in the various manuscript texts have been preserved and are recorded here just as they are found in the texts; *u/v* and *i/j* are also printed as they occur in the manuscripts. Normally all indentations and sub-divisions in the texts reflect the actual practices of the scribes. In the case of the alliterative debates (*Winner and Waster*, the *Parliament of the Three Ages*, and *Death and Life*), however, some paragraph indentations have been introduced to indicate major narrative divisions in the poems. If a poem receives a title in the manuscript, that title has been printed before the text of the poem. If a poem is untitled, a title has been supplied and placed within brackets.

Select Bibliography

This list includes the works cited in the Introduction and notes, as well as other critical materials pertinent to the study of medieval debate poetry.

Ackerman, Robert W. "The Debate of the Body and Soul and Parochial Christianity." *Speculum* 37 (1962): 541–65.

Alain de Lille. *The Complaint of Nature.* Trans. Douglas M. Moffat. Yale Studies in English 36 (1908); repr. Hamden, CT, 1972.

Batiouchkoff, T. "Le débat de l'âme et du corps." *Romania* 20 (1891), 1–55, 513–78.

Baugh, Nita S., ed. *A Worcestershire Miscellany.* Philadelphia, 1956.

Bazire, Joyce. "Mercy and Justice." *NM* 83 (1982), 178–91.

Benary, W., ed. *Salomon et Marcolfus.* Sammlung mittellateinischer Texte 8. Heidelberg, 1914.

The Bestiary: A Book of Beasts. Trans. T. H. White. New York, 1954.

Bestul, Thomas. *Satire and Allegory in Wynnere and Wastoure.* Lincoln, NE, 1974.

Biblia Sacra iuxta Vulgatam Clementiniam. Ed. Alberto Colunga and Lorenzo Turrado. 5th ed. Madrid, 1977.

Bishop Percy's Folio Manuscript: Ballads and Romances. Ed. John W. Hales and Frederick J. Furnivall. 3 vols. London, 1867–68.

Boase, T. S. R. *Death in the Middle Ages.* New York, 1972.

Böddeker, K., ed. *Altenglische Dichtungen des MS Harl. 2253.* Berlin, 1878.

Bossy, Michel-Andre. *Medieval Debate Poetry: Vernacular Works.* New York, 1987.

Braekman, W. L., and P. S. Macaulay. "The Story of the Cat and the Candle in Middle English Literature." *NM* 70 (1969), 690–702.

Brandl, Alois and O. Zippel, eds. *Mittelenglische Sprach- und Literaturproben.* Berlin, 1917.

Brown, Carleton. *English Lyrics of the XIIIth Century.* Oxford, 1932.

Brown, Carleton, and R. H. Robbins. *The Index of Middle English Verse.* New York, 1943.

Brunner, Karl. "Mittelenglische Todesgedichte." *Archiv* 167 (1935), 20–35.

————. "HS Mus. Additional 31042." *Archiv* 132 (1914), 319–21.

Bucholz, R. "Die Fragmente der Reden ser Seele an den Leichnam in zwei Handschriften zu Worcester und Oxford." *Erlanger Beiträge zur englischen Philologie* 6. Erlangen, 1890.

Carmina Burana. Ed. Wilhelm Meyers, et al. 2 vols. in 4 parts. Heidelberg, 1930–70.

Chaucer, Geoffrey. *The Parlement of Foulys*. Ed. D. S. Brewer. London, 1960.

———. *The Riverside Chaucer*. Gen. ed. Larry D. Benson. 3rd ed. Boston, 1987.

Child, Francis J., ed. *The English and Scottish Popular Ballads*. 5 vols. Boston, 1882–98.

Cleanness. Ed. J. J. Anderson. Manchester, 1977.

Cohen, Kathleen. *Metamorphosis of a Death Symbol: The Transi Tomb in the Late Middle Ages and the Renaissance*. Berkeley, 1973.

Conlee, John W. "*The Owl and the Nightingale* and Latin Debate Tradition." *The Comparatist* 3 (1980), 57–67.

Conybeare, J. J. *Illustrations of Anglo-Saxon Poetry*. London, 1826.

Cosquin, E. "Le Conte du Chat et de la Chandelle dans l'Europe du moyen âge et en Orient." *Romania* 40 (1911), 371–430.

Crisp, Frank. *Mediaeval Gardens*. Ed. Catherine C. Patterson. 2 vols. London, 1924; repr. New York, 1966.

Cursor Mundi. Ed. Richard Morris. EETS o.s. 57, 59, 62, 66, 99, 101. London, 1874–93.

Curtius, Ernst Robert. *European Literature and the Latin Middle Ages*. Trans. Willard R. Trask. New York, 1953.

Dauney, W., ed. *Ancient Scottish Melodies*. Edinburgh, 1838.

Davies, R. T., ed. *Medieval English Lyrics*. London, 1963.

Death and Liffe. James H. Hanford and J. M. Steadman, eds. *SP* 15 (1918), 221–94.

———. Joseph M. P. Donatelli, ed. Speculum Anniversary Monographs 15. Cambridge, MA, 1989.

Dickins, Bruce, ed. *The Conflict of Wit and Will*. Leeds Texts and Monographs 4. Leeds, 1937.

Dickins, Bruce, and R. M. Wilson. *Early Middle English Texts*. London, 1956.

Dudley, Louise. "The Grave." *MP* 11 (1913–14), 429–42.

Dunbar, William. *The Poems of William Dunbar*. Ed. W. Mackay Mackenzie. London, 1932.

———. *The Poems of William Dunbar*. Ed. John Small. STS 2. Edinburgh, 1898.

Dunn, Charles W., and Edward T. Byrnes. *Middle English Literature*. New York, 1973.

du Méril, E. *Poésies populaires latines antérieures au douzième siècle*. Paris, 1843.

Edward of Norwich, Second Duke of York. *The Master of the Game*. Eds. William A. and Florence N. Baillie-Groham. London, 1904.

Elbow, Peter. *Oppositions in Chaucer*. Middletown, CT, 1975.

Emerson, Oliver F., ed. *A Middle English Reader*. London, 1932.

Faral, E. "Les débats du clerc et du chevalier dans la litterature des XIIe au XIIIe siècles." *Romania* 41 (1912), 473 ff.

Fein, Susanna. "The Poetic Art of *Death and Life*." *The Yearbook of Langland Studies* 2 (1988), 103–23.

The Floure and the Leafe and *The Assembly of Ladies*. Ed. Derek A. Pearsall. Edinburgh, 1962.

Flügel, E. "Kleinere Mitteilungen aus Handschriften." *Anglia* 14 (1892), 471–76.

Ford, Boris, ed. *The New Pelican Guide to English Literature. I: Medieval Literature*. Harmondsworth, Middlesex, 1982.

Furnivall, Frederick J., ed. *Hymns to the Virgin and Christ, The Parliament of Devils, and Other Religious Poems*. EETS o.s. 24. London, 1867.

———, ed. *Jyl of Breyntford's Testament and Other Poems*. London, 1871.

———, ed. *The Minor Poems of the Vernon MS*. EETS 117 London, 1901.

Garbáty, Thomas J., ed. *Medieval English Literature*. Lexington, MA, 1984.

The Gest Hystoriale of the Destruction of Troy. Ed. G. A. Panton and D. Donaldson. EETS o.s. 39, 56. London, 1869, 1874.

Gilman, Stephen. *The Art of La Celestina.* Madison, WI, 1956.

Godman, Peter. *Poetry of the Carolingian Renaissance.* Norman, OK, 1985.

Gray, Douglas. *Themes and Images in the Medieval English Religious Lyric.* London, 1972.

Halliwell (-Phillips), James O. *Nugae Poeticae.* London, 1844.

Hammond, Eleanor P. "A Parliament of Birds." *JEGP* 7 (1908), 105–09.

Hanford, James Holly. "Classical Eclogue and Mediaeval Debate." *Romanic Review* 2 (1911), 16–31, 129–43.

———. "The Debate of the Heart and Eye." *MLN* 26 (1911), 161–65.

———. "The Mediaeval Debate between Wine and Water." *PMLA* 28 (1913), 315–67.

The Harley Lyrics. Ed. G. L. Brook. Manchester, 1948.

Harrington, David V. "The Personifications in *Death and Liffe,* a Middle-English Poem." *NM* 68 (1967), 35–47.

Haskell, Ann Sullivan, ed. *A Middle English Anthology.* Garden City, NY, 1969.

Hässler, Herbert. *The Owl and the Nightingale und die literarischen Bestrebungen des 12 and 13 Jahrhunderts.* Frankfurt, 1942.

Hazlitt, W. Carew, ed. *The Remains of the Early Popular Poetry of England.* 4 vols. London, 1864–66.

Hedberg, Betty Nye. "The Bucolics and the Medieval Poetic Debate." *Transactions of the American Philological Association* 75 (1944), 47–67.

Heningham, Eleanor K. *An Early Latin Debate of the Body and Soul.* New York, 1939.

Henryson, Robert. *The Poems and Fables of Robert Henryson.* Ed. H. Harvey Wood. Edinburgh, 1958.

———. *The Poems of Robert Henryson.* Ed. Denton Fox. Oxford, 1981.

Heist, W. W. *The Fifteen Signs Before Doomsday.* East Lansing, MI, 1952.

Hirsh, J. C. "Classical Tradition and the *Owl and the Nightingale.*" *Chaucer Review* 9 (1975), 145–52.

Horstmann, Carl, ed. *Sammlung Altenglische Legenden.* Heilbron, 1878.

Hume, Kathryn. *The Owl and the Nightingale: The Poem and Its Critics.* Toronto, 1975.

Huganir, Kathryn. *The Owl and the Nightingale: Sources, Date, Author.* Philadelphia, 1931.

Hussey, S. S. "Langland's Reading of Alliterative Poetry." *Modern Language Review* 60 (1965), 163–70.

James, Jerry D. "The Undercutting of Conventions in 'Wynnere and Wastoure.'" *Modern Language Quarterly* 25 (1964), 243–58.

James, Montague Rhodes, ed. *The Apocryphal New Testament.* Oxford, 1924.

Janofsky, Klaus. "A View into the Grave: 'A Disputacion betwyx þe Body and Wormes' in British Museum MS Add. 37049." *Taius* 1 (1974), 137–59.

Jeanroy, A. *Les origines de la poésie lyrique en France au moyen âge.* 3rd ed. Paris, 1925.

Kail, J., ed. *Twenty-six Political and Other Poems from the Oxford Mss Digby 102 and Douce 322.* EETS o.s. 124. London, 1904.

Kantorowicz, Ernst H. *The King's Two Bodies: A Study in Medieval Political Theology.* Princeton, 1957.

Kernan, Anne. "Theme and Structure in *The Parlement of the Thre Ages.*" *NM* 75 (1973), 253–78.

Kinghorn, A. M., ed. *The Middle Scots Poets.* Evanston, IL, 1970.

Kurvinen, Auvo. "Mercy and Righteousness." *NM* 73 (1972), 181–91.

Kyng Alisaunder. Ed. G. V. Smithers. EETS e.s. 227, 237. London, 1952–57.

Lampe, David E. "The Poetic Strategy of the *Parlement of the Thre Ages.*" *The Chaucer Review* 7 (1972), 173–83.

Langland, William. *Piers Plowman: The A Version*. Ed. George Kane. London, 1960.
————. *Piers Plowman: The B Version*. Ed. George Kane and E. Talbot Donaldson. London, 1975.
————. *Piers Plowman: An Edition of the C-text*. Ed. Derek Pearsall. Berkeley, 1979.
The Laud Troy Book. Ed. J. Ernst Wülfing. EETS o.s. 121, 122. London, 1902, 1903.
Linow, Wilhelm. "Þe Desputisoun bitwen þe Bodi and þe Soule." *Erlanger Beiträge* 1 (1889), 24–105.
Luria, Maxwell, and Richard L. Hoffman, eds. *Middle English Lyrics*. New York, 1974.
Lydgate, John. *The Minor Poems of John Lydgate*. Ed. Henry Noble MacCracken. Parts 1 and 2. EETS 107 e.s., 192 o.s. London, 1910, 1934.
Mannyng, Robert. *Robert of Brunne's Handlyng Synne*. Ed. Frederick J. Furnivall. EETS o.s. 119, 123. London, 1901, 1903.
Merrill, E. "The Dialogue in English Literature." *Yale Studies in English* 42. New Haven, 1911.
Middle English Dictionary. Ed. Hans Kurath, Sherman M. Kuhn, John Reidy, and Robert E. Lewis. Ann Arbor, 1952–.
Migne, Jacques-Paul. *Patrologia Cursus Completus. Series Latina*. Paris, 1857–66.
Morte Arthure. Ed. George Perry. EETS o.s. 8. London, 1865.
Morte Arthure: A Critical Edition. Ed. Mary Hamel. Garland Medieval Texts 9. New York, 1984.
Mum and the Sothsegger. Ed. Mabel Day and Robert Steele. EETS o.s. 199. London, 1936.
Nennius. *History of the Britons*. Trans. A. Wade-Evans. London, 1938.
Ong, Walter J. *Fighting for Life: Contest, Sexuality, and Consciousness*. Ithaca, NY, 1981.
Oulmont, Charles *Les débats du clerc et du chevalier dans la litterature poetique du moyen âge*. Paris, 1911.
Owen, Lewis J., and Nancy Owen, eds. *Middle English Poetry*. Indianapolis, 1971.
The Owl and the Nightingale. Ed. J. W. H. Atkins. Cambridge, 1922.
The Owl and the Nightingale. Ed. N. R. Ker. EETS o.s. 251. London, 1963.
The Owl and the Nightingale. Ed. E. G. Stanley. London, 1960.
The Owl and the Nightingale. Ed. J. E. Wells. Boston, 1907.
The Oxford Dictionary of English Proverbs. Ed. W. G. Smith and Janet E. Heseltine. 2nd ed. by Sir Paul Harvey. Oxford, 1948.
Padelford, Frederick M., and Allen Benham. "The Songs of Rawlinson MS C. 813." *Anglia* 31 (1908), 309–97.
Panofsky, Erwin. *Tomb Sculpture*. New York, 1964.
Parkes, J. W. *The Conflict of the Church and the Synagogue*. London, 1934.
The Parlement of the Thre Ages. Ed. Israel Gollancz. Select Early English Poems 2. London, 1915.
The Parlement of the Thre Ages. Ed. M. Y. Offord. EETS o.s. 246. London, 1959.
Patch, Howard R. *The Other World*. Cambridge, MA, 1950.
Peck, Russell A. "The Careful Hunter in *The Parlement of the Thre Ages*." *ELH* 39 (1971), 333–41.
Percy, Thomas. *Reliques of Ancient English Poetry*. Ed. Henry B. Wheatley. 3 vols. 1886; repr. New York, 1966.
Pinkerton, J., ed. *Ancient Scottish Poems*. 2 vols. London and Edinburgh, 1786.
Raby, Frederick J. E. *A History of Christian-Latin Poetry: From the Beginnings to the Close of the Middle Ages*. 2nd ed. Oxford, 1953.
————. *A History of Secular Latin Poetry in the Middle Ages*. 2 vols. Oxford, 1934.
Reiss, Edmund. "Conflict and its Resolution in Medieval Dialogues." *Arts Liberaux et Philosophie au Moyen Age*, Actes du quatrième Congres international de Philosophie médiévale. 1969, 863–72.

Ritchie, W. Tod, ed. *The Bannatyne Manuscript*. 4 vols. STS n.s. 23. Edinburgh, 1928–34.
Robbins, Rossell Hope, ed. *Secular Lyrics of the XIVth and XVth Centuries*. Oxford, 1952.
Robbins, Rossell Hope, and John L. Cutler. *Supplement to the Index of Middle English Verse*. Lexington, KY, 1965.
Robertson, D. W., Jr. *A Preface to Chaucer: Studies in Medieval Perspectives*. Princeton, 1963.
The Romance and Prophecies of Thomas of Erceldoune. Ed. James A. H. Murray. EETS 61. London, 1875.
The Romance of William of Palerne. Ed. Walter W. Skeat. EETS e.s. 1. London, 1887; repr. New York, 1981.
Ross, Thomas Wynne. "Five Fifteenth-Century 'Emblem' Verses from Brit. Mus. Addit. MS. 37049." *Speculum* 32 (1957), 274–82.
Rowland, Beryl. *Birds with Human Souls: A Guide to Bird Symbolism*. Knoxville, TN, 1978.
Sandison, Helen E. *The "Chanson d'Aventure" in Middle English*. Bryn Mawr College Monographs 12. Bryn Mawr, 1913.
Sargent, Helen C., and G. L. Kittredge, eds. *English and Scottish Popular Ballads*. Boston and New York, 1904.
Scattergood, V. J. "*The Boke of Cupide*—An Edition." *English Philological Studies* 9 (1965), 47–83.
———. "The Debate Between Nurture and Kynd—An Unpublished Middle English Poem." *Notes & Queries* 17 (1970), 244–46.
Scheirer, W. "Die vier Töchter Gottes," *Zeitschrift für deutsches Alt.*, n. f. 9 (1877), 414-ff.
Schröer, A. "The Grave." *Anglia* 5 (1882), 289–90.
Scott, Tom. *Dunbar: A Critical Exposition of the Poems*. Edinburgh, 1966.
Sibbald, J., ed. *Chronicle of Scottish Poetry*. Vol. 3. Edinburgh, 1802.
The Siege of Jerusalem. Ed. E. Kölbing and Mabel Day. EETS o.s. 188. London, 1932.
Sir Gawain and the Green Knight. Ed. J. R. R. Tolkien and E. V. Gordon. 2nd ed. Rev. by Norman Davis. Oxford, 1967.
Sir Orfeo. Ed. A. J. Bliss. Oxford, 1966.
Sir Tristrem. Ed. G. P. McNeill. STS 8. Edinburgh, 1886.
Skeat, Walter W., ed. *Chaucerian and Other Pieces . . . A Supplement to the Complete Works of Geoffrey Chaucer*. Vol. 7. 1897; repr. Oxford, 1963.
Small, John, ed. *The Poems of William Dunbar*. STS 2. Edinburgh, 1898.
Stengel, E. *Codicem Manu Scriptum Digby 86*. Halle, 1871.
Suchier, W. "L'Enfant Sage." *Gesellschaft für romanische Literatur* 24 (1910), 465–89.
Tavani, G. "Il dibattio sul chierico e il cavaliere nella tradizione mediolatina e volgare." *Romanistisches Jahrbuch* 15 (1964), 51–81.
Thorpe, Benjamin. *Analecta Anglo-Saxonica*. London, 1846.
Tobler, Alfred. "Streit zwischen Veilchen und Rose." *Archiv* 90 (1893), 152–58.
Tristram, Philippa. *Figures of Life and Death in Medieval Literature*. London, 1976.
Twiti, William. *The Art of Hunting*. Ed. B. Danielsson. Stockholm, 1977.
Utley, Frances L. "Dialogues, Debates, and Catechisms." *A Manual of the Writings in Middle English*. Ed. A. E. Hartung. Vol. 3, 669–745. Hamden, CT, 1972.
Varnhagen, Hermann. "Gustav Kleinert. Ueber den streit zwischen leib und seele. Ein beitrag zur entwicklungsgeschichte der Visio Fulberti." *Anglia* 3 (1880), 569–81.
———. "Zu dem streitgedichte zwischen drossel und nachtigall." *Anglia* 4 (1881), 207–10.
Vices and Virtues. Ed. Ferdinand Holthausen. EETS o.s. 89, 159. London, 1888, 1921.
Virgil. *The Aeneid of Virgil*. Trans. Allen Mandelbaum. Berkeley, 1971.
Vollmer, E. "Das me Gedicht The Boke of Cupide." *Berliner Beiträge zur germanischen und romanischen Philologie* 17 (1898), 28 ff.
Waldron, R. A. "The Prologue to *The Parlement of the Thre Ages*." *NM* 73 (1972), 786–94.

Walther, Hans. *Das Streitgedicht in der lateinischen Literatur des Mittelalters.* Quellen und Unter-
    suchungen zur Lateinischen Philologie des Mittelalters. Vol. 5, pt. 2. Munich, 1920.

The Wars of Alexander. Ed. W. W. Skeat. EETS e.s. 47. London, 1886.

Whiting, Bartlett J., ed. *Proverbs, Sentences and Proverbial Phrases from English Writings mainly
    before 1500.* Cambridge, 1968.

Winner and Waster. A Good Short Debate Between Winner and Waster. Ed. Israel Gollancz. 2nd
    ed. Oxford, 1930.

Woolf, Rosemary. *The Religious Lyric in the Middle Ages.* Oxford, 1969.

Wright, Thomas, ed. *The Latin Poems Commonly Attributed to Walter Mapes.* Camden Society
    Publications 16. London, 1841.

————, ed. *Specimens of Lyric Poetry composed in England in the Reign of Edward the First.* Percy
    Society 4. London, 1842.

Wright, Thomas, and J. O. Halliwell (-Phillips), eds. *Reliquiae Antiquae.* 2 vols. London,
    1841–45.

Abbreviations

Archiv	*Archiv für das Studium der neueren Sprachen und der Literaturen*
BL	British Library
CT	Chaucer's *Canterbury Tales*
DL	*Death and Life*
EETS	Early English Text Society
ELN	*English Language Notes*
e.s.	extra series
fol(s).	folio(s)
Index	*The Index of Middle English Verse*
LGW	Chaucer's *Legend of Good Women*
ME	Middle English
MED	*Middle English Dictionary*
MLN	*Modern Language Notes*
MS(S)	manuscript(s)
NM	*Neuphilologische Mitteilungen*
OF	Old French
O&N	*The Owl and the Nightingale*
o.s.	original series
Oxford	*The Oxford Dictionary of English Proverbs*
PF	Chaucer's *Parliament of Fowls*
R-C	Robbins-Cutler, *Supplement to the Index of Middle English Verse*
SGGK	*Sir Gawain and the Green Knight*
SP	*Studies in Philology*
STS	Scottish Text Society
TC	Chaucer's *Troilus and Criseyde*
Whiting	B. J. Whiting, *Proverbs, Sentences, and Proverbial Phrases*
WW	*Winner and Waster*

Middle English Debate Poetry

The Grave

The twenty-five alliterative verses recorded on the final leaf of MS Bodley 343, written primarily in a late twelfth-century hand, may represent the earliest extant example of a Middle English poem in the Body and Soul tradition, although its direct association with that tradition has been challenged (see L. Dudley, *MP* 11 [1913–14], 429–42). This poem, which Benjamin Thorpe first titled "The Grave," has often been praised for its powerful and imaginative portrayal of the inexorableness of death and the humiliations of the grave. But it has also provoked a good deal of controversy. It is not certain, for example, whether "The Grave" is a self-contained piece or merely a fragment of a longer piece; whether its final three verses, which are written in a slightly later hand, should be accepted as an integral part of the poem; or whether the voice that speaks throughout the poem is the Soul addressing its Body, or a personified abstraction such as Death, or the moralist-poet addressing an unspecified audience. It is certain, however, that the poem consists primarily of an elaborate metaphorical description of the grave as a house, a concept that occurs in medieval literature as early as the *Vercelli Homily* IX in the tenth century, and as late as the *Play of Lazarus* from the Towneley Cycle in the fifteenth century. The specific detail most often encountered in metaphoric descriptions of the grave as a house, the roof of the dead man's house resting on his chest (or his nose or chin), occurs here in line 10. But the most striking aspect of this poem is its austere tone, which is all the more unsettling for being completely dispassionate and for lacking the vituperation usually characteristic of a Soul berating its sinful Body. Verses 11–15, especially, place a chilling emphasis on the cold, dark confinement of the grave.

Regardless of the poem's unresolved questions, "The Grave" provides an important link between Old and Middle English literary traditions. Its general implications of *memento mori* (especially reminiscent of Job 17:11–16) and its use of specific themes and images found in the early Middle English death lyrics and Body and Soul poems associate "The Grave" with this important group of poems. The fact that "The Grave" is written in a form of alliterative verse which closely approximates the Anglo-Saxon alliterative line also establishes the poem as an important intermediary between Old English poetry and the fourteenth-century poems of the alliterative revival. "The Grave" generated considerable interest among nineteenth-century scholars — it was edited several times during the nineteenth century, and it inspired a translation by Longfellow — but it has not received as much attention in the twentieth century. "The Grave" is rarely anthologized, perhaps because it does not fall neatly into either the Old English period or Middle English period. Whether or not the poem is viewed as an "address to the body," it provides an appropriate starting point for a consideration of the Middle English Body and Soul tradition.

---

1)   Base Text: Bodleian Lib. MS Bodley 343 (Bodl. 2406), fol. 170v

2)   Other mss: none

3)   Selected Printed Texts: J. Conybeare, *Illustrations of Anglo-Saxon Poetry* (1826), 270.
B. Thorpe, *Analecta Anglo-Saxonica* (1846) 153.
A. Schröer, *Anglia* 5 (1882), 289.
R. Bucholz, *Erlanger Beiträge* 6 (1890), 11.

4)   *Index of Middle English Verse* 3497

[The Grave]

Ðe wes bold ȝebyld er þe iboren were,
Ðe wes molde imynt er ðu of moder come;
Ac hit nes no idiht ne þeo deopnes imeten,
Nes ȝyt iloced hu long hit þe were.

Nu me þe bringæð þer ðu beon scealt,   5
Nu me scæl þe meten & þa molde seoðða.
Ne bið no þin hus healice itinbred,
Hit bið unheh and lah þonne þu list þerinne;
Đe helewaȝes beoð laȝe, sidwaȝes unheȝe,
Þe rof bið ibyld þire broste ful neh.   10
Swa ðu scealt on molde wunien ful calde,
Dimme & deorcæ þet den fulæt on honde,
Dureleas is þæt hus & dearc hit is wiðinnen
Đær þu bist feste bidytt, & dæð hefd þa cæȝe.
Laðlic is þæt eorð hus & grim inne to wunien,   15
Đer ðu scealt wunine & wurmes þe to deleð.
Đus ðu bist ileȝd & ladæst þine fronden;
Nefst ðu nenne freond þe þe wylle faren to.
Đæt efre wule lokien hu þe þæt hus þe likie
Đæt æfre undon ðe wule ða dure   20
. . . . . . & þe æfter lihten,
For sone þu bist ladlic & lad to iseonne.

---

21. There is no indication in the ms that a half-line is lacking.

---

5. *me*: the indefinite pronoun "one" or "someone" or "men"; the line could be rendered in the passive voice —"Now you are brought where you shall be"— but the indefinite pronoun helps to promote a sense of impersonalness and callousness —"Now someone brings you . . . . Now someone . . . ."
9. The internal rhyme in this verse may be intentional, reflecting the tendency of early Middle English alliterative verse to divide into couplets.
11. This verse fails to alliterate, but the *molde/calde* rhyme may be intended to replace the alliteration.
15. This verse is also lacking in alliteration.
16. The image of the body as food for worms is a conventional feature of ME death lyrics and of the later Body and Soul poems, culminating in an actual disputation between the body and the worms.
17-22. The desertion of the body by its former friends is also stressed in the Body and Soul tradition, as it is elsewhere (cf. *Everyman*). Often the physical loathsomeness of the body is emphasized, accompanied by sardonic comments about the body's present lack of lovers. That aspect of the theme is not stated overtly here, but it is suggested in the three verses that were added to the original text.
22. Following this verse in the ms are three verses in what is probably an early thirteenth-century hand:

Translation

For you a house was built ere you were born, for you the earth was marked out ere you came from your mother. But it was not prepared, nor its depth measured, nor was it yet certain how long it should be. Now men bring you where you shall be, now men measure you and the earth thereafter. This house (for you) is not constructed upward, it is flat and low when you lie within it; the endwalls are low, the sidewalls not tall, the roof is built quite near your breast. Thus you shall dwell, quite cold in the earth, in dimness and darkness; that den soon decays. Doorless is that house and dark within where you shall dwell, and worms (shall) devour you. Thus are you laid away, and (thus) you leave your friends; never will a friend seek you out, who will journey to you, who will ever inquire how you like that house, who will ever undo the door for you . . . and afterward join you, for soon you are loathsome and hateful to see.

For sone bid þin hæfet faxes bireued
Al bid des faxes feirnes forsceden
Næle hit nan mit fingres feire stracien.

("For soon your head is deprived of hair, / All the fairness of your locks destroyed, / No more attached by fair fingers.")

Nou is mon hol and soint:
The Soul's Address to the Body

The theme of the humiliations of death and dying found in many early death lyrics is joined with an address of the Soul to the Body in the thirteenth-century poem *Nou is mon hol and soint.* The first half of the poem (ll. 1–12) describes the unexpected arrival of death in the midst of life, the preparations the Body receives for burial, and the callous treatment of the Body by the living. The second half of the poem (ll. 13–24) consists entirely of the Soul's denunciation of the Body at the moment when the two are parted. The Soul berates the Body for having failed in its religious obligations and then offers a final grim reminder of the Body's corruption in the grave. This latter portion of the poem reflects an early stage in the evolution of the Body and Soul materials, one which precedes the exchange of speeches between the Soul and the Body. *Nou is mon hol and soint* is recorded in Trinity College Cambridge MS 323, a miscellany of Latin, Anglo-Norman and English works, which also contains several other death lyrics and poems relating to the Body and Soul tradition. There are uncertainties about the text of the poem as we have it in the manuscript, particularly in its final verses, and it is possible that the poem is a fragment of a longer work.

---

1)   Base Text: Trinity College Cambridge MS 323 (B.14.39), fol. 27v (col. 2)

2)   Other mss: none

3)   Printed Texts: T. Wright, *Camden Society* 16 (1841), 322
                                      H. Varnhagen, *Anglia* 3 (1880), 577
                                      C. Brown, *English Lyrics of the Thirteenth Century* (1932),
                                         31
                                      R. T. Davies, *Medieval English Lyrics* (1963), 73–4

4)   *Index of Middle English Verse* 2336

[Nou is mon hol & soint]

Nou is mon hol & soint
& huvel him comit in mund;
Þenne me seint aftir þe prest
Þat wel con reden him to Crist.   4
Afteir þe prest boit icomin
Þe feirliche deit him hauit inomin;
Me priket him in on vul clohit
& legget him by þe wout.   8
A-moruen boþin sout & norit
Me nimit þat bodi & berrit hit forit;
Me grauit him put oþer ston,
Þer-in me leit þe fukul bon.   12

Letters have been lost from the ends of some lines through trimming of the ms leaf.

5. boit *ms*: bou
6. inomin *ms*: ino . . .
10. forit *added*

1–3. These verses capture with chilling effect the brevity of human existence: "now one
  is healthy and happy, and he succumbs to sin; and now [when he is no longer healthy
  and happy] it is time to send for the priest. . . ."
3. *me*: the indefinite pronoun, i.e. "one" or "someone"; the line could be rendered as a
  passive: "then the priest is sent for." The repetition of the impersonal "someone"
  throughout this stanza contributes to the poem's callous tone.
8. *wout*: the meaning is uncertain; R. Woolf has suggested "cellar" or "outhouse."
9. *sout & norit*: literally, "south and north," but the meaning is that the harsh realities
  of burial practices are the same, regardless of where one lives.

Þenne sait þe soule to þe licam:

[Soul]   "Wey, þat ic ever in þe com!

Þu noldes friday festen to non,

Ne þe setterday almesse don,   16

Ne þen sonneday gon to churche,

Ne cristene verkis wrche.

Neir þu never so prud

Of hude & of hewe ikud,   20

Þu salt in horþe wonien

& wormes þe to-cheuen

& of alle ben lot

Þat her þe vere y-lewe."   24

Translation

Now is man whole and sound, and evil comes into his mind; then someone sends for the priest who can guide him toward Christ. After the priest has come, sudden death has seized him; someone fastens him inside a foul shroud and lays him beside a vault. In the morning, both south and north, someone takes that body and carries it forth; someone digs him a pit or a tomb wherein someone lays the fickle bone(s).

Then says the Soul to the Body: "Alas that I ever came within you! You would not fast until noon on Friday, nor give alms on Saturday, nor go to church on Sunday, nor do Christian works. Never mind how proud you were, famous for your skin and complexion, you shall dwell in the earth, and worms shall chew you, and you shall be loathsome to all who were dear to you."

---

15. non *ms*: no . . .
17. churche *ms*: chu . . .
18. wrche *ms*: wrch . . .
20. ikud *ms*: i . . .
22. þe *added*; vere *ms*: ve . . . y-lewe *ms*: plewe

---

15. *to non*: "until noon"; that is, 3 p.m., the ninth hour, at which time he could break his fast.

In a þestri stude I stod:
A Dialogue between the Body and the Soul

In a þestri stude I stod is a fully-developed dialogue between the Body and
the Soul which also subsumes a homily on the signs of Doomsday and the
Last Judgment. Such a union of originally separate but thematically relat-
ed materials is not unusual in death and doomsday literature where the
didactic concerns—producing horror, shame, revulsion, and the peniten-
tial activity that stems from those responses—outweigh aesthetic ones.
Although *In a þestri* falls into two distinct sections, some degree of unity
is achieved through the contrast between the corrupt and false judgments
rendered by the Body during his lifetime and the true and absolute judg-
ment he will receive on the Day of Doom. On the whole *In a þestri* does
not generate the intense conflict characteristic of later Body and Soul de-
bates such as *Als I lay in a winteris nyt.*

The dialogue section of *In a þestri* includes many of the familiar themes
of death literature: the *ubi sunt* formula, the image of the grave as a paltry
house, descriptions of the Body's physical corruption, and even a hint of
the theme of the fallen heroes (l. 31). But at the same time the poem is not
devoid of fresh imaginative touches, such as the striking image of the worms
casting lots for the Body's flesh (l. 27). The Soul's homily to the Body on
the signs of Doomsday is a crude and simplified account of the coming of
the end of the world. It is related to the immensely popular tradition of
the fifteen signs of Doom, based on the various scriptural references (prin-
cipally from the Book of Revelations) relating to the Day of Judgment and
the events which immediately precede it. The poet's compression of these

events into seven days may be intended to parallel the seven days of the Creation, but his handling of this material seems confused and repetitious. It also seems somewhat peculiar for this homily on Doomsday to be spoken by a Soul whose own salvation remains in question.

In a pestri survives in three widely varying manuscript texts. In Bodleian MS Digby 86, which serves here as the base text, the poem is merged crudely with two additional poems, *Doomsday* and the *Latemeste Dai*, poems which usually occur as separate pieces. (For a fuller description of Digby 86, see the introduction to the *Thrush and Nightingale*.) The Trinity and Harley texts differ from Digby by appending a lengthy moralizing conclusion which is certainly a later accretion. The poem is composed in imitation of the Latin septenary, a staple of thirteenth- and fourteenth-century homiletic writing, which often includes variants with six stresses and occasionally shows influence of the four-stress alliterative long line. Here it is enriched with medial rhyme to create, in effect, an eight-line stanza (abababab) of alternating four and three stress lines. The manuscript, however, prints these pairs of four and three-stress lines as a single line, and that format has been retained here.

1) Base Text: Bodleian MS Digby 86 (Bodl. 1687), fols. 195v–200r

2) Other mss: Trinity College Cambridge MS 323, fol. 29v
                       Brit. Lib. MS Harley 2253, fol. 57v

3) Printed Texts: T. Wright, 16 (1841), 246–9
                       E. Stengle, *Codicem Manu Scriptum Digby 86* (1871), 93
                       Böddeker, *Altenglische Dichtungen*, pp. 235–43

4) *Index of Middle English Verse* 1461

Hic incipit carmen inter corpus & animam

Hon an þester stude I stod an luitel strif to here
Hof an bodi þat was oungod þer hit lai on þe bere.

1. *Hon an þester stude*: "in a dark place"; the settings of Body and Soul poems are often appropriate for the mood of the poem; night-time settings are common, possibly suggested by Matthew 10:27 and Job 33:15-7.

Þo spak þe gost mid dreri mod mid reuþfele chere:

[Soul]   "Wo worþe þi fleis, þi foule blod, wi liggest þou nou here?   4

In halle þou were ful kene, þe wile þou were on liue,
False domes to deme, to chaungen two to fiue;
Þat is me onsene ne worþi neuere mo bliþe;
Ful sore mai I me mene þenne þat ilke wile."   8

Þo spac þe bodi so dimme to þe wrecche gost:

[Body]   "I vende mi worldes blisse me wolde euere i-last;
Nes me of no senne þat bindeþ me ful fast;
Þe bondes þat ich am inne to erþe hoe wileþ me cast."   12

Þo spac þe gost mid rute red after ful, iuis:

[Soul]   "Wer is þi muchele pruide, þi ver and þi gris,
Þine palefreis ane þine steden and þi pourpre pris?
Ne shalt þou nout wiþ þe leden, wrecche, þer þou list?"   16

Þo spac þe bodi wiþ niþe of herte mid sunnes þer hit lai
srud:

---

4. "Woe betide thy flesh, thy foul blood"; the question in the second half of the line is
   sarcastic. Cf. *Als I lay in a winteris nyt*, 14–5.
5–6. The Soul depicts the Body as a wealthy landholder who presides over the affairs
   of his estate, deceitfully manipulating them to his own financial advantage; cf. also
   l. 31. This judgment scene in the Body's hall is echoed in ll. 87 ff. when he must
   face the Last Judgment in the Lord's hall.
6. *to chaungen two to fiue*: i.e. to falsify the accounts by increasing the amount due, per-
   haps by altering a Roman numeral II to a V; however, the expression may be figur-
   ative.
7–8. "It is clear to me that there will never be any more joy (for us); sorely may I lament
   concerning that same time."
10. *vende*: "thought;" (*v* for *w* is common in this text)
10–11. These verses are transposed in the other mss.
11. The text for this verse is flawed in all mss, but the meaning is: "I gave no thought
   to sins that bind me so fast."
13. "Then spoke the ghost with right (i.e. good) counsel after foul (counsel), indeed."
14. *þi ver and þi gris*: "your fur and your gray fur;" see *Thrush and Night*. 116–7 and the
   note to those lines for discussion of this formulaic expression.
15. Cf. *Als I lay* 36; *pourpre pris*: "valuable silks"
16. "You shall take nothing with you, wretch, (to the place) where you (will) lie."
17. *srud*: "shrouded"

[Body] "Nou is þis dai comen me to, wo is me bitid.
Ibounden beþ mine honden, min eien aren me hud;
I wende for to biden here, heuele is me bitid." 20

[Soul] "Bodi, þou hauest liued to longe; wo worþe þe, so swikel;
Þe riʒtte to þe wronge þou turndest al to mikel;
Wile þou vere in þis vourlde þine wordes weren false and
swikel;
Of pines harde and stronge miʒtt þou be ful siker." 24

[Body] "Wend awei nou, wrecche, hou longe sal þis strif laste?
Wormes holdeþ here strif and here domes faste,
I-mad hoe habbeþ here lotes mi fles for to caste;
Moni fre bodi schal rotien, ne bid I nout nou þe laste." 28

[Soul] "Bodi, maiʒt þou nout lepen to leiken ne to rage,
Wilde beres to beten, to binden leounes sauuage,
Poure men to þreten, binimen hem here heritage.
Ful lowe shalt þou fallen for alle þin heie parage." 32

[Body] "Wrecche gost, þou wend awei, ful vel const þou nou chide.
I wot wel þat I shal rotien for al mi pruide;
Wormes schulen eten mi þrote and mi wite side,
Min howen fles hoe shelen eten and onder erþe huide." 36

[Soul] "Uuas I neuere wrecche bote þoreu þin heuele redes,
Of þine sunnes me þinkeþ shome and of þine heuele dedes;

---

22. turndest *ms*: turdest
24. be *ms*: ben

---

21. *wo worþe þe, so swikel*: "woe betide thee, (that art) so treacherous"
24. "Of pains (both) hard and strong, you will (now) be quite certain."
27. "They have made their lots, to cast for my flesh."
28. The line contains a hint of the theme of the fallen heroes, developed more extensively elsewhere and later combined with the theme of the Nine Worthies.
29. "Body, (now) you may not leap nor play or rage."
30. The Soul's disparagement of the Body here takes the form of ironic overstatement.
31. Cf. the Body's mistreatment of the poor in *Als I lay* 69–78.
32. *for alle þin heie parage*: "in spite of your great nobility"
37. "I would never have become wretched if it weren't for your evil counsels."

         Wile were þou wilde, nou luitel me þe dredeþ.
         To Crist shal I clepien, he bete nou mi nede."   40

[Body]   "Wend auuei nou, vrec gost, mid þine longe tale,
         Me is vo i-nou þei þou ne houpbreide mi bale;
         I wot al to soþe wermes me eten sale;
         Mi dede me drou of mi riȝt stude into on depe dale."   44

[Soul]   "Bodi, wer beþ þine solers and alle þine toures,
         Þine feire cloþes and þine couertoures?
         Ful louue shalt þou fallen for alle þine boures.
         To Jhesu wille ich callen, he be mi socours."   48

[Body]   "Wrecche gost, þou vent auei, fare þer þou shalt fare;
         Me is wo i-nou, mine sides beþ colde and bare;
         Min hous is maked of cleie, þe woues beþ colde and bare;
         Þei þou chide niȝt and dai, ne sege ich þe namore."   52

[Soul]   "Bodi, wi neuedest þou þe biþout, þe wile þou miȝttest
         i-wolde
         Hof him þat makede ous alle of nout, wat hauest þou him
         i-holde?
         For hore sunnen and nout ffor his his fles he solde;
         Blodi he was on rode i-don, so þe profete hous tolde.   56

---

41. longe tale *ms*: loge tale

---

39. "For a while you were wild, (but) now I fear you very little."
40. Here and in l. 48 the Soul is deluding itself, for death literature stresses that it is
     too late to call on Christ after death has occurred.
42. "I would be miserable enough even if you didn't chide me."
43-4. "I know all too certainly (that) worms shall eat me, (that) my deeds have drawn
     me from my rightful place into a deep hole"; note the alliteration in l. 44.
45-8. The *ubi sunt* theme is briefly introduced. Cf. *Als I lay* 25–32. In the other mss this
     stanza follows line 36.
45. *solers*: a solarium was an upper chamber or "summer room"; cf. *Als I lay* 34.
52. It is curious that in the Trinity MS two additional stanzas of dialogue occur at this
     point — one spoken by the Soul, one by the Body — for the Body's intention to with-
     draw from any further discussion is clearly expressed at this point.
53-4. "Body, why were you never mindful — during the time you could have been — of
     Him who made us all from nothing, (and of) what you owed to Him."

Bodi, wilt þou nou lustnen I wille tellen þe
Of tuo miracles & fiue bifore domesdai shulen be.
Pe mon þat is on liue, þenne he mai se:
Penne is þat ilke wel þat þere mai fle.   60

Pe forme dai shal comen a red deu;
Hit shal bireuen ous alle boþe gomen and gleu;
Pe grene tre shal bleden þat oure louerd seu:
Penne is þat ilke wel þat ere hauet ben treu.   64

Pat oþer dai fuir shal brennen al þat hit foren stondeþ,
Ne mai no water hit quenchen ne nout þat hit ouer wondeþ;
Al þis world shal ouergon and al þi brode londe:
Penne shal houre louerd sen wose herede his wounde.   68

Pe þridde dai flod shal flouen þat al þis worlde shal illen;
Boþe in loue and in heie þe fulþe auei shal spillen
Herre þen heni hul into þer erþe millen:
Wel is him þat treue haueþ ben al þat ilke wile.   72

Pe ferþe dai wind shal bloven; so longe so he dures,
Castles shulen doun fallen and þe heye toures,

63–4. *These verses are transposed in the ms.*
64. þat *ms:* þa

---

57. "Body, if you will now listen, I will tell you"; at this point the Soul begins its homily
    on the Signs of Doomsday, a free adaptation of scriptural references to the apocalypse,
    taken mainly from Revelations. On the medieval tradition of the signs before dooms-
    day, see W. Heist, *The Fifteen Signs before Doomsday* (East Lansing, 1952).
60. "Then is the man fortunate who is able to escape."
61. Revelation 8:7(?)
62. *gomen and gleu:* "joy and pleasure," a common alliterating tag; cf. *Clerk and Nightingale*
    67 and *Thrush and Nightingale* 33 and 67.
63. Luke 23:31(?)
64. I.e., "then is the man fortunate who before had been true."
65. *oþer dai:* i.e., "the second day;" Rev. 8:8–9 or 11:5(?)
68. "Then shall our Lord see those who honored His wounds."
69–70. Rev. 8:10–11(?); *shal illen:* "shall cause harm"
71. "higher than any hill, miles upon the earth" (?)
73. The events described for the fourth, fifth, and sixth days seem to correspond to events oc-
    curring after the sounding of the seventh trumpet in Rev. 16:18–20; *he:* i.e., "it" (the wind).

Þe wode riȝt in to þe more wiþ þe harde shoures:
Þer shal euch mon cnouuen his and we shulen houre.   76

Þe fiffte dai hit shal ben liþe; aȝein þe wind shal saille,
Me ne þinkeþ noþin god to holden longe tale,
Þe wode into þer erþe, þe hul in to þe dale:
Ich holde him louerd and sire þa set seuene mai suale.   80

Þe seste dai aȝein þe non for aungles sulen wonden,
Blouen þat al þis world shal quakien wiþ hornes in honde;
If eni þing is on liue in watre oþer in londe,
Þer hi shulen arise and to þe dome ȝonge.   84

Þe seueþe dai shulen arisen, so þe boc ous tolde,
Hof here putte heuer ilke, boþe ȝonge and holde,
And comen in to þe halle, stronge domes to holde:
Þe mon þat haueþ ani god don wel hit is him i-holde.   88

Ne halt þe nout to chide ne holde domes stronge,
Þe aungles shulen quakien þat Crist makede wiþ his honde,
And þe tuelue aþostles þat woneden in þis londe,
And houre leue leuedi þat neuere ne louede wronge.   92

---

80. louerd *ms*: louer

---

75. "the forest onto the moor"
76. "There each man shall (come to) know his (fate) and we ours" (?).
78. A rhetorical device, essentially used as a filler, common in medieval narratives.
80. "I hold him (to be) Lord and Sire . . . ." The ms reading and the meaning of the second half of the line are uncertain.
81. "The sixth day before noon four angels shall sound (their horns)."
85–7. I Corinthians 15:52(?) On the seventh day the dead shall be summoned to their final judgment.
86. "from their graves every one, both young and old"
87. This line recalls ll. 5–6 and the judgments made *in halle* by the Body.
89. "nor will it help you at all to argue or to think the judgments (too) harsh"
92. "Our dear Lady, who never loved sin," will also be present at the Last Judgment.

Þenne clepeþ hore louerd Seinte Mari,
Hoe bringeþ þe rode þat stod opon þe Mounte Caluari;
Hy seþ þer his fet stondeþ his side is al blode;
For houre soule fode deþ he þolede witerli.   96

Þenne clepeþ hore louerd wiþhouten eni oupbreid:
'Comeþ blessede bernes þat in þis worlde weren sprad;
To paradis ȝe shulen alle, so þe profete hous rad,
Ha comeþ in to þis halle, mid blisse hi shulen ben lad.'   100

Þenne clepeþ houre louerd to Satanas þe hounhende:
'Awei fle þou, foul wit, mit þine acursede genge.
Awei fle þou henne, ne wone þou her no stounde,
Bote heuere bouten hende doun in helle grounde.'"   104

Þenne seiȝ þe gost, "weilavei" and þer affter "alas;
Wo werþe þat ilke stounde, bodi, þat þou boren was."

---

95. fet *ms*: fest
96. soule *ms*: foule
104. heuere bouten hende *ms*: heuere ho bouten hende

---

93. "Then our Lord will call Saint Mary."
95. "They see where his feet had stood, his bloody side."
96. "For our soul's nourishment he knowingly suffered death."
98–100. The summoning of the good souls to heaven contrasts sharply with the damnation of the wicked soul depicted in the concluding section of *Als I lay*.
100. *ha*: "who"
101–4. The judgment of Satan, from Rev. 20:1–3.
101. *Satanas þe hounhende*: "Satan, the un-courteous"
102. "Fly away, foul creature, with your accursed host."
104. *Bote heuere bouten hende*: "but ever without end"
106. "Accursed be that time, Body, when you were born"; at this point the Digby text concludes and, with no indication in the ms, there follows the text of a thematically related poem on Doomsday (*Index* 3967).

Als I lay in a winteris nyt:
A Debate between the Body and the Soul

The dramatic possibilities inherent in the mutual antagonisms of the Body and the Soul are fully realized in the Middle English debate *Als I lay in a winteris nyt*, the most impressive of the Body and Soul poems in English. *Als I lay* is unusual among Middle English poems for its combination of humor, pathos, and terror, and unusual among poems in the Body and Soul tradition for the very human qualities of its disputants and for the chilling effect of its conclusion, which causes the narrator to awaken in a cold sweat. *Als I lay* is more than a "brimstone thriller," however, for in addition to the poem's conventional admonition to repent before it is too late, the debate explores the intricacies of the Body and Soul relationship, stressing their mutual dependence and identifying the spiritual and physical sins for which they are accountable. The poem raises various moral and philosophical questions, not all of which are explicitly resolved.

Als I lay consists of three parts: the actual debate between the Soul and the Body, the vivid descriptive section which follows the debate, and the brief dream-vision framework which encloses the other two parts. The frame serves to establish a winter's night setting and to suggest the mental state in which the narrator experiences his vision. The disputation section consists of four lengthy exchanges between the Soul and Body, and is completely free from the artificial constraints of balance and parallelism so often imposed in the Latin and French debates. The debate begins with the newly-released Soul's denunciation of the Body, a speech which includes an extensive and sardonic *ubi sunt* passage, a description of the greed of those who stand to inherit the Body's possessions, and the Soul's declaration of its innocence. In responding to the Soul, the Body uses the theme of the fallen heroes to remind the Soul that death is common to all men; the Body concedes that it succumbed to worldly temptations, but it accuses the Soul of having failed to provide it with the proper moral guidance. The Soul rationalizes its failure to control the Body's impulses on the basis of the compassion it felt for the Body, whom it loved like a brother. In the final narrative section the torments inflicted on the damned Soul by the hell-hounds sent to fetch it away are depicted graphically. In a grim travesty of the hunts enjoyed by the knight during his lifetime, the Soul is forced by its tormentors to ride toward hell's entrance, where, in smoke and stench, it is swallowed up. Until their reunion on the Day of Judgment, the Soul will suffer in hell and the Body wili moulder in the grave. The narrator, terrified, awakens from his vision, acknowledges his sinfulness, prays for Christ's mercy, and urges other men to do likewise.

Seven texts of *Als I lay* are extant — more than are extant for any other debate poem in Middle English — indicating the fascination which the body and soul theme held for medieval audiences and perhaps also attesting to the literary merits of this particular poem. The earliest of the manuscripts is Laud Misc. MS 108 of the Bodleian Library, compiled near the end of the thirteenth century. The Laud text is easily the most attractive version of the poem from the standpoint of poetic qualities, as well as the most authoritative. Unfortunately, two manuscript leaves have been lost from this text. The text of the poem contained in the Auchinleck manuscript is second to the Laud text chronologically and in merit, but it contains many textual flaws, particularly toward the end of the poem. The other texts of *Als I lay* reflect substantial alterations and departures from the earlier versions and are distinctly inferior to them. The text of the poem which follows here is based upon the Laud manuscript, with 136 verses inserted from the Auchinleck manuscript to approximate those which have been lost from Laud. This is not an ideal solution, but it permits the Laud text to be presented in its entirety, while not sacrificing the "completeness" of the poem.

Bodleian Library MS Laud Misc. 109 (Bodl. 1486), although not as well known as Digby 86, Harley 2253, or the Auchinleck manuscript, is also one of the great manuscript anthologies compiled before the 1350–1400 era. In addition to containing didactic works such as the *Body and Soul* debate, the *South English Legendary*, and the *Vision of St. Paul*, it also contains texts of the thirteenth-century romances *King Horn* and *Havelok. Als I lay* is written in eight-line stanzas rhyming abababab.

1) Base Text: Laud Misc. 108 (Bodl. 1486), fols. 200r–203r (verses 1–48, 185–624)
Auchinlech MS (Advocates 19.2.1), fols. 31vb–34vb (verses 49–184)

2) Other mss: Vernon MS (Bodl. 3938), fol. 286rc
Digby 102 (Bodl. 1703) fol. 136r
BL MS Royal 18.A.x, fol. 61v
BL Addit. MS 22283, fol. 80va (verses 1–198 only)
BL Addit. MS 37787, fol 34r

3) Selected Printed Texts: W. Linow, *Erlanger Beiträge* 1 (1889), 24–105 (Laud 108, Bodl 1703 and 3938, and Auch.)
Thomas Wright, Camden Society 16 (1841), 334–46 (Laud 108 and Bodl 3938)
O. F. Emerson, *A Middle English Reader* (1948), 47–64 (Laud MS)
N. S. Baugh, *A Worcestershire Miscellany* (1956), 44 (BL Addit. 37787)
T. Garbáty, *Medieval English Literature* (1984), 603–19 (BL Addit. 37787)

4) *Index of Middle English Verse* 351

[The Debate between the Body and the Soul]

Als I lay in a winteris nyt,
In a droukening bifor þe day,
Vorsoþe I sauȝ a selly syt:

---

1. Als *ms*: ls (*The letters* ls *are preceded by a space for the capital letter which was never inserted.*)

---

1. Both the atmosphere and the symbolism of the poem are enhanced by the winter's night setting, which contrasts with the spring morning settings of the debates concerning love; scriptural passages such as Matt. 10:27 and Job 33:15–7 undoubtedly contributed to the choice of a night-time setting.
2. *In a droukening*: perhaps "in a troubled state of mind"; *droukening* is one of several obsolescent words in the Laud text which were altered in later Middle English versions of the poem.
3. "In truth I saw a wondrous sight."

A body on a bere lay 4
Þat hauede ben a mody knyȝt,
And lutel serued God to pay;
Loren he haued þe liues lyȝt,
Þe gost was oute and scholde away. 8

Wan þe gost it scholde go,
Yt biwente and withstod,
Bihelod þe body þere it cam fro,
So serfulli with dredli mod. 12

[Soul] It seide, "Weile and walawo!
Wo worþe þi fleys, þi foule blod!
Wreche bodi, wyȝ listou so,
Þat ȝwilene were so wilde and wod? 16

Þow þat were woned to ride
Heyȝe on horse in and out,
So koweynte kniȝt, i-kud so wide,
As a lyun fers and proud; 20
Ȝwere is al þi michele pride,

---

6. pay *ms*: payr
18. Heyȝe *ms*: heyre
19. kniȝt *ms*: knit

---

5. *mody*: "lusty" or "proud"
6. "and did little to please God"
7. *liues lyȝt*: literally his "life's light," but metaphorically his soul, the "ghost" of l. 8 — a suggestive phrase.
13. *Weile and walawo*: "alas and wellaway"
14. "Woe be to your flesh . . ."; i.e., "a curse on your foul flesh and blood"; cf. *In a þestri* 4; verses such as this one and ll. 21, 29, etc. suggest that *Als I lay* is an extensive re-working and elaboration of *In a þestri*, similar to what sometimes occurs among the ME religious lyrics.
15. "Wretched body, why lie you so?"
18. Cf. 415; riding "high on one's horse" indicates an exaggerated sense of self-importance; cf. Chaucer's Monk (*Cant. Tales* I 271) and Youth in *P3A* 111 and 170.
19. "so skillful a knight, so widely-known"
21. Cf. *In a þestri* 14

And þi lede þat was so loud?
ȝwi listou þere so bareside,
I-pricked in þat pore schroud?   24

ȝwere beon þi castles and þi toures,
Þi chaumbres and þi riche halles
I-peynted with so riche floures,
And þi riche robes alle?   28
Þine cowltes and þi couertoures,
Þi cendels and þi riche palles?
Wrechede is nouȝ þi bour!
Tomoruwe þouȝ schalt þer-inne falle!   32

ȝwere ben þi wurdli wedes,
Þi somers with þi riche beddes,
Þi proude palefreys and þi stedes
Þat þouȝ haddest in dester leddes?   36
Þi faucouns þat were wont to grede,
And þine houndes þat þou ledde?
Me þinkeþ God is þe to gnede
Þat alle þine frend beon fro þe fledde.   40

---

31. *an uncanceled* it *precedes* is
33. wurdli *ms*: murdli
37. wont *ms*: nouȝt

---

22. *lede*: "speech," i.e., voice
24. Cf. *Nou is mon* 7
25ff. The *ubi sunt* formula, used here sardonically, is a common feature in Body and
    Soul poetry.
29. Cf. *In a þestri* 46; *cowltes*: "quilts"
30. *cendals and palles*: costly fabrics, perhaps used as wall hangings
31-2. Cf. these verses with "Wen þe turuf is þi tuur" (*Index* 4044); the image of the grave
    as a paltry house has a long history (cf. *The Grave*); cf. ll. 76-80 below.
34. "your sumpter horses with rich trappings," or possibly "your summer rooms (i.e.,
    solaria) with rich beds" (cf. *In a þestri* 45)
36. *dester leddes*: "right-hand leads"
37. *grede*: "cry out"
39. "I think that God is too stingy to you."

Ʒwere ben þine cokes snelle
Þat scholden gon greiþe þi mete
With speces swete for to smelle,
Þat þouʒ neuere were fol of frete,   44
To do þat foule fleys to suwelle
Þat foule wormes scholden ete?
And þouʒ hauest þe pine of helle
With glotonye me bigete!   48

[Whare be þine glewemen þat schuld þe glewe,
Wiþ harp & fiþel & tabour bete,
Trumpours þat þine trumpes blewe?
Hem þou ʒeue ʒiftes grete,   52
Riche robes held & newe
For-to glewe þe þer þou sete;
Tregettours þat were vntrewe
Of þe hye hadde grete biʒete.   56

For to bere þi word ful wide
& maky of þe rym & raf,
Riche men for pamp & pride
Largeliche of þine þou ʒaf.   60
Þe pouer ʒede al bi side,

---

44. were *ms*: werere
58. rym *ms*: rune

---

41. *cokes snelle*: "quick (i.e., busy) cooks"
42. "that should prepare your food"
44. "(so) that you were never too full to eat"
45. *to do*: "to cause"
49–184. These verses, supplied from the Auchinleck MS, provide a good indication of what would have been found in the verses lost from the Laud MS.
49. *glewemen*: "gleemen," i.e., entertainers
53. *held*: "old"
55–6. "illusionists (i.e., magicians) that were untrue (i.e., skilled at deception), from you they had great rewards"
58. "and make for you rhyme and verse"; the phrase *rym and raf* is conceivably related to the comment of Chaucer's Parson that he cannot *rum, ram, ruf* (*Cant. Tales* I 42).
61–8. Pleas for the oppressed poor are commonly found in works with more overt political concerns, such as *Pierce the Ploughman's Creed*.

Euer þou hem ouer-haf,
& ʒif þai com in þine vnride,
Þai were y-stricken wiþ a staf.   64

Of þe pouer þou it nam
Þat mani a glotoun ete & drank;
Þou no rouʒest neuer of wham
No who þer-fore sore swank;   68
Þe riche was welcome þer he cam,
Þe pouer was beten þat he stank;
Now alle is gon in Godes gram
& þou hast, wreche, litel þank.   72

Tomorwe, anon as it is day,
Out of kiþ fram alle þine kin,
Alle bare þou schalt wende oway
& leuen al þine warldes winne.   76
Fram þe palays þat þou i lay,
Wiþ wormes is now y-taken þin in;
Þi bour is bilt wel cold in clay,
Þe rof schal take to þi chin.   80

Þou þat neuer in alle þi liue
Of þis warldes mock miʒtest be sad,
Now schaltow haue at al þi siþe
Bot seuen fet, vnneþe þat.   84

61–2. "The poor were pushed aside, (for) you always passed them by"; cf. *WW* 170
63. *vnride*: "path" (?)
65–6. "You took from the poor that (which) many a glutton ate and drank."
67. *no rouʒest neuer*: "didn't ever care"
68. *No*: "nor"; *sore swank*: "worked hard"
70. beaten until he was unable to control his bodily functions (?)
71. *gram*: "anger"
74. "away from all your kith and kin"
76. *warldes winne*: "worldly possessions," a common idiom
78. *þin in*: "thy lodging"
80. "The roof shall reach your chin"; cf. *The Grave* 10
82. "of this world's things might have your fill"
83. *siþe*: "journey" (?)

Þou miȝt y-se þe soþe & kiþe
Þat al is lorn þat þou biȝat;
No schaltow neuer make þe bliþe
Þer oþer men schal make hem glad. 88

Of alle þat þou togiders drouȝ,
Þou were harder þan þe flint,
Swiche schal make him large anouȝ
Þat þou wel litel haddest y-mint. 92
Þat þou madest it so touȝ,
Al þi bobaunce is now y-stint;
Ich may wepe þat þou bi louȝ,
For al mi ioie for þe is tint. 96

Þi fals air schal be ful fain
Þi fair fe to vnder-fo;
Now wele is him þis day y-sein
Þat litel gode schal for ous do. 100
He no wold nouȝt ȝiue oȝain,
To bring ous in-to rest & ro,
Of alle þi lond an acre or tvain
Þat þou so sinfuly com to. 104

Þi wiif no wil no more wepe;
Toniȝt no miȝt he haue no rest

---

85. *kiþe*: "know"
89. *drouȝ*: "drew"
91. *large anouȝ*: "free enough"
92. *y-mint*: "intended"
93. *madest it so touȝ*: i.e., "were so arrogant"; the meaning of the expression "to make it tough" varies according to its context, but "to act with cockiness" is attested elsewhere (cf. *As I stod on a dai* 29, and *Troilus & Criseyde* II 1025).
94. *bobaunce*: "pompousness"
95. *louȝ*: "low"
96. "For all my joy, because of you, is lost."
97–8. Note the running alliteration in these verses.
98. "your fair goods to receive"
101. "He wouldn't be willing to give (back) again."
104. *come to*: "came by"
105–10. "Neither will your wife weep anymore, nor will she have any rest nor sleep be-

No for fele þouȝtes slepe,
To wite what maner wiȝt be best   108
In þi stede for-to crepe;
Bi þis hye wot anoþer al prest:
Be þou be to-morwen doluen depe,
Anon þai schal be treweþe fest.   112

Now schul þine sekatours seck
Al þi gode when þou art ded;
Al to-gider schal go to wrek,
Haue men deled a litel bred.   116
Ich man pike what he may skek,
Hors & swine, schepe & net,
Gold & siluer, daþet who rec;
Ne be we boþe bi-tauȝt þe qued?   120

Now may þine neiȝbours liue,
Wreche, þatow hast wo y-wrouȝt;
Þou stintest neuer wiþ hem to striue
Til þai were to pouert brouȝt.   124
He was þi frende þat wald þe ȝiue
& þi fo þat ȝaf þe nouȝt;
Þe curs is comen þat now wil cliue
Þat mani a man haþ þe bi-souȝt.   128

Now beþ þe bedes on þe liȝt,
Wreche, þer y se þe lie,

---

cause of (her) many thoughts — contemplating what person (would) be best to creep
into your place; by now she has another all prepared." These verses (which Chaucer
may have known) bring to mind the Wife of Bath's marital stratagems (cf. *Cant. Tales*
III 567–74).
112. *treweþe fest*: i.e., "betrothed"
113. *sekatours seck*: "executors seek"; cf. *WW* 302–4
115–6. I.e., "It shall all be wasted, (just as if) men have divided up a piece of bread."
118. *net*: "cattle"
119. *daþet who rec*: "regardless of who cares"
120. "For aren't we both consigned to the Evil One?"
129. "Now have the prayers (of your enemies) come about."

Þat mani a man bad day & niȝt
& lay on her knes to crie.   132
Allas þat ich, wreched wiȝt,
Schal so gilteles abie
Þin misdedes & þine vntiȝt,
& for þe hard paines drie."   136

When þe gost wiþ reweful chere
Hadded y-maked þis michel mone,
Þe bodi þer it lay on bere,
A gastlich þing as it was on,   140
Lift vp his heued opon þe swere;
As it were sike it gan to gron,
[Body]   & seyd: "Wheþer þou art mi fere,
Mi gost þat is fro me gon?"   144

It seyd, "Wheþer þou be mi gast,
Þat me abreidest of min vnhap?
Vncomli, me þouȝt min hert brast
When deþ so diolfuli me drap.   148
Y nam þe first no worþ þe last
Þat haþ y-dronken of þat nap;
Nis non so kene þat he is cast,
Þe prodest arst may kepe his clap.   152

---

151. so *is written below line*
152. *the* l *in* clap *is written below the line*

---

135. *vntiȝt*: "vices"
136. *drie*: "endure"
137. In the Auchinleck MS each speech is introduced by a Latin rubric: e.g. *corpus respondit anime.*
138. *mikel mone*: "great complaint"
141. *heued*: "head"; *swere*: "neck"
143–6. "Is it true that you are my companion, my soul that has departed from me? Is it true that you are my soul, (you) who mock my unfortunate state?"
148. *drap*: "struck"
150. *nap*: "(drinking) cup"
152. "The proudest should be the first to hold his tongue."

Wele y wot þat y schal rote;
So dede Alisaunder & Cesar
Þat no man miȝt of hem finde a mot,
No of þe moder þat hem bar.   156
Wirmes ete her white þrote,
So schal hye mine, wele am y war;
When deþ so scharpliche schet his schot,
Þer nis non helpe oȝain to char.   160

Þer y seiȝe boþe clerk & kniȝt
& old man bi gates go,
Y was a ȝong man & liȝt
& euer wende to liui so.   164
Halles heiȝe & bours briȝt
Y hadde y-bilt & mirþes mo,
Mi woning here wel wele y-diȝt,
& now deþ haþ me dempt þer-fro.   168

Mi woning here wel worþli wrouȝt,
And wende to liui ȝeres fele;
Wodes, wones, watres y bouȝt,

---

158. hye *supplied*
160. helpe *supplied*; to *supplied*

---

154. The Body here introduces the theme of the fallen heroes, which is frequently found
    in Body and Soul literature.
157. Cf. *In a þestri* 35
159. The personified figure of Death commonly carries a dart or arrow; note the alliter-
    ation in this verse.
160. " . . . to turn toward"
161-2. Death striking down all classes of men indiscriminately is a common theme, es-
    pecially in ME lyrics concerning death; cf. *Index* 1387.
163-72. Theses verses reflect the "Pride of Life" theme, which is more fully explored
    in the *Parl. of Three Ages.*
167. "My dwelling here (I had) very sumptuously prepared."
168. *dempt*: "doomed"
171. *y*: "I"
171-2. Cf. the activities of Middle Age in the *Parl. of the Three Ages*

Wiþ al þat ich miȝt pike & spele.   172
Þe world is torned to-ȝain mi þouȝt,
When deþ þat stilly can stele
Haþ me dempt oway wiþ nouȝt,
& oþer welden alle mi wele.   176

Soule, ȝif þou it me wilt atwite
Þat we schul be boþe y-spilt,
ȝif þou hast schame & gret despite,
Al it is þine owhen gilt.   180
Y þe say at wordes lite,
Wiþ riȝt resoun, ȝif þatow wilt:
Þou berst þe blame & y go quite,
Þou scholdest fram schame ous haue yschilt.]   184

For God schop þe aftir His schaft
And gaf þe boþe wyt and skil;
In þi loking was I laft,
To wisse aftir þin oune wil.   188
Ne toc I neuere wyche craft,
Ne wist I ȝwat was guod nor il,
Bote as a wretche dumb and daft,
Bote as touȝ tauȝtest þer-til.   192

---

175. Haþ *ms*: & haþ
185. schaft *ms*: schap
191. daft *ms*: mad

---

172. *pik & spele*: "earn and save"
176. "and others wield all my wealth"
177. *atwite*: "blame"
183. *quite*: "free"
185. "For God created you in his image" (Genesis 1:26). It is at this point that the text in the Laud MS resumes.
187. *loking*: "care" or "keeping"
189. *wyche*: "wicked"
192. *touȝ*: "thou"; similarly *tou* (for *þou*) in lines 269, 293, 381

Set to seruen þe to queme,
Boþe at euen and amoruen,
Siþin I was þe bitauȝt to ȝeme
Fro þe time þat þouȝ was born.   196
Þouȝ þat dedes couþest deme
Scholdest habbe ben war biforn
Of mi folye, as it semet:
Nouȝ wiþ þi-selue þouȝ art forlorn."   200

[Soul]   Þe gast it seyde, "Bodi, be stille!
ȝwo haþ lered þe al þis wite,
Þat giuest me þese wordes grille,
Þat list þer bollen as a bite?   204
Wenestouȝ, wretche, þoȝ þouȝ fille
Wid þi foule fleichs a pite,
Of all dedes þouȝ didest ille
Þat þouȝ so litli schalt be quite?   208

Wenestou nou gete þe griþ
Þer þouȝ list roten in þe clay?
Þey þouȝ be rotin pile and pid
And blowen wiþ þe wind away,   212
ȝeot schaltouȝ come wiþ lime and lyþ
Agein to me on domesday,

---

198. ben *ms*: be
205. þoȝ *ms*: þor

---

193. *to queme*: "for pleasure"
195. "because I was taught to heed you"
197. *coupest deme*: "knew how to judge"
203. *grille*: "harsh"
204. *bollen as a bite*: "swollen as a (leather) bottle"
209. "Do you now expect to have peace?"
211. *pile and pid*: "peel and pith," i.e., outside and inside
213-6. The re-uniting of Soul and Body on the Day of Judgment is based upon such
     scriptures as I. Cor. 15:51-3, Rev. 11:18, and Rev. 20:12-5.
213. *lime and lyþ*: "limb and joint"

And come to court and I þe wiþ
For to kepen oure harde pay.   216

To teche were þouȝ me bi-tauȝt,
Ac ȝwan þouȝ þouȝtest of þe qued,
Wiþ þi teþ þe bridel þouȝ lauȝt;
Þouȝ didst al þat I þe forbed.   220
To sunne and schame it was þi drauȝt,
Til vntid and til wikkedehed;
Inouȝ I stod ageyn and fauȝt,
Bot ai þouȝ nome þin oune red.   224

Wan I þe wolde teme and teche
Ȝwat was uuel and ȝwat was guod,
Of Crist ne kirke was no speche
Bot renne aboute and breyd wod;   228
Inouȝ I miȝte preye and preche,
Ne miȝte I neuere wende þi mod
Þat þouȝ woldest God knouleche,
Bot don al þat þin herte stod.   232

I bad þe þenke on soule-nede,
Matines, masse, and euesong;
Þouȝ mostist first don oþere dede,
Þou seidist al was idel gong.   236

---

217. were *ms*: ȝwere
226. ȝwat *in margin*

---

216. "to receive our harsh reward"
217. "You were taught to learn from me."
218. *qued*: "evil"
219. "With your teeth you took the bridle"— perhaps related to the expression "to get the bit between your teeth."
221. *drauȝt*: "inclination"
224. "but always you took your own advice"
228. *breyd wod*: "brayed like a madman"
236. *idel gong*: "a useless journey," i.e., a wasted effort

To wode and water and feld þouȝ edest,
Or to court to do men wrong;
Bote for pride or grettore mede
Lutel þouȝ dust guod among.   240

Nouȝ mouwe þe wilde bestes renne
And lien vnder linde and lef,
And foules flie bi feld and fenne,
Siþin þi false herte clef.   244
Þine eiȝene blinde and connen nouȝt kenne,
Þi mouth is dumb, þin ere is def,
And nouȝ so lodly þouȝ list grenne —
Fro þe comeþ a wikke wef!   248

Ne nis no leuedi briȝt on ble,
Þat wel weren i-woned of þe to lete,
Þat wolde lye a-niȝth bi þe
For nouȝth þat men miȝte hem bihete.   252
Þouȝ art vnsemly for to se,
Vncomli for to cussen suwete;
Þouȝ ne hauest frend þat ne wolde fle,
Come þouȝ stertlinde in þe strete!"   256

[Body]   Þe bodi it seide, "Ic seyȝe,
Gast, þouȝ hast wrong, i-wys,
Al þe wit on me to leye
Þat þouȝ hast lorn þi mikil blis.   260

---

238. court *ms*: cour

---

237. Hunting here symbolizes the pursuit of worldly pleasure, as it also does in the *Parl.*
   of Three Ages and in the Monk's portrait in the *Gen. Prol.* of the *Canterbury Tales.*
248. *a wikke wef*: "a wicked whiff," i.e., a terrible stench
249. *briȝt on ble*: i.e., "fair of face," a common cliché in love lyrics and romances.
250. "that was accustomed to allow you to"
256. "if you came rushing down the street"
259. *wit*: "blame" (cf. *atwite* in l. 177)

Were was I bi wode or weyʒe,
Sat or stod or dide ouʒt mys,
Þat I ne was ay vnder þin eyʒe?
Wel þouʒ wost þat soth it ys.   264

Wedir I ede vp or doun,
Þat I ne bar þe on my bac,
Als þin as fro toun to toun,
Alse þouʒ me lete haue rap and rac?   268
Þat tou ne were and red roun,
Neuere did I þing ne spac;
Here þe soþe se men mouen
On me þat ligge here so blo and blac.   272

For al þe wile þouʒ were mi fere
I hadde al þat me was ned;
I miʒte speke, se, and here,
I ede and rod and drank and et;   276
Lodli chaunced is my chere
Sin þe tyme þat þouʒ me let;
Def and dumb I ligge on bere
Þat I ne may sterin hand ne fet.   280

I scholde haue ben dumb as a schep
Or as a nouwe or as a suyn,
Þat et and drank and lai and slep,
Slayn and passid al his pin;   284

---

268. Alse *ms*: Als se

---

261. *Were*: "Where"
268. *rap and rac*: "blows and blows"; redundant alliterating phrases also occur in ll. 309,
    391, 436, etc.
269–70. "Without you there to advise me, I was unable to think or speak."
277. "horribly changed is my appearance"
278. *let*: "left," i.e., departed
282. *a nouwe*: "a ewe"; cf. *a noxe* ("an ox"), l. 430
284. *pin*: "pain"

Neuere of catel he ne kep,
Ne wyste wat was water ne wyn,
Ne leyn in helle þat is so dep:
Neuere ne wist I of al þat was tin."   288

[Soul]   Þe gast yt seide, "Is no doute,
Abouten, bodi, þouȝ me bar;
Þou mostist nede, I was wiþoute
Hand and fot, I was wel war.   292
Bote as tou bere me aboute
Ne miȝt I do þe leste char;
Þorfore most I nede loute,
So doth he þat non oþer dar.   296

Of a wymman born and bredde,
Body, were we boþe tvo;
Togidre fostrid fayre and fedde
Til þou couþist speke and go.   300
Softe þe for loue I ledde,
Ne dorst I neuere do þe wo;
To lese þe so sore I dredde,
And wel I wiste to getin na mo.   304

For me þou woldest sumwat do
Wȝile þou were ȝong a litil first,

---

296. he *supplied*

---

285. "It never paid any attention to possessions."
288. A difficult verse; perhaps "Never would I have known the things that happen then" (i.e., in Hell).
294-6. "I couldn't make the slightest move; therefore I had to bow (to your wishes), as one who has no other choice."
301. "I led you gently, out of love for you"; the relationship between Body and Soul described here suggests the intimacy of brothers; the Soul, in the role of elder brother, has been lenient with his unruly younger brother, the Body, out of affection for him.
306-12. In these verses the Soul describes the Body's early cooperation and its initial willingness to do penance through the mortification of the flesh; later on, however,

For frendes eyʒe þat þe stod to,
Þe wile þouʒ were betin and birst;   308
Oc wan þouʒ were þriuen and þro
And knewe honger, cold, and uirst,
And ʒhwilk was eyse, rest, and ro,
Al þin oune wil þou dist.   312

I sau þe fair on fleychs and blod,
And al mi loue on þe I kest;
Þat þou þriue me þouʒte guod,
And let þe hauen ro and rest.   316
Þat made þe so sturne of mod
And of werkes so vnwrest,
To fiʒte with þe ne was no bot —
Me þat þouʒ bar in þi brest.   320

Gloterie and lecherie,
Prude and wicked coveytise,
Niþe and onde, and enuie
To God of heuene and alle hise,   324
And in vnlust for to lye —
Was ti wone not of þise?

---

309. Oc *ms*: or
326. ti *ms*: te; not *ms*: non

---

the Body preferred to follow an easier course; ll. 307–8 are difficult, but their mean-
ing seems to be, "because of the comforts of friendship that you enjoyed, (you be-
haved well during) the period of time that you were (often) chastised" (i.e., when
you were young).
309. *þriuen and þro*: "had thriven and become strong," i.e., were fully matured
317. *sturne of mod*: "obstinate"
318. *vnwrest*: "deceitful"
321–5. The Soul here lists the Seven Deadly Sins, each of which the Body indulged in.
323. *Niþe and onde*: "malice and anger," together comprising the sin of Wrath; this is a
common formula.
325. "to lie in slothfulness"
326. "Weren't your habits (comprised) of these?"

Þat I schal nouȝ ful dere abye!
A! Weyle! Sore may me grise!   328

Þou was warned her bifore
Ȝwat we boþe scholden haue;
Idel tale held tou þat þore
Þouȝ þou sauȝ fele bidun in graue.   332
Þou dist al þat þe werld þe bad
And þat þi fleys þe wolde craue;
I þolede þe and dide as mad,
To be maister and I þi cnaue."   336

[Body]   "I-weneste þouȝ, gost, þe geyned ouȝt
For to quite þe wiþal —
Þouȝ þat was so wordly wrouȝt —
To seye I made þe my þral?   340
Dud I neuere on liue nouȝt!
I ne rafte ne I ne stal
Þat furst of þe ne kam þe þouȝt:
Aby yt that abyȝe schal!   344

Ȝwat wist I wat was wrong or rith,
Wat to take or ȝwat to schone,
Bote þat þouȝ pottist in mi siȝth,

---

330. we *supplied*
332. þouȝ *supplied*; ȝwat we *canceled*
335. dide *supplied*
337. þe *supplied*; ouȝt *ms:* out

---

332. *bidun:* "defiled"
333. *þe werld:* "the world," the first of man's three tempters, along with the flesh and the devil; these three foes are treated more fully later in the poem.
335-6. "I suffered you and did as I was made (to do), (allowing you) to be the master and I the servant."
337-8. "Do you think, ghost, you have gained anything for to acquit you . . . ?"
339. *wordly:* "worthily"
344. "He shall pay who deserves to pay!"
346. *schone:* "shun"

Þat al þe wisdom scholdest cone?   348
Ȝwanne þouȝ me tauȝtist on vntiȝth
And me gan þeroffe mone,
Þanne dud I al my miȝth
Anoþer time to haue my wone.   352

Oc haddist þouȝ þat Crist it ovþe,
Giuen me honger, uurst, and cold,
And þouȝ witest me þat no guod couþe
In bismere ȝhan I was so bold,   356
Þat I hadde vndernomen in ȝouþe
I hauede holden hwan I was old;
Þou let me reykin north and south
And hauen al my wille on wold.   360

Þouȝ scholdist for no lif ne for lond,
Ne for non oþer worldes winne,
Haue soffrid me to lein on hond
Þat hauede torned to schame or sunne.   364
Oc for I þe so eise fond,
And þi wretche wit so þunne
Þat ay was wriþinde as a wond,
Þerfore couþe I neuere blinne.   368

---

350. And *ms*: an
358. hwan I was *supplied*
366. wit *ms*: with
368. þerfore *ms*: þefore

---

348. "(you) that all the wisdom should have known"
353. "but if you had (done as) Christ taught"
354. force me to do penance through the mortification of the flesh; cf. 310
355. "and (if) you had instructed me who knew no better"
356. *bismere*: "shame"
359. *reykin*: "wander"
360. "and let me obtain all my desires"
363. *to lein on hond*: "to undertake"
365. *eise fond*: "easy found"
366. *þunne*: "thin," i.e., weak
367. " . . . bending (or wavering) like a reed"

To sunne þouȝ wistist was my kinde,
As mankinne it is also,
And to þe wretche world so minde,
And to þe fend þat is ore fo.   372
Þouȝ scholdest er haue late me binde
Wan I misdede and don me wo.
Ac ȝwanne þe blinde lat þe blinde,
In dike he fallen boþe two."   376

Þo bigan þe gast to wepe,
[Soul]   And seide, "Bodi, allas, allas
Þat I þe louede euere ȝete,
For al mi loue on þe I las!   380
Þat tou louedest me þouȝ lete,
And madest me an houue of glas;
I dide al þat þe was sete
And þouȝ my traytor euere was.   384

Ho may more trayson do
Or is louerd betere engine
Þan he þat al is trist is to,

---

381. lete *ms*: le

369–72. Here the Body also alludes (as the Soul had earlier) to the traditional tempters
    of man: the flesh, the world, and the devil.
371. *so minde*: "(was) so mindful"
373. "You should have bound me sooner."
375–6. This well-known proverb (Whiting B350) is based on Matt. 15:14 (Luke 6:39);
    cf. also Bruegel's painting, "Parable of the Blind Men" (Gallerie Nationali di
    Capodimonte, Naples).
377. This section in the Soul's speech may be based on St. Bernard's "De tribus inimicis
    hominis, carne, mundo, et diabolo" (Migne, *PL* 184:503–5), as is the poem "St. Ber-
    nard on Man's Three Foes" in the Vernon MS (*Index* 2865).
380. *las*: "concentrated"
382. *houve of glas*: "a cap of glass," a helmet that creates the illusion of providing protec-
    tion, thus giving its wearer a false sense of security; see note to l. 81 of the *Clerk and
    the Nightingale II.*
383. *sete*: "sweet"

In and ouʒt as ovne hyn?   388
Ay seþþe þouʒ was þriuen and þro,
Mittis ded I alle mine
To porueʒe þe rest and ro,
And þouʒ to bringe me in pine.   392

Þe fend of helle þat haueþ enuiʒe
To mankune, and euere haþ had,
Was in vs as a spie,
To do sum god ʒwan I þe bad.   396
Þe werld he toc to cumpayniʒe,
Þat mani a soule haued for-rad;
Þey þre wisten þi folye,
And madin, wretche, þe al mad.   400

ʒwan I bad þe reste take,
Forsake sunne ay and oo,
Do penaunce, faste, and wake,
Þe fend seide, 'Þouʒ schalt nouʒt so';   404
Þos sone al þi blisse forsake
To liuen ay in pine and wo.
Ioyʒe and blisse I rede þouʒ make
And þenke to liue ʒeres mo.   408

ʒwan I bad te leue pride,
Þi manie mes, þi riche schroud,
Þe false world þat stod biside

---

404. fend *ms*: fe

---

388. "as completely as (your) own servant"
389–90. "Ever since you were grown and strong, I used all my might."
396. "when I commanded you to do good"
398. *for-rad*: "deceived"
399. *þey þre*: "those three," i.e., the world, flesh, and devil
402. *ay and oo*: "once and for all"
410. *mes*: "meals," i.e., feasts; *schroud*: "clothing"

Bad þe be ful quoynte and proud,   412
Þi fleychs with riche robes schride —
Nouʒt als a beggare in a clouʒt! —
And on heiʒe horse to ride
With mikel meyne in and ouʒt.   416

ʒwan I bad þe erliche to rise,
Nim on me, þi soule, kep,
Þouʒ seidest þou miʒtest a none wise
Forgon þe murie morweslep.   420
Wʒan ʒe hadden set your sise,
ʒe þre traytours, sore I wep;
ʒe ladde me wid ʒoure enprise
As te boþelere doth is schep.   424

ʒwan ʒe þre traitours at o tale
Togidere werein agein me sworn,
Al ʒe maden troteuale,
Þat I haued seid biforn.   428
ʒe ledde me bi doune and dale

---

422. ʒe *ms*: þe
423. ʒoure *ms*: oure
425. ʒe *supplied*
429. ʒe *ms*: þe

---

413. *schride*: "clothe"
414. *clouʒt*: "rag"
415. Cf. 18 and the note to l. 18.
416. *mikel meyne*: "a large retinue"
418. *þi soule* is an appositive.
421. *set your sise*: "made your compact"
423. *enprise*: "cleverness"
424. *boþelere*: "butler," but "butcher" (the reading of the Auchinleck MS) seems more appropriate.
425. *at o tale*: "in complete agreement"
427. *troteuale*: "idle or foolish behavior"; the meaning of this rare term can be inferred from its several occurrences in Robert Mannyng of Brunne's *Handlyng Synne* (47, 5971, etc.).

As a noxe bi þe horn,
Til þer as him is browen bale,
Þer his þrote schal be schorn.   432

For loue þi wille I folewede al,
And to min oune deth I drouȝ,
To foluwe þe þat was mi þral,
Þat euere were false and frouȝ.   436
Þouȝ it dist and I forhal,
We wistin wel it was wouȝ;
Þerfore mote we kepe ore fal,
Pine and schame and sorewe inouȝ.   440

Þeiȝ alle þe men nouȝ vnder mone
To demen weren sete on benche,
Þe schames þat vs schullen be done
Ne schuldin haluen del biþenke.   444
Ne helpeþ vs no bede ne bone,
Ne may vs nou no wyl towrenche;
Hellehoundes cometh nou sone,
Forþi ne mouwe we noyþer blenche."   448

Ȝwan þat bodi say þat gost
Þat mone and al þat soruwe make,

---

448. forþi *ms*: forbi

---

430. *a noxe*: "an ox"
431. *is browen bale*: "bale is brewed," i.e., harm is prepared
432. *schorn*: "cut"
436. *frouȝ*: "fickle"
437. *forhal*: "concealed (it)"
438. *wouȝ*: "evil"
441. *þeiȝ*: "though"; *vnder mone*: "under the moon," i.e., in the world
443-4. "the humiliations that shall be done to us — (they) could not think up half"
445. *no bede ne bone*: "neither prayer nor boon"
446. "nor may any trick now separate us (from what is coming to us)"
448. "therefore we may not, either of us, escape"

[Body]   It seyde, "Allas þat my lif hath last,

Þat I haue liued for sunne sake,   452

Þat min herte anon ne hadde to-borste

Ʒwan I was fram mi moder take;

I miʒte haue ben in erþe kest,

And i-leiʒen and i-roten in a lake.   456

Þanne haued I neuere lerned

Ʒwat was vuel ne ʒwat was guod,

Ne no þing with wrong ʒernd,

Ne pine þoled, as I mot,   460

Ʒwere no seint miʒye beren ore ernde

To Him þat bouʒte vs with is blod,

In helle ʒwanne we ben brend,

Of sum merci to don vs bot."   464

[Soul]   "Nay, bodi, nouʒ is to late

For to preiʒe and to preche;

Nou þe wayn is ate ʒate,

And þi tonge haþ leid þe speche.   468

O poynt of ore pine to bate

In þe world ne is no leche;

Al tegidere we gon o gate:

Swilk is Godes harde wreche.   472

Ac haddest þouʒ a lutel er,

Ʒwile vs was lif togidre lent,

453-4. "that my heart did not burst as soon as I was taken from my mother"; cf. Job 10:18-9; here the Body, like Job, has begun to despair.

460. "nor pain suffered, as I must"

461. *ore ernde*: "our petition"

467. "Now the wain (death wagon) is at the gate," a fairly common expression in poems concerning death; cf. l. 7 in "The Signs of Death" (*Index* 4045): "Al to late, al to late þen is te wayn atte ʒate."

468. *leid*: "laid (aside)," i.e., lost

469. *bate*: "abate"

472. *wreche*: "punishment"

473-88. These stanzas contain the central didactic message of the poem: "If only you had been mindful of your spiritual needs earlier! Now that death has taken us there is no remedy."

Þo þat was so sek and ser,
Vs schriuen and þe deuel schent,   476
And laten renne a reuly ter
And bihiȝt amendement,
Ne þorte vs haue friȝt ne fer
Þat God ne wolde His blisse vs sent.   480

Þey alle þe men þat ben o lyues
Weren prestes, messes for to singe,
And alle þe maidenes and þe wyues,
Wydewes, hondene for to wringe,   484
And miȝte suweche fyue
Als is in werld of alle þinge,
Siþin we ne mouwen vs suluen schriue,
Ne schulde vs into blisse bringe.   488

Bodi, I may no more duelle
Ne stonde for to speke with þe;
Hellehoundes here I ȝelle,
And fendes mo þan men mowe se   492
Þat comen to fette me to helle,
Ne may I noweder fro hem fle;
And þouȝ schalt comen with fleys and felle
A domesday to wonie with me."   496

Ne hauede it non er þe word i-seyd,
Þat wiste ȝwider it scholde go,

---

482. for *supplied*

---

477. "and let run a sorrowful tear"—i.e., demonstrated contrition
481. *Pey*: "Though"
485-6. "and might five times more than the total of things in the world"
487. I.e., "(even) then we may not be shriven."
497-576. There are many visual representations in medieval art corresponding to the
    events depicted in this passage, especially in manuscript illustrations, which attest
    to the fascination of the age with the grotesque and the horrific; see, for example,
    the illustrations in T. S. R. Boase's *Death in the Middle Ages* (New York, 1972), 19-58.
497. *non er*: "no sooner"

In abreken at a breid
A þousend deuelene and yet mo.   500
ȝwan þei haddin on him leyd
Here scharpe cloches alle þo,
Yt was in a sori pleyt,
Reuliche toyled to and fro.   504

For þei weren ragged, roue, and tayled,
With brode bulches on here bac,
Scharpe clauwes, longe nayled,
No was no lime withoute lac.   508
On alle halue it was asayled
With mani a deuel foul and blac;
Merci criende lutel auailede
ȝwan Crist it wolde so harde wrac.   512

Some þe chaules it towrasten
And ȝoten in þe led al hot,
And bedin him to drinke faste,
And senke abouten him a brod.   516
A deuil kam þer ate laste
Þat was maister, wel I wot;
A colter glowende in him he þraste
Þat it þoruȝ þe herte it smote.   520

Gleyues glowende some setten
To bac and brest and boþe sides
Þat in his herte þe poyntes mettin,

---

524. maden *in margin*

---

499. *at a breid*: "at a bound"
502. "their sharp claws all of them"
504. "pitifully pulled . . ."
508. *lime withoute lac*: "limb without claws" (or possibly "without deformity")
513. "Some pried open the Soul's jaws."
516. "and shook about him a goad"
519. *colter*: "plowshare"
521. *Gleyues*: "glaives," single-edged blades mounted on long handles, used for thrusting and for cutting

And maden him þo woundes wide;   524
And seiden him fol wel he lette
Þe herte þat was so fol of pride;
Wel he it hadde þat men him bihette,
For more scholde it bitide.   528

Wordly wedes for to were
Þei seiden þat he louede best;
A deueles cope for to bere
Al brennynde on him was kest,   532
With hoe haspes i-mad to spere,
Þat streite sat to bac and brest;
An helm þat was lutel to here;
Anon him kam an hors al prest.   536

Forth was brouȝt þerewith a bridel
A corsed deuel als a cote
Þat grisliche grenned and ȝenede wide
Þe leyȝte it lemede of his þrote;   540
With a sadel to þe mid-side
Fol of scharpe pikes schote,
Alse an hechele onne to ride;
Al was glowende, ilke a grote.   544

Opon þat sadil he was sloungen
As he scholde to þe tornement;
An hundred deuel on him dongen,
Her and þer þan he was hent;   548

---

525. "and said to him full well (must) he lose"
527–8. "Well had he (now) received that which men had promised him, (and) more was
    to come."
529. "costly clothes for to wear"
531. *cope*: "cloak"
533. *hoe*: "its"; *spere*: "fasten"
535. *here*: "praise"
538. "(by) a devil as cursed as a coot"
543. *hechele*: "flax comb"
544. *ilke a grote*: "each piece (of the saddle)"

With hote speres þoruȝ was stongen,
And wiþ oules al to-rent;
At ilke a dint þe sparkles sprongen
As of a brond þat were forbrent.   552

Ȝwan he hadde reden þat rode
Opon þe sadil þer he was set,
He was kest doun as a tode,
And hellehoundes to him were led   556
Þat broiden out þo peces brode,
Als he to helle-ward was fet;
Þer alle þe fendes fet it trode,
Men miȝte of blod foluwe þe tred.   560

He beden him hontin and blowen,
Crien on Bauston and Bewis,
Þe ratches þat him were woned to knowen,
He scholden sone blowe þe pris;   564
An hundred deuels, racches on a rowe,
With stringes him drowen, vnþanc his,
Til he kome to þat lodli lowe
Þer helle was, I wot to wis.   568

Wȝan it cam to þat wikke won,
Þe fendes kasten suwilk a ȝel

---

549. stongen *ms*: strongen
552. forbrent *ms*: forbrend

---

550. *oules*: "awls"
562. *Bauston and Bewis*: names of two of the Devil's hunting dogs; in some accounts of the hell-hounds each hound is sent in pursuit of sinners who indulged in a particular vice, e.g. *Bauwiz* (*Bewis*) specializes in tracking down lechers; see "Nicolas Bozon," *Histoire Littéraire de la France* 36, p. 405.
564. *blowe þe pris*: i.e., sound the hunting call indicating that the quarry (the "prize") has been captured.
566. *vnþanc his*: "for which he wasn't grateful"
567. *lodli lowe*: "awful cave"
568. " . . . I know for certain."
569. *wikke won*: "terrible dwelling place"

Þe erþe it openede anon;
Smoke and smoþer op it wel,   572
Boþe pich and brumston —
Men myȝte fif mile haue þe smel!
Louerd, wo schal him be bigon
Þat haþ þeroffe þe tenþe del!   576

Wȝan þe gost þe soþe i-sey,
Wȝider it scholde, it kaste a cri
[Soul]   And seide, "Ihesu Crist þat sittest on hey,
On me, þi schap, nouȝ haue merci!   580
Ne schope þouȝ me þat art so slyȝ?
Þi creature al so was I,
Als man þat sittes þe so ny,
Þat þou hauest so wel don by.   584

Þouȝ þat wistest al biforn,
Wȝi schope þou me to wroþer-hele,
To be þus togged and totoren,
And oþere to hauen al mi wele?   588
Þo þat scholden be forloren,
Wretches þat tou miȝtest spele —
A! Weile! Wȝi lestouȝ hem be born,
To ȝeue þe foule fend so fele!"   592

Agein him þe fendes gonnen criȝe,
[Devils]   "Caitif, helpeþ þe na more

---

572. wel *ms*: wal
585. biforn *ms*: bi for

---

581. "Did you not create me, You who are so wise?"
586. *to wroþer-hele*: "for an evil fate," i.e., destruction
587. " . . . tugged and torn"
588. *And oþere*: "And others"; this verse indicates that the Soul is still unable to reconcile itself to the loss of its worldly possessions.
589–90. "Those who shall be lost, wretches that You might spare —"

To calle on Ihesus ne Marie,
Ne to crie Cristes ore.   596
Loren þouȝ hauest þe cumpainye
Þou hauest serued vs so ȝore;
Þarfore nou þou schalt abye
As oþere þat leuen on oure lore."   600

Þe foule fendes þat weren fayn,
Bi top and tail he slongen hit
And kesten it with myȝt and mayn
Doun into þe deueles pit,   604
Þer sonne ne schal neuere be seyn;
Hemself he sonken in þer-mit;
Þer erþe himsulf it lek aȝeyn,
Anon þe donge it was fordit.   608

Wȝan it was forth, þat foule lod,
To helle wel or it were day,
On ilk a her a drope stod
For friȝt and fer þer as I lay.   612
To Ihesus Crist with mild mod
ȝerne I kalde and lokede ay,
ȝwan þo fendes hot fot
Come to fette me away.   616

I þonke Him þat þolede deth,
His muchele merci and is ore

---

607. himsulf *ms*: hemsulf

---

602. *he*: "they"
606–8. "Themselves they sank in there-with (i.e., with it); (and) there the earth locked itself again, (and) immediately the dungeon was closed."
608. Following this verse is the French rubric: *Sou ke parla cely ki ceste avision aveit weu e dit issi* ("below, he who had seen this vision spoke and said").
611. "On each hair stood a drop (of sweat)."
615. *hot fot*: "hot foot," i.e., quickly; cf. the expression *foot-hoot* in Chaucer's *Cant. Tales* (II 438) and *Book of the Duchess* 375.

Þat schilde me fram mani a qued,
A sunful man as I lai þore.   620
Þo þat sunful ben, I rede hem red
To schriuen hem and rewen sore:
Neuere was sunne i-don so gret
Þat Cristes merci ne is wel more.   624

---

621. *rede hem red*: "give them counsel"
624. Following this verse is a benediction in French:

> Sa grace ly doine Jhesu Crist
> Ki ce dite de meins escrit!
> De li server de quer parfit,
> A tous otreie ly seint espirit!
> ("May Jesus Christ give grace to him
> who speaks about my writing; may the
> Holy Spirit grant to all that they may
> be served in some perfect way by this.")

This final prayer is not found in the other Middle English texts of the poem; it may be the contribution of the scribe rather than the author.

A Disputation between the Body and the Worms

One of the final adaptations of the Body and Soul theme in Middle English literature occurs in *A Disputacione Betwyx The Body and Wormes*. Although lacking the dramatic force of the best Body and Soul debates, the *Body and Worms* is notable for its elaborate dream-vision framework, which sets the poem during one of the periodic outbreaks of the Black Death, and for its inclusion of the Nine Worthies topos, which complements the fuller accounts of the Worthies found in the *Parliament of the Three Ages* and the alliterative *Morte Arthure*. The *Body and Worms* also deviates significantly from previous poems in the Body and Soul tradition in that its fundamental purpose is to inculcate understanding rather than fear. This purpose is corroborated by the fact that the manuscript, British Library MS Additional 37049, of Carthusian provenance, is an early fifteenth-century collection of pieces of didactic instruction and meditation intended for a clerical audience, possibly for novitiates. This manuscript is also acclaimed for its vivid illustrations which accompany the various didactic pieces, producing an effective combination of instructional advice and visual application. (For information on this manuscript, see T. W. Ross, *Speculum* 32 [1957], 274–82.)

The *Body and Worms* possibly reflects a conscious attempt to invert the point of view exemplified by Body and Soul debates such as *Als I lay*, for here the traditional figure of the proud knight is replaced by that of a fine lady, the torments inflicted on the Soul are replaced by the suffering of the Body, and the didactic intention is no longer to induce repentance but to generate the humble acceptance of the realities of death. Like many late medieval poems on death, the *Body and Worms* is certainly macabre, and yet the description of the dissolution of the Body in the grave is less gruesomely realistic than those found in many of the thirteenth-century death lyrics. Indeed, the poem's catalogue of the attacking "worms," though fascinating, is not especially terrifying, and some modern readers may find it amusing. Although lacking in real drama, the *Body and Worms* captures the psychological movement within the mind of the lady, which results from her confrontation with the worms. Her initial repugnance toward death and the corruption of her body, and her nostalgic longing for past pleasures are replaced by her genuine acceptance of present realities and the recognition that death is a completely natural phenomenon. The poem is thus related thematically to *Death and Life*, with its even greater emphasis on St. Paul's defiant apostrophe: "O death, where is thy sting? O grave, where is thy victory?" (I Cor. 15: 55). (For an excellent critical discussion of the *Body and Worms*, see Klaus Jankofsky, *Taius* 1 [1974], 137–59.) In regard to the poetic style of the *Body and Worms*, it should be noted that the language of the narrative frame is far more ostentatious than that of the actual dialogue, and the style generally is reminiscent of the Lydgatian poetry of the mid-fifteenth century. The verse form is ostensibly rime royal, but it is closer to being rhymed prose.

---

1)   Base Text: British Library MS Additional 37049, fols. 33r–35r

2)   Other mss: none

3)   Printed Text: K. Brunner, *Archiv* 167 (1935), 30–5

4)   *Index of Middle English Verse* 1563

A Disputacione betwyx the Body and Wormes

In þe ceson of huge mortalitie,
Of sondry disseses, with þe pestilence
Heuely reynand, whilom in cuntre

1–5. Although the narrator indicates that his pilgrimage into the countryside is prompted by his conscience, the implication is clear that his flight from the Black Death is also expedient.

To go pylgramege mefed be my conscience,
And on my way went with spedily diligence.   5
In a holy day afore me I sawe a kyrk
Wher to go I dressed, my bedes to wirk,

In a wilsom felde standyng desolate,
Vn-to here a messe was my hole intent.
It was done & sayd be I come þerat;   10
Oppyn I fande þe dore & entre sone I hent;
I knelyd me downe & to my prayers went,
With lawe obeysaunce mekyd me downe
To ane ymage, with gret deuocione.

Bysyde me I sawe a towmbe or sepulture   15
Ful freschly forgyd, depycte, & depynte,
Compassed & made be newe coniecture,
Of sondre armes þer many a prynte;
Þe epytaf to loke was I not faynte:

---

4. way *in margin*

---

7. "where I prepared to go, to say my prayers"
10. *be I come*: "by the time I had come"
12–4. The ms illustration (folio 33 recto) depicts the kneeling figure of the narrator before the wounded body of Christ on the Cross; a doorway is in the background behind the cross.
15–23. These verses are illustrated in the ms by the painting of a double decker or transi tomb; on the upper tier lies the effigy of the woman, on the lower the decomposing body wrapped in a shroud and beset by an imposing host of worms and other crawling creatures. The woman is lying in state in a splendid gown and mantle, her head resting on a tasseled pillow; her eyes are open and her hands are folded on her breast in prayer. (For discussions and illustrations of such tombs, see for example Kathleen Cohen, *Metamorphosis of a Death Symbol: The Transi Tomb in the Late Middle Ages and the Renaissance*, 1974; Erwin Panofsky, *Tomb Sculpture*, 1964; Ernst H. Kantorowicz, *The King's Two Bodies*, 1957; and T.S.R. Boase, *Death in the Middle Ages*, 1972.)
18. Several memorial shields are depicted on the coffin in the ms illustration which precedes the poem; these coats of arms might offer some clue to the actual identity of the woman in the illustration, if the poet had an actual person in mind.
19. Beneath the ms illustration preceding the poem are the following verses, the epitaph

In gylt copyr with goldly schewyng þan,   20
With a fresche fygure fyne of a woman,

Wele atyred in þe moste newe gyse,
With long lokkes of þis disceyfyng.
In a slomer I slept, taken I was in syche wyse,
Rapt & rauesched fro my selfe beynge;   25
Betwyx þis body & wormes hyr fretynge,
Strangly ilk one oþer corespondynge,
In maner of a dyaloge it wente;
Þerfore to þis insawmpyl ȝe take intente.

---

21. fyne *ms*: syne

---

referred to here; the first four verses comprise the actual epitaph, and they convey
a feeling of having been taken directly from a tomb inscription:

> Take hede vnto my fygure here abowne
> And se how sumtyme I was fressche & gay
> Now turned to wormes mete & corrupcone
> Bot fowle erth & stynkyng slyme & clay
> Attend þerfore to þis disputacione written here
> And writte it wysely in þi hert fre
> Þat þer-at sum wisdom þou may lere
> To se what þou art & here aftyr sal be
> When þou leste wenes. venit mors te superare
> When þi grafe grenes. bonum en mortis meditari

22–8. This stanza of eight verses, the only one in the poem to deviate from the rime
royal scheme, is here printed as it occurs in the ms. It has very plausibly been sug-
gested, however, first by Brunner and then more fully by Jankofsky, that several verses
have been lost from the text. According to Jankofsky, "Brunner realized that some-
thing did not make sense from the point of view of content but did not look for cause.
Thus he prints stanza four as having eight lines instead of seven. A closer look, however,
shows that the lacuna spans two stanzas. Stanza four continues with the description
of the tomb begun in stanza three but stops abruptly with the description of the la-
dy's hair. It is relatively easy to see how the scribe . . . could have skipped a few lines,
picking up again with 'wyse' (a) — stanza five — continuing with the (b) rhymes. . . .
Thus crucial information for our understanding of the tomb and epitaph and their
iconographic classification is missing" (*Taius* 1 [1974], 159).

24–5. This depiction of the narrator being "taken" out of himself and transported into
a trance-like state may underscore the suggestion that his dream vision or somno-
lent meditation carries serious didactic significance.

Þe Body spekes to þe Wormes:

[Body]   "Wormes, wormes," þis body sayd,   30
            "Why do ȝe þus, what causes ȝow me þus to ete?
            By ȝow my flesche is horribilly arayed,
            Whilk was a fygure whylom fresche & feete,
            Right amyabyll & odorus & swete,
            Beste belofed of any creature,   35
            Lady & soferayne cald I ȝow ensure.

            Of bewte I was a lady precious,
            Of gentil blode desendyng, of right lyne
            Of Eve, and of trewe begynyng generows;
            Al hertes glad my plesaunce to dyuyne,   40
            Men of honour & of gret worschip al dyd declyne;
            And nowe here in erth mortal deth come me to—
            Emang ȝow wormes nakyd lyg I loo!

            Most vnkynde neghbours þat euer war wroght!
            Dynner mete & sowper al to lyte,   45
            Now fretyng & etyng ȝe hafe me þorow soght,
            With ane insaciabyll & gredy appetyte;
            No rest bot alway þe synk, sowke, & byte;
            Day tyme ne houre with ȝow is no abstynence,
            Bot ay redy agayne me with vyolence.   50

            When ȝe fyrst began to drawe me to,
            It semes me ȝe wer fed in a faynt pasture;

---

30. The dialogue which begins at this point is illustrated in the margins of ms folios
    33v to 35r. In the first two of these four illustrations the worms occupy a position
    at the top of the page; in the last two their positions have been reversed. In all four
    illustrations the lady's skeletal corpse stands erect, wearing only the headdress depicted
    in the tomb illustration.
37–43. These verses convey feelings and images that closely parallel those found in the
    powerful Middle English death lyric "Wen þe turuf is þi tuur," *Index* 4044.
52. The worms' insatiable appetite stems from the *faynt* or "meager" pasture of their re-
    cent feeding; cf. the similar use of this metaphor by Chaucer's Host when he re-
    marks on the *gentil pasture* in which the Monk has been feeding (CT VII, 1933).

Now fatte waxen & vgly rownde & gret also!
Of curtasy & gentilnes lefe of me ȝour cure
And with sum oþer dwelle & endure   55
Whilk may ȝow rewarde with better wardone,
For ner am I wasted, consumed, & gone."

Wormes spekes to þe Body:

[Worms]   "Nay, nay, we will not ȝit departe þe fro
While þat one of þi bones with oþer wil hange,
To we hafe scowred & pollysched to   60
And made als clene as we can þaim emange;
For our labour we aske no maner of þing to fange —
Gold, syluer, ryches, ne no oþer mede —
Bot onely vs wormes on þe to fede,

Whilk may not sauour ne smell in no wyse   65
Þine orrybyll flesche, rotyng & stynkynge,
Of al creatures hated to devyse,
Safe onely of vs wretchid wormes beyng;
If we, as bestes, had smellyng & tastynge,
Trows þou þat we wald towche þi caryone playne?   70
Nay, parde, we wald it voyde for certayne!"

Þe Body spekes to þe Wormes:

[Body]   "Parde, vncortes ȝe be vnto me,
Þus heuely to threte me & manace
And þus me lefe bot bare bones to see.
Now where be ȝe knyghtes, cum forth in place,   75

54–6. The lady attempts to dismiss the worms in the courtly phrases she would have
    used with her suitors during her life, suitors whose absence she laments in ll. 75–85
    below.
69–70. The distinction between the "worms" as creatures lacking senses of taste and smell
    and other beasts may be the poet's invention, made for its dramatic effect.
75–85. The lady's pleas for her suitors to come and defend her from the attacking worms
    continues her courtly rhetoric from the previous stanzas and also represents a varia-
    tion on the *ubi sunt* convention.

And ȝe worschiþful sqwyers, both hye & base,
Þat sumtyme to me offerd ȝour seruyse,
Dayes of ȝour lyfes, of hertes frawnchsyse,

Sayng permyttyng ȝour lyfe to myne avyse?
To do me seruys, cum & defende nowe me   80
Fro þies gret horribil wormes vgly to se,
Here gnawyng my flesche þus with gret cruelte,
Devowryng & etyng nowe as ȝe may se,
Þat sumtyme ȝe lufed so interly—
Now socour & defende here my body!"   85

Þe Wormes answers to þe Body:

[Worms]   "What suld þai do, lat se vs vnto;
Of þaim drede we noght, ne of þair mone,
For at þe vtteraunce we hafe had to do
With alle þat wer myghty, passed forth & gone
Afore þis tyme, hafyng þair dunacyone: 90
Emproure, kynge, & conqwerours alle,
Lords temperall and spyritualle;

Þe neyne worthy, Judas Machabeus sure,
Julyus Cesar, Godfray de Bolayne,
Alexander, Dauyd, Ector, & Arthure,   95

---

95. Arthure *ms*: Athure

78–79. "for the whole of your lives, from your hearts' generosity, saying that you would
    govern your lives according to my judgments"
88. *at þe vtteraunce*: i.e., "from the earliest time"
90. *dunacyone*: "donation," i.e. the gift of their bodies; Brunner reads *diuiacione*.
93–6. The Nine Worthies topos commonly occurs in conjunction with the *ubi sunt* motif
    and the theme of the impermanence of earthly glories. No attempt is made here to
    group the Worthies into the triads of Pagan, Old Testament, and Christian heroes.
    More extensive accounts of the Nine Worthies occur in the *Parliament of the Three Ages*
    (ll. 300–585) and the alliterative *Morte Arthure* (ll. 3260 ff.); for discussions of the Nine
    Worthies topos, see R. S. Loomis, *MP* 15 (1917), 19–27, and M. Y. Offord, ed., *Parl.*
    of the Thre Ages, *EETS* 246 (1959), xl.

Kyng Charls, Duk Josue þe captayne;
With al þe Troiane knyghtes most souerayne;
With fayr Elyn bewtyuows of vysage,
Pollysene, Lucres, Dydo of Cartage;

Þies & oþer war also fayr as ȝe,   100
ȝit durst þai not styr ne mofe in no wyse
When possession on þaim taken had we;
For al venomos wormes to devyse
Acowmpenyd ar to þat seruyse,
With vs for to halde ar þai set fully,   105
ȝow vnto devowre & waste vttyrly:

Þe cokkatrys, þe basilysk, & þe dragon,
Þe lyserd, þe tortoys, þe coluber,
Þe tode, þe mowdewarp, & þe scorpyon,
Þe vypera, þe snake, & þe eddyr,   110
Þe crawpaude; þe pyssemoure, & þe canker,
Þe spytterd, þe mawkes, þe evet of kynde,
Þe watyr leyche, & oþer ar not behynde."

Þe Body spekes to þe Wormes:

[Body]   "Remedy can I fynde none in no wyse,
          Socowre ne no relese in no stownde,   115

98–9. Because the body is that of a woman, the poet also includes examples of the tran-
sience of feminine beauty. The four he selects — Helen of Troy, Polyxena (the daugh-
ter of King Priam of Troy), Lucretia (a virtuous Roman wife who killed herself after
being raped), and Dido — are also among the female martyrs of love that Chaucer
selected for inclusion in the *Legend of Good Women*.

107–13. The nineteen creatures in the catalogue of the "worms" reflect the poet's familiarity
with bestiary lore. With the sole exception of the mole (*mowdewarp*), all of these crea-
tures appear in the bestiaries among the "reptiles and fishes." The cockatrise and bas-
ilisk, fabulous creatures like the dragon, were sometimes considered to be identical,
though a distinction is implied here. The basilisk was able to poison its victims merely
by a look. *Coluber*: snake; *mowdewarp*: mole (moldiwarp); *crawpaude*: crab; *canker*: crab;
spytterd: spider; *mawkes*: maggots; *evet*: newt. (On medieval bestiaries, see for example
The Bestiary: A Book of Beasts, ed. T. H. White [New York, 1954].)

114–20. In this single stanza the Body begins the process of resigning itself to the reali-
ties of the grave. It should be noted that the speeches assigned to the Body follow
a clear structural pattern; the first three have four stanzas, then two stanzas, then
one stanza; the second three consist of one stanza, then two stanzas, and finally four
stanzas. The two single stanza speeches represent the turning point in the disputation.

Bot in þis case must I go after þair devyse,
Þorowly gnawen my flesche & sore bownde,
For þai ar hateful to lyfes kynde fownde.
What sal I do bot lat þaim hafe þair wyll?
Aventure me must abyde þof þai do me spyll!"   120

Þe Wormes answers to þe Body:

[Worms]   "Þe fyrst day þow was borne our mesyngers we sende;
Vnto þaim we gaf in our commawndement
As in charge þai suld vs not offende,
Ne not departe fro þe to deth on þe went;
Þe to frete & to gnawe was oure intent,   125
And after come with þe to our regyowne,
Þi flesche here to hafe for þair warysowne,

Whilk has obeyde our commaundment,
Of þis may þou on no wyse say nay;
Bot þat sum both þi wombe & stomak hent,   130
Owdyr lyce or neytes in þi hede alway,
Wormes in þe handes, flees in þe bedde I þe say,
With oþer venomosnes, dyuers & sondry,
To warne ȝow of vs to make ȝow redy."

Þe Body spekes to þe Wormes:

[Body]   "Now knawe I wele ȝour mesyngers þai were,   135
Þe whilk with me in lyfe keþyd resydence;
No langer wil I dispute þis matere,
Nor debate, bot suffer ȝour violence.

---

135. mesyngers *ms*: mensyngers

130–7. The description of these harbingers of the death-worms provides a telling commentary on the inescapable realities of medieval life, even for fine ladies.

Do ȝour will with me at ȝour beneuolence;
Bot ȝit in the Sawter Dauid says þat alle   140
Sal be obedyent vnto mans calle."

Þe Wormes awnswers to þe Body:

[Worms]   "Þat power dures whils man has lyfe;
In þis wrechid warld here ar þai þe apon;
Now þi lyfe is gone, with vs may þou not stryfe;
Þou art bot as erthe & as þinge to noght gone;   145
Lyke as I þe sayd was in þine aduencione,
Of Lentyn comynge þe Ask Wedynsday,
When þe preste with asses crosses al way,

And with asses blisses, to hafe rememoraunce
What þou art & wher to þou sal turne agayne;   150
For asses þou was afore þis instaunce,
And asses sal þou be after for certayne.
Be þou lord, lady, or hye sufferayne,
To powder & dust in tyme to cum þou sall;
Of warldly goynforth swylk is þi entyrvall."   155

Þe Body spekes to þe Wormes:

[Body]   "Allas, allas, now knaw I ful well
Þat in my lyfe was I made lewyd & vnwyse,
With a reynawnde pryde so mykil for to mell,
For myne abowndant bewte to so devyse;
To prowde hafe I bene, to wanton, & to nyse,   160
In warldly pleasaunce gret delyte hafyng,
To be my comper none worthy þinkynge.

140-1. Psalms 8:4-8, especially verse 6.
143. "Here in this wretched world (i.e., the grave) they rule over you."
145-55. These verses reflect such passages of scripture as Gen. 3:19 and Eccles. 3:20,
    which underlie the liturgy for Ash Wednesday.
162. "thinking that no one was worthy to be my equal"

And now soget to wormes I am beynge
Beryng þair preue mesyngers dayly,
As loppes & lyce & oþer wormes right commerowsly,   165
Vnknawyng fro whyne þai come trewly.
To þis can I say no more vttyrly,
Bot arme me I must with gode sufferaunce
Oure Lordes will to abyde with al þe circumstaunce."

Þe Wormes awnswers to þe Body:

[Worms]   "By þis sufferaunce of vs no thanke gyt ȝee,   170
For by ȝour wil lyfed hafe euer ȝe walde;
Rememor ȝe sal with will of ȝour hert fre
In holy scripture, & ȝe wole behalde
Þat þe fayrnes of women talde
Is bot vayne þinge & transitory;   175
Women dredyng God sal be praysed holy."

Þe Body spekes to þe Wormes:

[Body]   "ȝa, now is to late tyme paste to call agayne,
As now at þis stownde, bot put me onely
In þe mercy of our Lord God most sufferayne,
Whilk is for þe best so to do sothely,   180
And þat þos on lyfe may hafe space to be redy
To rememor in þe same wyse also,
Contynewly þinkynge in þe tyme to cum þerto.

What he salbe & also what is he,
Be it he or sche, be þai neuer so fayr, bewar   185

---

164. mesyngers *ms*: mensyngers

---

165. *commerowsly*. The rhyme scheme calls for a word ending in -*ing*.
172–6. Proverbs 30:31.
185–8. Possibly a reference to Mark 7:20–3.

Of pryde with his felows þat noght be,
Þe whilk oft men brynges in to care,
As scripture mencion makes þe soth to declare;
Þerfore gode is to avoyde fleschly temptacone,
By þe feende our foo both wroght & done.   190

Þis þat I hafe complened & sayd,
In no displesyng take it ȝow vnto.
Lat vs be frendes at þis sodayn brayde,
Neghbours, & luf as before we gan do;
Let vs kys & dwell to-gedyr euermore,   195
To þat God wil þat I sal agayn vpryse
At þe day of dome before þe hye justyse,

With þe body glorified to be,
And of þat nowmbyr þat I may be one,
To cum to þat blis of heuen in fee,   200
Þorow þe mene & þe mediacione
Of our blissed Lord, our verry patrone,
Þar in abilite to be for his hye plesaunce.
Amen. Amen. pour charite at þis instaunce."

Now spekes he þat sawe þe vysion:

[Narrator] With þis I woke fro slepe sompnolent,   205
Or of a slomery meditacone;

---

199. of *in margin*

---

186. "(Beware of) Pride and his good-for-nothing companions" (the other six of the Seven
    Deadly Sins).
193. *at þis sodayn brayde*: i.e., "for this brief time"
193–5. Cf. Job 17:14.
195. The Body's invitation to kiss the worms symbolizes the full awareness she has achieved
    of the need for Christian reconciliation. She has transcended entirely her initial repug-
    nance of these agents of physical corruption.
196–7. Cf. Job 19:26; Psalm 49:14; I Cor. 15:51–5.
196. *to þat*: i.e., "until that time when"

To a holy man of hye excellent
Mefed I þis dreme & strange vysion,
Whilk bad me put it vndir scripcion,
Als nere as I cowde remembyr me verely,   210
In als fayir langage as I cowde godely,

Vnto þe reders þinge delectabyll,
And a monyscyon both to styr & to mefe
Man & woman to be acceptabyll
Vnto our Lord, & al lustes for to lefe   215
Of warldly þinges, whilk dos þaim grefe,
And þe more rather to call vnto mynde
Oure Saueour & to Hym vs bynde. Amen.

Winner and Waster

Winner and Waster, the first of the three Middle English alliterative debates, is also one of the earliest works of the Alliterative Revival. The poem's many references to contemporary social and historical matters point to 1353 as a likely date of composition, a specificity in dating which is unusual for medieval texts. *Winner and Waster* is also unusual in synthesizing elements from several genres and modes — debate, dream vision, allegory, satire, the political-historical poem, and the complaint about the times. Like many of the poets in the alliterative tradition, the *Winner and Waster* poet is skilled in sustaining vivid passages of description, but he is exceptional among them for his ability as a satirist; at times he attacks the object of his anger with the directness of Langland, at times he manifests a satiric subtlety and wittiness that is almost Chaucerian. *Winner and Waster* is a sophisticated poem, to be sure, and it is also a difficult one. Some of its contemporary allusions are still obscure, and the only extant text of the poem is incomplete and thus inconclusive. Still, there can be little doubt that the poet's primary object is to decry the social and economic instability of the times, a state of affairs largely resulting from Edward III's commitment of resources to the Hundred Years War with France.

The somber prologue establishes the poem's tone of moral condemnation. In the manner of a "complaint against the times" (cf. Chaucer's lyric "Lak of Stedfastnesse"), the speaker inveighs against the present perversion of traditional values and ideals, even suggesting that the end of the world may be approaching. The corruption of the age is also reflected, he suggests, in its failure to value the work of true poets, which has given way to more frivolous forms of entertainment. The speaker is confident, nevertheless, that in the end true poets will receive their due. Following the Prologue the poet employs the *chanson d'aventure* device to provide a transition into the dream-vision section of the poem. The narrator, wandering alone in the country, experiences the sounds and sights of nature, but in this case with a difference. Whereas normally in the dream-vision the narrator is lulled to sleep by the singing of the birds and the murmuring brook, here the elements of nature produce a cacophony which only delays his slumber. The implication seems to be that the social disorder described in the Prologue extends beyond human society, even into the wider realm of nature.

Transported in his dream to a beautiful green meadow surrounded by forests, the narrator observes two armies poised on the brink of combat. The ranks of one are formed by churchmen, lawyers, and merchants; the ranks of the other by members of the aristocracy, the landed gentry, and the professional military. The former army is described at length, with each of its sub-groups identified by a "heraldic" banner. These are the legions of Winner, dedicated to accruing wealth, and chief among them are the various orders of the friars, which are particularly singled out for satirical comment. The second army, that of Waster, receives little treatment, a curious but possibly significant structural discrepancy. The representatives of these two groups are summoned by the King's messenger (probably Edward the Black Prince, son of Edward III), and the personified figures of Winner and Waster appear before the king to state their cases.

In the ensuing debate Winner contends that Waster consumes the nation's material goods without concern for the present or the future, that agricultural production has been brought to a standstill, and that vital resources such as the forests are being destroyed. Waster in turn accuses Winner of being concerned only with making profits and with safeguarding his accumulated goods, and Waster alleges that his own consumption actually benefits society by creating jobs and a greater demand for goods. Their arguments throughout the debate are largely self-serving, yet they also contain elements of truth. Despite their superficial resemblance to the Ant and the Grasshopper of Aesop's fable, Winner and Waster cannot be fairly equated with that pair of characters, nor is it fair to apply to them Langland's comments on the virtues of winning and the evils of wasting from *Piers Plowman*. For while Waster may indeed be guilty of prodigality, Winner's extreme thriftiness is itself a form of the sin of avarice. It should be observed, then, that in the debate between Winner and Waster one immoderate view is pitted against an equally immoderate view. From the poet's observations in the Prologue and the debaters' observations in the debate section of *Winner and Waster*, it is clear that the times are seriously out of joint and that the prevailing social and economic ills stem from Edward III's own policies and actions. The poem may be construed, then, as a plea for the king to act responsibly in an effort to bring these contradictory forces under control. Perhaps the king's decisions — to send Winner abroad to reside with the Pope, and to locate Waster in the Cheapside section of London — represent the first steps toward doing that. Another view, however, is that these actions do not really represent an attempt to provide a remedy but are simply an expedient means of preserving the status quo. But before the king's instructions to the two can be completed the text breaks off, and thus we do not know how the poem would have ended. As the poem stands, the words of the preacher in Ecclesiastes 3:6 would seem to provide an appropriate gloss: there is a time for gathering things together and a time for using them up. As the king himself observes, saving and expending are both necessary, for "every Winner needs a Waster."

Winner and Waster is a signal work in the Middle English alliterative tradition. It is one of the earliest poems to re-introduce alliterative verse in the form of the "alliterative long line" and to reflect a vocabulary peculiar to the works of the Alliterative Revival. The influence of *Winner and Waster* is considerable and may be seen not only in the two subsequent alliterative debates (the *Parliament of the Three Ages* and *Death and Life*) but in the even greater poetry of William Langland. The text of *Winner and Waster*, in its incomplete state, is preserved only in British Library MS Addit. 31042, one of the two "Thornton Manuscripts," a manuscript recorded in the fifteenth century. The text contains many errors, some of which may have existed in the scribe's copy text. In his edition of the poem Sir Israel Gollancz proposed a great many emendations, only some of which have been incorporated here. Since the 1960s there have been many valuable critical discussions of *Winner and Waster*, the most comprehensive of which is T. H. Bestul's fine study, *Satire and Allegory in Wynnere and Wastoure* (1974).

---

1) Base Text: British Library Additional MS 31042, fols. 176v–183v

2) Other mss: none

3) Selected Printed Texts: I. Gollancz, *Select Early English Poems*, 3 (1920)
                             A. S. Haskell, *A Middle English Anthology* (1969),
                             382–407

B. Ford, *The New Pelican Guide to English Literature*
(1982), 1:398–415 (text edited by T. Turville-Petre)

4)   *Index of Middle English Verse* 3137

Here Begynnes A Tretys And god Schorte refreyte
by-twixe Wynnere And Wastoure

[Prologue]

Sythen that Bretayne was biggede and Bruyttus it aughte,
Thurghe the takynge of Troye with tresone with-inn,
There hathe selcouthes bene sene in seere kynges tymes,
Bot neuer so many as nowe by the nynde dele.
For nowe alle es witt and wyles that we with delyn,   5
Wyse wordes and slee, and icheon wryeth othere;

---

4. nynde *ms*: nyne

---

1. "Since Britain was built (i.e., founded) and Brutus possessed it"; cf. *SGGK* 20; the
   notion that Britain was founded by Brutus (the grandson or great-grandson of Aeneas)
   apparently originates with Nennius' *Historia Brittonum*; it is an idea reiterated throughout
   the chronicle tradition, and in later Middle English literature passing references to
   Brutus are common, especially in the romances; cf. *SGGK* 13 and *P3A* 407.
2. In medieval English treatments of the Troy story, (which derive from Benoit de Sainte-
   Maure's *Roman de Troie* and Guido de Columnis' *Historia Trojana*), the fall of Troy results
   from treachery from within; usually implicated in this treachery are such figures as
   Antenor and Aeneas, who negotiated privately with the Greeks in order to insure
   the safety of their families and possessions; in Aeneas's case, however, he ran afoul
   of the Greeks later on when he attempted to conceal Polyxena from them; cf. *SGGK*
   1–5 and the account in the *Laud Troy Book*.
3. *selcouthes*: "strange happenings"; cf. *Piers* C.1.5
4. *nynde dele*: "ninth part"
5. *witt and wyles*: "cleverness and cunning"; most editors emend *wyles* to *wylle*, and there
   is some justification for preferring that common ME collocation (i.e., "wit and will")
   to the text as it is written; but in this instance it seems more likely that these terms
   are used to describe two closely related aspects of man's deceitfulness, and not the
   contrastive characteristics usually indicated by the phrase "wit and will."
6. "wise words and sly (words)," probably in apposition to *witt and wyles* in l. 5; *icheon
   wryeth othere*: "each one (i.e., each man) betrays the other," or possibly "each (man's)
   word conceals another (meaning)"

And now es no frenchipe in fere bot fayntnesse of hert.
Dare neuer no westren wy, while this werlde lasteth,
Send his sone southewarde to see ne to here,
That he ne schall holden by-hynde when he hore eld es.   10
For-thi sayde was a sawe of Salomon the wyse —
It hyeghte harde appone honde, hope I no noþer —
When wawes waxen schall wilde and walles bene doun,
And hares appon herthe-stones schall hurcle in hire fourme,
And eke boyes of no blode, with boste and with pryde,   15
Schall wedde ladyes in londe and lede hir at will,
Thene dredfull domesdaye it draweth neghe aftir.
Bot who-so sadly will see and the sothe telle
Say it newely will neghe or es neghe here.
Whylome were lordes in londe þat loued in thaire hertis   20

---

7. *This verse occurs in the ms between l. 21 and l. 22.*
15. no *supplied*
17. one hande *cancelled after* draweth

---

7. *in fere*: "in company" (i.e., among companions); *feyntnesses of hert* may imply a mutual lack of trust even between friends, a theme voiced by Chaucer in his poem "Lak of Stedfastnesse."
8–10. The phrase *while this werlde lasteth* is the first of the several references in the Prologue to the possibility that the Apocalypse may be approaching; these verses also reflect a provincial bias against the urbanized South and Southeast of England.
8. *westren wy*: "man of western (England)"
10. "that he should hold behind (at home) when he is hoary with age"
12. "It comes hard upon hand (i.e., is near at hand), I can believe nothing else"; the "it" which is approaching is the end of the world.
14. "And hares shall crouch upon hearth-stones (as if they were) in their lair"; this specific detail is attested elsewhere in medieval prophecies concerning the Day of Doom (e.g. *Thomas of Erceldoune*, EETS 61 [1875], xvii).
15–6. This contemptuous reference to marriages between *boyes* (young men of low birth) and *ladyes* is another indication of the social disorder of the times.
16. *lede hir at wille*: "lead (them) according to their (own) wishes," i.e., control them
18. *sadly*: "soberly," i.e., clearly
19. "say it will soon approach or is (now) nearly here"
20–30. In his inventory of the abuses of the times, the narrator now deals more specifically with the hard times which have befallen genuine poets; it is their misfortune to live in an age in which true art fails to receive proper recognition; cf. *Piers* B.prol.33–7.

To here makers of myrthes þat matirs couthe fynde,
Wyse wordes with-inn þat wroghte were neuer,
Ne redde in no romance þat euer renke herde;
Bot now a childe appon chere, with-owtten chyn-wedys,
Þat neuer wroghte thurgh witt thre wordes to-gedire,   25
Fro he can iangle als a iaye and iapes telle,
He schall be leuede and louede and lett of a while
Wele more þan þe man that made it hym-seluen.
Bot neuer þe lattere, at the laste when ledys bene knawen,
Werke witnesse will bere who wirche kane beste.   30

[I]

Bot I schall tell ȝow a tale þat me by-tyde ones,
Als I went in the weste wandrynge myn one,
Bi a bonke of a bourne, bryghte was the sone,

---

25. thre *ms*: thies

---

21. "to hear poets of poems who could find (suitable subject) matters"
22. "wise words (from) within, that were never written down"; this verse pays tribute
    to the skillfullness of oral poets who composed their works extemporaneously—and
    thus their works were not available to be read (1.23).
23. "nor (were) read in any romance that (any) man heard"
24. *appon chere*: "in appearance"; *chin-wedys*: "chin clothing," i.e., a beard
25. "who never created through (his) own skill three words together"
26. *Fro*: "from (the time that)"; *iangle als a iaye*: "jangle as a jay," i.e., mindless chattering
    or perhaps reciting from memory (cf. 1. 28); jays could be taught to repeat words
    which they heard over and over (cf. *Cant. Tales* I 642–3).
27. "He shall be believed and loved and honored for a time."
28. *Wele*: "much"
29–30. "But nevertheless, when at last men are known (for what they really are), the
    works (themselves) will bear witness to who can work the best."
32. The "west"—where it is often the wont of narrators (especially those in alliterative
    poems) to wander; *myn one*: "by myself"
33–44. It is generally the case in dream visions that the murmuring stream and the
    singing of the birds promote the narrator's somnolence; here, however, nature's lack
    of harmony seems to mirror the social discord already described; and rather than
    lulling the narrator to sleep, this natural cacophony actually delays the narrator's
    slumbers.

Vndir a worthiliche wodde by a wale medewe;
Fele floures gan folde ther my fote steppede. 35
I layde myn hede one ane hille, ane hawthorne be-syde;
The throstills full throly they threpen to-gedire,
Hipped vp heghwalles fro heselis tyll othire,
Bernacles with thayre billes one barkes þay roungen,
Þe iay ianglede one heghe — iarmede the foles! 40
Þe bourne full bremly rane þe bankes by-twene;
So ruyde were þe roughe stremys and raughten so heghe,
That it was neghande nyghte or I nappe myghte,
For dyn of the depe watir and dadillyng of fewllys.
Bot as I laye at the laste, þan lowked myn eghne, 45
And I was swythe in a sweuen sweped be-lyue.

Me thoghte I was in the werlde, I ne wiste in whate ende,
One a loueliche lande þat was ylike grene,
Þat laye loken by a lawe the lengthe of a myle.
In aythere holte was ane here in hawberkes full brighte, 50
Harde hattes appon hedes and helmys with crestys,

---

50. attyrede *cancelled after* hawberkes

---

34. *worthiliche*: "lovely"; *wale*: "pleasant"
36. The narrator in *Death and Life* also falls asleep beneath a hawthorne (*DL* 31, 33).
37. "The thrushes squabbled vigorously . . ."; cf. *P3A* 14.
38. "Highwalls (i.e., woodpeckers) hopped up from the hazels to other (trees)"; it seems probable that *hipped* describes the movements of the birds ("hopped") rather than their calls, although that is a possibility.
39. *Bernacles*: "wild geese"
40. *iarmede the foles*: "the fowls (birds) clamored," a comment summarizing ll. 37–40.
41. *full bremly*: "quite noisily"
42. *raughten*: "reached"
43. *or*: "ere"
44. *dadillying of fewllys*: "chattering of (the) birds"
45. *lowked*: "locked," i.e., shut tightly
46. "And I was quickly swept up into a dream."
47. *whate ende*: i.e., "what part"; cf. *Piers* B.prol.12 and *Pearl* 65
48. *lande*: "meadow"; *ylike*: "entirely"
49. *loken by a lawe*: "enclosed by a hill"
50. "In each wood was an army . . ."; *hawberkes*: "hauberks," coats of mail
51. *crestys*: "crests," devices (often in the form of decorative animals) attached to the top of helms, by which the wearers could be recognized

Brayden owte thaire baners, bown for to mete,
Schowen owte of the schawes, in schiltrons þay felle;
And bot the lengthe of a launde thies lordes by-twene.
And I prayed for the pese till the prynce come,   55
For he was worthiere in witt than any wy elles,
For to ridde and to rede and to rewlyn the wrothe
That aythere here appon hethe had vn-till othere.
At the creste of a clyffe a caban was rerede,
Alle raylede with rede the rofe and the sydes,   60
With Ynglysse besantes full brighte, betyn of golde,
And ichone gayly vmbygone with garters of inde,
And iche a gartare of golde gerede full riche.
Then were thies wordes in þe webbe werped of he,
Payntted of plunket, and poyntes by-twene,   65

---

55. I *ms*: alle
58. hethe *ms*: hate
64. thies *ms*: thre

---

52. "unfurled their banners, ready to meet (in battle)"
53. *Schowen*: "shoved," i.e., rushed; *schiltrons*: "squadrons"
54. *launde*: a meadow or lawn
55. *I*: the ms reads *alle*, but that seems to contradict the eagerness of these forces to have at each other; *the prince*: i.e., the king (who will soon be identified as Edward III).
57–8. "for to rid (i.e., prevent) and to reconcile and to govern the wrath that each army upon the heath had toward the other"
59. *caban*: i.e., pavilion; *rerede*: "reared," i.e., set up
60. *raylede*: "decorated"; cf. *P3A* 119
61. *Ynglysse besantes*: the bezant, a small gold Byzantine coin, was commonly used in Europe from the ninth century on; but the "English besant" is probably the gold noble, first minted by Edward III in 1344; the reference here seems to be to ornaments designed in imitation of Edward's coin; in any case, it provides one indication that this king is Edward III; cf. *P3A* 123.
62. "and each one gaily surrounded by garters of (indigo) blue," in reference to the Order of the Garter, established by Edward III in the mid 1340s; the Order originally included the king, his son Edward the Black Prince (the Prince of Wales), and twenty-four knights.
63. *gerede*: "adorned"
64. "Then were these words woven into the banner raised on high."
65. *plunket*: a light shade of blue, contrasting with the darker blue (inde) in l. 62; *poyntes*: "points," i.e., periods

Þat were fourmed full fayre appon fresche lettres,
And alle was it one sawe appon Ynglysse tonge:

[The   "Hethyng haue the hathell þat any harme thynkes."
Armies]   "Now the kyng of this kythe—kepe hym oure Lorde!"

Vpon heghe one the holt ane hathell vp stondes,   70
Wroghte als a wodwyse, alle in wrethyn lokkes,
With ane helme one his hede, ane hatte appon lofte,
And one heghe one þe hatte ane hatefull beste,
A lighte lebarde and a longe, lokande full kene,
ȝarked alle of ȝalowe golde in full ȝape wyse.   75
Bot that þat hillede the helme by-hynde in the nekke
Was casten full clenly in quarters foure,
Two with flowres of Fraunce be-fore and be-hynde,
And two out of Ynglonde with sex grym bestes,
Thre leberdes one lofte, and thre on lowe vndir;   80

---

73. hatefull *ms*: hatt full

---

67. *one sawe*: "a saying"

68. "Shame have the man who thinks any evil (of it)," an English rendering of the motto of the Order of the Garter: *Honi soit qui mal y pense.*

69. "The king of this country—now may our Lord keep him (safe)!"— shouted in unison by the assembled armies; it reflects the devotion which both armies have for the king, perhaps the only point in which their attitudes coincide.

70–82. It isn't made clear who the *hathell* ("man") described in these verses is, but he is possibly the Garter Herald.

70-1. "High up in the woodlands a man rises up, / Dressed as a wild man of the woods, with twisted locks (of hair)"; cf. the *wodwos* with whom Gawain contends in *SGGK* 721.

72. *ane hatte appon lofte*: a "cap of maintenance" above the helmet, perhaps like the one on the helmet of the Black Prince's effigy at Canterbury Cathedral.

73. *hatefull beste*: "an angry-looking beast"

74. *lighte*: i.e., "graceful"; *lokande full kene*: "looking (i.e., staring) fiercely"

75. *ȝarked*: "made"; *ȝape*: "skillful"

76-80. "But that which covered the neck behind the helm"—a cloth or floating veil hanging down the back of the helm, embellished with heraldic designs; this veil (or "mantling") bears the royal arms of the Plantagenets which were designed in 1337, when Edward III lay claim to the crown of France; the upper left and lower right quarters (i.e., *be-fore* and *be-hynde*) show lilies (*flowres of Fraunce*, the fleur de lys), while the upper right and lower left quarters show the six grim beasts of England, which in heraldic terms are *lions leopardes*, or *lions passant-gardant*—lions walking and looking about, presented full-faced, in contrast to lions rampant, whose faces are seen in profile; the lilies are gold on a field of blue, the lions gold on a field of red.

At iche a cornere a knoppe of full clene perle,
Tasselde of tuly silke tuttynge out fayre.
And by þe cabane I knewe the knyghte that I see,
And thoghte to wiete, or I went, wondres ynewe.
And als I waytted, with-inn I was warre sone   85
Of a comliche kynge crowned with golde,
Sett one a silken bynche, with septure in honde,
One of the louelyeste ledis, who-so loueth hym in hert,
That euer segge vnder sonn sawe with his eghne.
This kynge was comliche clade in kirtill and mantill,   90
Bery-brown as his berde, broudered with fewlys,
Fawkons of fyne golde flakerande with wynges,
And ichone bare in ble blewe, als me thoghte,
A grete gartare of ynde gered full riche.
Full gayly was that grete lorde girde in the myddis,   95
A brighte belte of ble, broudirde with fewlys,
With drakes & with dukkes, daderande þam semede,
For ferdnes of fawcons fete, lesse fawked þay were.
[Narrator]   And euer I sayde to my-selfe, "full selly me thynke

---

83. knyghte *ms*: kynge
91. als *ms*: was
94. gerede full riche *ms*: girde in the myddes

---

81. *knoppe*: "nob" or "button"
82. *tuly silke*: red silk, perhaps reflecting the fact that silk of this kind was originally im-
    ported from Toulouse (cf. *SGGK* 858); *tuttynge out*: "flaring out"
84. "And (I) expected to experience, before I went, wonders a-plenty."
85. *waytted*: "watched"; *warre*: "aware"
91. "berry-brown as his beard, embroidered with birds" (cf. *SGGK* 878–9); the palfrey
    ridden by Chaucer's Monk is also "berry-brown" (*CT* I, 207).
92. *flakerande*: "flapping"
93. "and each one carried in blue color, it seemed to me"
94. *ynde*: indigo blue
95. *girde in the myddis*: "belted about the middle"
96. Cf. line 91
97. *daderande*: "trembling (with fright)"
98. *ferdnes*: "fear"; *lesse fawked*: "lest seized"
99–100. "And ever I said to myself, it would be quite surprising (to me) if this man doesn't
    sometimes ride to the river"; the phrase "ride to the river" is an idiom which

<table>
<tr><td></td><td>Bot if this renke to the reuere ryde vmbestounde."</td><td>100</td></tr>
</table>

     Bot if this renke to the reuere ryde vmbestounde."   100
       The kyng biddith a beryn by hym þat stondeth,
     One of the ferlyeste frekes, þat faylede hym neuer:

[King]   "Thynke I dubbede the knyghte with dynttis to dele!
     Wend wightly thy waye, my willes to kythe;
     Go bidd þou ʒondere bolde batell þat one þe bent houes,
     That they neuer neghe nerre to-gedirs;
     For if thay strike one stroke, stynte þay ne thynken."

[Knight]   "ʒis, lorde," said þe lede, "while my life dures."
     He dothe hym doun one þe bonke & dwellys a while,
     Whils he busked and bown was one his beste wyse.   110
     He laped his legges in yren to the lawe bones,
     With pysayne & with pawnce polischede full clene,
     With brases of broun stele brauden full thikke,
     With plates buklede at þe bakke þe body to ʒeme,
     With a iupown full iuste, ioynede by the sydes,   115
     A brod chechun at þe bakke, þe breste had anoþer,
     Thre wynges in-with, wroghte in the kynde,

---

means to go hawking (cf. *P3A* 208 and *Sir Orfeo* 308); Edward III's passion for hawk-
ing was well known, and thus here is yet another clue to this king's identity.

101–2. The *beryn* ("man" or "knight") addressed by the king, although he is never ex-
plicitly identified, appears to be Edward III's eldest son, Edward the Black Prince.

102. "one of (the) most marvelous of men . . ."

103. *Thynke*: i.e., "Remember (that); *the*: "thee"; *dynttis*: "blows"

104–6. "Go quickly (on) your way, my wishes to make known; tell yonder brave forces
that on the field approach, that they (must) never draw nearer together."

105. Cf. line 143

107. Cf. lines 195–6

109. *dothe hym*: i.e., "takes himself"

110. *busked and bown*: "dressed and equipped"

111–8. Elaborate descriptions of the arming of a knight occur often in medieval works,
especially in the romances (cf. *SGGK* 568–89 and 2015–29).

111. *yren*: leg armor, usually called "greaves"

112. *pysane*: neck armor; *pawnce*: body armor

113. *brases*: "braces," armor for the arms; *brauden*: i.e., woven

114. *ʒeme*: "protect"

115. *iupown*: "jupon," a sleeveless tunic, tight about the upper body but loose around
the hips; it was usually laced up the sides.

116. *chechun*: "escutcheon"

117. "three wings (i.e., feathers) within (the escutcheon), depicted naturally (i.e., realisti-
cally)"; these feathers are the emblem of the Prince of Wales.

          Vmbygon with a gold wyre—whee, I þat gome knewe!
          What! he was ʒongest of ʒeris and ʒapest of witt
          Þat any wy in this werlde wiste of his age.   120
          He brake a braunche in his hande & caughten it swythe,
          Trynes one a grete trotte, & takes his waye
          There bithe thies ferdes folke in the felde houes.
[Knight]   Sayd, "Loo, the kyng of this kyth—þer kepe hym oure
          Lorde!—
          Send his erande by me, als hym beste lyketh,   125
          That no beryn be so bolde, one bothe his two eghne,
          Ones to strike one stroke, ne stirre none nerre,
          To lede rowte in his rewme, so ryall to thynke
          Pertly with ʒoure powers his pese to disturbe.
          For this es the vsage here and euer schall worthe: 130
          If any beryn be so bolde with banere for to ryde
          With-inn þe kyngdom riche, bot the kynge one,
          That he schall losse the londe and his lyfe aftir.

---

127. ne *ms*: no

---

118. *whee*: the ms reads *when*, but an exclamation such as "why!" seems likely, as the narrator realizes that he knows the identity of this young knight.
119. *What*: "indeed"; *ʒapest*: "liveliest"
121. The branch is the traditional symbol of peace, originating in the olive branch of Genesis 8:11 (cf. *SGGK* 265-6).
122. *Trynes*: "hurries"
123. *ferdes folke*: i.e., "armed groups"
125. For the sake of alliteration, *erande* ("message") is usually emended either to *bodworde* or *bidding*.
126. *one bothe his two eghne*: "at the risk of having both his eyes put out"(?)
127-9. "once to strike a stroke, nor to stir any nearer, to lead a company in his realm, (or) so regal to think (yourself) (that) proudly with your powers (you) disturb his (the king's) peace"
130-3. The consequences for "breaking the king's peace" by armed conflict or rebellion within the kingdom are clearly spelled out in these verses; they appear to be a direct reflection of the Statute of Treasons, passed in 1352, which prohibited private groups from bearing arms without royal sanction.
133. "that his property shall be confiscated by the state and then he shall be executed"

Bot sen ȝe knowe noghte this kythe of the kynge-ryche,
He will forgiffe ȝe this gilt of his grace one."   135
   Full wyde hafe I walked amonges thies wyes one,
Bot sawe I neuer siche a syghte, segges with myn eghne;
For here es alle þe folke of Fraunce ferdede be-syde,
Of Lorreyne, of Lumbardye, and of Lawe Spayne,
Wyes of Westwale þat in were duellen,   140
Of Ynglonde, of Yrlonde, Estirlynges full many,
Þat are stuffede in stele, strokes to dele.
   And ȝonder a banere of blake þat one þe bent houes,
With thre bulles of ble white brouden with-inn,
And iche one hase of henppe hynged a corde,   145
Seled with a sade lede—I say, als me thynkes,

---

134. the kythe of this kynge-ryche *ms*: this kythe ne the kynge-ryche
137. segges *ms*: segge
143. a banere *in margin*
144. bulles *ms*: bibulles

134–5. The king's willingness to excuse their breach of the peace may be due to the fact that this law has only recently been enacted (and thus they can be assumed to be acting in ignorance of it), or more likely, because he is reluctant to come down too hard on two of his particular favorites.
136–96. Most editors include these verses in the knight's address to the two armies; but given the satirical nature of many of the descriptions and editorial comments in this passage, it seems much more likely that these are the narrator's observations, not the knight's.
136. " . . . among these men on my own"
138–42. The first sub-group within the army of Winner comprises the international merchants who were welcomed in England by Edward III; this is the only group for whom there is no "heraldic" banner.
138. *ferdede be-syde*: i.e., "were mustered together"
139. *Lawe*: "low"
140. *Westwale*: Westphalia; *were*: "war"
141. *Estirlynges*: "Easter-lings," i.e., Hanseatic merchants from eastern Germany
142. *þat*: "who," referring to the whole assemblage of merchants; the image of these merchants *stuffede* into armor is intentionally comic.
142–8. The second sub-group is associated with the Pope, at this time Pope Clement VI, whose papal seat was at Avignon. Their banner is black (possibly suggesting the Pope's association with the Benedictines or "Black Monks"), with three white papal bulls (i.e., documents) from which cords with lead seals hang.

That hede es of Holy Kirke, I hope he be there,
Alle ferse to the fighte with the folke þat he ledis.
    Anoþer banere es vp-brayde with a bende of grene,
With thre hedis white-herede with howes one lofte,   150
Croked full craftyly and kembid in the nekke:
Thies are ledis of this londe þat schold oure lawes ȝeme,
That thynken to dele this daye with dynttis full many;
I holde hym bot a fole þat fightis whils flyttynge may helpe,
When he hase founden his frende þat fayled hym neuer.   155
    The thirde banere one bent es of blee whitte,
With sexe galegs, I see, of sable with-inn,
And iche one has a brown brase with bokels twayne:
Thies are Sayn Franceys folke, þat sayen alle schall fey   159
worthe.
    They aren so ferse and so fresche, þay feghtyn bot seldom;

---

157. galegs *ms*: galeys

---

147. "that (he who) is head of Holy Church, I expect that he's there"
149–55. Lawyers make up the third sub-group, and their banner is green, probably in reference to the "green wax," used by lawyers to seal revenue-raising documents (cf. the reference in the "Song of the Husbandman" [*Index* 696], l. 38). The satire against the legal establishment contained in these verses is fairly overt — their vanity (150–1), their hypocrisy (152) and their untrustworthiness (155).
150. *howes one lofte*: "hoods on high"; cf. the Ellesmere MS portrait of Chaucer's Man of Law
151. "folded quite skillfully and combed (i.e., placed in layers) on the neck"
154. *flyttynge*: "argument" or "legal debate," with no implication of the verbal abuse or ridicule which later became the hallmark of a "flytting."
155. This verse is ironic, for medieval lawyers had a reputation for accepting bribes and were notoriously untrustworthy, even toward their own clients; cf. ll. 349–53 in the poem "The Simonie" (*Index* 1992).
156–62. The four orders of friars also march in Winner's company; first come the Franciscans, whose white banner displays three pairs of fur-lined "galoshes," sandals with straps and buckles; (cf. *Pierce the Ploughman's Creed* 298–9 for a comment on the buckled shoes of the Franciscans). This portrait of the Franciscans emphasizes the disparity between what these friars preached and how they lived themselves.
157. *galegs*: "sandals"
158. *brase*: "brace," i.e., strap
159. "These are St. Francis' folk, who preach that all things shall pass away," alluding to their fire and brimstone sermons.
160. "They are so fierce and so fresh (because) they seldom fight."

I wote wele for wynnynge they wentten fro home—
His purse weghethe full wele that wanne thaym all hedire.
  The fourte banere one the bent was brayde appon lofte,
With bothe the brerdes of blake, a balle in the myddes,
Reghte siche as the sonne es in the someris tyde,   165
When it hase moste of þe maȝne, one Missomer Euen.
Thynkes Domynyke this daye with dynttis to dele—
With many a blesenande beryn his banere es stuffede!
And sythen the pope es so priste thies prechours to helpe,
And Frounceys with his folke es forced besyde,   170
And alle the ledis of the lande ledith thurgh witt,
There es no man appon molde to machen þam agayne,
Ne gete no grace appon grounde, vndir God hym-seluen.
  And ȝitt es the fyfte appon þe folde þe faireste of þam alle:

---

164. balle *ms*: balke
166. maȝne *ms*: maȝe
167. Thynkes *ms*: That was

161-2. The narrator states that despite their vows of poverty, the Franciscans are devoted to the cause of making money.
163-8. The Dominican friars, or Black Friars, come next; displayed on their black-bordered banner is a ball that blazes like the mid-summer sun, suggesting their love of ostentation and their lack of humility.
163. *brayde appon lofte*: "unfurled aloft"
164. "with both borders in black," in reference to the border on the banner and the border surrounding the escutcheon displayed on the banner
166. "when it has its greatest strength, on Mid-summer's Eve"
167-8. "Dominic expects this day to deal with dints (i.e., to do battle); with many a 'blessing-warrior' (i.e., the Dominican friars) his banner is stuffed"; the phrase *blesenande beryn* effectively captures the incongruity the poet is aiming for.
169-73. These verses suggest that the Dominicans received preferential treatment from the Pope, to the detriment of the Franciscans (170), which allowed the Dominicans to attain positions of prominence and influence.
169. *thies prechours*: "these preachers"; the Dominicans were often called the "Friar Preachers."
170. *es forced besyde*: i.e., "is pushed out of the way"
171. "and all the men of the country (the Dominicans) control through (their) cleverness"
173. "nor (who) obtains any favor anywhere . . ."
174-9. The Carmelites or White Friars, also called "Mary's Men" (177), carry a banner displaying three boars' heads; the boars' heads reflect the Carmelites' reputation for gluttony; cf. *Pierce the Plowman's Creed* 92-4.

A brighte banere of blee whitte with three bore-hedis;   175
Be any crafte þat I kan, Carmes thaym semyde,
For þay are the ordire þat louen oure Lady to serue.
If I scholde say þe sothe, it semys no nothire
Bot þat the freris with othere folke schall þe felde wynn.
The sexte es of sendell, and so are þay alle,   180
Whitte als the whalles bone, who-so the sothe tellys,
With beltys of blake bocled to-gedir,
The poyntes pared off rownde, þe pendant a-waye,
And alle the lethire appon lofte þate one lowe hengeth
Schynethe alle for scharpynynge of the schauynge iren.   185
The ordire of þe Austyns, for oughte þat I wene,
For by the blussche of the belte the banere I knewe.
And othere synes I seghe sett appon lofte,
Some witnessee of wolle, and some of wyne tounnes,
Some of merchandes merke, so many and so thikke   190

---

176. *This verse occurs in ms as l. 186.*
186. *This verse occurs in ms as l. 176.*
189. Some wittnesse *ms*: some of wittnesse
190. merkes *ms*: merke

---

176. Lines 176 and 186 have been transposed in the ms.
178–9. These verses support the assignment of 136–96 to the narrator, for it seems un-
   likely that an editorial comment such as this would be made by the Black Prince.
178. *it semys no nothire*: i.e., "nothing else seems possible"
180–7. Last among the four orders of friars are the Augustinians or Austin friars; dis-
   played on their banner is a belt, which the Austin friars used as a shaving-strop.
180. *sendelle*: a fine silk fabric; *and so are þay alle*: either a reference to the material out
   of which all of the friars' banners are made, or more likely, a reference to the Austin
   friars' fastidiousness about their appearance.
183. The ends of the leather belts were rounded, and there were no pendants.
184–5. The hanging portion of the belt displayed on the banner shines from its frequent
   use as a shaving-strop.
185. *schauyng iren*: i.e., razor
187. *the blussche*: "the shininess"
188–92. The standards of several others are also among the assembled forces of Win-
   ner, including the wool and wine merchants.
189. *some*: "some (of the banners)"
190. *merchandes merkes*: "merchants' marks," the emblems displayed on the banners of the
   various merchants

That I ne wote in my witt, for alle this werlde riche,
Whatte segge vnder the sonne can the sowme rekken.
　　And sekere one þat other syde are sadde men of armes,
Bolde sqwyeres of blode, bowmen many,
Þat if thay strike one stroke, stynt þay ne thynken   195
Till owthir here appon hethe be hewen to dethe.

[Knight]　"For-thi I bid ȝow bothe that thaym hedir broghte
That ȝe wend with me are any wrake falle,
To oure comely kyng that this kythe owethe;
And, fro he wiete wittirly where þe wronge ristyth,   200
Thare nowthir wy be wrothe to wirche als he demeth."
　　Of ayther rowte ther rode owte a renke, als me thoghte,
Knyghtis full comly one coursers attyred,

---

201. wy *ms*: wyes; demeth *ms*: doethe

---

192. *the sowme rekken*: "the sum reckon"
193-6. Waster's army receives only minor attention, in comparison to the lengthy ac-
count of Winner's army. Bestul suggests that this abbreviated treatment may be par-
tially explained by the fact that there was "no well-developed satiric tradition aimed
at prodigality to correspond to the venality satire that gives life and richness to the
poet's report of Winner's army" (p. 73). That is possibly the case, but it also seems
to underestimate the originality of this poet. The poet's decision to omit a compara-
ble satiric attack on those who support Waster may be a reflection of his own atti-
tudes, or more likely, those of the audience or specific patron for whom he is writing.
In any event, the three groups that he does identify within Waster's army — knights,
squires, and bowmen — constitute the same social unit with which Chaucer begins
his catalogue of the Canterbury pilgrims. In the war against France, the English
army was largely drawn from these three groups.
193. "And firmly on that other side are sober men of arms (i.e., knights)."
194. *of blode*: i.e., of noble birth; cf. line 15
195. Cf. line 107
196. "until one of the armies upon the heath is hacked to death"
197. The knight's address to the two armies is here resumed; *For-thi*: "Therefore," in refer-
ence to ll. 126-35; the two being addressed (i.e., *ȝow bothe*), who have brought their
armies *hedir* ("hither"), are Winner and Waster.
198. " . . . ere any harm befalls"
199. *this kythe owethe*: "this land owns (i.e., rules)"
200-1. "And, from (the time that) he knows precisely where the wrong rests, let neither
man be reluctant to act as he commands."

And sayden, "Sir sandisman, sele the be-tyde!
Wele knowe we the kyng; he clothes vs bothe,   205
And hase vs fosterde and fedde this fyve and twenty
wyntere.
Now fare þou by-fore and we schall folowe aftire."
And now are þaire brydells vp-brayde, and bown one þaire
wayes.
Thay lighten doun at þe launde, and leued thaire stedis,
Kayren vp at the clyffe, and one knees fallyn.   210
The kynge henttis by þe handes & hetys þam to ryse,
[King]   And sayde, "Welcomes, heres, as hyne of oure house
bothen."
The kynge waytted one wyde and the wyne askes;
Beryns broghte it anone in bolles of siluere;
Me thoghte I sowpped so sadly it sowede bothe myn eghne.
And he þat wilnes of this werke to wete any forthire,   216
Full freschely and faste, for here a fitt endes.

---

215. sowede *ms*: sowrede

---

204. "and said, 'Sir Envoy, blessings be-tide thee'"
205–6. If the figure of twenty-five years is to be taken literally, then the present date
is 1352 (Edward III having ascended the throne in 1327). These verses also indicate
the privileged status which each group has long enjoyed.
208. "And now are their bridles taken up, and (now have they) set forth on their way."
209. *þe launde*: the lawn or meadow; cf. 48–9
210. "(they) go up to the cliff, and on (their) knees fall"
211. *henttis*: "takes (them)"
212. This verse further attests to the king's fondness for both Winner and Waster and
the positions of prominence (*hyne*: "retainers") they have enjoyed within his house.
213. *waytted one wyde*: "looked about"
214. *bolles*: "bowls," i.e., cups
215. "I imagined that I (too) supped so deeply that it sored (i.e., bleared) both my eyes";
cf. *P3A* 286.
216–7. This embellishment is used to suggest a "minstrel's call" in an actual oral perfor-
mance, in addition to signaling a division of the narrative; cf. the note to l. 96 of
Mercy and Righteousness.
217. *full*: i.e., "fill up (your bowls)"; *fitt*: a term used to designate a section within a narra-
tive work, most often in popular romances; cf. line 367 and *Sir Thopas* (*CT* VII, 888).

[II]

[King]	Bot than kerpede the kynge, sayd, "Kythe what ʒe hatten,
	And whi the hates aren so hote ʒoure hertis by-twene.
	If I schall deme ʒow this day, dothe me to here." 220
[Winner]	"Now certys, lorde," sayde þat one, the sothe for to telle,
	"I hatt Wynnere, a wy that alle this werlde helpis,
	For I lordes can lere, thurgh ledyng of Witt.
	Thoo þat spedfully will spare and spende not to grete,
	Lyve appon littill-whattes, I lufe hym the bettir; 225
	Witt wendes me with and wysses me faire;
	Aye when I gadir my gudes, than glades myn hert.
	Bot this felle false thefe þat by-fore ʒowe standes
	Thynkes to strike or he styntt, and stroye me for-euer.
	Alle þat I wynn thurgh witt, he wastes thurgh pryde — 230
	I gedir, I glene, and he lattys goo sone;
	I pryke and I pryne, and he the purse opynes —
	Why hase this cayteffe no care how men corne sellen?

---

224. spende *cancelled after* will
227. I *supplied*

---

218. *Kythe what ʒe hatten*: "Make known what you are called."
220. *dothe*: "allow"
221–45. In his opening remarks Winner first congratulates himself for being a model
   of frugality; he then denounces Waster for spending his wealth on self-indulgent pleas-
   ures and on weapons, and for selling his farm equipment and failing to fulfill his
   agricultural responsibilities.
222. Winner, like the disputants in many a medieval debate poem, is quick to call at-
   tention to the ways in which he benefits mankind; Waster will do much the same
   later on.
223. *lere*: "learn," i.e., teach; *Witt*: "wit," which usually implies "knowledge" or "clever-
   ness," but here it seems to mean "common sense"
224–5. "Those who will save thriftily and not spend too greatly, (and) live upon small
   portions, I love them the better."
226. "Witt accompanies me and guides me wisely."
228. " . . . this false, evil thief," i.e., Waster; cf. 242
231. *lattys goo sone*: "lets go soon," i.e., quickly dissipates
232. "I stitch up and pin together, and he opens the purse."

His londes liggen alle ley, his lomes aren solde,

Downn bene his dowfehowses, drye bene his poles,   235

The deuyll wounder one the wele he weldys at home—

Bot hungere and heghe horses and howndes full kene!

Safe a sparthe and a spere sparrede in ane hyrne,

A bronde at his bede-hede, biddes he no noþer

Bot a cuttede capill to cayre with to his frendes.   240

Then will he boste with his brande & braundesche hym ofte,

This wikkede weryed thefe that Wastoure men calles,

That, if he life may longe, this lande will he stroye.

For-thi deme vs this daye, for Drightyn's loue in heuen,

To fighte furthe with oure folke to owthire fey worthe."   245

[Waster]   "Ʒee, Wynnere," quod Wastoure, "Thi wordes are hye;

---

237. horses *ms*: howses

---

234. "His lands lie fallow, his equipment is sold off."

235. *dowfehowses*: "dove-cots"; *poles*: "pools"

236. "The devil (may) wonder at the wealth he wields at home" (because he has spent it all on outside interests).

237. *heghe horses and howndes*: "high horses and hounds . . . ," used to typify Waster's self-indulgent amusements; the phrase "high horse" also suggests pride, as in *P3A* 111 and *Als I lay* 18. (For a dramatic account of Hunger's revenge on wasters, see Passus 6 of the B text of *Piers Plowman*.)

238-40. "Except for a halberd (a long-shafted axe with a spike on top) and a spear kept in a corner, a sword at his bed's head, he asks for nothing more than a gelded nag to ride with his friends."

239. A person's most prized possessions were often kept at his "bed's head"; cf. *Cant. Tales* I 293 and 3211.

240. Cf. *P3A* 189

242. *weryed*: "accursed"

244. *Drightyn's*: "God's"

245. *to owthire fey worthe*: "until one of us is destroyed"; cf. *P3A* 485

246-62. In his response to Winner's charges, Waster poses the question, what would become of Winner's wealth if it weren't put to use? (It is typical of this debate that each disputant, instead of defending himself against the other's charges, attempts to deflect those charges by introducing counter-charges.) Here Waster emphasizes Winner's failure to feed the poor (a virtue he will later ascribe to himself), and he invokes the scriptures in condemning Winner's miserly habits, a technique which will also be used by Winner.

246. *hye*: "high," i.e., lofty

Bot I schall tell the a tale that tene schall the better.
When thou haste waltered and went and wakede alle þe nyghte,
And iche a wy in this werlde that wonnes the abowte,
And hase werpede thy wyde howses full of wolle sakkes — 250
The bemys benden at the rofe, siche bakone there hynge,
Stuffed are sterlynges vndere stelen bowndes —
What scholde worthe of that wele, if no waste come?
Some rote, some ruste, some ratons fede.
Let be thy cramynge of thi kystes, for Cristis lufe of heuen!
Late the peple and the pore hafe parte of thi siluere;
For if thou wyd-whare scholde walke and waytten the sothe,
Thou scholdeste reme for rewthe, in siche ryfe bene the pore.
For and thou lengare thus lyfe, leue thou no noþer,
Thou schall be hanged in helle for that thou here spareste;
For siche a synn haste þou solde thi soule in-to helle, 261
And there es euer wellande woo, worlde with-owtten ende."

[Winner]   "Late be thi worde, Wastoure," quod Wynnere the riche.
"Thou melleste of a mater, thou madiste it thi-seluen;

---

264. thou *ms*: tho

---

247. *that tene schall the better*: "that shall trouble you the more"
248. "when you have tossed and turned and (lain) awake all night"; cf. *P3A* 257
249. *wonnes the abowte*: "dwells near you"
250. *werpede*: "filled"
252. *sterlynges*: "(pounds) sterling," i.e., coins; *bowndes*: "bands"
253. *worthe*: "become"; *wele*: "wealth"
254. Matthew 6:19; *ratons*: "rats"
255. *kystes*: "chests"
257. *wyd-whare*: "far and wide"
258. "You would weep for pity, in such numbers are the poor."
259. *leue*: "believe"
260. *spareste*: "save up" or "store away"
261. The sin Waster has in mind is avarice.
262. *wellande woo*: "welling woe," i.e., continual suffering
263–93. Winner's second speech is almost entirely a re-statement of his initial criticisms of Waster.
264. "You speak of a matter (i.e., problem) you created yourself"— in reference to Waster's suggestion that Winner's wealth would be worthless if it wasn't put to use.

With thi sturte and thy stryffe thou stroyeste vp my gudes,
In playinge and in wakyng in wynttres nyghttis,   266
In owttrage, in vnthrifte, in angarte pryde.
There es no wele in this werlde to wasschen thyn handes
That ne es gyffen and grounded are þou to getyn haue.
Thou ledis renkes in thy rowte wele rychely attyrede,   270
Some hafe girdills of golde þat more gude coste
Than alle þe faire fre londe that ȝe by-fore haden.
ȝe folowe noghte ȝoure fadirs þat fosterede ȝow alle
A kynde heruestes to cache, and cornes to wynn,
For þe colde wyntter and þe kene with gleterand frostes,   275
Sythen dropeles drye in the dede monethe.
And thou wolle to the tauerne by-fore þe toune-hede,
Iche beryne redy with a bolle to blerren thyn eghne,
Hete the whatte thou haue schalte and whatt thyn hert
lykes —
Wyfe, wedowe, or wenche þat wonnes there aboute.   280
There bott 'fille in' and 'feche forthe Florence to schewe,'
'Wee-hee' and 'worthe vp'—wordes ynewe!

---

270. rychely *ms*: ryhely
274. caste *cancelled before* cache

---

265. *sturte*: "stirrings," i.e., pleasurable activities
266. *wakynge*: "holding wakes," i.e., celebrating
267. *owttrage*: i.e., "outrageous excesses"; *angarte pryde*: "arrogant pride" (cf. *SGGK* 681 and *Dest. Troy* 9745)
268. *wele*: "wealth," perhaps with a play upon "well"
269. "that isn't given (away) and used up once you have gotten hold of it"
276. "afterward (comes) the rain-less drought in the dry season"
277. "but you would rather (go) to the tavern beyond the edge of town"; establishments of the kind described here were often located just beyond the town boundaries.
279–80. "(and) promises (to give) you whatever you wish to have or your heart desires — (whether) wife, widow, or wench (i.e., younger woman) that lives there about"
281. *fille in*: "fill up (the cup)"; Florence was a conventional name for a woman of loose morals, and in this instance she is probably a prostitute.
282. *Wee-hee*: the whinnying sound of a horse is sometimes used to indicate sexual arousal (cf. *Piers* B.4.22 and *Cant. Tales* I 4066), a symbolism probably stemming from Jeremiah 5:7–8.

Bot when this wele es a-waye, the wyne moste be payede
fore:
Than lympis ȝowe weddis to laye, or ȝoure londe selle.
For siche wikked werkes, wery the oure Lorde!   285
And for-thi God laughte that he louede, and leuede þat
oþer;
Iche freke one felde oghe þe ferdere be to wirche.
Teche thy men for to tille and tynen thyn feldes,
Rayse vp thi rent-howses, ryme vp thi ȝerdes —
Owthere hafe as þou haste done, and hope aftir werse: 290
Þat es firste þe faylynge of fode, and than the fire aftir,
To brene the alle at a birre, for thi bale dedis.
The more colde es to come, als me a clerke tolde."
[Waster]   "ȝee, Wynnere," quod Wastoure, "Thi wordes are vayne.
With oure festes and oure fare we feden the pore;   295

---

288. tynen *ms*: tymen

---

284. "Then it comes to pass that you must pawn your clothes . . ."
285. *wery the* . . .: "(may) our Lord take vengeance on you"
286-7. "And because God took the one that he loved, and left the other, each man in
the field ought to be the more eager to work"; probably a reference to Matthew 24:40
(Luke 17:35).
288-93. The lack of sufficient agricultural production in the 1350s — due to the demands
of the war and the consequences of the Black Death — is here suggested, although
Winner blames only Waster for this failure.
288. *tynen*: "harrow"
289. *ryme up*: "clear away"; *yerdes*: "enclosed lands"
290. "or have as you have done (i.e reap what you have sown), and expect the worst"
291-2. These verses probably contain a reference to Revelation 18:8, and thus Winner
associates the destruction of Waster with the destruction of Babylon.
292. "to burn you all in an instant, for your evil deeds"
293. This reference to a "greater cold" that is to come may relate to ll. 275-6, but it
may also be a reference to the actual winter of 1352-53, which was especially bitter;
this is one more piece of "evidence" which points to 1353 as *W & W's* likely date
of composition. This verse also carries apocalyptic overtones, recalling verses 13-17;
cf. also Proverbs 20:4.
294-323. In his second speech Waster argues that his banquets benefit the poor by keeping
money in circulation; he also argues that days of fasting such as Fridays and the
eves of saints' days should be abolished so that he could feast more often, thus benefit-
ing the poor even more! Waster also offers harsh criticisms of the legal profession.

It es plesynge to the Prynce þat paradyse wroghte;
When Cristes peple hath parte, Hym payes alle the better,
Then here ben hodirde and hidde and happede in cofers
That it no sonn may see thurgh seuen wyntter ones;
Owthir freres it feche when thou fey worthes,   300
To payntten thaire pelers or pergett with thaire walles.
Thi sone and thi sektours ichone sewes othere;
Maken dale aftir thi daye, for thou durste neuer
Mawngery ne myndale, ne neuer myrthe louediste.
A dale aftir thi daye dose the no mare   305
Þan a lighte lanterne late appone nyghte,
When it es borne at thi bakke, beryn, be my trouthe.
Now wolde God that it were als I wisse couthe
That thou, Wynnere, thou wriche, and Wanhope thi brothir,
And eke ymbryne dayes, and euenes of sayntes,   310

---

300. Owthir freres it feche *ms*: owthir it freres it feche
302. sewes *ms*: slees

---

297. Cf. such scriptures as Matt. 19:21 and 25:35–46; *hym payes*: "it pleases Him"
298. "than for it here to be hoarded and hidden and locked up in chests"
299. *sonn*: "sun"; *ones*: "once" (i.e., "not once")
300–1. These verses contribute to the poem's anti-fraternal satire.
300. *Owthir*: "or (else)"; *fey worthes*: "become fated," i.e., die
301. *pelers*: "pillars"; *pergett*: "plaster"
302. *sektours*: "executors"; *sewes*: "sues"
303–4. These are difficult verses. Perhaps they mean, "They make expenditures (or charitable gifts?) after your (death) day, for you never dared (to have) feasts, nor memorial drinks, nor ever loved mirthful events."
305. *dale*: "dole," i.e., payments (or charitable gifts?); *dose the no mare*: "does you no more (good)"
308. "Now (I) wish to God that it were as I could arrange."
309. *wriche*: "wretch"; *Wanhope*: i.e., Despair (cf. note to l. 109 in *Mercy and Righteousness*); Winner and Wanhope are "brothers," perhaps because of the state of wretchedness in which they live due to their similar fears—Winner because he fears the loss of his goods, Wanhope because he fears the loss of salvation; both are dour fellows.
310. *ymbryne dayes*: "Ember Days," special fast days occurring on the Wednesday, Friday, and Saturday during Lent, and following Whitsunday, Holy Cross Day (Sept. 14), and St. Lucia's Day (Dec. 13).

The Frydaye and his fere one the ferrere syde,
Were drownede in the depe see there neuer droghte come,
And dedly synn for thayre dede endityde with twelue.
And thies beryns one the bynches with howes one lofte,
That bene knowen and kydde for clerkes of the beste,   315
Als gude als Arestotle or Austyn the wyse,
That alle schent were those schalkes, and Scharshull it-wiste
Þat saide I prikkede with powere his pese to distourbe.
For-thi, comely kynge, that oure case heris,
Late vs swythe with oure swerdes swyngen to-gedirs;   320
For now I se it es full sothe þat sayde es full ʒore:
The richere of ranke wele, the rathere will drede,
The more hauande þat he hathe, the more of hert feble."
[Winner]   Bot than this wrechede Wynnere full wrothely he lukes,
Sayse, "Þis es spedles speche to speken thies wordes!   325
Loo, this wrechide Wastoure that wyde-whare es knawenn,
Ne es nothir kaysser ne kynge ne knyghte þat the folowes,

---

311. "Friday and his companion on the farther side (i.e., Saturday)"; this is not a refer-
ence to Good Friday and Holy Saturday but to Fridays in general and to fasts kept
on Saturdays in honor of the Virgin Mary, whose votive mass was said on Saturday.

312. *there . . .* : "where drought never comes," a striking example of litotes

313. "and were convicted of Deadly Sin for their deed by a jury of twelve"

314-8. Waster's attack on the legal profession, begun in 149–55, is continued here, pick-
ing up on the trial metaphor of 313.

314. *howes*: "hoods" (judges' caps); cf. 150

315. *kydde for*: "reputed to be"

316. *Arestotle or Austin*: Aristotle or St. Augustine, a sarcastic use of hyperbole; (in *P3A*
586–93 Aristotle is briefly treated, in his role as one of the world's wisest men).

317-8. William de Scharshull became a justice of the King's Bench in 1333 but was dis-
missed and imprisoned in 1340; he was restored to his office in 1342, and in 1350
he became Chief Justice of the King's Bench, a position he held until 1357; in Janu-
ary of 1352, before parliament, Scharshull accused the military nobility of being waste-
ful and of growing rich, which may explain Waster's animosity towards him; this
reference to Scharshull provides corroborative evidence for dating the poem to 1352-3.

317. "(would) that all those fellows were destroyed, and Scharshull among them"

322. "The richer in abundant wealth, the sooner will dread."

323. *hauande*: "havings," i.e., possessions

325-65. Winner's third speech is entirely devoted to describing the banquet given by
Waster for a few friends. Winner's detailed catalogue of the various dishes indicates
his disgust, but it may also suggest a perverse fascination.

325. *spedles*: "worthless"

327. *ne es nothir*: "(there) is neither"

Barone ne bachelere ne beryn that thou loueste,
Bot foure felawes or fyve that the faythe owthe;
And he schall dighte thaym to dyne with dayntethes so
many　　　　　　　　　　　　　　　　　　　　　　　330
Þat iche a wy in this werlde may wepyn for sorowe.
The bores hede schall be broghte with plontes appon lofte,
Buk-tayles full brode in brothes there be-syde,
Venyson with the frumentee and fesanttes full riche,
Baken mete ther-by one the burde sett,　　　　　　335
Chewettes of choppede flesche, charbiande fewlis,
And iche a segge þat I see has sexe mens doke.
If this were nedles note, anothir comes aftir,
Roste with the riche sewes and the ryalle spyces,
Kiddes cleuen by þe rigge, quarterd swannes,　　　340
Tartes of ten ynche — þat tenys myn hert
To see þe borde ouer-brade with blasande disches,
Als it were a rayled rode with rynges and stones!
The thirde mese to me were meruelle to rekken,
For alle es Martynmesse mete þat I with moste dele,　　345
Noghte bot worttes with the flesche, with-owt wilde fowle,

---

328. *bachelere*: "young knight"; *that thou loueste*: "that loves you"
329. *that the fayth owthe*: "that owes you allegiance"
330. *dayntethes*: "dainties," i.e., delicacies
332-61. Waster's banquet may be compared with Arthur's feast for the Roman ambassadors in the alliterative *Morte Arthure* 176-215.
332. *plontes*: "plants," i.e., herbs used as decorative garnishes
334. *frumentee*: wheat boiled in milk
335. *Baken mete*: "baked foods," e.g. pies; *burde*: "board," i.e., table
336. *chewettes*: small pieces of meat (cf. Prince Hal's comment to Falstaff in *I Henry IV* (V.i.29)); *charbiande fewlis*: "grilled birds"
337. *sexe mens doke*: "portions of duck (suitable for) six men"(?)
338. *nedles note*: "unnecessary" or "useless" (cf. *Patience* 220 and *Cleanness* 381); *anothir*: "another (course)"
339. *sewes*: "sauces"; *ryalle*: "royal"
340. "kids split along the back bone . . ."
343. "as (if) it were a cross adorned with rings and (precious) stones"
344. *mese*: "mess," i.e., course
345-7. Winner here describes his own frugal diet.
345. *Martynmesse mete*: i.e., salted meat (which would normally be eaten only during the winter)
346. *worttes*: "vegetables"

Saue ane hene to hym that the howse owethe.
And he will hafe birdes bownn one a broche riche,
Barnakes and buturs and many billed snyppes,
Larkes and lyngwhittes, lapped in sogoure,   350
Wodcokkes and wodwales full wellande hote,
Teeles and titmoyses to take what hym lykes;
[Caude]ls of conynges & custadis swete,
[Daryo]ls & dische-metis þat ful dere coste,
[Mawm]ene þat men clepen, ȝour mawes to fill,   355
[Iche] mese at a merke by-twen twa men,
[Thog]he he bot brynneth for bale ȝour bowells with-in.
[Me te]nyth at ȝour trompers, þay tounen so heghe,
[Pat a gome in þe gate goullyng may here;
[Pan] wil þay say to þam-selfe, as þay samen ryden,   360
ȝe hafe no myster of þe helpe of þe heuen kyng.
Þus are ȝe scorned by skyll & schathed þeraftir,
Þat rechen for a repaste a rawnsom of siluer.
Bot ones I herd in a haule of a herdmans toung:

353–60. *A corner of the ms leaf is missing.*
364. ones *ms*: one

---

347. "except for a hen for him who owns the house"
348-9. "And he (Waster) will have birds prepared on a spit richly, wild geese and bitterns and . . .snipes."
350. *lyngwhittes*: "linnets"; *lapped*: "covered"
353-60. Ellipsis is used in these verses to indicate where letters are missing as a result of a tear in the ms; Gollancz's conjectural emendations are supplied in the notes which follow.
353. [*Caudel*]*s of conynges*: "rabbit stews"
354. [*Daryo*]*ls*: "pasties"
355. [*Mawm*]*ene*: a wine sauce
356. "Each course (was placed) at a spot between two men."
357. *for bale*: "with painful discomfort"
358. [*Me te*]*nyth*: "I am angry at"
359. "that a man by the gate (i.e., standing outside in the street) the blaring can hear"
361. *myster*: "need"
362. *by skyll*: "quite rightly"; *schathed*: "insulted"
363. *rechen*: "reach," i.e., give or pay out

'Better were meles many þan a mery nyghte.'"   365
And he þat wilnes of þis werke for to wete forther,
Full freschely & faste, for here a fit endes.

[III]

[Waster]   "3ee, Wynnere," quod Wastour, "I wote wele my-seluen
What sall lympe of þe, lede, within fewe 3eris;
Thurgh þe poure-plenty of corne þat þe peple sowes,   370
Þat God wille graunte of his grace to growe on þe erthe,
Ay to appaire þe pris & passe nott to hye,
Schal make þe to waxe wod for wanhope in erthe,
To hope aftir an harde 3ere, to honge þi-seluen.
Woldeste þou hafe lordis to lyfe as laddis on fote?   375
Prelates als prestes þat þe parischen 3emes?
Prowde marchandes of pris as pedders in towne?
Late lordes lyfe als þam falles —
Þay þe bacon & beefe, þay botours & swannes,

---

366. forther *ms*: forthe

---

365. "Better to have many meals than one merry night"; probably proverbial
367. *full*: "fill"; cf. 217
368–91. In his third speech Waster briefly assails Winner again for his constant worry-
   ing; he then argues in favor of preserving the traditional hierarchical order of socie-
   ty, which was being threaten by the rising middle class; and finally he points out
   the fundamental reality that Winners need Wasters.
369. *lympe of þe*: "happen to you"
370–4. The sense of these difficult verses seems to be that over-farming the land results
   in driving down the value of what is produced, whereas under-farming results in
   a scarcity — and either condition causes Winner to despair.
370. *poure plente*: "pure plenty," i.e., great abundance
372. "always to impair the price so that it raises not too high"
373. "shall cause you to go mad with despair . . ."
376. *þe parischen 3emes*: "the parishioners watch over"
377. *pedders*: "pedlars"
378. "Let lords live as they wish, lads as it befalls them."
379. "they (the commoners) the bacon and beef (i.e., plain fare), they (the aristocrats)
   bitterns and swans (i.e., delicacies)"

Pay þe roughe of þe rye, þay þe rede whete,   380
Pay þe grewell gray, & þay þe gude sewes —
& þen may þe peple hafe parte in pouert þat standes,
Sum gud morsell of mete to mend with þair chere.
If fewlis flye schold forthe & fongen be neuer,
& wild bestis in þe wodde wone al þaire lyue,   385
& fisches flete in þe flode & ichone ete oþer,
Ane henne at ane halpeny by halfe ȝeris ende,
Schold not a ladde be in londe a lorde for to serue.
Þis wate þou full wele witterly þi-seluen:
Who-so wele schal wyn, a wastour moste he fynde,   390
For if it greues one gome, it gladdes anoþer."

[Winner]   "Now," quod Wynner to Wastour, "me wondirs in hert
Of thies poure penyles men þat peloure will by,
Sadills of sendale with sercles full riche.
Lesse & ȝe wrethe ȝour wifes, þaire willes to folowe,   395
Ȝe sellyn wodd aftir wodde in a wale tyme,
Bothe þe oke & þe assche & all þat þer growes;
Þe spyres & þe ȝonge sprynge ȝe spare to ȝour children,

---

390. moste *in margin*

---

381. *grewell*: "gruel"; *sewes*: "sauces"
382-3. "And then may the people that stand in poverty have (their) part, some good
    morsel of meat to improve their condition."
384-8. Waster is attempting to rationalize his hunting excursions on economic grounds — if
    the wealthy folk didn't reduce the wild game population, he reasons, then the poor
    people could live just by eating wild game, in which case they wouldn't need to work.
387. "a hen (would be worth only) a halfpenny within six months"
389. "You know this full well yourself."
390. "whoever wishes to win wealth . . ."; proverbial (Whiting W142)
392-422. In his fourth and last speech Winner contrasts Waster's pride — symbolized
    by the wide-hanging sleeves of his and his lady's gowns — with the humility of the
    Virgin Mary.
393. *peloure*: "fur"
394. *sercles*: i.e., rings
395. "so as not to anger your wives . . ."
396. *wodd*: "wood"; *wale*: "short"
398. "the sprouts and young saplings you save for your children"

& sayne God wil graunt it his grace to grow at þe last
For to saue to ȝour sones—bot þe schame es ȝour ownn! 400
Nedeles saue ȝe þe soyle, for sell it ȝe thynken.
ȝour forfadirs were fayne, when any frend come,
For to schake to þe schawe & schewe hym þe estres,
In iche holt þat þay had ane hare for to fynde,
Bryng to þe brode lande bukkes ynewe,   405
To lache & to late goo, to lightten þaire hertis.
Now es it sett & solde, my sorowe es þe more,
Wastes alle wilfully, ȝour wyfes to paye.
That are had lordes in londe & ladyes riche,
Now are þay ny-sottes of þe new gett, so nysely attyred, 410
With wyde slabbande sleues, sleght to þe grounde,
Ourlede all vmbtourne with ermyn aboute;
Þat es as harde, as I hope, to handil in þe derne
Als a cely symple wenche þat neuer silke wroghte!
Bot who-so lukes on hir lyre, oure lady of heuen,   415
How scho fled for ferd ferre out of hir kythe

---

404. holt *in margin*
411. wyde *ms*: elde

---

403. "to rush off to the forest and show him the inner places"
405. *brod launde*: "wide meadow"
406. "to catch and to let go (again) . . ."
407. "now it is (either) leased or sold . . ."
408. *paye*: "please"
409–11. "(Those) who formerly had lords in the land and ladies rich (i.e., were the ser-
     vants of lords), now are 'near-fools' (or 'new-fools'?) of the new mode, so foolishly
     attired, with wide hanging sleeves, straight to the ground, bordered all around with
     ermine."
410. *new gett*: "new mode," i.e., latest fashion; this phrase also occurs in Chaucer's por-
     trait of the Pardoner (*CT* I 682).
411. Cf. the Ellesmere MS illustration of Chaucer's Squire, whose sleeves are "longe and
     wyde" (*CT* I 93).
413. *as I hope*: i.e., "I imagine"; *derne*: "dark"
414. "as an inexperienced young peasant-girl who has never handled silk"; an intriguing
     simile.
415. *lyre*: "face"
416. *kythe*: "country"; the reference is to Matt. 2:13–4.

Appon ane amblande asse, with-owtten more pride,
Safe a barne in hir barme, & a broken heltre
Þat Iosephe held in hys hande, þat hend for to ȝeme,
Alle-þofe scho walt al þis werlde, hir wedes wer pore;   420
For to gyf ensample of siche, for to schewe oþer
For to leue pompe & pride—þat pouerte ofte schewes."
　　　Than þe Wastoure wrothly castes vp his eghne
[Waster]　& said, "Þou Wynnere, þou wriche, me woundirs in hert,
What hafe oure clothes coste þe, caytef, to by,   425
Þat þou schal birdes vp-brayd of þaire bright wedis,
Sythen þat we vouche-safe þat þe siluer payen!
It lyes wele for a lede his lemman to fynde
Aftir hir faire chere, to forthir hir herte;
Then will scho loue hym lelely as hir lyfe one,   430
Make hym bolde & bown with brandes to smytte,
To schonn schenchipe & schame þer schalkes ere gadird;
& if my peple ben prode, me payes alle þe better
To fee þam faire & free to-fore with myn eghne.

---

420. wedes *ms*: wordes

---

418. "except for a babe on her bosom, and a broken halter"; the detail of the broken
　　halter is added by the poet (perhaps to fulfill the alliterative needs of the verse).
419. " . . . that gentle one (i.e., Mary) to guide"
420. *walt*: "wielded," i.e., ruled; *wedes*: "clothing"
422. " . . . poverty often demonstrates that"
423. Cf. 324, where Winner is similarly described.
424–55. In his final speech Waster attempts to justify his expenses for clothing, and he
　　accuses Winner once again of wasting his goods by storing them away.
426. *birdes*: "maidens"
427. "since we who pay the silver (for their clothes) agree (to do so)"
428–9. "It well befits a man to maintain his lady-love, to please her according to her wishes."
430. " . . . loyally as her own life"
431–2. Waster here expresses the conventional view that love has the power to inspire
　　noble behavior.
432–4. "to shun dishonor and shame where warriors are assembled; and if my people
　　are proudly arrayed, it pleases me all the more, to award them fairly and freely be-
　　fore my eyes (i.e., personally)"

& ȝe negardes appon nyghte, ȝe nappeid so harde,   435
Routten at ȝour raxillyng, raysen ȝour hurdes;
ȝe beden wayte one þe wedir, þen wery ȝe þe while
Þat ȝe hade hightilde vp ȝour houses, & ȝour hyne raysed.
For-thi, Wynnere, with wronge þou wastes þi tyme;
For gode day ne glade getys þou neuer.   440
Þe deuyll at þi dede-day schal delyn þi gudis,
Þe þou woldes þat it were, wyn þay it neuer;
Þi skathill sectours schal seuer þam aboute,
& þou hafe helle full hotte for þat þou here saued.
Þou tast tent one a tale þat tolde was full ȝore: 445
I hold hym madde þat mournes his make for to wyn —
Hent hir þat he haf schal, & hold hir his while;
Take þe coppe as it comes, þe case as it falles;
For who-so lyfe may lengeste lympes to feche
Woodd þat he waste schall, to warmen his helys,   450
Ferrere þan his fadir dide by fyvetene myle.

---

447. hym *ms*: hir

435–8. Perhaps these difficult verses may be rendered: "and you misers in the night-
time, you sleep so deeply (i.e., not deeply at all), (you) yawn while you stretch your-
self, you raise your haunches (?), you order (your men) to wait on the weather, then
you curse the time that you didn't repair your buildings and improve your servants'
(living) conditions."
439. *with wronge*: i.e., "wrongfully"
441–4. Cf. Waster's similar comments in lines 259–62 and 302.
442–3. "Those (whom) you wish to have it, they (will) never enjoy it; your wicked exe-
cutors shall disperse them (i.e., your goods)."
445–51. In these verses Waster espouses his hedonistic philosophy of living for the mo-
ment and taking what life has to offer.
445–7. "You (should) take heed of an adage that was told of yore: I hold him (to be)
mad that worries about winning his mate — he who wants her should take her and
(should) keep her as long as he wishes." These not especially refined sentiments pro-
vide an insight into Waster's belief that he can do as he likes and take what he wants.
448. Probably proverbial
449–51. "For whoever may live the longest is obliged to fetch (the) wood that he shall
use to warm his heels, farther than his father did by fifteen miles"; Waster is arguing
in favor of living a full but brief life, one in which the inconveniences of old age won't
have to be experienced.

Now kan I carpe no more, bot, Sir Kyng, by þi trouthe,
Deme vs where we duell schall; me thynkes þe day hyes.
3it harde sore es myn herte, & harmes me more
Euer to see in my syghte þat I in soule hate."   455
    The kynge louely lokes on þe ledis twayne,

[King]   Says, "Blynnes, beryns, of 3oure brethe and of 3oure brode
wordes,
And I schal deme 3ow this day where 3e duelle schall,
Aythere lede in a lond þer he es loued moste.
Wende, Wynnere, þi waye ouer þe wale stremys,   460
Passe forthe by Paris to þe Pope of Rome;
Þe cardynalls ken þe wele, will kepe þe ful faire,
& make þi sydes in silken schetys to lygge,
& fede þe & foster þe & forthir thyn hert,
As leefe to worthen wode as þe to wrethe ones.   465
Bot loke, lede, be þi lyfe, when I lettres sende,
Þat þou hy þe to me home, on horse or one fote;
And when I knowe þou will come, he schall cayre vttire,

---

454. herte *supplied*
468–73. *ms is defective*
468. come *ms*: co

---

453. *the day hyes*: "the day hastens"; this verse conveys a sense of urgency, suggesting that
there is little time left in which to apply a remedy; cf. the haste with which the poacher
leaves the forest at the conclusion of the *Parl. of the Three Ages*.
455. *þat*: "that (which)" or "he (whom)," in reference to Winner
456. *louely lokes*: "looks lovingly"; this verse provides another indication of the king's affection
for both of the disputing parties.
457. "He says, 'Cease, men, your arguing and your open accusations.'"
459. *Aythere lede*: "each man"
460. *wale stremys*: "swift currents"
461–5. The Pope of Rome: the papal court of Clement VI, the "Pope of Rome," located
at this time in Avignon, France; Clement died near the end of 1352, and was suc-
ceeded by Pope Innocent VI. Clement's fondness for comforts of the kind described
in these verses was well-known.
463. *schetys to lygge*: "sheets to lie"
465. "as lief to go mad as to make you be angry (even) once"
468–73. Due to the condition of the ms, the final letters of these verses have been lost.
468. *he schall cayre vttire*: "he (Waster) shall go farther away"

And lenge with anoþer lede til þou þi lefe [taketh],
For þofe þou bide in þis burgh to þi ber[ying-day],   470
With hym happyns þe neuer a fote for . . . .
       And thou, Wastoure, I will þat þou won[ne þer euer]
Þer moste waste es of wele & of wyng . . . till.
Chese þe forthe in-to þe Chepe, a chambre þou rere,
Loke þi wyndowe be wyde, & wayte þe aboute,   475
Where any potet-beryn þurgh þe burgh passe;
Teche hym to þe tauerne till he tayte worthe;
Doo hym drynk al ny3te þat he dry be at morow,
Sythen ken hym to the crete to comforth his vaynes,
Brynge hym to Bred Strete, bikken þi fynger,   480
Schewe hym of fatt chepe scholdirs ynewe,
Hotte for þe hungry, a hen oþer twayne,
Sett hym softe one a sege, & sythen send aftir,
Bryng out of þe burgh þe best þou may fynde,
& luke thi knave hafe a knoke bot he þe clothe sprede;   485

---

469. taketh *is supplied*
470. berying-day *ms*: ber
472. *Gollancz's emendation is supplied in brackets.*
485. sprede *ms*: spr

---

469. *lenge*: "linger," i.e., stay
471. The sense of this damaged verse is that Winner and Waster must not be permitted
    to come in contact with each other.
472. *won[ne þer euer]*: "dwell where ever"
474–5. "Take yourself forth into Cheapside (a district in the City of London) and take
    a room (there), see (to it) that your window is (kept) wide open, and keep on the
    lookout for."
476. *potet-beryn*: a "tippler"(?), or simply a "well-heeled fellow"(?)
477. *Teche*: "show"; *tayte worthe*: "becomes tight"
478. *Doo*: "make"
479. "Then introduce him to the (wine of) Crete to comfort his veins."
480. *Bred Strete*: Bread Street, near Cheapside, where there were many places to eat; *bik-
    ken*: "beckon"
481. *chepe*: "sheep"
482. *oþer twayne*: "or two"
483. *sege*: "seat"; *send aftir*: "sent out for (more)"
485. "And see that your serving boy receives a blow unless he spreads the cloth"; using
    a table cloth would have been considered something of a luxury.

Bot late hym paye or he passe, & pik hym so clene
Þat fynd a peny in his purse & put owte his eghe!
When þat es dronken & don, duell þer no lenger,
Bot teche hym owt of the townn to trotte aftir more.
Then passe to þe Pultrie, þe peple þe knowes,   490
And ken wele þi katour to knawen þi fode —
The herouns, þe hasteleteȝ, þe henne wele serued;
Þe pertrikes, þe plouers, þe oþer pulled byrddes,
Þe albus, þis oþer foules, þe egretes dere —
Þe more þou wastis þi wele, þe better þe Wynner lykes!   495
& wayte to me, þou Wynnere, if þou wilt wele chese,
When I wende appon werre my wyes to lede;
For at þe proude pales of Parys þe riche
I thynk to do it in ded, & dud þe to knyghte,
& giff giftes full grete of golde & of siluer   500
To ledis of my legyance þat lufen me in hert;

---

500. siluer *ms*: si

---

486. *or he passes*: "before he departs"
490. *Pultrie*: Poultry, another street in Cheapside, where birds were sold
491. "and teach well your caterer . . ."
492-4. Cf. Winner's similar catalogue, 348-52.
492. *hasteleteȝ*: "haslets," meats (usually the entrails of animals) roasted on a spit (cf. *SGGK* 162)
493. *pertrikes*: "partridges"; *pulled*: "plucked"
494. *albus*: "bullfinches"
495. The king's comment here is in conflict with the views expressed so vehemently by Winner, but it accords with Waster's assertion in l. 390 that a Winner must find a Waster.
496-7. "And attend upon me, Winner, if you choose well, when I go to lead my men into war"; apparently the king, having completed his instructions to Waster, turns here once again to Winner.
498. *pales of Parys*: "the palace of Paris," i.e., the Louvre
501. *legyance*: "allegiance"
502. "and then to go as I came . . ."

& sythen kayren as I come, with knyghtis þat me foloen,
To þe kirke of Colayne þer þe kynges ligges. . . ."

---

503. The king is probably referring to the Shrine of the Three Kings in Cologne
Cathedral, which Edward III specially reverenced; he may have planned to go there
to pray for success in his impending military campaign. In any event, it is at this
point that the text breaks off. If the king's final speech is as neatly structured as the
speeches of the debaters, then the king would have gone on to address Waster once
more, after concluding his second set of remarks to Winner. At that point, presuma-
bly, there would have been a brief concluding frame in which the narrator would
have been awakened from his dream, perhaps followed by a brief reflection on his
dream experience and then a few benedictory verses—a concluding section much
like those found in the *Parliament of the Three Ages* and Chaucer's *Book of the Duchess* and
Parliament of Fowls.

The Parliament of the Three Ages

Chaucer's Miller is not alone in observing that "youthe and elde are often at debaat" (*CT* I 3230), for references to the strife between the Ages of Man are common in Middle English literature. Yet only a few Middle English poems deal with this subject specifically. Robert Henryson's short poem "The Ressoning Betuix Aige and Yowth" is a late example of such a work, but the major poem devoted to this theme is the fourteenth-century alliterative debate *The Parliament of the Three Ages*. Whereas some medieval treatments of the Ages of Man identify seven or even ten phases through which human beings pass, the *Parliament* poet concentrates on the three basic periods of adulthood—*Youthe* (Young Adulthood), *Medill Elde* (Middle Age), and *Elde* (Old Age)—emphasizing the shifting values and preoccupations of each. The poet's conception of his first two personified figures, Youth and Middle Age, accord entirely with conventional medieval stereotypes. Youth is preoccupied with his appearance and with his leisure activities, Middle Age with his profits and the accumulation of material assets, and neither of them can see beyond his immediate interests. Youth resembles such figures as Waster in *Winner and Waster* and Chaucer's Squire; Middle Age manifests a kinship with such figures as Winner and Chaucer's Merchant ("His resons he spak ful solempnely, / Sownynge alwey th'encrees of hys wynnyng" *CT* I 275–6). The poet's conception of Old Age, however, is more complicated. In this case two contradictory medieval stereotypes were available: Old Age depicted as a wise and disinterested speaker of truth; and Old Age depicted as an embittered and garrulous old dodderer. The *Parliament* poet appears to draw upon both of these stereotypes, with the result that *Elde* is an ambiguous figure, and one whose views do not necessarily reflect the views of the poet, an assumption which is sometimes made.

The *Parliament of the Three Ages* begins with a May-morning deer hunting sequence which is remarkable for its realism and its enveloping atmosphere of stealth. The descriptions of the forest at dawn, of the magnificent buck and his watchful younger companion, and of the hunter's prowess seem fresh and vivid, and they also suggest a poet who was himself an experienced outdoorsman. Particularly striking in this regard are the poet's detailed descriptions of the deer's antlers and the "breaking of the deer," passages which also reflect the poet's knowledge of medieval hunting manuals such as *The Master of Game* (written by Edward, the second Duke of York) and *The Art of Hunting* (written by William Twiti). The immediate function of this introductory poaching episode is to provide a realistic context for the narrator's dream vision, but it also anticipates, through the sudden and dramatic slaying of the deer, the didactic concerns of the dream vision; there is probably an implicit suggestion in this opening sequence of the motif of the hunter who is himself hunted by Death.

Once the narrator enters his dream he focuses directly upon the three figures who stand before him. His portrait of youth emphasizes Youth's robust physical appearance and his splendid clothing, his briefer portrait of Middle Age concentrates on his preoccupation with work and money, and the portrait of Old Age focuses on his physical decrepitude, his religious preoccupation, and his unpleasant disposition. Each of these figures is assigned a symbolic color — green for Youth, gray for Middle Age, and black for Old Age — and a symbolic age — 30 for Youth, 60 for Middle Age, 100 for Old Age. The actual debate section of the *Parliament* is surprisingly meager. The only genuine exchanges take place between Youth and Middle Age, as Youth celebrates his joyous life as a young courtier (including a lengthy and specific description of the courtly pastime of hawking) and as Middle Age roundly criticizes him for wasting his time and resources on such frivolous pursuits. When a full-fledged debate fails to materialize, Old Age intervenes, denounces the values of both Youth and Middle Age, and offers an extended meditation on man's mortality. To illustrate his *vanitas vanitatum* theme, Old Age discourses first upon the Nine Worthies and then more briefly upon the world's wisest men and most famous lovers. Although Old Age's moral sentiments are largely conventional, on the whole his sermon is an eccentric and prolix performance, filled with digressions, irrelevancies, and errors of fact. Because of the length of his "homily" — it takes up more than half the poem — some critics believe that it constitutes a major structural flaw in the *Parliament*; and because the homily strikes a somewhat different note from what precedes it, some have suggested that it may be the work of a second poet, but this seems unlikely.

In addition to reflecting the poet's familiarity with hunting and hunting manuals, the poem also reflects his familiarity with an extensive body of medieval romance literature, in French and in English. The centerpiece of Old Age's sermon, the Nine Worthies topos, was widely popular in the later Middle Ages, making one of its earliest appearances in Jacques de Longuyon's *Voeux du Paon* (c. 1312). It occurs in several other Middle English poems, most notably the alliterative *Morte Arthure*, the prologue to the *Cursor Mundi*, and the *Disputation between the Body and the Worms*.

The *Parliament of the Three Ages* occupies a central position among the works of the Alliterative Revival. It has close ties with the alliterative poems on political and didactic matters (e.g. *Piers Plowman*, *Mum and the Sothsegger*, and *Death and Life*), as well as with the alliterative poems in the historical-epic tradition (e.g. *Sir Gawain and the Green Knight*, *The Destruction of Troy*, the *Morte Arthure*, and the *Siege of Jerusalem*). The *Parliament* has an especially close relationship with *Winner and Waster*. Both are alliterative works of substantial length and complexity, and in both poems the clash of personified abstractions occurs within a narrator's dream vision. The *Parliament* differs from *Winner and Waster* in its basic concerns, which are moral rather than political, and in its failure to generate the animated exchanges and dramatic force of the earlier poem. The two poems are recorded side by side in British Library MS Additional 31042, one of the two Thornton manuscripts. A second and fragmentary text of the *Parliament* is recorded in British Library MS Additional 33994 (the Ware manuscript).

---

1)   Base Text: BL MS Addit. 31042, ff. 169r–176v

2)   Other mss: BL MS Addit. 33994, ff. 19r–26v

3)   Selected Printed Texts: I. Gollancz, *Early English Poems*, 2 (1915)
          M. Y. Offord, *The Parlement of the Thre Ages*, EETS 246 (1959), (contains both the Thornton text and the fragmentary Ware text)
          C. W. Dunn and E. T. Byrnes, *Middle English Literature* (1973), 238–70
          A. S. Haskell, *A Middle English Anthology* (1969), 408–42

4)   *Index of Middle English Verse* 1556

The Parlement of the Thre Ages

In the monethe of Maye when mirthes bene fele,
And the sesone of somere when softe bene the wedres,
Als I went to the wodde my werdes to dreghe,
Into þe schawes my-selfe a schotte me to gete
At ane hert or ane hynde, happen as it myghte;   5
And as Dryghtyn the day droue frome þe heuen
Als I habade one a banke be a bryme syde,
There the gryse was grene, growen with floures —
The primrose, the pervynke, and piliole þe riche —
The dewe appon dayses donkede full faire,   10
Burgons & blossoms & braunches full swete,

---

1. monethe *ms*: monethes

---

1. In contrast to *Winner and Waster* and *Death and Life*, the *Parliament of the Three Ages* has no "prologue" but begins immediately with the narrator's May-morning adventure; line 1 is a formulaic verse; cf. line 12,969 in the *Destr. of Troy*: "Hit was the moneth of May when mirthes begyn" (EETS 39, p. 424).
2. Cf. the opening verse in *Piers Plowman* ("In a somer sesoun whan softe was the sonne") and l. 2343 of the *Destr. of Troy* ("In the season of somer, er the sun rose"), which initiates Paris's hunting expedition in which he too experiences a dream-vision.
3. *My werdes to dreghe*: i.e., "to try my luck" or "to take my chances"; but the phrase may also carry the implication of "tempting fate," in which case the spiritual significance of the hunter's adventure may be foreshadowed.
3–5. These verses provide the first hint that the narrator is a poacher, and it will soon be apparent that his hunting activities violate several laws: e.g. he is hunting in a private preserve (see ll. 92–9); he is using a crossbow, a weapon whose use was restricted to persons of property (which he is not, presumably); and he is hunting indiscriminately for either male or female deer (during May) although doe season (according to the *Master of the Game*) extends only from September 14 to February 2.
6. Although this verse might be read to suggest that the narrator's adventures begin as night is falling, they probably begin just before sunrise (cf. 15–6) and conclude just after sunset, enclosing the period of the natural day, which is often used to symbolize life from birth to death. Line 6 may be rendered: "As the Lord, from heaven, was driving forth (i.e., bringing forth) the day."
7. *habade*: "abided"; *one*: "on"
7–16. The sounds of the river, the fragrance of the flowers, and the singing of the birds usually contribute to the narrator's drowsiness, but that is not the case in the *Parliament*.
11. Cf. *DL* 71

And the mery mystes full myldely gane falle;
The cukkowe, the cowschote, kene were þay bothen,
And the throstills full throly threpen in the bankes,
And iche foule in that frythe faynere þan oþer   15
That the derke was done & the daye lightenede.
Hertys and hyndes one hillys þay gonen,
The foxe and the filmarte þay flede to þe erthe;
The hare hurkles by hawes & harde thedir dryves,
And ferkes faste to hir fourme & fatills hir to sitt.   20
    Als I stode in that stede one stalkynge I thoghte;
Bothe my body and my bowe I buskede with leues
And turnede to-wardes a tree & tariede there a while;
And als I lokede to a launde a littill me be-syde,
I seghe ane hert with ane hede, ane heghe for the nones: 25
Alle vnburneschede was þe beme, full borely þe mydle,
With iche feetour as thi fote, for-frayed in the greues,
With auntlers one aythere syde egheliche longe.

---

14. "And the thrushes scolded (each other) quite vigorously on the banks"; cf. *WW* 37
15. "And each bird in the forest was gladder than the others."
17. *gonen* (or *gouen*?): in the context of ll. 17–20, a verb describing movement seems likely; however, *gouen* can mean "to gaze about," which would be consistent with the vigilance of the deer in the verses soon to follow; this verse could then be rendered, "harts and hinds gazed about (themselves) on the hillsides."
18. Cf. *Cleanness* 534
19–20. Cf. *WW* 14
19. 19. *hurkles by hawes*: "crouches by hedges"
20. Cf. *DL* 30
21–99. There are many descriptions of deer hunts in Middle English literature, especially in the romances (e.g. *SGGK, The Awntyrs off Arthure, Sir Tristrem*, etc.), but such descriptions invariably depict courtly hunting parties riding to the hunt. This description is exceptional in presenting a solitary hunter who hunts on foot, with only his dog to assist him. The care which he takes throughout this passage to insure that he remains undetected by others suggests that he is a poacher, not a likely avocation for a courtier.
24. *launde*: "a clearing" or "meadow"
25. *ane hegh for the nones*: "a high one indeed"
26. The beam, the main stem of the newly-grown antlers, is "unburnished" because it has not yet been rubbed completely free of its skin-like covering; *full borely*: "very strong"
27. "with each tine, (looking) like your foot, frayed (against the trees) in the grove"; the covering on the upper portions of the antlers has been partially rubbed away.
28–30. According to the *Master of the Game* the tines nearest the deer's head are called the "auntelers," the ones just above those are the "rialls," and the uppermost ones are the "susreals" (*MG* 17).

The ryalls full richely raughten frome the myddes
With surryals full semely appon sydes twayne;   30
And he assommet and sett of vi and of fyve
And þerto borely and brode and of body grete,
And a coloppe for a kynge, cache hym who myghte.
Bot there sewet hym a sowre þat seruet hym full ȝerne,
That woke & warned hym when wynde faylede   35
That none so sleghe in his slepe with sleghte scholde hym
dere,
And went the wayes hym byfore when any wothe tyde.
   My lyame than full lightly lete I doun falle,
And to the bole of a birche my berselett I cowchide;
I waitted wiesly the wynde by waggynge of leues,   40
Stalkede full stilly no stikkes to breke,
And crepite to a crabtre and couerede me ther-vndere;
Then I bende vp my bowe and bownede me to schote,
Tighte vp my tylere and taysede at the hert.

---

31. v *cancelled before* fyve

---

31. One side of the antlers has six branches, the other side five; since the deer has achieved
   his full growth (that is to say, he is *sett*), when his antlers are "summed" (*assommet*)
   he can be seen to be a "Hart of eleven points" (Twiti, *Art of Hunting*, 47); this would
   make him older than six years since in his sixth year a male deer becomes a "Hart
   of the first head" with ten points to his antlers.
33. *a coloppe*: "a tasty morsel"; since the poacher may be hunting in a royal preserve,
   irony is probably intended in this verse.
34. "But there followed after him a soar (a fourth-year male) that served him full eager-
   ly"; this younger deer, who serves as lookout for the older deer, is portrayed as fulfill-
   ing the role of a young squire to an older knight.
36. *dere*: "harm"
37. *wothe tide*: "danger betided"
38–9. The hunter quietly drops his dog's leash (*lyame*) and stations him behind a tree;
   he doesn't actually unleash the dog until l. 61; the dog is a berselett, a hunting dog
   which was small in stature and especially adept at moving through dense undergrowth.
40. *waitted wiesly*: i.e., "judged carefully"
44. "Raised up the stock (of my crossbow) and took aim at the hart"; the *tyler* is the stock
   or main beam of the crossbow; its central groove guides the arrow (or quarrel). The
   kinds of crossbows which were used in hunting are described in an appendix to the
   Master of the Game entitled "Arms of the Chase."

Bot the sowre þat hym sewet sett vp the nese,   45
And wayttede wittyly abowte & wyndide full ȝerne.
Then I moste stonde als I stode and stirre no fote ferrere,
For had I myntid or mouede or made any synys,
Alle my layke hade bene loste þat I had longe wayttede.
Bot gnattes gretely me greuede and gnewen myn eghne,   50
And he stotayde and stelkett and starede full brode;
Bot at the laste he loutted doun & laughte till his mete,
And I hallede to the hokes and the hert smote;
And happenyd that I hitt hym by-hynde þe lefte scholdire,
Þat þe blode braste owte appon bothe the sydes;   55
And he balkede and brayed and brusched thurghe þe greues,
As alle had hurlede one ane hepe þat in the holte longede;
And sone the sowre þat hym sewet resorte to his feris,
And þay, forfrayede of his fare, to þe fellys þay hyen;
And I hyede to my hounde and hent hym vp sone,   60
And louset my lyame and lete hym vmbycaste.
The breris and the brakans were blody byronnen,
And he assentis to þat sewte and seches hym aftire,
There he was crepyde in-to a krage and crouschede to þe
erthe.
Dede als a dore-nayle doune was he fallen.   65

---

48. myntid *ms*: mytid
56. leues *cancelled before* greues

---

46. "and looked carefully about and sniffed the wind quite eagerly"
49. *layke*: i.e., "sport"
51. "And he (the soar) paused and moved cautiously and looked about widely."
53. *hallede to the hokes*: "drew back the hooks" (in order to release the bow cord)
56. "And he bucked and jerked and brushed (i.e., crashed) through the groves"; the verb
    brayed probably describes the hart's movements rather than his cries.
57. "as if all (the beasts) had been hurled in a heap that dwelled in that wood"
59. "And they, frightened by (the wounded hart's) behavior, hastened to the moors."
61. "and loosed my leash and let him cast about"; cf. 38–9
63. *sewte*: "pursuit"
64. *There*: "where"; *he*: i.e., the hart
65. This simile also occurs in *William of Palerne* (628 and 3396) and in *Piers Plowman*
    (C.2.184); wooden doors were commonly studded with nails in the Middle Ages, but

And I hym hent by þe hede and heryett hym vttire,
Turned his troches & tachede thaym in-to the erthe,
Kest vp that keuduart and kutt of his tonge,
Brayde owte his bewells my bereselet to fede;
And I slitte hym at þe assaye to see how me semyde,   70
And he was floreschede full faire of two fyngere brede.
I chese to the chawylls chefe to be-gynn,
And ritte doun at a rase reghte to the tayle,
And þan þe herbere anone aftyr I makede;
I raughte the righte legge by-fore, ritt it þeraftir,   75
And so fro legge to legge I lepe thaym aboute;
And þe felle fro þe fete fayre I departede,

---

69. owte *supplied*
70. slitte *ms*: sisilte

---

it is unclear why a "door nail" should be deader than any other nail; one guess is
that the deadest nail is the particular doornail which is repeatedly struck by the door
knocker.
66–99. Even though the hunter might be expected to be in something of a hurry, he
very carefully follows the "rules" for the breaking (or brittling) of the deer as they
are recorded in medieval hunting manuals. The specific stages in the breaking of
a deer are described in even greater detail in *SGGK* (1323–64) and *Sir Tristrem* (452–515).
66. *heryett hym vttire*: "dragged him out" (from where he had crept to)
67. The hunter first anchors the deer to the ground by means of the sharp points (*troches*)
of his antlers.
68. *keuduart.*: This is the only occurrence of this word in Middle English, and its mean-
ing is unknown. The context indicates something to do with raising the deer's head
or opening his mouth. The deer's tongue was considered to be a delicacy.
69. The entrails were customarily given to the hounds; cf. *SGGK* 1329.
70–1. The "assay" is the place in the hart's chest where his fatness can be measured;
here, as in *SGGK* (1329), it is of two fingers' breadth, a substantial amount.
72. "I selected the jowls as the place to begin."
73. "and ripped down with a rush . . ."
74. In both this poem and *SGGK* "making the erber" is the initial stage in disembowel-
ing the deer. It involves removing the deer's first stomach, which is then opened,
emptied, and re-filled with blood and fat from the paunch. It is then sewn up with
thread.
75–8. The hunter skins the deer in the traditional manner: from a length-wise cut ex-
tending from throat to tail (73), the hide is slit outward along each of the forelegs
and hindlegs. The hide is then flayed (*flewe*) outward toward the backbone (*rigge*);
cf. *SGGK* 1332.

And flewe it doun with my fiste faste to the rigge.
I tighte owte my trenchore and toke of the scholdirs,
Cuttede corbyns bone and keste it a-waye.   80
I slitte hym full sleghely and slyppede in my fyngere,
Lesse the poynte scholde perche the pawnche or the guttys;
I soughte owte my sewet and semblete it to-gedire,
And pullede oute the 'pawnche and putt it in an hole.
I grippede owte the guttes and graythede thaym be-syde,   85
And than the nombles anone name I there-aftire;
Rent vp fro the rygge reghte to the myddis,
And then the fourches full fayre I fonge fro þe sydes,
And chynede hym chefely and choppede of the nekke,
And þe hede and the haulse homelyde in sondree.   90
Þe fete of the fourche I feste thurghe the sydis,
And heuede alle in-to ane hole and hidde it with ferne,
With hethe and with horemosse hilde it about,
Þat no fostere of the fee scholde fynde it ther-aftir;
Hid the hornes and the hede in ane hologhe oke,   95
Þat no hunte scholde it hent ne haue it in sighte.
I foundede faste there-fro for ferde to be wryghede,
And sett me oute one a syde to see how it cheuede,

---

81. sleghely *ms*: cleghely
84. pawnche *ms*: pawche
89. chynede *ms*: chynade

---

80. The *corbyns bone* is a piece of gristle on the end of the sternum. It is referred to as the "corbyns fee" or *corbeles fee* (*SGGK* 1355 and *Sir Tristrem* 502–4); it is thrown up into a tree as an offering to the crows.
83. *sewet*: the suet or fat
86. "And then the entrails soon after I took"; the *nombles* include organs such as the liver and kidneys, considered to be delicacies.
88–91. The haunches (*fourches*) are cut off, and then after the neck and head have been removed, they are re-fastened to the sides of the deer.
92–6. The hunter's attempt to remove all traces of his activity is a clear indication of its illegality. The *foster of the fee* he wishes to avoid is the forester, an officer who has inherited his position (he is said to have it *in fee*). Chaucer's Yeoman is a professional forester (*CT* I 117).
97. "I worked quickly, therefore, for fear of being discovered."

To wayte it frome wyldes swyne that wyse bene of nesse.
And als I satte in my sette the sonne was so warme,   100
And I for slepeles was slome, and slomerde a while;
And there me dreme in that dowte a full dreghe sweuynn,
And whate I seghe in my saule the sothe I schall telle.

I seghe thre thro men threpden full ȝerne,
And moten of myche-whate and maden thaym full tale.   105
And ȝe will, ledys, me listen ane hande-while,
I schall reken thaire araye redely, for-sothe,
And to ȝowe neuen thaire names naytly there-aftire.
The firste was a ferse freke, fayrere than thies othire,
A bolde beryne one a blonke, bownne for to ryde,   .   110
A hathelle on ane heghe horse with hauke appon hande.
He was balghe in the breste and brode in the scholdirs,
His axles and his armes were i-liche longe,
And in the medille als a mayden menskfully schapen;
Longe legges and large and lele for to shewe.   115

---

99. *wayte*: i.e., "guard"
101. "And because I was heavy with sleepiness I slumbered a while."
102. *dreghe sweuynn*: "long dream"
103. This important verse seems to indicate that the narrator's dream is a form of self-
     exploration.
104–5. "I saw three determined men (who) contended in earnest, and who spoke of many
     things and expressed them with vigor"; the phrase *maden thaym full tale* is unrecorded
     elsewhere and is difficult to render. The omission of an "understood" relative pronoun
     occurs often in the poem (cf. 152, 275, 427, etc.).
106. *And*: "if"; *ledys*: "men"
109–35. In this portrait of the personified figure of Youth the medieval theme of the
     "Pride of Life" receives particular emphasis (see I John 2:15–7); in this regard the
     portraits of Youth and of Chaucer's Squire may be compared. Youth also bears some
     general likenesses to the figure of the Green Knight in *SGGK* (136 ff.), but these resem-
     blances are probably coincidental.
110. Cf. *The Siege of Jerusalem* 271
111. Riding "on a high horse" is a common metaphor for an exaggerated sense of self-
     importance; cf. the descriptions of the Body in *Als I lay* (18 and 451) and that of Chau-
     cer's Merchant (*CT* I 271); cf. also WW 237.
114. Knights in romances are often portrayed as slim-waisted (e.g. *SGGK* 144 and *Wars
     of Alexander* 4923), a characteristic which Chaucer parodies by giving Sir Thopas *sydes
     smale* (*CT* VII 836), a phrase more appropriate for a heroine than a hero.

He streghte hym in his sterapis and stode vp-rightes,
He ne hade no hode ne no hatte bot his here one:
A chaplet one his chefe-lere, chosen for the nones,
Raylede alle with red rose, richeste of floures,
With trayfoyles and trewloues of full triede perles,   120
With a chefe charebocle chosen in the myddes.
He was gerede alle in grene, alle with golde by-weuede,
Enbroddire alle with besanttes and beralles full riche;
His colere with calsydoynnes clustrede full thikke,
With many dyamandes full dere dighte one his sleues.   125
Þe semys with saphirs sett were full many,
With emeraudes and amatistes appon iche syde,
With full riche rubyes raylede by the hemmes;
Þe price of that perry were worthe powndes full many.
His sadille was of sykamoure that he satt inn,   130
His bridell alle of brente golde with silke brayden raynes,
His cropoure was of tartaryne þat traylede to þe erthe;

---

116. Cf. the Ellesmere MS portrait of Chaucer's Squire, whose long legs are also straight in his stirrups.

117-21. Youth's only headwear is a chaplet which is adorned with red roses and decorated with *trayfoyles and trewloues* —"trefoils (three-lobed leaves) and true-love knots," popular ornamental figures — and studded with gem stones. In ll. 178-81 Youth explains why he refrains from wearing any hat or hood at this time.

122. Youth's green clothing symbolize his age, just as the grey clothing worn by Middle Age and the black clothing of Old Age symbolize their ages; Youth's green apparel, with golden ornamentations woven into the fabric, recalls the dress of the Green Knight (*SGGK* 615).

123. "Embroidered entirely with bezants (designs resembling gold coins of Byzantium) and beryls"; Chaucer's Squire also wears colorfully embroidered garments (*CT* I 89).

124. Youth's dress, and particularly the style of collar he wears, has been used as evidence for dating the poem to the fourth quarter of the fourteenth century (see R. E. Lewis, *NM* 69 (1968), 380-90).

129. *perry*: "jewelry"; the gems which adorn Youth's clothing indicate his aristocratic standing and his personal wealth, and they reflect his desire to display himself as ostentatiously as possible; also their permanence may provide an ironic comment on the fleetingness of youth.

130. Medieval saddles were sometimes made of wood, apparently.

132. *cropoure*: "crupper," leather or cloth straps passing beneath the horse's tail and attached to the saddle; cf. the Ellesmere portraits of the Squire, Knight, Prioress, Monk, and Wife; of these, the Squire's come the nearest to "trailing to the earth."

And he throly was threuen of thritty ʒere of elde,
And ther-to ʒonge and ʒape, and ʒouthe was his name—
And the semelyeste segge that I seghe euer.   135
    The seconde segge in his sete satte at his ese,
A renke alle in rosette þat rowmly was schapyn,
In a golyone of graye girde in the myddes,
And iche bagge in his bosome bettir than othere.
One his golde and his gude gretly he mousede,   140
His renttes and his reches rekened he full ofte,
Of mukkyng, of marlelyng, and mendynge of howses,
Of benes of his bondemen, of benefetis many,
Of presanttes of polayle, of pufilis als;
Of purches of ploughe-londes, of parkes full faire,   145
Of profettis of his pasturs, that his purse mendis;
Of stiewardes of storrours, stirkes to bye,
Of clerkes of countours, his courtes to holde;

---

135. semelyeste *ms*: semely
147. stiewardes *ms*: stiewarde

133-4. "And he was splendidly grown to thirty years of age, and accordingly was young and lively, and Youth was his name"; thirty seems to reflect the age of a fully mature "youth," in contrast to more immature youths of twenty such as Chaucer's Squire and the dreamer in the *Roman de la Rose*; the monk Daun John in the *Shipman's Tale* is thirty and is described as being young (*CT* VII 1215-18), and Isaac in the York play of *Abraham's Sacrifice of Isaac* is thirty while Abraham is 100 years old, the age of Old Age in this poem.

137. *rossette*: a coarse woolen fabric, often reddish-brown ("russet") in color, though here perhaps grayish, if *rossette* is the material of the *golyone* ("tunic") of l. 138; cf. 182, where it is stated that Middle Age is "all in gray"; Middle Age's corpulent physique is indicated by the phrase *þat rownly* ("roundly") *was schapyn*.

139. *bagge*: i.e., "money bag"; Middle Age's values are clearly indicated here; he is quite similar to the figure of Winner in *Winner and Waster*, and like Winner he reflects elements of the personified vice of Avarice.

141. *reches rekened*: "riches counted"

143. "of the wages of his laborers . . ."

144. *polayle*: "poultry"; *pufilis*: possibly "furs," if the word is a form of *purfil*, but Offord prefers "small pieces of land"

147. "of stewards of the stores, heifers to buy"

148. *clerkes of countours*: the treasury clerks who oversee Middle Age's financial transactions

And alle his witt in this werlde was one his wele one.
Hym semyde for to see to of sexty ȝere elde—   150
And þer-fore men in his marche Medille Elde hym callede.
    The thirde was a laythe lede, lenyde one his syde,
A beryne bownn alle in blake, with bedis in his hande,
Croked and courbede, encrampeschett for elde;
Alle disfygured was his face and fadit his hewe,   155
His berde and browes were blanchede full whitte,
And the hare one his hede hewede of the same.
    He was ballede and blynde and alle babirlippede,
Tetheles and tenefull, I tell ȝowe for sothe;
And euer he momelide and ment and mercy he askede,   160
And cried kenely one Criste and his crede sayde,
With sawtries full sere tymes to sayntes in heuen;
Envyous and angrye—and Elde was his name.
I helde hym be my hopynge a hundrethe ȝeris of age,

---

157. his *in margin*

---

149. *his witt*: "his thought"; *one his wele one*: "on his wealth only"
150. *to see to*: "to look at"; just as thirty is the "mature" stage of Youth, sixty reflects the
    mature stage of Middle Age.
152. "The third was a foul-looking fellow (who) leaned on his side."
153-9. Old Age is dressed in black, completing the color scheme for the three ages of
    man, and his decrepit physical state is described in detail. His preoccupation with
    religious concerns, first indicated by his *bedis* ("prayer beads"), contrasts with the worldly
    concerns of Youth and Middle Age.
158. *ballede*: "bald"; *babirlippede*: this term is usually applied to thick or loosely hanging
    lips, but here it may indicate Old Age's trembling lips or that he is mumbling to
    himself.
159. *tenefull*: "peevish"
160. *momelide and ment*: "mumbled and moaned"
163. Old Age is often portrayed as being envious, angry, and *tenefull* (159); Chaucer's
    Reeve observes that "Elde" is characterized by "Avauntyng, liyng, anger, coveitise"
    (*CT* I 3884-5).
164. *be my hopynge*: "by my reckoning"; Old Age is 100, completing the age scheme of
    thirty, sixty, and 100, an unusual series of numbers; it does have a parallel in the
    biblical parable of the sower (Matthew 13:3-23, particularly 13:8), a usage which
    doesn't appear to be especially pertinent here.

And bot his cruche and his couche he carede for no more.   165
   Now hafe I rekkende ȝow theire araye, redely the sothe,
And also nameded ȝow thaire names naytly there-aftire,
And now thaire carpynge I sall kythe, knowe it if ȝowe liste.

   Now this gome alle in grene so gayly attyrede,
This hathelle one this heghe horse with hauke one his fiste,   170
He was ȝonge and ȝape and ȝernynge to armes,
And pleynede hym one paramours and peteuosely syghede.
He sett hym vp in his sadill and seyde theis wordes:
[Youth] "My lady, my lemman, þat I hafe luffede euer,
My wele and my wirchipe, in werlde where þou duellys,   175
My playstere of paramours, my lady with pappis full swete,
Alle my hope and my hele, myn herte es thyn ownn!
I by-hete the a heste and heghely I a-vowe,
There schall no hode ne no hatt one my hede sitt
Till þat I ioyntly with a gesserante iustede hafe with onere,   180
And done dedis for thi loue, doghety in armes."

---

166. I *supplied*
168. kythe *in margin*
173. seyde *ms:* seyden
180. *second* with *supplied*

---

165. The only worldly possessions of value to Old Age are his crutch and his couch, in marked contrast to Youth and Middle Age.
166-7. Cf. *CT* I 715-6: "Now have I toold you shortly, in a clause, / Th'estaat, th'array, the nombre, and eek the cause. . . ."
168. "And now their conversation I shall relate, listen if you wish."
170. The hawk on Youth's fist anticipates his discourse on the joys of hawking (208-38).
171-2. These are perhaps the two most essential characteristics of the medieval personi-fication of Youth — his *ȝernyng to armes* and his love-longing.
172. "And he lamented upon his beloved and piteously sighed."
176. *playstere of paramours:* "healer of love-longing"
180. "until I have firmly jousted with honor in a coat of mail"
181. Youth's sentiments recall the desire of Chaucer's Squire to perform knightly feats in order "to stonden in his lady grace" (*CT* I 88).

        Bot then this gome alle in graye greued with this wordes

[Middle And sayde, "Felowe, be my faythe, þou fonnes full ȝerne,

Age]   For alle es fantome and foly that thou with faris.

        Where es þe londe and the lythe þat þou arte lorde ouer?   185

        For alle thy ryalle araye renttis hase þou none,

        Ne for thi pompe and thi pride penyes bot fewe;

        For alle thi golde and thi gude gloes one thi clothes,

        And þou hafe caughte thi kaple, þou cares for no fothire.

        Bye the stirkes with thi stede and stalles thayme make;   190

        Thi brydell of brent golde wolde bullokes the gete;

        The pryce of thi perrye wolde purches the londes;

        And wonne, wy, in thi witt, for wele neghe þou spilles."

        Than the gome alle in grene greued full sore,

[Youth] And sayd, "Sir, by my soule, thi conselle es feble.   195

        Bot thi golde and thi gude thou hase no god elles;

        For be þe lorde and the laye þat I leue inne,

        And by the Gode that me gaffe goste and soule,

        Me were leuere one this launde lengen a while,

        Stoken in my stele-wede one my stede bakke,   200

---

184. es *supplied*

---

182. The values reflected in Youth's conventional love-complaint provoke a response from Middle Age, initiating the relatively brief section of the poem in which a debate actually takes place.

183. *fonnes full ȝerne*: i.e., "are quick to play the fool"

184. Cf. the Middle English lyric beginning, "Al es bot fantum þat we with ffare" (*Index* 189).

185–93. Compare Middle Age's attack on the irresponsibility of Youth with Winner's attack on the activities of Waster (*WW* 228–45).

189. *kaple*: "a caple," a nag or packhorse; Middle Age is speaking disparagingly of Youth's fine horse; cf. *WW* 240.

190. *Bye the stirkes*: "Buy yourself heifers."

193. "and live, sir, by using your mind, for you are very near ruin"

196. *Bot*: "except for"; *no god elles*: i.e., "no other god"

199. Cf. *Siege of Jerusalem* 83

200. *stele-wede* ("steel-clothing," i.e., armor) and *here-wedys* ("war-dress") in 201 are metaphors reminiscent of Old English poetic diction; cf. *SGGK* 260, *Destr. of Troy* 9634, and *Wars of Alex.* 1010.

Harde haspede in my helme and in my here-wedys,
With a grym grownden glayfe graythely in myn honde,
And see a kene knyghte come cowpe with my-seluen,
Þat I myghte halde þat I hafe highte and heghely avowede,
And parfourme my profers and prouen my strengthes,   205
Than alle the golde and the gude that thoue gatt euer,
Than alle the londe and the lythe that thoue arte lorde ouer.
    And ryde to a reuere redily there-aftir,
With haukes full hawtayne that heghe willen flye;
And when þe fewlis bene founden, fawkoneres hyenn   210
To lache oute thaire lessches and lowsen thaym sone,
And keppyn of thaire caprons, and casten fro honde;
And than the hawteste in haste hyghes to the towre,
With theire bellys so brighte blethely thay ryngen,   214
And there they houen appon heghe as it were heuen angelles.
Then the fawkoners full fersely to floodes þay hyen,
To reuere with thaire roddes to rere vp the fewles,
Sowssches thaym full serely to seruen thaire hawkes.

---

204. halde *in margin*

---

202. *glayfe*: "glaive," a single-edged blade used for both cutting and thrusting, usually
    mounted on a long staff; here perhaps used simply to mean sword.
208–45. This hawking episode testifies to the poet's knowledge of the procedures and
    terms of this popular aristocratic sport as it was practiced during the later Middle
    Ages. Although hawking was a form of entertainment, it was governed by rules which
    were strictly adhered to. Medieval hawking developed a specialized vocabulary in
    which every process, every piece of equipment, and every part of a bird's anatomy
    was given a distinctive term.
210. A falconer was usually a high-ranking servant who oversaw the tending of the birds
    and their mews and who was also in charge of the hunt. Here *fawkoners* seems to refer
    to the several servants who handle the birds during the hunt.
212. *keppyn of thaire caprons*: "pull off their hoods"
213. "Then the proudest in haste hurries into flight."
214. Bells of differing tones were fastened to a bird's legs, and their sounds could be
    heard even when the hawk was too high up to be seen.
216. *floodes*: "waters"
217. *roddes*: "beating rods," used to frighten the water foul into flight
218. *sowssches*: "beats"? i.e., "swings the rods at them"; probably an onomatopoetic verb
    used to suggest the sound of the rods as they swing through the air

Than tercelettes full tayttely telys doun stryken,
Laners and lanerettis lightten to thes endes,   220
Metyn with the maulerdes and many doun striken;
Fawkouns þay founden freely to lighte,
With hoo and howghe to the heron þay hitten hym full ofte,
Buffetyn hym, betyn hym, and brynges hym to sege,
And saylen hym full serely, and sesyn hym there-aftire.   225
Then fawkoners full fersely founden þam aftire,
To helpen thaire hawkes thay hyen thaym full ȝerne,
For the bitt of his bill bitterly he strikes.
They knelyn doun one their knees and krepyn full lowe,
Wynnen to his wynges and wrythen thaym to-gedire,   230
Brosten the bones and brekyn thaym in sondire;
Puttis owte with a penn þe maryo one his gloue,
And quopes thaym to the querrye that quelled hym to þe
dethe.
He quyrres thaym and quotes thaym, quyppeys full lowde,
Cheres thaym full chefely ecchekkes to leue,   235
Than henttis thaym one honde and hodes thaym ther-aftire,

---

233. quopes *ms*: quotes
235. cheres thaym *ms*: cheresthe hym

---

219. *tercelettes*: a term sometimes used for male hawks generally, but which strictly speaking applies only to male peregrine falcons
220. The *laner* (female) and the *lanneret* (male) are a smaller species of hawk which was imported from Italy and Greece; *lightten to thes endes*: "light upon (i.e., swoop down upon) the ducks."
223–33. In this brief episode the heron is the hawks' quarry; *hoo* and *howghe*: the cries of the falconers as they direct the attack of the hawks upon the heron; when the heron has been brought to bay (*to sege*), it is capable of inflicting serious damage to the hawks (228), for which reason the falconers protect their birds by twisting the heron's wings together (230). The marrow from the heron's large wing bones is fed to the hawks on the thick glove worn on the falconer's left hand (232).
233. "and whoops (i.e., calls) them (the hawks) to the quarry which they had crushed to death"
234–5. "He quarries them (i.e., allows them to eat the quarry) and gluts them, (then) whips (i.e., signals) quite loudly, / urges them especially to ignore lesser quarry (e.g. crows or pies)."

Cowples vp thaire cowers thaire caprouns to holde,
Lowppes in thaire lesses thorowe vertwelles of siluere.
Þan he laches to his luyre and lokes to his horse,
And lepis vpe one the lefte syde als þe laghe askes.   240
Portours full pristly putten vpe the fowlis,
And taryen for theire tercelettis þat tenyn thaym full ofte,
For some chosen to þe echecheke, þoghe some chefe bettire.
Spanyells full spedily þay spryngen abowte,
Be-dagged for dowkynge when digges bene enewede.   245
    And than kayre to the courte that I come fro,
With ladys full louely to lappyn in myn armes,
And clyp thaym and kysse thaym and comforthe myn hert;
And than with damesels dere to daunsen in thaire chambirs,
Riche romance to rede and rekken the sothe   250
Of kempes and of conquerours, of kynges full noblee,
How thay wirchipe and welthe wanne in thaire lyues;
With renkes in ryotte to reuelle in haulle,
With coundythes and carolles and compaynyes sere,

---

252. thay *ms*: thaire

237–8. "draws tight the thongs to secure their hoods, / loops in their leases through rings
of silver"
239. *laches to his luyre*: "takes up his lure"; the lure was made of bright feathers inserted
into leather or cloth which surrounded a piece of raw meat attached to a block of wood.
243. "For some choose the lesser quarry but some choose the better."
245. *be-dagged*: in clothing which has been "dagged" the edges hang down in sharp points;
the wet, muddy coats of the dogs give this impression; *when digges bene enewede*: "when
ducks have been driven to hiding" (through fear of the hawks); *enewede* is an example
of the technical vocabulary of hawking with which the poet is familiar.
246. *kayre*: "return"
247–8. conventional romance phraseology; cf. *Morte Arthure* 3292
250–1. These romances of kings and conquerors which Youth either reads or listens to
anticipate the heroic stories which Old Age recounts in his attempt to demonstrate
the futility of human accomplishments..
254. *coundythes and carolles*: "conduts" were songs sung in parts, usually with three voices;
"carols" were sung as plainsong (a single melodic line sung in unison); "conduts" were
of liturgical origin (cf. *Owl and Nightingale* 483), but they became secularized (cf. *SGGK*
1655), and like carols they were commonly sung in conjunction with dancing.

And chese me to the chesse that chefe es of gamnes;   255
And this es life for to lede while I schalle lyfe here.
And thou with wandrynge and woo schalte wake for thi gudes,
And be thou doluen and dede thi dole schalle be schorte,
And he that thou leste luffes schalle layke hym there-with,
And spend that thou haste longe sparede, the deuylle spede
hym elles."   260
  Than this renke alle in rosett rothelede thies wordes:
[Middle He sayde, "Thryfte and thou haue threpid this thirtene wynter;
Age] I seghe wele samples bene sothe that sayde bene full ȝore:
Fole es that with fole delys; flyte we no lengare."
  Than this beryn alle in blake bownnes hym to speke   265
[Old And sayde, "Sirres, by my soule, sottes bene ȝe bothe.
Age] Bot will ȝe hendely me herken ane hande-while,
And I schalle stynte ȝour stryffe and stillen ȝour threpe.
I sett ensample bi my-selfe and sekis it no forthire:
While I was ȝonge in my ȝouthe and ȝape of my dedys,   270
I was als euerrous in armes as ouþer of ȝoure-seluen,
And as styffe in a stourre one my stede bake,
And as gaye in my gere als any gome elles,
And as lelly by-luffede with ladyse and maydens.
My likame was louely es lothe nowe to schewe,   275
And as myche wirchipe I wane, i-wis, as ȝe bothen.

---

262. ȝere *cancelled before* wynter

---

257. *wandrynge*: "wondering," i.e., worrying; *wake for*: "keep watch over"
258. "And when you are buried and dead, the grieving for you shall be brief."
259. *layke hym*: "amuse himself"
261. *rothelede*: "rattled off"?; or "spoke angrily"?
262. Perhaps "thirteen" has been chosen as much for alliteration as for sense.
263. *samples*: i.e., "proverbs"; cf. *WW* 321
264. proverbial (Oxford F 486); *delys*: "deals"; *flyte*: "argue"
269–89. In this brief "autobiography" Old Age, like the Wife of Bath, draws upon his
 own experience rather than upon learned authorities.
269. Cf. *Wars of Alex.* 3879
272. *styffe in a stourre*: "firm in a battle"
275. "My body (that) was lovely is now loathsome to look at."

And aftir irkede me with this, and ese was me leuere,
Als man in his medill elde his makande wolde haue.
Than I mukkede and marlede and made vp my howses,
And purcheste me ploughe-londes and pastures full noble,   280
Gatte gude and golde full gaynly to honde,
Reches and renttes were ryfe to my-seluen.
Bot elde vndire-ȝode me are I laste wiste,
And alle disfegurede my face and fadide my hewe,
Bothe my browes and my berde blawnchede full whitte —   285
And when he sotted my syghte, than sowed myn hert —
Croked me, cowrbed me, encrampeschet myn hondes,
Þat I ne may hefe þam to my hede ne noghte helpe my-seluen,
Ne stale stonden one my fete bot I my staffe haue.

    Makes ȝoure mirrours bi me, men, bi ȝoure trouthe;   290
This schadowe in my schewere schunte ȝe no while.
And now es dethe at my dore that I drede moste;
I ne wot wiche daye, ne when, ne whate tyme he commes,
Ne whedirwardes, ne whare, ne whatte to do aftire.
Bot many modyere than I, men one this molde,   295
Hafe passed the pase þat I schall passe sonne;
And I schall neuen ȝow the names of nyne of the beste

---

297. ix *cancelled before* nyne

---

277. *irkede me*: "I became displeased"; *me leuere*: "dearer to me"
279. *mukkede and marlede*: "manured and fertilized"
283. "But old age undermined me before I least expected it."
286. *sotted*: "dulled"; *sowed*: "stung" ? or "soured"?
288. *ne may hefe*: "cannot raise"
291. "This shadow in my mirror you cannot avoid for long"; the shadow is either the physical consequences of old age, or death itself.
292. Cf. 654 and *DL* 10
293–4. Such sentiments are often encountered in the Middle English lyrics concerning death; cf. "Whan I thenke thynges three" (*Index* 3969).
297. The "nine of the best" are the heroes known as the Nine Worthies: Hector, Alexander, and Caesar, the three Pagan Worthies of classical lore; Joshua, David, and Judas Maccabeus, the three Jewish Worthies of the Old Testament; and Arthur, Charlemagne, and Godfrey of Bouillon, the three Christian Worthies of "modern" history.

Þat euer wy in this werlde wiste appon erthe,
Þat were conquerours fulle kene and kiddeste of oþer.
   The firste was Sir Ector, and aldeste of tyme,   300
When Troygens of Troye were tried to fighte
With Menylawse þe mody kynge and men out of Grece,
Þat þaire cite assegede and sayled it full ȝerne,
For Elayne his ownn quene that there-inn was holden,
Þat Paresche the proude knyghte paramours louede.   305
Sir Ectore was euerous, als the storye telles,
And als clerkes in the cronycle cownten þe sothe:
Nowmbron thaym to x and ix mo by tale
Of kynges with crounes he killede with his handes,
And full fele oþer folke, als ferly were ellis.   310
Then Achilles his adversarye vndide with his werkes,
With wyles and no wirchipe woundede hym to dethe,
Als he tentid to a tulke þat he tuke of were.

---

308. x and ix *ms*: xix and ix

---

299. "who were conquerors full bold and the most famous of all"

300-31. Old Age briefly recounts the story of Troy's fall, paying tribute to Hector's prowess before describing his death through the wiles of Achilles. However, greater emphasis is placed here on the tragic consequences which occur after Hector's death than it is on Hector's own achievements; even more curious is the speaker's list of Trojan heroes who were felled by the Greeks, a list which includes Ulysses and Hercules, among other "Trojan" notables. (A much fuller account of the fall of Troy occurs in the Middle English *Destruction of Troy*, an adaptation of Guido de Columna's *Historia Trojana*.)

303. *sayled*: "assailed"

305. *paramours*: "passionately"; here, as in 612, this word is used adverbially.

308. *x and ix*: i.e., "nineteen"; the ms reads *xix and ix*; Offord, following the reading of the less authoritative Ware MS, emends to *nynety and ix*; but since only eighteen kings are listed in the *Destr. of Troy*, it seems likely that the first *xi* in *xix and ix* is an uncancelled scribal error.

310. "and a great many others, (who were) just as wonderful"; this line occurs again at 566.

311-3. Cf. *Destr. of Troy* 8643-60, where Hector's death is more fully described; there, as here, Achilles stabs Hector while he is attending to a prisoner he has captured.

313. "as he attended to a warrior he had taken in the battle"; *of were*: "of war," i.e., as a prisoner of war

And he was slayne for that slaughte, sleghely þeraftir,
With the wyles of a woman as he had wroghte by-fore.   315
Than Menylawse þe mody kynge hade myrthe at his hert
Þat Ectore hys enymy siche auntoure hade fallen;
And with the Gregeis of Grece he girde ouer the walles,
Þe prowde paleys dide he pulle doun to þe erthe,
Þat was rialeste of araye and rycheste vndir the heuen.   320
And þen the Trogens of Troye teneden full sore,
And semblen þaym full serely and sadly þay foughten;
Bot the lure at the laste lighte appon Troye:
For there Sir Priamus the prynce put was to dethe,
And Pantasilia þe quene paste hym by-fore,   325
Sir Troylus, a trewe knyghte þat tristyly hade foghten,
Neptolemus, a noble knyghte at nede þat wolde noghte fayle,
Palamedes, a prise knyghte and preued in armes,
Vlixes and Ercules þat full euerrous were bothe,
And oþer fele of þat ferde fared of the same,   330
As Dittes and Dares demeden to-gedir.

---

322. serely *ms*: sorely
331. demeden *ms*: demedon

314–5. Accounts of Achilles' death vary, but there is poetic justice here in having Achilles' own death be due to the treachery of another; *slaughte*: "slaughter."
317. *auntoure*: "adventure" (i.e., misadventure)
323. "But defeat at last fell upon Troy."
324. *Sir Priamus the prynce*: King Priam
325. *Pantasilia þe quene*: Penthesilea, a queen of the Amazons who fought on the side of Troy during the war, was also slain by Achilles.
326. The death of Troilus is described in the *Destr. of Troy* 10,290–311 and in Chaucer's *Troilus and Criseyde* V 1800–6.
327. *Neptolemus*: Neoptolemus (also called Pyrrhus), the son of Achilles, entered the Trojan War after his father's death and became the slayer of Priam; his inclusion here makes no sense for he wasn't killed during the war, and even if he had been, he wouldn't belong in a list of Trojan heroes.
328. Palamedes was a Greek who was stoned to death by other Greeks, an event engineered by Ulysses.
329. Perhaps the point that Old Age is making is that all of the ancient heroes, not just the Trojans, ultimately experienced the same fate.
331. *Dittes and Dares* were the authors of what were believed to be eyewitness accounts

Aftir this Sir Alysaunder alle þe worlde wanne,
Bothe the see and the sonde and the sadde erthe,
Þe iles of the Oryent to Ercules boundes,
Ther Ely and Ennoke euer hafe bene sythen, 335
And to the come of Antecriste vnclosede be þay neuer;
And conquered Calcas knyghtly ther-aftire,
Ther ientille Iaȝon þe iewe wane þe flese of golde.
Then grathede he hym to Gadres the gates full righte,
And there Sir Gadyfere þe gude the Gaderayns assemblet, 340
And rode oute full ryally to rescowe the praye;
And þan Emenyduse hym mete and made hym full tame,
And girdes Gadyfere to the grounde, gronande full sore;
And there that doughty was dede, and mekill dole makede. 344

---

339. grathede *ms*: grathode
340. Gadyfere *ms*: godfraye; Gaderayns *ms*: goderayns

---

of the Trojan War; the *Ephemeris Belli Trojani* of Dictys Cretensis reflects a pro-Greek bias while the *De Excidio Trojae Historia* of Dares Phrygius favors the Trojans; in fact, the probability is that the two works were written late in the Roman era. Benoit de Sainte-Maure's *Roman de Troie* (c. 1160) and Guido de Columna's *Historiana Trojana*, from which later medieval Troy literature dervives, supposedly drew upon the works of Dares and Dictys.

332–403. Romances celebrating Alexander the Great were very popular in the Middle Ages; what Old Age presents, however, is a garbled digest of miscellaneous adventures drawn from several of these romances; there is no single source for them, but some seemed to be derived from Jacques de Longuyon's *Voeux du Paon* (c. 1312), the work which contains the earliest known treatment of the Nine Worthies topos.

333. *sadde*: "solid"

334. *Ercules boundes*: "The Pillars of Hercules," standing at the western end of the world; i.e., the Straits of Gibraltar

335. *Ely and Ennoke*: Elias and Enoch who, according to legend, wait in the earthly paradise for the coming of the Antichrist, with whom they will do battle; but Old Age may be confusing them with the Gog and Magog of the Alexander stories.

337. *Calcas*: Colchis, the Asian country to which Jason and the Argonauts went in their search for the golden fleece

338. *Iaȝon þe iewe*: "Jason the Jew" is just one of the many curiosities that Old Age produces in his sermon; perhaps his mind has slipped ahead to "Joshua the Jew" (430, 436, 438).

339–44. These verses concern the "Foray of Gadifer," an episode in which the brave knight Gadifer is killed by Emenidus who then laments his death (344).

Then Alixander the Emperour, þat athell kyng hym-seluen,
Arayed hym for to ryde with the renkes þat he hade:
Ther was the mody Meneduse, a mane of Artage —
He was Duke of þat douthe and a dussypere —
Sir Filot and Sir Florydase, full ferse men of armes,
Sir Clyton and Sir Caulus, knyghtis full noble,   350
And Sir Garsyene the gaye, a gude man of armes,
And Sir Lyncamoure thaym ledys with a lighte wille.
        And than Sir Cassamus thaym kepide, and the kyng prayede
To fare in-to Fesome his frendis to helpe.
For one Carrus the kynge was comen owte of Inde,   355
And hade Foȝome affrayede and Foȝayne asegede
For Dame Foȝonase the faire that he of lufe by-soughte.
The kynge agreed hym to goo and graythed hym sone
In mendys of Amenyduse þat he hade mys-done.
Then ferde he to-warde Facron and by the flode abydes,   360
And there he tighte vp his tentis and taried there a while.
There knyghtis full kenely caughten theire leue
To fare in-to Foȝayne, Dame Foȝonase to see,
And Idores and Edease, alle by-dene;
And there Sir Porus and his prynces to the poo avowede —   365
Was neuer speche by-fore spoken sped bettir aftir,
For als þay demden to doo thay deden full euen.
For there Sir Porus the prynce in-to the prese thrynges,

---

347. "There was the proud Emenidus, a man of Arcadia."
348. *douthe*: "noble company"; *dussypere*: one of the twelve peers
353. *kepide*: "detained"
354. *Fesome*: Epheson
356. "and had frightened Fesonas (the daughter of Gadifer of Larris) and had besieged Epheson"; the similar proper names, one referring to a lady and one to a place, are confusing.
359. "in amends for what Emenidus had done" (the slaying of Gadifer the elder)
360. *Facron*: presumably a river
364. *Idores and Edease*: nieces of Fesonas held captive with her; *all by-dene*: "all (three of them) together"
365. *to the poo avowede*: "made vows to the peacock"; the story of the vows is related in the second part of Jacques' work: at a banquet Porrus and his companions vow to achieve certain things in the battle which is about to take place against Alexander's forces; in the subsequent fight each of them fulfills his vow.

And bare the batelle one bake and abaschede thaym swythe;
And than the bolde Bawderayne bowes to the kynge,   370
And brayde owte the brighte brande owt of the kynges hande,
And Florydase full freschely foundes hym aftir,
And hent the helme of his hede and the halse crakede.
Than Sir Gadefere the gude gripis the axe,
And in-to the Indyans ofte auntirs hym sone,   375
And thaire stiffe standerte to stikkes he hewes.
And than Sir Cassamus the kene, Carrus releues —
When he was fallen appon fote he fet hym his stede.
And aftyr that Sir Cassamus Sir Carus he drepitt,
And for þat poynte Sir Porus perset hym to dethe.   380
And than the Indyans ofte vttire þam droghen,
And fledden faste of the felde and Alexandere suede.
When þay were skaterede and skayled and skyftede in sondere,
Alyxandere, oure athell kyng, ames hym to lenge,
And fares in-to Foȝayne festes to make,   385
And weddis wy vn-to wy that wilnede to-gedire.
Sir Porus, the pryce knyghte, moste praysed of othere,
Fonge Foȝonase to fere and fayne were thay bothe;
The bolde Bawderayne of Bade-rose, Sir Cassayle hym-seluen,
Bele Edyas the faire birde, bade he no noþer;   390
And Sir Betys the beryne, the beste of his tyme,
Idores his awnn lufe aughte he hym-seluen;
Then iche lede hade the loue that he hade longe ȝernede.

---

369. "and forced the battle-line back and astonished them quickly"
370-3. Baudrain, who had vowed to disarm Alexander himself, manages to do so, only to be killed by Floridas.
374. *Sir Gadefer*: son of the Gadifer killed in 343–4
377-9. Cassamus fulfills his vow — to set Clarus back on his mount if he found him unhorsed — but having done so this once, when Cassamus encounters Clarus later in the battle he kills him.
380. *poynte*: "deed"; *perset*: "pierced"
381. *vttire þam droghen*: i.e., "drew themselves out (of the battle)"
384. *oure athell kyng*: "our noble king," an epithet which seems appropriate when used in reference to King Arthur in l. 484, but which seems mis-applied here to Alexander (perhaps it is a form of anachronism); *ames hym to lenge*: "aims (i.e., plans) to linger"
386. "and weds person unto person who wished to be together"
390. *bade he no noþer*: "he asked for no other"

Sir Alixander oure Emperour ames hym to ryde,
And bewes to-wardes Babyloyne with the beryns þat were
leuede,   395
By-cause of Dame Candace that comforthed hym moste;
And that cite he by-segede and assayllede it aftire,
While hym the ȝatis were ȝete and ȝolden the keyes;
And there that pereles prynce was puysonede to dede —
Þare he was dede of a drynke as dole es to here,   400
That the curssede Cassander in a cowpe hym broghte.
He conquered with conqueste kyngdomes twelue,
And dalte thaym to his dussypers when he the dethe tholede;
And thus the worthieste of this werlde went he to his ende.

Thane Sir Seȝere hym-seluen, thatt Iulyus was hatten,   405
Alle Inglande he aughte at his awnn will,
When the Bruyte in his booke Bretayne it callede.
The trewe toure of Londone in his tyme he makede,
And craftely the condithe he compaste there-aftire,   409
And then he droghe hym to Dovire and duellyde there a while,

---

396. Candace *ms*: Candore
401. cr *cancelled before* curssede

---

396. Alexander's love affair with Candace is treated in *Kyng Alexander* (6648 ff.) and in
the *Wars of Alex.* (5075 ff.); cf. 627.
399–401. Alexander's death by treachery (from drinking a poisoned cup of wine) is
described in *Kyng Alex.* (7810 ff.) and in the *Prose Life of Alexander* (EETS 143, pp. 110–3).
405–20. This account of Caesar, the third of the Pagan Worthies, is quite brief; perhaps
the poet had little information to draw on, since Caesar is not celebrated in medieval
romance in the way that Hector and Alexander are; the few scraps which are put
together here may stem from local folklore rather than from literary sources.
407. The name "Brut" occurs in various titles (e.g. Wace's *Roman de Brut* and Layamon's
Brut) but Brut is not an author, as indicated here, but the mythical founder of Bri-
tain (i.e., Brutus), whose exploits are chronicled at length by Geoffrey of Monmouth.
408. Caesar's association with the building of the Tower of London is sometimes en-
countered, as here, and it is likely that the medieval Tower was actually constructed
on the site of earlier Roman fortifications.
409. *the condithe he compaste*: "the aquaduct he constructed"
410–3. Dover Castle, like the Tower of London, belongs to the medieval era; but Caesar
undoubtedly did "dwell there a while" at Dover, and it is also likely that he provi-
sioned an encampment there.

And closede ther a castelle with cornelles full heghe,
Warnestorede it full wiesly, als witnesses the sothe,
For there es hony in that holde holden sythen his tyme.
Than rode he into Romayne and rawnsede it sone,
And Cassabalount þe kynge conquered there-aftire;   415
Then graythed he hym in-to Grece and gete it be-lyue.
The semely cite Alexaunder seside he ther-aftire,
Affrike and Arraby and Egipt the noble,
Surry and Sessoyne sessede he to-gedir,
With alle the iles of the see appon iche a syde.   420
Thies thre were paynymes full priste and passed alle othire.
      Of thre Iewes full gentill iugge we aftir,
In the Olde Testament as the storye tellis,
In a booke of the Bible that breues of kynges,
And renkes þat rede kane Regum it callen.   425
      The firste was gentill Iosue þat was a Iewe noble,
Was heryet for his holynes in-to heuen-riche.
When Pharaoo had flayede the folkes of Israelle,
Thay ranne into the Rede See for radde of hym-seluen;

---

416. it *ms*: hym

---

414. *Romayne*: "Roman territory," here probably referring to the area in Britain which
was soon to come under Roman control.
415. *Cassabalount*: Cassivellaunus, the British tribal chieftain who ruled the Catuvellau-
ni, in the region of present-day Berkshire, Buckinghamshire, and Hertfordshire; he
opposed Caesar's invasion in 54 B.C. but was defeated; he is treated as a hero by
Geoffrey of Monmouth.
417. *Alexaunder*: Alexandria
419. *Surry and Sessoyne*: Syria and Saxony
424-5. The stories concerning David are contained in the books of *Primum Regum* and
Secundum Regum in the Latin Vulgate (which in the protestant Bible are 1 and 2 Samuel),
but the stories concerning Joshua occur in the books of Exodus and Joshua, and
those concerning Judas Maccabeus in 1 and 2 Maccabees.
428-37. Old Age attributes the parting of the Red Sea (Exodus 14:21-9) to Joshua rather
than to Moses; perhaps he is confusing this event with Joshua's later parting of the
Jordan River (Joshua 3); in any case, this remarkable error may support the sugges-
tion that the poet intends to portray Old Age as partially senile.
428. *had flayede*: "had put to flight"
429. *for radde of hym-seluen*: "for fear of him"

And than Iosue the Iewe Ihesu he prayed,   430
That the peple myghte passe vnpereschede that tyme;
And than the see sett vp appon sydes twayne,
In a manere of a mode walle that made were with hondes,
And thay soughten ouer the see, sownnde alle to-gedir;
And Pharaoo full fersely folowede thaym aftire;   435
And efte Iosue þe Iewe Ihesus he prayede,
And the see sattillede agayne and sanke thaym there-inn—
A soppe for the Sathanas, vnsele haue theire bones!
And aftire Iosue þe Iewe full gentilly hym bere,
And conquerede kynges and kyngdomes twelue,   440
And was a conqueroure full kene and moste kyd in his tyme.
     Than Dauid the doughty, thurghe Drightynes sonde,
Was caughte from kepyng of schepe & a kyng made.
The grete grym Golyas he to grounde broghte,
And sloughe hym with his slynge & with no sleghte elles.   445
The stone thurghe his stele helme stong into his brayne,
And he was dede of that dynt—the deuyll hafe that wreche!
And than was Dauid full dere to Drightyn Hymseluen,
And was a prophete of pryse and praysed full ofte.
Bot ȝit greued he his God gretely ther-aftire,   450

---

442. Drightynes *ms*: drightyn
446. stong *ms*: stongen
447. wreche *ms*: reche

---

430. Joshua's prayer to Jesus is a typical example of anachronism.
433. *mode*: "mud"
434. *sownnde*: "sound," i.e., safe
438. *the Sathanas*: Satan
440-1. Old Age here claims that Joshua conquered twelve kingdoms, the same number
    conquered by Alexander; he omits any mention of Joshua's death.
442. *Drightynes sonde*: "the Lord's command"
444. *Golyas*: Goliath
445. *no sleghte elles*: "no other skill"
447. *hafe that wreche*: "have the wretch"; cf. 438

For Vrye his awnn knyghte in aventure he wysede,
There he was dede at that dede, as dole es to here;
For Bersabee his awnn birde was alle þat bale rerede.
   The gentill Iudas Machabee was a Iewe kene,
And there-to worthy in were and wyse of his dedis;   455
Antiochus and Appolyne, aythere he drepide,
And Nychanore, anoþer kynge, full naytly there-aftire;
And was a conquerour kydde and knawen with the beste.
Thies thre were Iewes full ioly and iusters full noble,   459
That full loughe haue bene layde sythen gane full longe tyme:
Of siche doughety doers looke what es worthen.
   Of the thre Cristen to carpe couthely there-aftir,
Þat were conquerours full kene and kyngdomes wonnen,
Areste was Sir Arthure and eldeste of tyme,
For alle Inglande he aughte at his awnn will,   465
And was kynge of this kythe and the crowne hade.
His courte was at Carlele comonly holden,
With renkes full ryalle of his rownnde table,
Þat Merlyn with his maystries made in his tyme,
And sett the sege perilous so semely one highte,   470
There no segge scholde sitt bot hym scholde schame tyde,
Owthir dethe with-inn the thirde daye demed to hym-seluen,
Bot Sir Galade the gude that the gree wanne.

---

451. "For he sent Uriah, his own knight, into misfortune (i.e., unto his death)"; 2 Samuel 11: 14–5
452. *There*: "where"; *dede at that dede*: "killed during that event"
453. "For Bathsheba his own lady was all that evil brought about."
454–8. Judas Maccabeus receives a mere five verses, probably reflecting a lack of familiarity (or a lack of interest) with him and his exploits, which are recorded in 1 and 2 Maccabees.
456. Judas Maccabeus did defeat the armies of Antiochus, but Antiochus himself died from a hideous disease (cf. Chaucer's *Monk's Tale, CT* VII 2575–630).
460. "that full low have been laid since a very long time has passed"
461. *es worthen*: "has become"
462. *carpe couthely*: "speak knowingly"
467. *Carlele*: Carlisle
469. *maystries*: "masteries (magical powers)"; cf. *SGGK* 2448
471. "where no knight should sit unless disgrace should befall him"

There was Sir Launcelot de Lake full lusty in armes,
And Sir Gawayne the gude that neuer gome harmede,   475
Sir Askanore, Sir Ewayne, Sir Errake fyt3 Lake,
And Sir Kay the kene and kyd of his dedis,
Sir Perceualle de Galeys þat preued had bene ofte,
Mordrede and Bedwere, men of mekyll myghte,
And othere fele of that ferde, folke of the beste.   480
Then Roystone þe riche kyng, full rakill of his werkes,
He made a blyot to his bride of the berdes of kynges,
And aughtilde Sir Arthures berde one scholde be;
Bot Arthure oure athell kynge anoþer he thynkes,
And faughte with hym in the felde till he was fey worthen. 485
And þan Sir Arthure oure kyng ames hym to ryde;
Vppon Sayn Michaelles Mounte meruaylles he wroghte,

---

481. Roystone *ms*: Boystone
482. a blyot *ms*: ablyot

---

473. *gree wann*: "the highest award won," though here perhaps implying "achieved the Grail"
474–80. The Knights of the Round Table listed here are all well-known figures, with the exception of Sir Askanore, who is more obscure; he is mentioned a few times in passing in Malory and once in the alliterative *Morte Arthure* (1739), and he may correspond to the knight Sir Escanor who appears in a few French romances; his inclusion here may be just for the sake of the alliteration, but he seems very out of place in a list of Arthur's ten most illustrious knights.
475. *Gawayne the gude*: this is a common epithet for Sir Gawain in alliterative poetry, and it reflects the highly favorable view of Gawain that is encountered in most Arthurian works in Middle English, in contrast to the less favorable view of Gawain that is sometimes encountered in French romances and to an extent in Malory.
476. *Errake*: Erec
479. *Bedwere*: Bedivere
481–9. These accounts of Arthur's fights with a giant and a dragon seem somewhat muddled. *Roystone* probably corresponds to Geoffrey's *Retho* and Malory's *Royns*, giants who wished to add Arthur's beard to their collections of royal beards; but Arthur did not fight a dragon on St.Michael's Mount (although there is a legend that he fought one at Greve de St-Michel in Brittany, near Morlaix); and it is also odd that Arthur sails over the sea *after* the St. Michael's Mount episode, not before it.
482. "He made a bleaunt (gown) for his bride out of the beards of kings"; in all other versions the beards are intended for the giant's own mantle.
485. *was fey worthen*: "had become fated (to die)"; cf. 496
487–8. Arthur's adversary on St. Michael's Mount should be a giant, not a dragon.

There a dragone he drepe þat drede was full sore.
And than he sayled ouer the see in-to sere londes,
Whils alle the beryns of Bretayne bewede hym to fote.   490
Gascoyne and Gyane gatt he there-aftir,
And conquered kyngdomes and contrees full fele.
Than ames he in-to Inglonde in-to his awnn kythe;
The gates to-wardes Glassthenbery full graythely he rydes;
And ther Sir Mordrede hym mett by a more syde,   495
And faughte with hym in the felde to alle were fey worthen,
Bot Arthur oure athell kyng and Wawayne his knyghte.
And when the felde was flowen & fey bot thaym-seluen,
Than Arthure Sir Wawayne athes by his trouthe
That he swiftely his swerde scholde swynge in the mere,   500
And whatt selcouthes he see the sothe scholde he telle.
And Sir Wawayne swith to the swerde and swange it in the
mere,
And ane hande by the hiltys hastely it grippes,
And brawndeschet that brighte swerde and bere it a-waye;
And Wawayne wondres of this werke, and wendes by-lyue   505
To his lorde there he hym lefte, and lokes abowte,
And he ne wiste in alle this werlde where he was by-comen.
And then he hyghes hym in haste and hedis to the mere,
And seghe a bote from the banke and beryns there-inn.

---

490. "while all the nobles of Brittany bowed at his feet"
491. *Gascoyne and Gyane*: Gascony and Guienne
494. "The ways toward Glastonbury at once he rides"; Glastonbury, according to tradi-
tion, is Arthur's place of burial, and it is also believed to be "Avalon."
496. Cf. 485
497. *Wawayne*: i.e., Gawain
498–512. In this account of the "Passing of Arthur," Gawain plays the part usually as-
signed to Bedivere (although in all standard versions of the legend Gawain's death
precedes Arthur's).
499. *athes*: "(makes) promise"
500. *his swerde*: i.e., Excalibur
501. Cf. *Piers* B.12.133
502. *swith*: "(went) quickly"; in most accounts the knight's reluctance to part with the
sword leads him to disobey the king until the king's third request, when he finally
complies.
507. Cf. *William of Palerne* 222 and *WW* 47.

There-inn was Sir Arthure and othire of his ferys,   510
And also Morgn la Faye that myche couthe of sleghte;
And there ayther segge seghe othir laste, for sawe he hym no
more.
 Sir Godfraye de Bolenn siche grace of God hade
Þat alle Romanye he rode and rawnnsunte it sone.
Þe Amorelle of Antyoche aftire he drepit,   515
Þat was callede Corboraunt, kiluarde of dedis;
And aftir he was callede kynge and the crownn hade
Of Ierasalem and of the Iewes gentill to-gedir;
And with the wirchipe of this werlde he went to his ende.   519
 Than was Sir Cherlemayne chosen chefe kynge of Fraunce,
With his doghty doussypers to do als hym lykede:
Sir Rowlande the riche, and Duke Raynere of Iene,
Olyuer, and Aubrye, and Ogere Deauneys,
And Sir Naymes at the nede that neuer wolde fayle,
Turpyn, and Terry, two full tryed lordes,   525

---

511. la Faye *ms*: lafaye

---

510. *ferys*: "companions"; normally Arthur is borne away by four queens, one of whom
 is Morgan le Fay (511).
512. "And there each man saw the other for the last time . . ."
513–9. Godfrey of Bouillon, like Caesar and Judas Maccabeus, receives only cursory
 treatment; also, Old Age deviates from the proper chronology by presenting God-
 frey before Charlemagne.
514. *rawnnsunte it sone*: "put it to ransom at once"
515. *Amorelle*: i.e Emir
516. *kiluarde*: "infamous"
520–79. Old Age's extended treatment of Charlemagne reveals his familiarity with a
 large number of miscellaneous episodes directly or indirectly involving Charlemagne.
 This account, like those of Alexander and Arthur, seems to be a pastiche created
 from the speaker's recollections of various literary materials.
521. *doussypers*: "the twelve peers," but the term is often applied rather loosely to groups
 of noble knights; cf. 403 and *Awntyrs of Arthure* 4.
522–30. Lists of the twelve peers vary from work to work; only three of the twelve listed
 here are among the twelve named in *The Song of Roland* (Roland, Oliver, and Sam-
 son), but Turpin, Thierri, Naimes, and Ogier the Dane are often included among
 the twelve, as here.

And Sir Sampsoune hym-selfe of the Mounte Ryalle,
Sir Berarde de Moundres, a bolde beryn in armes,
And gud Sir Gy de Burgoyne, full gracyous of dedis,
The katur fitȝ Emownteȝ, were kydde knyghtes alle,
And oþer moo than I may myne or any man elles.   530
    And then Sir Cherlles þe chefe ches for to ryde,
And paste to-wardes Polborne to prouen his strengthe.
Salamadyne the Sowdane he sloghe with his handis,
And þat cite he by-segede and saylede it full ofte,
While hym his ȝernynge was ȝett and the ȝates opynede;   535
And Witthyne thaire waryed kynge wolde nott abyde,
Bot soghte in-to Sessoyne socoure hym to gete;
And Cherlemayne, oure chefe kynge, cheses in-to the burghe,
And Dame Nioles anone he name to hym-seluen,   539
And maried hir to Maundevyle þat scho hade myche louede;
And spedd hym in-to hethyn Spayne spedely there-aftire,
And fittilled hym by Flagott faire for to loge.

---

529. knyghtes *ms*: kings
534. cite *supplied*

---

529. *The katur fitȝ Emownteȝ*: "the four sons of Aymon'; if the four are considered collec-
    tively, they bring the total to twelve; their inclusion is unusual; *kynghtes*: this is the
    reading of the Ware MS, which makes better sense than the reading *kynges* in the
    Thorton MS.
530. "and others, more than I can bring to mind, . . ."; cf. 630.
532. *Polborne*: perhaps Paderborn in Saxony
533. *Salamadyne the Sowdane*: "Salamadine (a blending together of Soliman and Saladin?)
    the Sultan"; Charlemagne was never involved with either Soliman or Saladin — perhaps
    another instance of Old Age's memory playing tricks.
534. *saylede*: "assailed"
535. "until his desire was achieved and the gates (were) opened"
536. *Witthyne*: Witikind or Widukind, a Westphalian chieftain who led a revolt against
    Charlemagne
537. *Sessoyne*: Saxony
538. *cheses*: "goes"
539–40. This is the only known reference to the lovers Nioles and Maundevyle; they
    may be the writer's or speaker's invention.
541–57. These verses relate some of the dramatic events found in the most popular of
    all the Charlemagne romances, *Fierabras* or *Sir Ferumbras*.
542. *Flagott*: a river in Spain

There Olyuer the euerous aunterde hym-seluen,
And faughte with Sir Ferambrace & fonge hym one were;
And than they fologhed hym in a fonte and Florence hym
callede.   545
And than moued he hym to Mawltryple Sir Balame to seche,
And that Emperour at Egremorte aftir he takes,
And wolde hafe made Sir Balame a man of oure faythe,
And garte feche forthe a founte by-fore-with his eghne;   549
And he dispysede it and spitte and spournede it to the erthe,
And one swyftely with a swerde swapped of his hede;
And Dame Floripe þe faire was cristened there-aftire,
And kende thaym to the Corownne þat Criste had one hede,
And the nayles anone nayttly there-aftire,   554
When he with passyoun and pyne was naylede one the rode.
And than those relikes so riche redely he takes,
And at Sayne Denys he thaym dide, and duellyd there foreuer.
    And than bodworde vn-to Merchill full boldly he sendys,
And bade hym Cristyne by-come and one Criste leue,
Or he scholde bette doun his borowes and brenn hym
there-inn;   560
And garte Genyone goo that erande that greuede thaym alle.
Thane rode he to Rowncyuale, þat rewed hym aftire,

---

544. *fonge hym one were*: "captured him in battle"
545. "And then they baptized him in a font and (from then on) called him Florence"
    (the name which Ferumbras assumes as a Christian).
546. *Mawltryple*: a town with a bridge crossing the Flagot; *Sir Balame*: the Emir of
    Aigremorte (547) and the father of Sir Ferumbras
549. "and had a font brought forth in front of his eyes"
551. *one*: i.e., "a man" (the indefinite "someone")
552. *Dame Floripe*: Sir Ferumbras' sister
553. *kende thaym*: "revealed to them"
553-7. Charlemagne is credited in various works with having regained important relics
    of the Passion — here the crown of thorns and the nails driven into the cross; cf. *Morte
    Arthure* 3426-9 and the OF poem *La Pèlerinage de Charlemagne* 160-81.
557. "And he took them to St. Denis, where they remained forever."
558-70. These verses present a summary of major events in *The Song of Roland*.
558. *Merchille*: Marsile, the saracen king of Spain
561. *Genyone*: Ganelon, whose name is synonymous in medieval literature with treachery
562. "Then he (Charlemagne) rode to Roncesvalles, which he later regretted"; note the
    use of litotes.

There Sir Rowlande the ryche Duke refte was his lyfe,
And Olyuer, his awnn fere that ay had bene trewe,
And Sir Turpyn the trewe that full triste was at nede,   565
And full fele othir folke, als ferly were elles.
Then suede he the Saraȝenes seuen ȝere and more,
And the Sowdane at Saragose full sothely he fyndis;
And there he bett downn þe burghe and Sir Merchill he tuke,
And that daye he dide hym to the dethe als he had wele
seruede.   570
Bot by than his wyes were wery and woundede full many,
And he fared in-to Fraunce to fongen thaire riste,
And neghede to-warde Nerbone that noyede thaym full sore;
And þat cite he asseggede appone sere halfues,
While hym the ȝates were ȝette & ȝolden the keyes,   575
And Emorye made Emperour euen at that tyme,
To haue it and to holde it to hym and his ayers.
And then thay ferden in-to Fraunce to fongen thaire ese,
And at Sayn Denys he dyede at his dayes tyme.

     Now hafe I neuened ȝow the names of nyne of þe beste   580
Þat euer were in this werlde wiste appon erthe,

---

570. hym *supplied*
577. haue *ms*: kepe
580. nyne *ms*: ix nyne

---

566. Cf. 310
568. *full sothely*: "quite truly"; a filler phrase
573. *Nerbone*: Narbonne
574-7. Charlemagne's siege of Narbonne is described in the *Aymeri de Narbonne*, an OF cycle of *chansons de geste*.
574. *sere halfues*: "many sides"
575. "until the gates were given up (i.e., surrendered) and the keys (were) yielded to him"
576. *Emorye*: Aymeri of Narbonne
583-611. Following his lengthy disquisition on the Nine Worthies, Old Age goes on to a briefer discussion of the world's wisest men, selecting two wise men from the ancient world (Aristotle and Virgil), one from the Old Testament world (Solomon), and one from the Christian world (Merlin); his point once again is that human achievements, in this case the possession of great wisdom, are of little avail when Death arrives, as it inevitably does.

And the doghtyeste of dedis in thaire dayes tyme:
Bot doghetynes when dede comes ne dare noghte habyde.
Of wyghes þat were wyseste will ʒe now here,
And I schall schortly ʒow schewe and schutt me ful sone.   585
Arestotle he was arste in Alexander tyme,
And was a fyne philoʒophire and a fynour noble,
The great Alexander to graythe and gete golde when hym liste,
And multiplye metalles with mercurye watirs,
And with his ewe ardaunt and arsneke pouders,   590
With salpetir and sal-ieme and siche many othire,
And menge his metalles and make fyne siluere,
And was a blaunchere of the beste thurghe blaste of his fyre.
Then Virgill thurgh his vertus verrayle he maket,
Bodyes of brighte brasse full boldely to speke,   595
To telle whate be-tydde had and whate be-tyde scholde,
When Dioclesyane was dighte to be dere Emperour;
Of Rome and of Romanye the rygalte he hade.
Than Sir Salomon hym-selfe sett hym by hym one;
His Bookes in the Bible bothe bene to-gedirs: 600

---

593. blaunchere ms: plaunchere
594. verrayle ms: veruayle or vernayle

---

587. *philoʒophire*: used here in the sense of "alchemist," which is how Aristotle was per-
    ceived during the Middle Ages; he was the reputed author of the *Secreta Secretorum*,
    which was written at the request of Alexander; *a fynour noble*: "an excellent refiner of
    precious metals."
589–93. This passage incorporates a series of alchemical terms, similar to those encoun-
    tered in Chaucer's *Canon's Yeoman's Tale*.
590. *ewe ardaunt*: "ardent spirit" (alcohol)
591. *sal-ieme*: "gem salt," i.e., rock salt
593. *blaunchere*: one who "whitens" metals (in this case converts them to silver)
594–8. Virgil is often portrayed in medieval literature as engaging in the necromantic
    arts. In one of the legends associated with Virgil he creates a talking head of brass
    which speaks prophetically. (See for example the tale of "Vergilius" in the *Seven Sages
    of Rome*, EETS 191, ll. 1997–2008.)
597. *Dioclesyane*: the Roman Emperor Diocletian who ruled A.D. 284–313; he is a central
    figure in the *Seven Sages of Rome*.
599. "Then Sir Solomon set himself apart."
600–2. Solomon's two books are probably Ecclesiasticus and the Book of Wisdom of
    the Old Testament Apocrypha, not Ecclesiastes and the Book of Proverbs.

That one of wisdome and of witt wondirfully teches,
His sampills and his sawes bene sett in the toþer;
And he was the wyseste in witt that euer wonnede in erthe,
And his techynges will bene trowede whilles þe werlde standes,
Bothe with kynges and knyghtis and kaysers ther-inn.   605
     Merlyn was a meruayllous man and made many thynges,
And naymely nygromancye nayttede he ofte,
And graythed Galyan a boure to kepe hyr þer-in,
That no wy scholde hir wielde ne wynne from hym-seluen.   609
Theis were the wyseste in the worlde of witt þat euer ȝitt were,
Bot dethe wondes for no witt to wende were hym lykes.
     Now of the prowdeste in presse þat paramoures loueden
I schalle titly ȝow telle and tary ȝow no lengere.
Amadase and Edoyne, in erthe are they bothe,
That in golde and in grene was gaye in thaire tyme;   615

---

608. graythed *ms*: Graythen

---

607. "And especially necromancy he often practiced."
608. *Galyan*: apparently a reference to the lady more often known as Nynyve, Nimiane, or Viviane, with whom Merlin became infatuated; in the Middle English Prose *Merlin* and in Lovelich's verse *Merlin* Merlin creates an orchard of fruits and flowers for her; later she uses the knowledge she has acquired from Merlin to free herself from his unwanted attentions.
611. "But death doesn't hesitate because of any man's intelligence to go where he wishes"; cf. 632.
612-30. Old Age moves on to a third group of illustrious persons, the world's most famous lovers. Except for Samson and Delilah, these pairs of lovers are all found in medieval romances. There are rhetorical qualities to this brief section which set it apart from what has gone before and which may suggest that the speaker takes particular relish in the demises of these youthful lovers. The poem takes on a darker tone as the speaker approaches the end of his homily.
613. In addition to serving notice that his sermon is nearly finished, this verse conveys a sense of urgency; cf. 585.
614. *Amadase and Edoyne*: Amadas and Idoine — well-known lovers in French romance who are often included in lists of famous lovers; they are alluded to in Thomas of Hailes' *Love Rune* (67), where they are listed in company with Paris and Helen and Tristan and Isolde.
614. Phrases such as "in earth are they both" become a kind of litany in this section; cf. 617, 619, 621, etc.
615. The colors gold and green, so prominent earlier in the description of Youth, are here emblematic of health and youthful vigor.

And Sir Sampsone hym-selfe, full sauage of his dedys,
And Dalyda his derelynge, now dethe has þam bothe.
Sir Ypomadoun de Poele, full priste in his armes,
& þe faire Fere de Calabre, now faren are they bothe.
Generides þe gentill, full ioly in his tyme,   620
And Clarionas þat was so clere, are both nowe bot erthe.
Sir Eglamour of Artas, full euerous in armes,
And Cristabelle the clere maye es crept in hir graue;
And Sir Tristrem the trewe, full triste of hym-seluen,
And Ysoute his awnn lufe, in erthe are þay bothe.   625
Whare es now Dame Dido was qwene of Cartage,
Dame Candace the comly was called quene of Babyloyne,
Penelopie that was price and pasten alle othere,

---

617. & *deleted before* now; bothe *ms*: boghte
618. his *ms*: hir
619. & *supplied*
627. Candace *ms*: Candore

616-7. The story of Samson and Delilah occurs in Judges 13-6; cf. Chaucer's *Monk's Tale* VII 2015-94.
618-9. The adventures of Ipomadon of Apulia are recorded in a twelfth-century Anglo-Norman romance and in three Middle English works adapted from it; after great trials and tribulations, Ipomadon finally wins the love of his lady, who is known only as La Fiere, "the Proud One" of Calabria.
620-1. The story of this pair of less well-known lovers is told in the fifteenth-century Middle English romance *Generides* (EETS o.s. 55, p. 70); no earlier versions survive in English or French.
621. *þat were so clere*: "who was so beautiful"
622-3. The several mss and early printed texts of *Sir Eglamour* attest to the popularity of the story in England during the later Middle Ages; there are no French versions of this romance.
624-5. The tragic love of Tristan and Isolde, or Tristrem and Iseult, though often referred to in Middle English works, is celebrated only in the Middle English romance *Sir Tristrem* (Scottish Text Society 8) and in Malory's *Morte D'Arthur*.
626-8. These three women suffered as a result of their lovers' absences — one as a result of his desertion (Aeneas), one through his death (Alexander), and one because of war (Ulysses).
627. Cf. 394-401
628. Penelope, along with Alceste, was viewed in the Middle Ages as a perfect exemplar of wifely fidelity; cf. Chaucer's *TC* V 1778 and the *CT* V 1443-4.

And Dame Gaynore the gaye?—nowe grauen are thay bothen,
And othere moo than I may mene or any man elles.   630
   Sythen doughtynes when dede comes ne dare noghte
habyde,
Ne dethe wondes for no witt to wende where hym lykes,
And ther-to paramours and pride puttes he full lowe;
Ne there es reches ne rent may rawnsone ȝour lyues,
Ne noghte es sekire to ȝoure-selfe in certayne bot dethe,   635
And he es so vncertayne that sodaynly he comes,
Me thynke þe wele of this werlde worthes to noghte.
Ecclesiastes the clerke declares in his booke,
Vanitas vanitatum et omnia vanitas,
Þat alle es vayne and vanytes and vanyte es alle.   640
For-thi amendes ȝoure mysse whilles ȝe are men here,
Quia in inferno nulla est redempcio,
For in helle es no helpe, I hete ȝow for sothe.
Als God in his gospelle graythely ȝow teches,
Ite ostendite vos sacerdotibus,   645
To schryue ȝow full schirle and schewe ȝow to prestis.
Et ecce omni munda sunt vobis,
And ȝe þat wronge wroghte schall worthen full clene.

---

640. es *supplied*

---

629. *Gaynore*: Guinevere
630. Cf. 530
631-2. These verses reiterate 583 and 611, verses used to conclude separate sections within
    Old Age's homily.
634. "Nor are there riches or rents that can ransom your lives."
635. *noghte es sekire*: "nothing is assured"
636. *vncertayne*: i.e., "unpredictable"
637. "It seems to me that the wealth of this world turns to nothing."
639-40. Ecclesiastes 1:2 (and 12:8)
641. "Therefore make amends for your misdeeds . . ."
642-3. Job 7:9; in *Piers Plowman* (B.18.149) this verse is cited by Truth as she debates
    with her sister Mercy.
645-6. Luke 17:14: "Go show yourselves to the priests"
647. "And behold, all the world is yours" (a paraphrase of Luke 17:21).

Thou man in thi medill elde, hafe mynde whate I saye.
I am thi sire and thou my sone, the sothe for to telle,   650
And he the sone of thi-selfe þat sittis one the stede,
For Elde es sire of Midill Elde and Midill Elde of ʒouthe;
And haues gud daye, for now I go — to graue moste me wende.
Dethe dynges one my dore, I dare no lengare byde."
   When I had lenged and layne a full longe while,   655
I herde a bogle one a bonke be blowen full lowde,
And I wakkened ther-with and waytted me vmbe.
Than the sone was sett and syled full loughe;
And I founded appon fote and ferkede to-warde townn.
And in the monethe of May thies mirthes me tydde,   660
Als I schurtted me in a schelfe in þe schawes faire,
And belde me in the birches with bewes full smale,
And lugede me in the leues þat lighte were & grene.
There dere Drightyne this daye dele vs of Thi blysse,
And Marie þat es mylde qwene, amende vs of synn.
amen.amen.   665

Thus Endes the Thre Ages

---

654. Cf. 292–4 and *DL* 10

656. The bugle call which wakens the dreamer may be compared with the ringing of
   the bells which awakens Chaucer's dreamer in the *Book of the Duchess*; in both cases
   these realistic details also convey funereal overtones, and in the case of the bugle,
   the call to the Last Judgment (the "last trump") may also be suggested; Death's sum-
   moning trumpet occurs often in late medieval literature, in poems such as "Ffare
   well, this world" (*Index* 769), and in morality plays such as *Everyman* and *The Castle
   of Perseverance*.

657. *waytted me vmbe*: "looked around me"

658. *syled full loughe*: "sailed (sunk) quite low"

659. "And I leapt to my feet and hurried toward town"; this verse concludes the narra-
   tive action in the poem, leaving many questions unanswered: what causes the narra-
   tor to rush into town? where is he going and what does he intend to do there? has
   he simply abandoned the deer over which he had expended such efforts earlier? what
   effect has his visionary experience had upon him? This ambiguous conclusion is some-
   what like those found in Chaucer's *Book of the Duchess* and *Parliament of Fowls*.

660. This verse provides a return to the beginning of the poem.

661–3. This description of the deer hunter in hiding is more elaborate than the one in
   97–8; *schurtted*: perhaps "hid" or "camouflaged"; *belde me: i.e.,* "built myself a blind";
   bewes: "boughs"; *lugede*: "sheltered"

664–5. The benediction; *There*: "thus" or "and therefore"

Death and Life

The last of the three Middle English alliterative debates is *Death and Life*, a difficult but powerful and rewarding poem. The difficulties arise primarily from the corrupt state of the text, which is extant only in the Percy Folio, a manuscript compiled near the middle of the seventeenth century, more than two hundred years after *Death and Life's* likely date of composition. Chief among the poem's virtues are its vivid descriptions, particularly the portraits of the personified antagonists, Lady Life and Lady Death; the passages depicting the regenerative power and nurturing qualities of Life set against the malevolence and destructive power of Death; and the account of Death's "joust with Jesus" and the aftermath of that momentous event. The subject of the poem — the eternal struggle between the force which seeks to create and sustain life and the force which seeks to eradicate it — is one well-suited to poetry on the grand scale.

Death and Life begins with a brief introduction which is both an invocation to Christ and an expression of the speaker's anxiety concerning death. Following a conventional *chanson d'aventure* opening, the narrator is transported into a visionary world where he witnesses Lady Life, a splendidly beautiful woman, instilling renewed vitality in all living things; for a brief time her creatures experience the joys of life, but their pleasures are cut short by the unexpected arrival from the north of Lady Death, an ugly, vicious being who relishes her destructive enterprise. In the face of Death's onslaught, Lady Life prays for God's mercy; her prayer is heard, and God sends Sir Countenance to halt Death's ravages.

The second major section of the poem, the actual debate, then begins as Lady Life rebukes Lady Death for her senseless destruction. Death defends her actions as the natural consequence of the sin of Adam and Eve. Life insists that Death is an agent of Satan, but Death counters with the argument that she actually deters men from sinning. Sensing a victory in their battle of words, Death claims to be invincible, and she lists the names of notable heroes whom she has vanquished. She overreaches herself, however, when she includes Christ among the conquered. At the mention of Christ's name all creatures, including Death, fall to their knees (Philippians 2:10). Lady Life then recounts the true events of Christ's passion, in which Death was vanquished by Christ in their joust on the cross; she also relates Christ's subsequent harrowing of hell, when the Old Testament patriarchs and prophets were freed from Satan's bondage. Lady Life then turns to her creatures and comforts them with the knowledge that life is eternal as well as temporal; she raises from death those whom Death had ravaged earlier, and in a reversal of the *danse macabre* motif, she leads them into the eternal realm. The narrator awakens from his dream and offers a brief benediction.

Death and Life provides an important complement to *Winner and Waster* and the *Parliament of the Three Ages*, after which it is quite likely patterned. Its more specific inspiration, however, is probably to be found in the confrontation between Life and Death in *Piers Plowman* (C.20.28–70). *Death and Life* provides an elaborate gloss upon the passage, much in the way that biblical narratives such as *Cleanness* provide imaginative elaborations of scriptural texts. In addition to *Piers Plowman*, *Winner and Waster*, the *Parliament of the Three Ages*, the apocryphal *Gospel of Nicodemus*, and numerous passages of scripture, the poem also reflects the poet's familiarity with Alain de Lille's *De Planctu Naturae*. The *Death and Life* poet is directly indebted to Alain's portrait of the goddess Natura for many of the specific details in his own portrait of Lady Life. But as the poem makes clear, despite their similarities, Lady Life and the goddess Natura are not entirely identical. Lady Life is a dual figure, with both temporal and eternal dimensions, and she is subject to the laws of nature only in her temporal manifestation. The personified figure of Death (cf. Rev. 6:8) also reflects a duality; for while she serves as an agent of Satan, she also functions within God's scheme, and paradoxically (as she herself observes), she provides a dramatic warning to men to eschew sin. The fact that Death is portrayed as a woman is fairly unusual among medieval representations of death, where death is normally a skeletal or dessicated figure, either male or of indeterminate sex; nevertheless, she provides an effective parallel to the personified figure of Lady Life. It is also possible that the poet's conception of Lady Death reflects the influence of Virgil's depiction of Alecto (one of the three classical Furies) in Book IV of the *Aeneid*.

Death and Life is surely intended to be an inspirational poem, and in this regard it may be intended to provide a counter to the *vanitas vanitatum* message of the *Parliament of the Three Ages*. The description of Christ's dramatic triumph over Death, and Lady Life's resurrection of her creatures, provide concrete representations of the sentiments expressed in Hosea 13:14 —"O death, I will be thy plagues; O grave, I will be thy destruction"— and in I Corinthians 15:55 —"O death, where is thy sting? O grave, where is thy victory?"

---

1)   Base Text: BL MS Addit. 27879 (the Percy Folio), pp. 384–90

2)   Other mss: none

3)   Printed Texts: J. H. Hanford and J. M. Steadman, *SP* 15 (1918), 221–94
          I. Gollancz and M. Day, *Select Early English Poems*, 3 (1930)
          Joseph M. P. Donatelli, Speculum Anniversary Monographs 15 (1989)

4)   *Index of Middle English Verse* 603

Death & Liffe

2 fitts

Christ, Christen King, that on the crosse tholed,
Hadd paines & passyons to deffend our soules,

1–87. These verses are recorded in the ms as 174 short lines; after l. 87 they are written as alliterative long lines.

1–21. The design and intent of these opening verses seems somewhat confused; ll. 1–4 clearly begin the narrator's invocation to Christ, which is concluded in ll. 20–21; but ll. 7–18 seem to belong more appropriately to a homily than to a prayer, especially 13–16 which are clearly admonitory; perhaps there are some omissions in the text — possibly between lines 4–5 or 5–6 — and perhaps some of the verses in this opening

Giue vs grace on the ground the greatlye to serve
For that royall red blood that rann ffrom thy side;
& take away of thy winne word as the world asketh,   5
That is richer of renowne, rents or others.
For boldnesse of body, nor blytheness of hart,
Coninge of clearkes, ne cost vpon earth,
But all wasteth away & worthes to nought,
When Death driueth att the doore with his darts keene.   10
Then noe truse can be taken, noe treasure on earth;
But all lordshipps be lost & the liffe both.
If thou haue pleased the Prince that paradice weldeth,
There is noe bearne borne that may thy blisse recon.
But if thou haue wrongffully wrought & will not amend,   15
Thou shalt byterlye bye or else the booke ffayleth.
Therfore begin in God to greaten our workes,
& in His ffaythfull Sonne that ffreelye Him ffolloweth,
In hope of the Holy Ghost that yeeld shall neuer.

---

passage have been mis-arranged. In any case, this "prologue" passage provides an introduction to the human problem which the poem addresses, man's fear of death, a fear which the narrator shares.

1. With the opening verse of *DL* cf. verses 1–11 of the alliterative *Morte Arthure* and the first verse of the alliterative poem *The Crowned King* (*Index* 605).

3. *on the ground*: "in the world"; cf. *WW* 173

4. Cf. *Morte Arthure* 3990

5–6. These verses are confusing, perhaps because of scribal error; one would expect to find here a phrase such as "that taketh away the sins of the world"; verses 5–6 seem out of place in an invocation, and they do not provide a smooth transition into verses 7–12.

6. Cf. *P3A* 634

8. "cunning (i.e., knowledge) of clerks, nor wealth upon earth"

9. *worthes to nought*: "becomes as nothing," i.e., is destroyed; cf. *P3A* 637

10. Cf. *P3A* 292 and 654

11. *truse*: probably "truce," but possibly "package" (from OF *trusse*)

12. "But all earthly titles (must) be relinquished and life also."

13. Cf. *WW* 296 and *Scotish Feilde* 203

14. *bearne*: "man" or "person"; *recon*: "reckon," i.e., comprehend

16. *bye*: "buy," i.e., pay; cf. *Piers* A.3.236

17–9. These verses suggest that Christian salvation may be achieved through believing in the three parts of the Holy Trinity, which are themselves associated with the Christian virtues of charity, faith, and hope. The phrase *greaten our workes* ("increase" or "strengthen" our works) implies acts or deeds of a charitable nature.

God that is gracyous & gouerneth vs all,   20
Bringe vs into blisse, that brought vs out of ball.

[I]

Thus ffared I through a ffryth where fflowers were manye,
Bright bowes in the banke breathed ffull sweete,
The red rayling roses, the richest of fflowers,
Layd broad on their bankes with their bright leaues,   25
& a riuer that was rich runn ouer the greene
With still sturring streames that streamed ffull bright.
Over the glittering ground as I there glode,
Methought itt lenghtened my liffe to looke on the bankes.
Then among the fayre flowers I fettled me to sitt,   30
Vnder a huge hawthorne that hore was of blossomes;

---

20. gouerneth *ms*: gouerne
22. where *ms*: were
25. layd *ms*: land
30. fettled *ms*: settled

---

21. " . . . who brought us out of sorrow"
22–38. This conventional *chanson d'aventure* opening sets the stage for the narrator's dream vision; his weariness from wandering, the fragrance of the flowers, the singing of the birds, and the murmuring of the stream combine to induce his slumbers.
22. The word *Thus* has no clear point of reference; since the narrator's anxiety concerning death serves to precipitate his dream, perhaps the implication is, "with these (morbid) thoughts weighing heavily upon me, *thus* I wandered through a forest . . . ."
23. *bowes*: "boughs"
24. Cf. *P3A* 119
25. The ms reads *land*, not *layd*, but *layd* seems the more likely reading (cf. l. 63).
27. "with gently murmuring streams that brightly flowed"
28. *glode*: "glided," i.e., moved
29. *lenghtened*: perhaps should be emended to "lightened" (i.e., "raised my spirits"; cf. *WW* 406), but in view of the poet's concern with the briefness of man's life, *lenghtened* may be correct.
30. *fettled*: "prepared"; the ms reads *settled*, but cf. *P3A* 20; the AAAx pattern of alliteration, though not followed universally in *DL*, is clearly the rule; AAbb alliteration is unusual.
31. The dreamer in *Winner and Waster* also falls asleep beneath a hawthorn (WW 36).

I bent my backe to the bole & blenched to the streames.
Thus prest I on apace vnder the greene hawthorne.
Ffor breme of the birds & breath of the fflowers,
& what for waching & wakinge & wandering about,   35
In my seate where I sate I sayed a-sleepe;
Lying edgelong on the ground, list all my seluen,
Deepe dreames and dright droue mee to hart.
     Methought walking that I was in a wood stronge,
Vpon a great mountaine where mores were large,   40
That I might see on euerye side 17 miles,
Both of woods & wasts & walled townes,
Comelye castles & cleare with caruen towers,
Parkes & pallaces & pastures ffull many,
All the world full of welth winlye to behold.   45
I sett me downe softlye and sayd these words:
"I will not kere out of kythe before I know more."
& I wayted me about, wonders to know,
& a ffayrlye beffell soe fayre me bethought:

---

45. winlye *ms*: vunlye
49. a *ms*: I

---

32. Cf. *Piers* B.1.9; *blenched to*: "turned towards"
33. This verse makes little sense in this context and is surely mis-placed or mis-written. If the second half of the line is correct, the stressed words of the first half-line should probably alliterate on "g," though not necessarily. No satisfactory emendations have been proposed.
35–8. Cf. *Piers* C.1.6–8
36. *sayed*: "slumbered"; cf. 454
37. *list all my seluen*: " . . . left all (by) myself," or "(I) lost myself entirely (to my dream)" (?)
38. *dright*: "noble"(?); *droue mee to hart*: i.e., "drove (deeply) in my heart"; cf. *P3A* 103: "And whate I seghe in my saule the sothe I schalle telle."
39. "I thought that I was walking in an immense forest"; cf. *WW* 47
41. *17* was probably chosen to supply the "s" alliteration, in addition to indicating "a very great distance."
45. *winlye*: "lovely" or "blissful"; the ms reads *vunlye*, but cf. verses 75, 80, and 428.
48. *wayted*: "looked"; cf. *P3A* 46 and 657 and *WW* 213
49. This verse is probably corrupt; cf. *Piers* B.prol.6: "Me byfel a ferly of fairy me thouȝte."

I saw on the south syde a seemely sight,   50
Of comelye knights full keene & knights ffull noble,
Princes in the presse proudlye attyred,
Dukes that were doughtye & many deere erles,
Sweeres & swaynes that swarmed ffull thicke.
There was neither hill nor holte nor haunt there beside   55
Butt itt was planted ffull of people, the plaine and the roughte.
    There ouer that oste estward I looked
Into a boolish banke, the brightest of other,
That shimered and shone as the sheere heauen
Throughe the light of a Ladye that longed therin.   60
Shee came cheereing ffull comlye with companye noble,
Vpon cleare clothes, were all of cleare gold,
Layd brode vpon the bent with brawders ffull riche,
Before that ffayre on the ffeeld where shee fforth passed.
Shee was brighter of her blee then was the bright sonn,   65

---

50. The "south" suggests sunlight, warmth, and fertility, in contrast to the cold sterility
of the "north" (in l. 142).

51-6. These verses present the full spectrum of human society, from the higher nobility
on down, but in contrast to Langland's "fair field full of folk," all of the people found
here are very attractive.

51. The first use of *knights* is possibly an error for *kings*; cf. 76-9.

52. *in the presse*: "among the throng"

53. Cf. *Destr. of Troy* 84

56. Cf. *Piers* C.1.20; the second half of l. 56 refers to the geography (i.e., "the flat lands
and the hillsides"), not to the people; in l. 79 the people are divided into the poor
and the rich.

57. The east suggests dawn and the coming of day, freshness, renewal, regeneration;
in *Piers* (C.1.14) Truth's tower is located in the east.

58. *a boolish bank*: "a rounded hillock"(?)

60-8. The personified figure of Lady Life belongs to the medieval dream-vision tradi-
tion of personified ladies; she has much in common with such figures as Lady
Philosophy in Boethius' *Consolation of Philosophy*, Reason in the *Roman de la Rose*, Holy
Church in *Piers*, and especially Natura in Alain de Lille's *The Complaint of Nature* (*De
Planctu Naturae*).

60. *longed therin*: "belonged (i.e., lived) there"

61. *cheering*: probably "moving" (from the verb *keren*) though possibly "comforting"

62-4. Lady Life moves over the golden "cloths" which have been laid on the fields for
her like a carpet, a striking metaphorical description of the rays of the morning sun.

63. *bent*: "field"; *brawders*: "borders," or "embroideries" (?)

64. *that ffayre*: "that beautiful (one)"

65. *blee*: "complexion"

Her rudd redder then the rose that on the rise hangeth,
Meekely smiling with her mouth & merry in her lookes,
Euer laughing for loue as she like wold;
& as shee came by the bankes, the boughes eche one
They lowted to that Ladye & layd forth their branches.   70
Blossomes & burgens breathed ffull sweete,
Fflowers fflourished in the frith where she fforth stepedd,
& the grasse that was gray greened beliue.
Breme birds on the boughes busilye did singe,
& all the wild in the wood winlye the ioyed.   75
Kings kneeled on their knees knowing that Ladye,
& all the princes in the presse & the proud dukes,
Barrons & bachelours, all they bowed ffull lowe;
All profrereth her to please, the pore and the riche.
Shee welcometh them ffull winlye with wordes ffull hend,   80
Both barnes & birds, beastes & fowles.
    Then that lowly Ladye, on land where schee standeth,
That was comelye cladd in kirtle & mantle
Of goodlyest greene that euer groome ware,
For the kind of that cloth can noe clarke tell;   85
& shee the most gracyous groome that on the ground longed;

---

66. *rudd*: "face"
68. *like wold*: "would like"
69–81. These verses describe the renewal of the natural world and the homage paid to Lady Life by all living creatures; the description moves progressively up the scale of life, from plants to birds to animals to human beings, much as Chaucer does in the opening verses of the *Canterbury Tales*.
70. *lowted*: "bowed"
71. Cf. *P3A* 11 and *Destr. of Troy* 2736
74. *Breme*: "lively"
75. "And all the wild (creatures) in the wood happily rejoiced."
78. *bachelours*: "young knights"; *all*: "all (of them together)"
81. Perhaps *fowles* should be *ffishes* (cf. 111–2).
82. *lowly*: probably "lovely" rather than "humble"
83. Cf. 445 and *WW* 90; *kirtle*: "gown"
84. Here Lady Life's green clothing indicates her association with the rebirth of nature and with the freshness and vitality of youth. (The personification of Youth in *P3A* is clad in green, as is Chaucer's Yeoman, who is a forester.)
85. "For no clerk can explain the nature of that cloth."
86. *groome*: here (and in l. 84 also, probably) *groome* is used in the general sense of "person" rather than in the more specific sense of "servant"; *that on the ground longed*: "that lived on earth"

Of her druryes to deeme to dull be my witts,
& the price of her perrie can no person tell,
& the colour of her kirtle was caruen ffull lowe,
That her blisfull breastes bearnes might behold, 90
With a naked necke that neighed her till,
That gaue light on the land as beames of the sunn.
All the kings christened with their cleere gold
Might not buy that ilke broche that buckeled her mantle,
& the crowne on her head was caruen in heauen, 95
With a scepter sett in her hand of selcoth gemmes.
Thus louely to looke vpon on land shee abydeth.
   Merry were the meanye of men that shee had,
Blyth bearnes of blee bright as the sunn:
Sir Comfort that carues when the court dineth, 100
Sir Hope and Sir Hind, yee sturdye beene both,
Sir Liffe & Sir Likinge & Sir Loue alsoe,
Sir Cunninge & Sir Curtesye that curteous were of deeds,
& Sir Honor ouer all vnder her seluen,
A stout man & a staleworth, her steward I-wisse. 105
She had ladyes of loue longed her about:

---

88. perrie *supplied*; person *ms*: P, *with mark through stem indicating* -er
100. carues *ms*: knight
101. that *ms*: yee

---

87. "My wits are too dull to describe her treasures."
88. *perrie*: "jewelry"; cf. *P3A* 129 and 192
89. *colour of hir kirtle*: "collar (i.e., neckline) of her gown"
90. Lady Life's breasts are an obvious symbol of her nurturing qualities.
91. "with a naked neck (visible) to those who were near her" (?)
92. Perhaps *beames* should be *leames*, but there are other examples of AAxx verses in the poem.
98–109. The attendants of Lady Life's court are especially similar to the personified attendants commonly encountered in works in the "love tradition," for example, Chaucer's *Parliament of Fowls*, poems which follow the model established in the *Roman de la Rose*.
98. *meanye*: "retinue"
101. *Sir Hind*: i.e., "Sir Hende," who seems to overlap with "Sir Courtesy" of l. 103.
102. *Sir Liffe* is surely incorrect; perhaps "Sir Lief"?
103. *Sir Cunninge*: "Sir Good Sense" or "Sir Knowledge"

Dame Mirth & Dame Meekenes & Dame Mercy the hynd,
Dallyance & Disport, 2 damsells ffull sweete,
With all beawtye & blisse bearnes to behold.
There was minstrelsye made in full many a wise,   110
Who-soe had craft or cuninge kindlye to showe,
Both of birds & beastes & bearnes in the leaues;
& ffishes of the fflood ffaine of her were;
Birds made merrye with their mouth, as they in mind cold.
Tho I was moued with that mirth that maruell mee thought;
What woman that was that all the world lowted,   116
I thought speedylye to spye, speede if I might.
    Then I kered to a knight, Sir Comfort the good,
Kneeling low on my knees curteouslye him prayed.
I willed him of his worshipp to witt me the sooth   120
Of yonder Ladye of loue & of her royall meanye.
[Sir   Hee cherished me cheerlye by cheeke & by chin,
Com-   & sayd, "Certes, my sonne, the sooth thou shalt knowe.
fort]   This is my Lady Dame Liffe that leadeth vs all;
Shee is worthy & wise, the welder of ioye,   125

---

109. & *supplied*
117–9. *These three verses are written as four in the ms.*
119. prayed *ms*: praysed

---

108. *Dallyance & Disport*: the presence of these two ladies, who would not be out of place
    in the court of Venus, suggests that the pursuit of sexual pleasure is a natural part
    of life.
109. "with every beauty and delight (for) men to behold"; cf. 242
110–4. This description of the harmoniousness of nature is in striking contrast to what
    the narrator experiences in *WW* prior to falling asleep.
111. *kindlye to showe*: "to describe naturally"
114. *in mind cold*: "in mind could," i.e., as they knew how
116. *lowted*: "reverenced"
117. "I hoped quickly to discover, if succeed I might."
118. *kered*: "approached"; Sir Comfort may have his origin in such scriptures as Isaiah
    40:1 and Psalms 23:4.
120. "I asked him respectfully to teach me the truth."
122. "He touched me lovingly . . ."
125. *welder*: "wielder"

Greatlye gouerneth the ground & the greene grasse.
Shee hath ffostered & ffed thee sith thou was ffirst borne,
& yett beffore thou wast borne shee bred in thy hart.
Thou art welcome, I-wisse, vnto my winn Ladye.
If thou wilt wonders witt, feare not to ffraine,   130
& I shall kindlye thee ken, care thou noe more."
Then I was fearfull enoughe & ffaythffullye thought
That I shold long with Dame Liffe & loue her for euer;
There shall no man vpon mold my mind from her take,
For all the glitteringe gold vnder the god of heauen.   135
Thus in liking this liuinge — the longer the more —
Till that it neighed neere noone & one hower after,
There was rydinge & revell that ronge in the bankes;
All the world was full woe winne to behold.
Or itt turned from 12 till 2 of the clocke,   140
Much of this melodye was maymed & marde.

  In a nooke of the north there was a noyse hard
As itt had beene a horne, the higheste of others,
With the biggest bere that euer bearne wist,
& the burlyest blast that euer blowne was   145
Throughe the rattlinge rout runge ouer the feelds;

---

126. *greatlye*: "completely"
129. *winn*: "joyful"
130. *ffraine*: "ask"
132-5. These verses recall the similarly naive desire of the dreamer in *Pearl* to remain
  with the Pearl-maiden (*Pearl* 283-8).
135. Cf. 430 and *Scotish Feilde* 103
136. I.e., "the longer it lasted the more I liked it"
139. This verse, written here as it appears in the ms, makes little sense; but no plausible
  or helpful emendations have been proposed.
140. *Or*: "ere"
142. The north is the region or direction commonly associated with the Devil in medieval
  literature (e.g. *Piers* C.2.112-22 and *Cant. Tales* III 1413-4), a symbolism possibly sug-
  gested by Jeremiah 1:14 and 4:6; since Death is Satan's minion and often his own
  progeny (cf. l. 235), associating Death with the north is entirely appropriate.
143-6. Death's trumpet-call occurs frequently in medieval literature (see note to *P3A*
  656). Here it is suggestive of both a literal call to battle and an apocalyptic sounding
  of the "last trump"; cf. Jeremiah 4:5 and Joel 2:1.
146. *rattinge rout*: "noisy crowd" (presumably in reference to Life's minions, not those in
  Death's retinue)

The ground gogled for greefe of that grim dame.
I went nere out of my witt for wayling care.
Yett I bode on the bent & boldlye looked;
Once againe into the north mine eye then I cast.   150
I there saw a sight was sorrowfull to behold,
One of the vglyest ghosts that on the earth gone.
There was no man of this sight but hee was affrayd,
Soe grislye & great & grim to behold.
& a quintfull queene came quakinge before,   155
With a carued crowne on her head, all of pure gold,
& shee the ffoulest ffreake that formed was euer,
Both of hide & hew & heare alsoe.
Shee was naked as my nayle both aboue and belowe;
Shee was lapped about in linenn breeches;   160
A more fearffull face no freake might behold,

---

151. saw *ms*: saye

---

147. This verse may be out of place since Lady Death has not yet been described; or,
    as suggested by Gollancz, perhaps *dame* should be *dance*, in which case the line refers
    to the Dance Macabre; *gogled for greefe*: "shook with fear."
149. *bode on the bent*: "abided on the field"
151-74. This description of Lady Death, which counter-balances the earlier portrait of
    Lady Life (61-98), is somewhat unusual, for Death is more commonly portrayed
    in medieval literature as male, or as being of indeterminate sex; although this strik-
    ing description of Death has no real parallel elsewhere, medieval literature contains
    many examples of loathly ladies, and the descriptions of Guinevere's ghostly mother
    in the *Awntyrs off Arthure* and Dame Ragnell in *The Wedding of Sir Gawain* seem especial-
    ly pertinent. It is also possible that the poet is indebted to Virgil's depiction of the
    Fury Alecto in Book IV of the *Aeneid* (ll. 447-532). The painting "Mad Meg," some-
    times ascribed to Bruegel, provides a striking visual analogue.
152. *ghosts*: i.e., "creatures"; *gone*: i.e., (has ever) gone
155. The *quintfull* ("haughty") queen who precedes Lady Death is Pride (cf. 183); in *Piers*
    (C.22.69-70) Pride carries the banner of the Antichrist, not the banner of Death,
    which is carried by Elde (95-6).
157. The *shee* is Lady Death, not the *quintfull queene* of l. 155; cf. *Morte Arthure* 781.
158. *heare*: "hair"
159-60. These verses seem contradictory, but they probably mean that Death is naked
    except for a linen grave shroud; "Naked as my nail" is a proverbial expression (*Ox-
    ford*, 554).

For shee was long & leane & lodlye to see.
There was noe man on the mold soe mightye of strenght
But a looke of that Lady & his liffe passed.
Her eyes farden as the fyer that in the furnace burnes; 165
They were hollow in her head, with full heauye browes;
Her cheekes were leane, with lipps full side,
With a maruelous mouth full of long tushes,
& the nebb of her nose to her navell hanged,
& her lere like the lead that latelye was beaten. 170
Shee bare in her right hand an vnrid weapon,
A bright burnisht blade all bloody beronen,
& in the left hand, like the legg of a grype,
With the talents that were touchinge & teenfull enoughe. 174
With that shee burnisht vp her brand & bradd out her geere;
& I for feare of that freake ffell in a swond.
Had not Sir Comfort come & my care stinted,

---

165. Her *ms*: His
171. an *ms*: &
181. selcothes *ms*: selclothes

---

162. *lodlye*: "loathly"
163–4. Cf. 177–8
165. Fiendish or ghostly beings are often described as having glowing red eyes; cf. Grendel in *Beowulf*, the Green Knight in *SGGK*, and Guinevere's mother in the *Awntyrs off Arthure*; Alecto's eyes are described as flaming in the *Aeneid* (IV.448).
167. *full side*: "quite wide," i.e., thick
168. *tushes*: "tusks," i.e., fangs
170. *her lere*: "(the color of) her face"
171. *vnrid*: "enormous"
172. *bloody beronen*: "be-run with blood," a common phrase in alliterative poetry (cf. *P3A* 62)
173. The verse appears to be flawed; either a noun phrase was omitted after &, or it is Death's left hand that is described; *grype*: "griffin"
174. *talents*: "talons"; *touchinge & teenfull*: i.e., the claws were "touching" (i.e., close together) and were "sharp"
175. " . . . she polished her sword and readied her (war) gear."
176–8. The dreamer's death from fright is prevented by Sir Comfort, even though he has looked upon Lady Death, which no man is supposed to be able to do and survive (163–4). Perhaps he enjoys special status by virtue of the fact that he is merely a visitor to this visionary world; cf. Chaucer's dreamer in the *Parl. of Fowls* (148–63); cf. also Revelation 1:17.

I had beene slaine with that sight of that sorrowfull Ladye.
Then he lowted to me low & learned me well;
[Sir C.] Sayd, "Be thou not abashed, but abyde there a while;   180
Here may thou sitt & see selcothes ffull manye.
Yonder damsell is Death that dresseth her to smyte.
Loe, Pryde passeth before & the price beareth,
Many sorrowffull souldiers following her fast after:
Both Enuye & Anger, in their yerne weeds, .   185
Morninge & Mone, Sir Mischeefe his ffere,
Sorrow & Sicknesse & Sikinge in Hart;
All that were lothinge of their liffe were lent to her court.
When she draweth vp her darts & dresseth her to smite,
There is no groome vnder God may garr her to stint."   190
    Then I blushed to that bearne & balefullye looked;
She stepped forth barefooted on the bents browne,
The greene grasse in her gate she grindeth all to powder,
Trees tremble for ffeare & tipen to the ground,

---

186. Mischeefe *ms*: Misheefe
192. She *ms*: he

---

182. *dresseth*: "readies herself"; cf. 189
183. Cf. 155-6
185-9. Lady Death's entourage comprises personified vices and emotional and physical
    conditions which are antithetical to those found in the court of Lady Life. Some of
    these figures may also be found among the portraits on the outside of the wall sur-
    rounding the garden in the *Romance of the Rose*.
185. *yerne weeds*: "iron clothing," i.e., armor; "steel weeds" is a more common alliterative
    phrase, but here "vowel alliteration" with Enuye & Anger is needed.
186. *his ffere*: "his companion"
188. The verse may imply those people who are contemplating suicide.
189-90. Cf. *WW* 107 and 195-6
190. *garr*: "cause"
191. "Then I turned toward the creature and sorrowfully watched."
192-209. Lady Death's massive and apocalyptic destruction of all living things seems
    to imply an unnatural occurrence of catastrophic proportion, an event such as the
    Plague; in the natural scheme of things Death should not make her appearance until
    the close of day, rather than as here, in the middle of the afternoon.
192-3. The language of these verses suggests that Death is negating Life's earlier ac-
    complishments (cf. 72-3).

Leaues lighten downe lowe & leauen their might,   195
Fowles faylen to fflee when the heard wapen,
& the ffishes in the fflood ffaylen to swimne,
Ffor dread of Dame Death that dolefullye threates.
With that shee hyeth to the hill & the heard ffindeth;
In the roughest of the rout shee reacheth forth darts.   200
There shee fell att the first fflappe 1500
Of comelyest queenes with crowne & kings full noble;
Proud princes in the presse prestlye shee quellethe;
Of dukes that were doughtye shee dang out the braynes;
Merry maydens on the mold shee mightilye killethe;   205
There might no weapon them warrant nor no walled towne;
Younge children in their craddle they dolefullye dyen;
Shee spareth ffor no specyaltye but spilleth the gainest;
The more woe shee worketh, more mightye shee seemeth.

    When my Lady Dame Liffe looked on her deeds   210
& saw how dolefullye shee dunge downe her people,
Shee cast vp a crye to the hye King of heauen.
& He hearthneth itt hendlye in His hye throne;

---

202. comlyest ms: comelyes

196–8. As Lady Death approaches, the creatures become paralyzed with fear.
196. *when the heard wapen*: "when they heard (the sound of her) blows"; *wapen* is apparent-
    ly an onomatopoetic verb used to suggest the sounds made by rapid movements
    through the air (cf. 217).
199. *with that*: i.e., "having destroyed the birds and fishes"; Death's destruction of living
    things also moves up the scale of life, although when she reaches mankind she slays
    kings and queens first and then works down to babies in the cradle; *heard*: "herd (of
    beasts)"
200. "in the midst of the group (of assembled creatures) . . ."
201. *fflappe*: "swing"
203. *prestlye*: "quickly"
204. *dang*: "dashed"
206. *warrant*: "preserve"
208. *spilleth the gainest*: "destroys the best"
211. *dunge*: "knocked"

Hee called on Countenance & bade his course take:

[God]   "Ryde thou to the reschew of yonder wrought Ladye."   215

Hee was bowne att his bidd & bradd on his way,

As wight as the wind that wappeth in the skye.

He ran out of the rainebow through the ragged clowds

& light on the land where the lords lay slaine,

& vnto dolefull Death he dresses him to speake;   220

[Sir C.] Sayth, "Thou wratthefull Queene that euer woe worketh,

Cease of thy sorrow thy soueraigine comandeth,

& let thy burnished blade on the bent rest,

That my Lady Dame Liffe her likinge may haue."

Then Death glowed & gran for gryme of his talke,   225

But shee did as he dained, durst shee noe other;

Shee pight the poynt of her sword in the plaine earth,

& with a looke full layeth shee looked on the hills.

[II]

Then my Ladye Dame Liffe shee looketh full gay,

Kyreth to Countenance & him comelye thankes,   230

---

217. as *ms*: that
219. lay *supplied*
225. his *ms*: her
226. he *ms*: she

---

214. Sir Countenance is derived from scriptures such as Psalms 4:6 and 89:15, and from Revelation 1:16–8.

216. "He was ready at (God's) bidding and set out on his way."

218-9. The rainbow symbolizes man's hope, established through God's covenant with Noah following the flood (Genesis 9:12–7); Sir Countenance is also the physical embodiment of the rainbow which is described as surrounding the throne of God in Revelation 4:3.

221. *Queene*: the alliterative pattern would normally require a word beginning with "w" such as *wrecche* or *wight*.

222. *sorrow*: i.e., "sorrowful deeds"

225. "Then Death glowed (glowered?) and ground (her teeth) in rage at his speech."

226. *dained*: "ordained," i.e., decreed; Death has no choice but to obey a command which comes from God.

Kissed kindlye that knight, then carped she no more;
But vnto dolefull Death dressed her to speake;
[Life]   Sayth, "Thou woefull wretch, weaknesse of care,
Bold birth full of bale, bringer of sorrowe,
Dame daughter of the devill, Death is thy name.   235
But if thy fare be the fairer, the feend haue thy soule!
Couldest thou any cause ffind, thou kaitiffe wretch,
That neither reason nor right may raigne with thy name?
Why kills thou the body that neuer care rought?
The grasse nor the greene trees greeued the neuer,   240
But come fforth in their kinds Christyans to helpe,
With all beawtye & blisse that barne might devise.
But of my meanye thou marreth, marveild I haue
How thou dare doe them to death, eche day soe manye,
& the handy worke of Him that heauen weldeth.   245
How keepeth thou His comandement, thou kaytiffe retch!
Wheras banely Hee them blessed & biddeth them thriue,

---

236. the *ms*: thy
238. right *ms*: wright
242. barne *ms*: harme
246. comandement *ms*: comandements

233–55. Here the actual debate between Lady Life and Lady Death begins. In her open-
ing speech Life rebukes Death for the sorrow she causes to innocent creatures, and
she challenges Death to justify her existence.
233. *weakness of care*: a perplexing phrase, probably the result of scribal error; a word
such as *wakener* or *wielder* would suit the context better.
234. The phrase "birth full of bale" is probably meant to be figurative, but it can also
be taken literally.
235. Satan's "fathering" of Death is described by Milton in *Paradise Lost* (II.746–87); it
is a concept that originates in James 1:15.
236. "Unless your dealings become fairer, the fiend have your soul."
237–8. "Can you explain, you miserable wretch, why neither reason nor right can be
linked with your name?"
239. " . . . that never did harm"
240–1. Cf. Genesis 1:11
242. *barne*: "man"
246. A reference to the Sixth Commandment (Exodus 20:13)
247–8. Cf. Genesis 1:28
247. *banely*: "promptly"

Waxe fforth in the world & worth vnto manye,
& thou lett them of their leake with thy lidder turnes.　　249
But with wondering & with woe thou waiteth them full yorne,
& as a theefe in a rout thou throngeth them to death,
That neither Nature nor I ffor none of thy deeds
May bring vp our bearnes, their bale thee betyde.
But if thou blinn of that bine, thou buy must full deere;
Thou may wary the weeke that euer thou wast fformed."　　255
　　Then Death dolefullye drew vp her browes,
Armed her to answer & vpright shee standeth,
[Death] & sayd: "O louely Liffe, cease thou such wordes.
Thou payneth thee with pratinge to pray me to cease.
Itt is reason & right that I may rent take,　　　　　　　260
Thus to kill of the kind both kings & dukes,
Loyall ladds & liuely, of ilke sort some;
All shall drye with the dints that I deale with my hands.
I wold haue kept the comandement of the hye King of heauen,
But the bearne itt brake that thou bred vp ffirst,　　　265
When Adam & Eue of the earth were shapen,
& were put into paradice to play with their selues,

---

248. world *ms*: word
255. Thou *ms*: they

---

248. *worth vnto manye*: "become many," i.e., multiply
249. "But you keep them from their pleasure with your evil tricks."
250. *wondering*: "wandering" or "confusion" (?); *yorne*: "eagerly"
251. Cf. 1 Thessalonians 5:2-3
252. Lady Life and the goddess Natura are in very close accord, but as this verse indicates, they are not synonymous.
254. "But unless you stop from (doing) that (wickedness ?), you will pay for it dearly"; *bine* is possibly an error for *bane* or *birre*; cf. 236.
255. "You may rue the week in which you were created."
260. Death is here responding to the question posed by Lady Life in 238-9.
263. *drye with*: "deal with" or "experience"
264. Cf. 246
265-77. Death points out that it was the sin originally committed by Adam and Eve which permitted her to come into existence; Genesis 2:16-3:19.

& were brought into blisse, bidd if the wold.
He warned them nothing in the world but a wretched branche
Of the ffayntyest ffruit that euer in ffrith grew.   270
Yett his bidding they brake, as the booke recordeth,
When Eue ffell to the ffruite with ffingars white,
& plucked them of the plant & poysoned them both.
I was ffaine of that ffray, my ffawchyon I gryped,
& delt Adam such a dint that hee dolue euer after.   275
Eue & her ofspring I hitt them I hope;
For all the musters that they made, I mett with them once.
Therfore Liffe, thou me leaue, I loue thee but a litle;
I hate thee & thy houshold & thy hyndes all.
Mee gladdeth not of their glee nor of their gay lookes;   280
Att thy dallyance & thy disport noe dayntye I haue;
Thy ffayre liffe & thy ffairenesse ffeareth me but litle;
Thy blisse is my bale breuelye of others,
There is no game vnder heauen soe gladlye I wishe
As to haue a slapp with my ffawchyon att thy fayre state."   285
    Then Liffe on the land ladylike shee speakes,
[Life]   Sayth: "These words thou hast wasted, wayte thou no other;
Shall thy bitter brand neuer on my body byte.
I am grounded in God & grow for euermore;
But to these men of the mold marvell methinketh   290

---

268. *bidd if the wold*: i.e., "(what they might want was theirs) ask if they would"
269. *warned them*: "prohibited (to) them"
270. *ffayntyest*: i.e., "most meager"
274. "I was pleased by that fray, my falchion I gripped."
275. *dolue*: "delved"; cf. Genesis 3:23
276. *I hope*: i.e., "I hope (to tell you)," a filler phrase
277. *musters*: i.e., "maneuvers"
278. *thou me leaue*: "believe me"
281. Cf. 108; *noe daynte*: "no pleasure"
283. *breuelye*: "briefly," but perhaps the reading should be *bremelye* ("fiercely").
285. *state*: "estate" (?); perhaps *slapp* should be *fflapp* and *state* should be *fface*.
287. *wayte thou no other*: "think nothing else"
289. *grounded*: "rooted," an apt metaphor; this verse also provides the first indication that
    Lady Life is eternal as well as temporal.
290-1. " . . . I wonder in what hole in your heart you keep the wrath (that you feel)
    toward these men."

In whatt hole of thy hart thou thy wrath keepeth.
Where ioy & gentlenesse are ioyned together
Betweene a wight & his wiffe & his winne children,
& when ffaith & ffellowshipp are ffastened ffor aye,
Loue & charitye, which our Lord likethe,   295
Then thou waleth them with wracke & wratheffully beginneth;
Vncurteouslye thou cometh, vnknowne of them all,
& lacheth away the land that the lord holdeth,
Or woryes his wiffe, or walts downe his children.
Mikle woe thus thou waketh where mirth was before.   300
This is a deed of the devill, Death, thou vsest.
But if thou leaue not thy lake & learne thee a better,
Thou wilt lach att the last a lothelich name."
[Death]   "Doe away, damsell," quoth Death, "I dread thee nought.
Of my losse that I losse, lay thou noe thought;   305
Thou prouet mee full prestlye of many proper thinge;
I haue not all kinds soe ill as thou me vpbraydest.
Where I wend on my way the world will depart:
Bearnes wold be ouer-bold bales ffor to want,
The 7 sinnes for to serue & sett them full euer,   310

---

293. a wight *ms*: his wight

---

294. *ffor aye*: "forever"
296. *waleth . . . wracke*: "afflict . . . misery"
298. *lacheth*: "snatch"; *the lord*: "the man" (not God); possibly *land* and *lord* have been trans-
    posed, and it is the lord who is snatched away by Death.
299. *woryes*: "attacks"; *walts downe*: "knocks down," i.e., kills
302. *lake*: "wicked custom"
303. *lach*: "possess"
305. "That I might lose my good reputation, don't give it a thought."
306. *prouet*: i.e., "accuse"; *prestlye*: "vigorously"; *proper*: "separate"
307. This verse may be flawed, but the sense is clear: "I am not as evil as you say."
308. *the world*: i.e., the temptation represented by the things of this world; Death is claiming
    in these verses (308–11) that man's awareness of her existence provides a deterrent
    against his natural inclination to commit sin.
309–10. These are difficult verses; a rough paraphrase might be, "men would be over-
    bold (i.e., foolhardy) to want to receive torment (in hell), by serving the Seven Sins
    and becoming committed to them."

& giue no glory vnto God, that sendeth vs all grace.
If the dint of my dart deared them neuer,
To lett them worke all their will itt were litle ioy.
Shold I for their fayrnesse their ffoolishnes allowe?
My Liffe (giue thou me leaue), noe leed vpon earth 315
But I shall master his might, mauger his cheekes,
As a conquerour keene, biggest of other,
To deale dolefull dints & doe as me list;
For I fayled neuer in fight but I the ffeild wan,
Sith the ffirst ffreake that formed was euer, 320
& will not leaue till the last bee on the beere layd.
But sitt sadlye, thou Liffe, & the soothe thou shalt know.
If euer any man vpon mold any mirth had,
That leaped away with thee, Liffe, & laughed me to scorne,
But I dang them with my dints vnto the derffe earthe. 325
Both Adam & Eue & Abell I killed,
Moyses & Methasula & the meeke Aronn,
Iosua & Ioseph & Iacob the smoothe,
Abraham & Isace & Esau the roughe;
Samuell, for all his ffingers, I slew with my hands, 330

---

315. *The parentheses occur in the ms.*
318. me *ms*: my
322. thou Liffe *ms*: thy Liffe

---

312. *deared*: "harmed"
315. *noe leed*: "(there is) no man"
316. *mauger . . .*: "in spite of his checks" (despite all he may do), a filler phrase.
317. *biggest of other*: i.e., "greater than (all) others"; (cf. 143)
318. *me list*: "I wish"
324. " . . . and laughed at me in scorn"
326–47. Death's catalogue of vanquished heroes includes the patriarchs of the Old Testament, several of the Nine Worthies, and the greatest of the Arthurian heroes; cf. the similar lists in the *Cursor Mundi* (330ff.) and the *Body and Worms* (93–9); Death overreaches herself, however, when she includes "Iesu of heauen" in the list of those she has slain.
330–1. Saul was Jonathan's father, not Samuel, an error possibly resulting from reading *Saul* as an abbreviation for *Samuel*; the phrase *for all his ffingers* probably means "despite the great strength of his hands," not that he was abnormally endowed; it is possible that *ffingers* should be *slingers*, but such a reading would eliminate the probable word play on *fingers* and *hands*.

& Ionathan his gentle sonne in Gilboa hills;
David dyed on the dints that I delt oft,
Soe did Salomon his sonn that was sage holden;
& Alexander alsoe, to whom all the world lowted,
In the middest of his mirth I made him to bow;   335
The hye honor that he had helped him but lite,
When I swange him on the swire to swelt him behoued.
Arthur of England & Hector the keene,
Both Lancelott & Leonades, with other leeds manye,
& Gallaway the good Knight & Gawaine the hynde,   340
& all the rowte I rent ffrom the round table;
Was none soe hardye nor soe hye, soe holy nor soe wicked,
But I burst them with my brand & brought them assunder.
How shold any wight weene to winn me on ground?
Haue not I iusted gentlye with Iesu of heauen?   345
He was frayd of my fface in ffreshest of time.
Yett I knocked Him on the crosse & carued throughe His
hart."

    & with that shee cast of her crowne & kneeled downe lowe,
When shee minned the name of that noble Prince.
Soe did Liffe vpon land & her leeds all,   350
Both of heauen & of earth & of hell ffeends;
All they lowted downe lowe, their Lord to honor.
Then Liffe kneeled on her knees with her crowne in her hand,

---

349. nemned *ms*: minned

---

334. Death plays on the words *lowted* ("bowed") and *bowed* in l. 335.
338. Hector is probably Hector of Troy (like Arthur, one of the Nine Worthies), although
    Gollancz suggested Ector de Maris, Lancelot's brother.
339. Leonades is probably Leonidas, the Spartan king who was killed at Thermopylae,
    but the Arthurian knight "Ladynas of the forest sauvage" has been proposed.
340. Gallaway is surely an error for Galahad; "Gawaine the courteous."
341. "and all that company I ripped from the Round Table"
344. "How should any man on earth expect to conquer me?"
345. *iusted*: "jousted"; cf. *Piers* C.20.17 and 26
348–52. This passage is based on Philippians 2:10: "That at the name of Jesus every
    knee should bow, of things in heaven, and things in earth, and things under the earth."

& looketh vp a long while towards the hye heauen;
She riseth vpp radlye & dresseth her to speake;   355
She calleth to her companye & biddeth them come neere,
Both kings and queenes & comelye dukes:

[Life] "Work wiselye by your witts my words to heare,
That I speake ffor your speed & spare itt noe longer."

Then shee turned from them & talketh these words: 360
She sayth, "Dame Death, of thy deeds now is thy doome
    shapen,
Through thy wittles words that thou hast carped,
Which thou makest with thy mouth & mightylye avowes.
Thou hast blowen thy blast breemlye abroade;
How thou hast wasted this world sith wights were first,   365
Euer murthered & marde, thou makes thy avant.
Of one point lett vs proue or wee part in sunder:
How didest thou iust att Ierusalem with Iesu my Lord?
Where thou deemed His death in one dayes time,
There was thou shamed & shent & stripped ffor aye.   370
When thou saw the King come with the crosse on His
    shoulder,
On the top of Caluarye thou camest Him against;
Like a traytour vntrew, treason thou thought.
Thou layd vpon my leege Lord lotheliche hands,

---

355. radlye *ms*: rudlye
360. from *ms*: to
364. breemlye *ms*: breenlye (?)
369. death *ms*: deat

---

364. Cf. 142–6; here, though, the "blast" that Life is referring to is Death's exaggerated claims, not the earlier sounding of her trumpet.
366. *marde*: "marred"; *avant*: "boast"
368–429. Medieval accounts of Christ's descent into hell — the so-called "Harrowing of Hell"—derive from the apocryphal work *The Gospel of Nicodemus* (see M. R. James, *The Apocryphal New Testament*). This description of Christ's victory over Death provides an important analogue to Langland's account of the harrowing of hell in *Piers* C.20 (B.18).
368. Cf. *Piers* C.20.17

Sithen beate Him on His body & buffetted Him rightlye,   375
Till the railinge red blood ran from His sides;
Sith rent Him on the rood with ffull red wounds.
To all the woes that Him wasted (I wott not ffew),
Thou deemest to haue beene dead & dressed for euer.
But, Death, how didst thou then with all thy derffe words,   380
When thou prickedst att His pappe with the poynt of a speare,
& touched the tabernackle of His trew hart,
Where my bower was bigged to abyde for euer?
When the glory of His godhead glented in thy face,
Then was thou feard of this fare in thy false hart;   385
Then thou hyed into hell hole, to hyde thee beliue;
Thy fawchon flew out of thy fist, soe fast thou thee hyed.
Thou durst not blushe once backe, for better or worse,
But drew thee downe ffull in that deepe hell,
& bade them barre bigglye Belzebub his gates.   390
Then thou told them tydands that teened them sore,
How that King came to kithen his strenght,
& how He had beaten thee on the bent & thy brand taken,
With euerlasting Liffe that longen Him till.
Then the sorrow was ffull sore att Sathans hart;   395
Hee threw ffeends in the ffyer, many ffell thousands;
& Death, thou dange itt on whilest thou dree might;

---

379. Thou *ms*: tho
391. Thou *ms*: the
393. He *ms*: shee; the *ms*: thy

---

379. "You thought (that He) was dead and addressed (i.e. dealt with) forever."
385. *feared of this fare*: "frightened by this turn of events"
388. *blushe*: "look" or "glance"
390. *barre bigglye*: "bar tightly"; cf. 418; *Belzebub*: Beelzebub, Lucifer's chief lieutenant
391. " . . . tidings that grieved them sorely"
392. *to kithen*: "to make known"
394. *longed Him till*: "belonged to Him"
397-8. "And Death, you hit with it (your sword) while you might endure; (then) because of the default (i.e. lack) of your falchion, you fought (on) with your hand" (see ll. 173-4 for a description of this "hand"); these verses are very possibly misplaced.

For ffalte of thy ffawchyon, thou fought with thy hand.
Bost this neuer of thy red deeds, thou ravished bitche!
Thou may shrinke for shame when thou the sooth heares.   400
   Then I leapt to my Lord that caught me vpp soone,
& all wounded as Hee was, with weapon in hand,
He fastened ffoote vpon earth & ffollowed thee ffast
Till He came to the caue that cursed was holden.
He abode before Barathron, that Bearne, while He liked,   405
That was euer merke as midnight with mourninge & sorrowe;
He cast a light on the land as beames of the sunn.
Then cryed that King with a cleere steuen,
[Christ] 'Pull open your ports, you princes within;
Here shall come in the King crowned with ioy,   410
Which is the hyest burne, in battell to smite.'
There was ffleringe of ffeends throughe the fyer gaynest,
Hundreds hurled on heapes in holes about.
The broad gates all of brasse brake all in sunder,
& the King with His crosse came in before.   415
He leapt vnto Lucifer that Lord Himselfe;
Then He went to the tower where chaynes were manye,
& bound him soe biglye that hee for bale rored.
Death, thou daredst that day & durst not be seene
Ffor all the glitering gold vnder God Himseluen.   420

---

406. mourninge *ms*: mournige

401–4. These verses sound like a passage out of medieval romance.
404–29. The poet heightens the drama of this confrontation by omitting the lengthy
   conversations which occur in the *Gospel of Nicodemus*.
405. *Barathon*: Barathrum, the abyss of hell
407. Cf. 92
409–10. Cf. *Piers* C.20.273–6; from *Nicodemus* 18, as based on Psalm 23:7.
412–3. Christ's words cause a general panic among the hell-fiends, who make futile at-
   tempts to hide or flee.
417 and 421. Quite possibly line 417 was copied here by mistake, as a result of scribal
   eye-slip (from *Himselfe* in 416 to *Himseluen* in 420) and then copied again in its proper
   place as 421. Nevertheless, poetic justice is served by having Lucifer imprisoned in
   his own dungeon.

Then to the tower Hee went where chanes are many;
Hee tooke Adam & Eue out of the old world,
Abraham & Isaac & all that Hee wold,
David & Danyell & many deare bearnes
That were put into prison & pained ffull long.   425
Hee betooke me the treasure that neuer shall haue end,
That neuer danger of death shold me deere after.
Then wee wenten fforth winlye together
& left the dungeon of devills, & thee, Death, in the middest —
& now thou prickes ffor pride, praising thy seluen!   430
        Therfore bee not abashed, my barnes soe deere,
Of her ffauchyon soe ffeirce nor of her ffell words.
Shee hath noe might, nay no meane, no more you to greeue,
Nor on your comelye corsses to clapp once her hands.
I shall looke you ffull liuelye, & latche ffull well,   435
& keere yee ffurther of this kithe aboue the cleare skyes.
If yee loue well the Lord that light in the mayden,
& be christened with creame & in your creede beleeue,
Haue no doubt of yonder Death, my deare children,
For yonder Death is damned with devills to dwell,   440
Where is wondering & woe & wayling ffor sorrow."
Death was damned that day, daring ffull still.
Shee hath no might, nay no maine, to meddle with yonder ost,
Against euerlasting Liffe that Ladye soe true.
        Then my Lady Dame Liffe with lookes soe gay,   445

---

437. loue *supplied*; Lord *ms*: Ladye
440. Death *supplied*

---

426. "He gave me the treasure that never shall have end"—the gift of eternal life.
427. *deere*: "endure" (?)
430. Perhaps an oblique reference to I Cor. 15:55 —"O death, where is thy sting?"
435-6. "I shall watch over you always, and keep you well, and take you away from this
    world beyond the clear skies."
437. "if you love well the Lord that was placed within the Maiden"
441. *wondering*: "wandering"

That was comelye cladd with kirtle and mantle,
Shee crosses the companye with her cleare ffingers.
All the dead on the ground doughtilye shee rayseth,
Fairer by 2 ffold then they before were.   449
With that shee hyeth ouer the hills with hundreds ffull manye.
I wold have ffollowed on that faire, but no further I might;
What with wandering & with woe I waked beliue.
    Thus fared I throw a ffirth in a ffresh time,
Where I sayd a-sleepe in a slade greene.
There dreamed I the dreame which dread all befrighted.   455
But Hee that rent all was on the rood, riche itt Himseluen.
& bringe vs to His blisse with blessings enowe.
Therto, Iesu of Ierusalem, grant vs Thy grace,
& saue there our howse holy for euer! Amen.

ffinis.

---

446. kirtle *ms*: christall

---

447. *crosses*: i.e., makes the sign of the cross over them
449-50. Cf. I Cor. 15:51-4
450. This image of Lady Life leading her resurrected minions off over the hills, as if in a dance of eternal life, may be an intentional inversion of the *danse macabre*.
454. *sayd*: "slumbered"; cf. 36
455. "There I dreamed the dream which frightened away all (my) fear," in reference to the narrator's initial anxiety concerning death.
456-9. These verses are the poet's benediction.
456. *riche itt*: "interpreted it," i.e., provided an explanation of the dream, suggesting divine revelation
459. This verse permits several interpretations: e.g. "and there preserve (for us) a holy habitation"; or "and there save (i.e., grant salvation to) our house entirely (i.e., our collective family)."

Jesus and the Masters of the Laws of the Jews

Among the several dialogues and debates in the Vernon manuscript are two which belong to the medieval tradition of the conflict between Church and Synagogue — the *Disputisoun Bitwene Child Jesu and Maistres of the Lawe Of Jewes* and the *Disputisoun By-twene a Christenmon and a Jew*. As noted in the headnote to the latter poem, both poems are popular manifestations of the confrontation between Christianity and Judaism, and like their predecessors in this tradition they are concerned with depicting the ultimate triumph of the faith over the Jewish faith. Central to both poems is the fundamental significance of the Trinity, a theological concept that occurs only in the New Testament. A second important concern in *Jesus and the Masters* is the reconciling of the Virgin Birth as recorded in the New Testament with the messianic prophecies of the Old Testament, particularly those found in Isaiah.

Jesus and the Masters also belongs to the medieval tradition of biblical narratives, poems in which specific episodes from the scriptures are imaginatively recounted. Such poems were composed throughout the earlier and later English Middle Ages: for example, the Old English *Genesis B* and *Exodus*; and the Middle English *Ormulum, Jacob and Joseph*, the *Southern Passion*, the *Cursor Mundi, Patience, Cleanness*, and *Susannah*. In the case of *Jesus and the Masters*, the biblical source is a mere eleven verses of scripture (Luke 2:41–51) depicting the twelve-year-old Christ confounding the learned doctors in the temple. Although these few verses are the only ones in the canonical gospels to reveal anything of the boyhood of Christ, Christ's infancy and boyhood were subjects of great curiosity in the Middle Ages. The apocryphal infancy gospels, in particular the *Gospel of Thomas* (see M.R. James, *The Apocryphal*

New Testament), which spawned numerous popular tales and legends, describe some of Christ's alleged activities between the nativity and the beginning of his ministry. This brief account of the boyhood of Christ in Luke also provided the basis for the imaginative elaborations on Christ's early life found in the *Cursor Mundi* (EETS 62, ll. 12,577–632) and in the "Christ and the Doctors" plays of the York, Wakefield, Chester, and Ludus Coventriae mystery cycles.

In the Vernon manuscript text of *Jesus and the Masters* there are 215 verses, arranged in eight-line stanzas rhyming abababab. Nearly half of the verses alliterate on two, three, or four syllables, and there is also occasional use of internal rhyme.

---

1)   Base Text: Bodl. MS 3938 (Vernon MS), Fol. 301r (col. iii)–301v (col. ii)

2)   Other mss: BL MS Addit. 22283 (Simeon MS), fol. 91r (ll.
                                   1–104 only)
                                   BL MS Harl. 3954, fol. 70v (ll. 37–92 and 109–82
                                      of *Jesus and the Masters* are here embedded in a
                                      longer work on the infancy of Christ, ll. 197–328)

3)   Printed Texts: F. J. Furnivall, *The Minor Poems of the Vernon MS.*
                                   EETS 117, pp. 479–84
                                   Carl Horstmann, *Sammlung Altenglischer Legenden* (1878),
                                      104–5 (for the verses embedded in Harl. 3954)

4)   *Index of Middle English Verse* 1887

---

her is a disputison bitwene child jhu & maistres of þe lawe of jewes

Lustneþ lordes leoue in londe,
Soþeli sawes I wol ʒou telle
Of gentyl Jhesu, I vnderstonde,
Þe ffalse ffei fonded to felle.   4
ffor wo ne wrake ne wolde he wonde

---

1. *Lustneþ lordes*: a common opening phrase found in both romances and religious poetry; *leoue in londe*: i.e., "loved throughout the land."

Of Trinite trewe to Jewes telle;
He sat in see, he nolde not stonde,
As best of barnes þat bar þe belle.   8

Þe gospel seiþ in þis manere,
Whon Jhesu was of twelf ȝer age
In to þe temple he com to lere
Wrangful wrecches þat wrouȝt outrage.   12
Maystres wondrede, þat þer were,
Þat lawes lerede in heore langage,
[masters]   And seide, "Child, what destou þere?
Þou sittest stalled in vre stage."   16

A mayster seide to Jhesu:
[a master]   "Þou scholdest lerne and nouȝt teche,
Þou spillest speche — what seystou!
Þi wrangful wordes worcheþ wreche;   20
Þou repungnest in pres aȝeyn vr prou,
As preised prophete þe peple preche.

---

7. *see*: "seat"; in the biblical account in Luke (2:46) it is emphasized that Jesus sat in the midst of the doctors: *sedentem in medio doctorum*; in early paintings and in illustrated devotional books of the 15th century, the Christ child is usually seated, though occasionally standing, but placed above the several doctors. In some instances he sits or stands on a kind of raised pulpit; cf. also ll. 15–6.

8. *bar þe belle*: an idiom expressing his superlative qualities; cf. *Troilus & Criseyde* 3.198; its original, literal meaning is disputed; the most common suggestion associates the phrase with "bellwether"—i.e., "one who leads a flock"; but some link it to a prize for winning a competition. For other occurrences of the phrase see Whiting, p. 37.

9. The story is found only in the gospel of Luke (2:41–51).

10. Twelve is also the age specified for other prodigious boys in medieval literature, such as Alexander, who at twelve succeeded in riding Bucephalus (*Kyng Alisaunder*, EETS 227, pp. 46–7), and Ipotis (also in the Vernon *ms*), who like Jesus in this poem reflects the motif of the wise child (see Suchier).

13. *Maystres*: "masters," which in the later Middle Ages denotes doctors of law or divinity

17. In this text of the poem none of the masters is identified and no distinctions are drawn among them. In the analogous text printed by Horstmann, however, the master who begins speaking at l. 18 and who disputes with Jesus until l. 92 is identified as "Cayfas"; thus in that text the master is linked with the high priest Caiaphas in Matt. 26, who presides over the council that condemns Jesus.

21–2. "You speak among the throng to our disadvantage, like an acclaimed prophet (you) preach to the people."

Stunt a stounde þi sawe of Gru,
Þi wit to teche may not reche.   24

Þow schuldest lerne A. B. C.
ffor þe fayleþ a foundement;
Þou tellest tales of Trinite,
In wonderwyse þi wit is went.   28
Ʒif þou wolt leorne þou miht þhe
ffor wonder wit on þe is sent;
Of bales boote þou miht be
Ʒif þou neore in errour hent."   32

[Jesus]   Jhesu seide: "I may wel se
Þi bok is blynt and þou art blent;
Þou farest foule, so þynkeþ me,
ffor lewed lore on þe is lent.   36
Whi is A. bi-fore B.?
Tel me þat, spekest in present,
Or I schal tymeli teche þe
Þi reson raþe þe schal repent."   40

Þe maister wiþ wel wikked wille
Spake in pres of people, apliht:
[master]   "Jhesu, þou art a grameful gille;
I rede raþe þou lerne a-riht;   44
And bote þou stonde a stounde stille,
To betyng bare þou schalt be diht."
[Jesus]   Qwaþ Jhesu, "Þat is no skille,
I com not hider for to fiht.   48

---

23. "Cease for a while your Greek (i.e., incomprehensible) saying."

25–40. The same rhyme alternation is maintained throughout these two stanzas.

37. The question posed by Jesus concerning the letter A, and his later explanation (ll. 54–68), recall the "many allegories of the first letter spoken by the young child" in the *Gospel of Thomas* (see M.R. James, *The Apocryphal New Testament*, p. 51).

38–40. After posing his first question, Jesus asserts his authority by insisting upon an immediate public response, in the phrases *spekest in present*, *tymeli*, and *rape*.

42. *apliht*: probably a shortened form of *I thee aplight*, "I assure you" or "in faith," used here to provide the rhyme and fill out the verse; cf. l. 119.

3it," quaþ Jhesu, "of myn askyng
Þou ne 3iuest non onswere.
I am ful old þeih I be 3ing;
A louely lore I wol þe lere,   52
Tak þis tale of my teching:
A. is prys wiþ-oute pere,
Lettre of þreo and is o þing:
Þreo partyes A. haþ knet i-fere.   56

Bi A. biginneþ þe lettrure,
ffor A. is lyk þe Trinite:
Þreo partyes A. haþ of mesure,
Knet in knotte on A. wol be.   60
3if þou wolt lerne þou miht hure
Hou A. is lyk þe deite:
Þe deite is, þis is sure,
Þreo and on in maieste,   64
And euer her-after heo schul dure
In-departable alle þre.
Nou hastou lerned, tac þou cure,
Hou A. is most of dignite."   68

Þe maister seide in þat stounde,
[master]   "What artou lettrure to lere?
Bi Moyses lawe nis not founde

---

50. 3iuest *ms*: 3uiest
57. ffor *ms*: ffo

---

51. The line suggests the topos of the *puer senilis* or *puer senex* (Curtius, pp. 98–100), and
    it also recalls Rev. 1:11: "I am Alpha and Omega, the beginning and the ending. . .
    which is and which was, and which is to come. . . ."
57–68. The only twelve-verse stanza in the poem.
70. "Who are you to teach us the alphabet!"
71–2. The concept of the Trinity, which is absent from the Mosaic constitution and the
    laws and commandments of the Pentateuch, indeed, from the Old Testament entire-
    ly, would have seemed to the masters a blatant contradiction of their basically
    monotheistic tenets. It is noteworthy, though, that in the Middle Ages prefigurings

Þe lawes þat þou tellest heere.   72
Þou seist in þis ilke grounde
Þou art old and ȝong i-feere;
Þi sawe soþli nis not founde,
Þerfore þou art me no-þing dere.   76

Stond þou stille swiþe I seye,
And louely lustne to my lore,
And þou miht bi alle weye
Beo ful wys for euer-more.   80
Þou hast wit in memorie,
And wel ȝong þi wit is core;
Hit is medlet wiþ ffolye
And þat greueþ me grimly sore.   84

Of Moyses vr lawe we had,
And nou newe þow wolt teche;
Of þi sawe swiþe am I sad,
Of þe Trinite to spille speche.   88
Þou greuest me, I am not glad;
With luþer lawes þou luþer leche;
Þou spekest of godhed as child al mad,
fforþer þen þi wit wol reche."   92

A-noþer mayster seide in hiȝe,
[another   "Child, her is a wonder þing;
master]   Þow kennest comeli clergye,
And ȝit to teche þou art to ȝyng;   96
Þou hast not lerned, as men seye;
Hou hastou þenne þi connyng?
Dueles demeþ mon to dyȝe,
Þi tonge haþ tast of heore teching.   100

---

of the Trinity were sometimes seen in the Old Testament. In *Piers Plowman* (B.16.167ff.),
for example, Abraham reveals a partial understanding of the Trinity from his en-
counter with the three angels.
74. The master is referring to the paradox in l. 51.
78. *louely*: "lowly," i.e., "humbly"
95. "You know theological doctrine very well."

Þi wrongful wordes worcheþ wrake;
Þow seist þat God is on and þre.
I bede þin errour þou forsake,
Þou spekest of þing þat mai not be.   104
As ouercome þou worth of take
Þat al þis peple hit schal se,
Þis qwestion to þe I make:
Tel me what is þe Trinite?"   108

Jhesu, as best þat bar þe belle,
Wolde wite riht a-non
Ʒif he couþe o þing telle
Of prechynge prophetes, wonder won,   112
Þat seide Crist scholde dwelle
Her on eorþe a-mong his fon,
[Jesus]   "Alle ʒor lawes to fulfelle;
Þis wol ʒor lawes euerichon.   116

Crist is liht of God Almiht
And of Godes liht i-core;
Ysaye spac herof, apliht,
Of a Mayden he scholde be bore.   120
Þou miʒt wel wite hit is riht
He schal bugge þat is forlore;
God is þe ffader, Crist sone & liht,
Þe sone is geten wiþ-outen hore.   124

ffor as þe sonne ʒiueþ his leem
Ʒif he wiþ cloudes is not let,
So com Crist as sonne beem

105–6. "so that you will be defeated, which all these people shall see"
109–16. In this stanza what begins as indirect discourse slips unobtrusively into direct
    speech, a frequent occurrence in medieval texts.
120. Isaiah 7:14
124. "The Son is begotten without sin"; the phrase *wiþouten hore* is sometimes used to
    describe the Virgin Mary, meaning "immaculate."
125–8. This metaphysical portrayal of the incarnation of Christ in Mary is found in
    both Latin and vernacular poetry and in late medieval art (see D. Gray, pp. 100–1).

In to þat buirde þat bales bet.   128
3if þou take wel good 3eem
Hou þe sonne beem euere is set
Vndeparted, so is þe strem
Of Crist with God mid knottes knet.   132

Now tak herto good entent:
Þe ffader liht in þe sone schalbe,
Þe ffader liht 3it nis nou3t blent:
Al is o liht in deite.   136
Þen is hit proued bi argument
Þat ffader and sone o liht beoþ he;
Þe holy spirit wiþ hem present,
Heo þreo beoþ God in Trinite.   140

ffor þe Trinite, I þe seye,
A. is lettre of alle cheef;
Þerfore he is in alle weye
Put bi-fore, her is good preef.   144
Þe Trinite þei schal seo wiþ e3e
Alle men þat ben him leof;
Þen is mon a preised prei3e
Þat to þe Trinite doþ no greef."   148

Þe maistres seide of þe lawe
Þat deueles tauhte him clergye.
[masters]   "A Mayde," þei seide, "bi prophetes sawe,
Schal bere Crist, kyng of glorie.   152
Wel we witen and wel is knawe
Þe olde Joseph weddet Marie;

151-2. Isaiah 7:14

153. The gospels offer no explicit indication of Joseph's age, but since Joseph is not men-
tioned during Christ's ministry, the implication is that he was considerably older than
Mary. In apocryphal writings, however, the concept of "old Joseph" is firmly estab-
lished; in the *Book of James*, for example, Joseph is reluctant to wed Mary: "and Joseph
refused, saying: I have sons, and I am an old man, but she is a girl: lest I become
a laughing-stock to the children of Israel" (ed. M.R. James, p. 42).

Oþer record cunne we non drawe:
He nis not Crist bi prophecie."   156

Jhesu spac with mylde chere
To Jewes þat gonne grede & crie:
[Jesus]   "ffareþ feire, ffrendes deore,
ʒe ffareþ foule wiþ folye.   160
And o þing a-non ʒe schul heere:
What seiþ þe prophete Ysaye?
Heo schal be wedded wiþoute pere,
Þe Mylde Mooder of Messye.   164

Ysaye seiþ a-noþer þing:
Crist in þe lawe schal be bore
And þat mot ben in weddyng,
And elles Cristes lawe is lore.   168
Prophetes speeke of his comyng,
At Jesse bi-gon þe more,
ʒit haþ Crist no bi-gynning
Al-þauʒ þat Crist be mon i-core.   172
Ioseph uirga floruit fatu Ysaye;
Coniunx, lex ut monuit, mater fit Messye."

Þe maystres and Jewes mo
Of ʒonge Jhesu hedde meruayle,   176
Hou þat he was comen hem to
Wiþ wit and clergye to assayle.
Of hem hedde Jhesu mony a fo,
ffor heore wit gon sone fayle;   180
Monye with-drawe and gonne go
Whon heore clergye hem nolde vayle.

___

161, 166. I can find no such references in Isaiah.
170–1. Jesse, the father of David and the root of "the tree of Jesse," is also the progenitor
   of Christ, though as the poet points out, Christ is without beginning or ending.
173–4. "The rod of Joseph flourished, according to Isaiah [cf. Isa. 11:10]; his wife, as
   the law foretold, became the mother of the messiah."

In-to þe temple com Marie,
Heo sayȝ hire sone in see was set   184
And tauȝte þe peple bi clergye,
Of loueli lawe wiþ-oute let.
To Him heo seide riht in heiȝe,

[Mary]   "Now is my bale myd boote i-bet!   188
Þi ffader and I wel sorie
Þe haueþ souȝt, & nouȝwher met.
Ego & pater tuus dolentes querebamus te."

Jhesu seide in þat stounde,   192
[Jesus]   "Mi ffader wille is þat I do;
I wol vn-bynde þat was bounde,
Mi ffader wole þat hit beo so.
Þe peple I preche wiþ facounde   196
And I teche ffrend and fo;
Mi sarmoun is boþe soþ & sounde,
On me is ffader and sone also.

Mi ffader lawe I wol fulfelle,   200
Þerfore I am hider i-sent;
Douȝter and Moder, to þe I telle,
Elles weore þe world i-schent.
Mi ffader wol, with-oute dwelle,   204
Þat I teche ow in present;
Þe ffendes fare doun to felle
Þat haþ with wrong þe world went."

Romayns þer were wonder won   208

189–93. These lines include vernacular paraphrases of portions of Luke 2:48–9, and
the Latin in l. 191 approximates the Vulgate text; the technique of interspersing the
Latin text and a vernacular translation is used also in *Piers Plowman* and the *Parl.
of the Three Ages*.
191. Luke 2:48: "your father and I have sought you sorrowing."
200–1. Perhaps an allusion to Matt. 5:17.
205. *ow*: "you" (thee)
208–9. "The Romans that were present, who were well-versed in theology, were won-
drously amazed"; there is no mention of Romans in the account in Luke or in any

Þat cunnynge were of clergye;
Bi prophecie heo wusten vchon
Þat he was Crist, with-outen lye,
Honourede him for Crist anon,   212
ffor his miht & his maistrie.
Preye we Crist þat we so don,
To geten þe gle in his glorie. Amen.

---

of the analogous materials. It is possible they are the poet's invention, functioning as knowledgeable witnesses who attest to the Christ child's supremacy over the masters.

A Disputation between a Christian and a Jew

A Disputation Between a Christian and a Jew falls squarely in the tradition of the conflict between Church and Synagogue (on this tradition see M. Schlauch, *Speculum* 14 [1939], 448–64), but the poem is more an extended *exemplum* than a true debate. The importance of the poem's narrative elements, drawn largely from romance literature and from folklore, far outweighs the importance of its use of dialogue, and the final conversion of the Jew results more from the power of the Christian's "magic" than from the power of his arguments. The narrative reflects several themes commonly encountered in the Celtic tradition: the subterranean passage into the Other World, a magic fairy castle, the danger posed for a mortal by a sumptuous fairy feast, and an unexpected and instantaneous return to earthly reality. Such narrative elements, when added to the rhetorical embellishments characteristic of oral performance, give the poem a distinctly romantic flavor, and yet the skill with which these elements are adapted to the poem's religious purposes should also be noted — for example the substitution of the host for the magic talisman which preserves its possessor while in the Other World. The doctrinal matters of the poem are also commonly encountered in the didactic literature of the Middle Ages. The joy that results from the salvation of a repentant sinner is stressed at the beginning and ending of the poem (cf. *Mercy and Righteousness*), but as the narrative unfolds, greater emphasis is placed on the importance of the mass and miraculous power of the eucharist, the embodiment of the three-fold God.

A few analogues to this story have been identified (see C. Brown, *MLN* 25 [1910], 141–4) — e.g. in the eighth-century life of St. Wulfram by Jonas of Fontanelles and in Thomas Cantimpre's *Bonum Universalis de Apibus* — but none of them seems to be directly related to this poem. Although it is probable that *Christian and Jew* was once contained in the Simeon manuscript, the only surviving text of the poem is in the Vernon manuscript, where it follows *Jesus and the Masters* and precedes a work on how to hear mass. The poem is written in tail-rhyme stanzas of sixteen verses, rhyming aaab cccb dddb eeeb, the metrical form of romances such as *Sir Degrevaunt*.

1) Base Text: Bodl. 3938 (Vernon MS), fols. 301v (col. iii)–302r (col. iii)

2) Other mss: none

3) Printed Texts: F. J. Furnivall, EETS 117, pp. 484–93
                     Carl Horstmann, *Sammlung Altenglischer Legenden*, pp. 204–8

4) *Index of Middle English Verse* 167

A disputisoun bytwene a cristenmon and a jew

Alle bliþe mote þei be
Þat folyes bleþeliche wole fle.
How hit bitidde biȝonde see
    Þe soþe I wol ȝow say.   4
In þe toun of Parys
Þat is a citee of prys,
Twey men mette þat weore wys,
    And wente bi þe way.   8
Þei weore clerkes of Diuinite,
Crafti men in heore degre;
Eiþer maister wolde be
    ffoondeþ, ȝif þei may.   12
Þus þei desputed so faste

12. ffondeþ *ms*: ffondey

5. The confrontation of Christian and Jew occurs in Paris, the major center for theological study in the Middle Ages; but the poet indicates that the Christian (identified in l. 306 as Walter of Berwick) later became an important Church official in Rome.
9. divinity students
11–2. Here *maister* probably indicates their desire to achieve mastery over their opponent, not as in l. 24 a Doctor of Divinity.

While þe day mihte laste;
Nouþer oþer couþe caste
   Beo rihtwys lay.   16

Þe ton was of Engelonde,
A cristene mon, Ich vnderstonde;
He hedde i-souht ouer þe sonde
   Wondres to se;   20
He hedde i-lernd of clergys,
As men doþ þat beoþ wys;
Þe mon þat most is of prys,
   Maister moste be.   24
Þe toþer was a Jeuȝ riht,
A mon muchel of his miht;
To his trouþe helde he tiht,
   Trewe as þe tre.   28
Þat wol I apertly preue —
Þulke lay þat he on leeue —
ffor no gold þat men mihte him ȝeue
   Chaunge wolde not he.   32

---

14. mihte *ms*: mihti
27. helde *ms*: hedde
31. men *supplied*

15–6. Neither of them was able to best the other, following proper debate procedure.
    Perhaps the phrase *rihtwys lay* ("righteous law") is meant to emphasize the contrast
    between the Jew's upright behavior on this first day and the trickery he resorts to
    on the next.
23–4. "The man of greatest worth must be(come) a Doctor of Divinity."
25. *a Jeuȝ riht*: "a just Jew"
26–32. The strength of the Jew's religious convictions, here emphasized, makes his sub-
    sequent conversion that much more impressive, as well as helping to account for his
    attempt to win the contest by unfair means.
27. "He held firmly to his beliefs."
28. If *þe tre* ("the tree") implies "the cross," the comparison is ironic in this context.
30. "that same law in which he believed," i.e., the Old Testament laws

Þe cristene mon seide as he þou3t,

[Christian] "Lo, 3onde vr God þat vs bou3t!

Oþer trouwe þou hit nou3t,

    Bi daye nor bi niht!   36

Certeynliche, 3onde is he

Þat for vs di3ede on þe tre,

And also bouwed him to be

    In a buyrde briht,   40

As heo wemles was,

Seþþe cler as þe glas;

Bitwene oxe and an as

    I-bore was þat kniht   44

At þe 3ol ful 3are,

Al for vr welfare;

Woldest þou leeue on my lare

    Þi lykyng were liht."   48

Þe Jeu3 sone seide þare,

[Jew] "Ar we fforþere fare,

Þer is o God and no mare,

    Hei3ly in holde;   52

And as I trowe in þe trone,

He schop þe sonne and þe moone,

But he hedde neuer no sone

    ffor synful was solde.   56

Þe grete God calle we

Þat is semely to se;

Oþer may þer non be,

    3onger ne olde.   60

---

35. i.e., "don't believe anything else"

40-2. The Christian emphasizes New Testament concepts such as the Virgin Birth throughout the poem.

48. "Your happiness would be easily achieved" (?); or, "your present beliefs would be readily abandoned" (?); perhaps *lykyng* should be emended to *lyvyng*.

51. One of the crucial concerns here, as in *Jesus and the Masters*, is the Christian's belief in the Holy Trinity (cf. also ll. 139–40 and 277–80), which the Jew of course rejects.

51. *o*: "one"

52. "firmly in control" (?)

Wharto makestou þi mone?
I trouwe þi wit beo þe wone!
Al mis artou gone
    Heer on þis wolde."   64

Þe cristen mon stondeþ stille,
And seþþen he talkeþ him tille
[Christian]   And seiþ þat "þi wikked wille
    Schal worche þe ful wo.   68
Þou leuest not in þe Mes
Þat euer God þer in is;
ffor þi lyking is þe les
    And loren artou so,   72

And al þi careful kynde
Þat euer bicom of his strende.
Men schal in baret þe bynde
    And bete þe ful blo;   76
Whon þou schalt of þis world wende,
Þou schalt be tauȝt to þe fende
And euermore wiþouten ende
    In-to þe pyne go."   80

Þe Jeuȝ bigon him to greue:
[Jew]   "Þat wol I apertly preue
Boþe of Adam and Eue,
    Of hem we weore alle i-wrouht.   84
And I dar wage wiþ þe
Tonnes of wyn þre

---

64. Emending *wolde*, "(earthly) realm," to *molde*, "world," suggested by Horstmann, seems unnecessary.

69-70. "You do not believe in the mass, that God is ever therein"; i.e. the Jew does not accept the sacrament of communion or the doctrine of transubstantiation.

73-4. "and all your sorrowful race (*careful kynde:* the Jewish people) that have ever come from its strain"

85-96. By demonstrating that Jesus is at his beck and call, the Jew will be proving his claim that the Christian God is not all-powerful.

86. "three tuns (casks) of wine"—just the sort of wager one would expect from university students

Þat I schal lete þe him se
    Þou seist þat þe bouht, 88
Boþe þe vuel and þe gode,
Hou he was don on þe Roode,
And alle þat bi him stoode
    Whon he to deþe was brouht. 92
So const þou not do
ffor al þi clergye þerto;
As haue I reste oþer ro,
    Þi reson is nouȝt." 96

Þe cristen mon mildely gon malt:
[Christian] "I telle þe, truwaunt fortalt,
Men schal in prison þe palt
    And putte þe to pyne; 100
But ȝif þou lete me him se
Þat for vs dyede on þe tre,
Seþþe þe maystrie ȝeue I þe,
    To þe and alle þyne. 104
Loke þow holde þat we say;
To-morwe, set we þat day,
We schal wende on vr way
    To winne vs þe wyne. 108
Þe mon þat fayles of his fare,
Al loren is his lare;
He may droupe and dare
    Þat schal his trouþe tyne." 112

Þus þei woke al þe niht
Til on þe morwen at day-liht
Þe cristene mon ros riht
    And radly gon say 116
His matyns in þe mornyng;
Seþþe his masse gon he syng;
He þonked vr lord in alle þing
    As he þat moste may. 120
Soone þei metten, as þei miht.
[Jew] "Haue i-don," he seide, "artou diht
ffor to holde þat þou hiht?

Þis is vr day   124
Oþer a nay or a ȝa;
Soone tel þou me swa."
Him grauntes for to ga
And went on heore way.   128

Þe cristen mon seide son,
Whon his masse was don,
[Christian]   "I wol take God me vppon
And bere him wiþ me   132
Boþe in lond and in leode —
Al þe lasse is my dred;
Þe mon þat to Him takeþ hede,
Þe better he may be.   136
Þer nis non enemy in helle,
Non so fers ne so felle,
And he here of vre lord telle
Þat on is in þre;   140
ffor al þe gold in þe grounde
He wolde not byde him a stounde
Þat he nolde freschly founde
And awey fle."   144

fforþ heo wenten on þe ffeld
To an hul þei biheold;
Þe eorþe cleuet as a scheld
On þe grounde grene.   148
Sone fond þei a stih;
Þei went þeron radly;
Þe cristene mon hedde ferly

131-3. These enigmatic lines are explained later when the Christian reveals that he is "carrying God with him" in the form of the mass wafer.

139. "if he were to hear of our Lord"

147-8. The passing of travellers into the Other World through an opening in a hill is a common feature in romances stemming from Celtic tradition; cf. works such as *Sir Orfeo*, *Thomas of Erceldoun*, and Marie de France's *Yonec*, and see H.R. Patch, *The Other World* (1950), esp. pp. 46-59, 231-319.

What hit mihte mene. 152
After þat stiȝ lay a strete
Clene i-pauet wiþ grete.
Þei fond a maner þat was meete
    Wiþ murþes ful schene, 156
Wel coruen and wrouht,
Wiþ halles heiȝes vppon loft.
To a place weore þei brouht
    As paradys þe clene. 160

Þer was foulene song,
Muche murþes among:
Hose lenge wolde long,
    fful luitel him þouht. 164
On vche a syde of þe halle,
Pourpul, pelure and palle;
Wyndouwes i þe walle
    Was wonderli i-wrouht. 168
Þer was dosers on þe dees:
Hose þe cheef wolde ches,
Þat neuere ricchere wes
    In no sale souht. 172
Boþe þe mot and þe molde
Schon al on red golde.
Þe cristen mon hedde ferli of þat folde
    Þat þider was brouȝt. 176

Þer was erbes growen grene,
Spices springynge bitwene;

---

161. As Patch points out (pp. 54–5), birds and their songs are often significant in Other World adventures.
163–4. "Whoever would linger there for long would think it but a short while"; Thomas of Erceldoun believes he has been in the Other World no more than three days when in fact it has been more than three years; see Patch, p. 58 and p. 232.
166. cf. the *Corpus Christi Carol* l. 6 (*Index* 1132)
167. *i*: "in"; cf. also l. 307; cf. *o*: "on" in l. 188 and l. 272.
170–2. "Whoever would choose the best of them would find none better in any hall."
173. *þe mot . . . þe molde*: i.e., the castle and its grounds
178. cf. *Pearl* l. 35.

Such hedde I non sene,
    ffor soþe, as I say.   180
Þe þrestel song ful schille,
He newed notes at his wille
ffeire ffloures to fille,
    ffeire in þat ffey.   184
And al þe rounde table good,
Hou Arthur in eorþe 30d,
Sum sat and sum stod
    O þe grounde grey;   188
Hit was a wonderful siht!
. . . .
As þei weore quik men diht,
    To seo hou þey play.   192

Þe Jew3 sone in þat tyde
He spak þer a word of pryde:
Hose wol lenge and abyde
    May lusten and lere.   196
Til a nonnerie þei came
But I knowe not þe name;
Per was mony a derworþ dame
    In dyapre dere,   200
Squi3ers in vch a syde,
In þe wones so wyde:
Heer schul we lenge and abyde,
    Auntres to heere.   204
Penne swiþe spekeþ he

179–80. The narrator speaks as if he too were present.

181–4. These lines suggest that the singing of the thrush assists in the blossoming of the flowers, an idea also suggested in the opening verses of the *Thrush and Nightingale*.

183–92. Cf. Arthurian legends concerning Avalon; ll. 187–8 especially recall the catalogue of the "taken" in *Sir Orfeo*, ll. 387–404.

186. The verse appears to be defective but seems to mean, "as it was when Arthur trode the earth."

190. This verse is lacking in the ms.

191. "They were arrayed as if they were alive."

205. *he*: i.e., the Jew

Til a ladi so fre
And biddeþ þat he welcome be,
    Sire Water, my feere.   208

Þer was bordes i-cloþed clene
Wiþ schire cloþes and schene.
Seþþe awasschen, I weene,
    And wente to þe sete.   212
Riche metes was forþ brouht
To alle men þat good þouht;
Þe cristen mon wolde nouht
    Drynke nor ete.   216
Þer was wyn ful clere
In mony a feir maseere,
And oþer drynkes þat weore dere
    In couþes ful gret.   220
Siþþe was schewed hem bi
Murþe and munstralsy,
And preyed hem do gladly
    Wiþ rial rehet.   224

By þe bordes vp þei stode
Or þei forþere ʒode;
So weore þei war of a Rode
    fful raþe, as I rede,   228
And a bodi þer vppon
Þat woundes hedde mony on.
Bi him stod Marie and Jon,
    Wepynde good spede;   232
Oþur apostles of prys,
Þoul and peter þe wys,

215–6. The Christian, like other venturers into the realm of faerie (cf. *Thomas of Erceldoun* ll. 177–92), wisely refrains from eating; there is surely meant to be a contrast, too, between those who sup with the devil and those who partake of God's supper, represented by the mass wafer.
217–20. Remarkable cups and drinking vessels often appear in other-worldly adventures.

And seint Jon þe baptys,
   Was douhti of dede.   236
Whon he was schewed to þe siht,
Boþe of leom and of liht,
Þe mon þat most was of miht
   His woundes gon blede.   240

   Þe Jeuȝ sone seide he,
[Jew]   "Holden is þat I hihte þe."
[Christian] Þe toþer seide, "Þat schal I se,
   Certeynly, ful sone."   244
Þe cristen mon hedde a derworþ þinge
On his bodi, he gon hit brynge
Þat a prest schulde wiþ synge
   Whon masse schulde be don.   248
[Christian] "Ȝif þou be God so fre
Þat for me diȝed on þe tre,
Here þi sone mai þou se,"
   And heold him a-bouen.   252
Whon he was schewed to þe siht
He barst þe buyldynge so briht;
Boþe was derk as þe niht —
   Heore sonne and heore mone.   256

---

232. *Wepynde good spede*: "weeping openly"

236. "who was doughty of deeds," a romance cliché applied to John the Baptist; his presence at the crucifixion is indeed curious, possibly providing a clue to the false-ness of the scene.

242. "Held (i.e., fulfilled) is that which I promised you"; the Jew is claiming to have won the wager.

245-8. The Christian's *derworþ þinge* is finally identified in ll. 247-8 as the consecrated host.

249-51. It isn't clear whether the Christian's speech is addressed to the figure on the cross or to the mass wafer he is holding before him (l. 252).

253-8. The demonic spell is immediately shattered through the power of the true God. This dramatic return to ordinary reality and to their original location (ll. 271-2) parallels events in works such as *Pearl*, some of the grail romances, and the *Thomas the Rhymer* poems.

256. Is "sun" an error for "stars"? or is the meaning, "One moment there was sunshine, then only the light of the moon"? Usually the brightness in the Other World stems from unnatural sources, which have here been extinguished.

Al þe gere þat was gay
Was þenne i-wasted away.
Þe cristene mon gon say,

[Christian]   "Beon þeos þi godes here?"   260
Þe Jeuh onswerde him wiþ nay
And ofte merci gon him pray.

[Jew]   "I wol leue my lay
And on þi lore lere.   264
Sore I doute me of dred
I haue i-lost my wed;
Þo þat are forþ fled
Was fendes in feere;   268
Non good but al ille."
No more he tented hem tille.
Heo þo stoden o þe hulle
Þer þey furst were.   272

Þus he ȝeldes him ȝare
Al for his welfare.

[Jew]   He seide, "Of blisse I haue be bare
Seþþen I was furst born.   276
Now knowe I wel þat hit mai be
Þat o-fold God is in þre,
Whuch þat þou brouȝt wiþ þe
Þis day at morn.   280
He is vre heuene kyng,
Makere of all þyng,
And schop þe fruit for-to spryng,
Boþe curnel and corn."   284
Þus he rapes of his res,

---

272. þer *corrected in ms from* þei

---

268. *fendes in feere*: "a company of fiends"; a common phrase; cf. *Thrush and Nightingale*, l. 18.
285. "Thus he alters his course . . ."

To vre God he him ches,
Let al his luþernes,
    Was poynt to be lorn.   288

Seþþe þei wente to þe cite,
Acordet as þei scholde be;
Who was payed bote he
    And eiþer of oþer.   292
He þonked God his swete sonde
Þat he hedde brouȝt out of bonde,
Wel i-wonne to his honde
    Blyþely his broþer.   296
Mete and drynke þei hedde at wille,
Wiþouten grucchyng or grille,
In trouþe tenten þei þer tille
    And lafte al þat oþer.   300
Þe mon þat haþ synne i-wrouȝt
And siþen repentes him ouȝt
God is apayed þat vs bouȝt —
    Leeue we non oþer.   304

What was þe monnes nome i-lyk
But Sir Water of Berewyk.
He was wonynge i þe ryk
    At Roome was called.   308
Þe pope ȝaf him pouste
Þat mony mon miht se,

---

288. i.e., "(he who) was nearly lost"

293–6. Apparently the Jew is thanking God for His messenger (i.e., the Christian), who has brought the Jew out of his bondage and has become his brother in the Christian faith.

301–4. The basis of this doctrine rests in such gospel parables as the Prodigal Son (Luke 15:11–32) and the Lost Sheep (Luke 15:4–7).

306. Sir Walter of Berwick has not been positively identified, although he was undoubtedly an historical personage. Clearly the poem is meant to be highly complimentary to him, just as the *O&N* is to Nicholas of Guildford.

Penitauncer for to be
    Of ȝonge and of olde, 312

Seþþe to soyle and to schriue
Boþe to mon and to wyue,
Eke to mende heore lyue
    And to þe trouþe holde. 316
Penne tok þei þe Jeuȝ,
Anon cristend hym neuȝ;
Pus to vre God he hym kneuȝ
    And ȝeply him ȝolde. 320

---

313. to *ms*: two
316–8. *These three verses are written as two in the ms, the scribe having mistakenly incorporated* þenne tok *into l. 316 and* þei þe Jeuȝ *into l. 318.*

---

311. *penitauncer*: a penancer or penitentiary is a priest appointed to hear confession and impose penance, duties described in ll. 313–6. The Christian's appointment to this position is consistent with his having received the Jew's confession in the poem.
319–20. "And thus he came to know our God, and eagerly yielded himself to Him."

A Dialogue between the Part Sensitive
and the Part Intellective

Several works in Middle English reflect the medieval tradition of the *psychomachia*, the struggle for domination among the various faculties of the human soul or psyche. The fragmentary *Conflict of Wit and Will* (*Index* *3783.5; see B. Dickins, *Leeds Texts and Monographs*, 4) is one of the most explicit examples in Middle English of the *psychomachia*, and many of the Body and Soul poems are related to that tradition in a more general way; prose treatises such as the *Vices and Virtues* (EETS 89) and Chaucer's *Tale of Melibee* reflect aspects of this tradition as well. This late Middle English dialogue between the *Part Sensitive and Part Intellective* is also a variety of the *psychomachia* debate in which separate aspects of the psyche give voice to their contrasting beliefs; the opponents represent the human faculties variously described in medieval literature as Reason and Desire, Wit and Will, or the Intellect and the Appetite, two of the three or four distinctive faculties that combine to make up the human soul.

The *Part Sensitive and Part Intellective* is not an especially distinguished piece; no real conflict or dramatic force is created by the speakers' exchanges of views, and the alternating speeches are not framed at the beginning or the end. But the poem's didactic intention, with its emphasis on the theme of the vanity of human wishes, stemming from Ecclesiastes 1:2, is supposed to be taken to heart. The earthly pleasures and successes enumerated by the Part Sensitive, which comprehend a wide range of human desires, may be loosely based on Ecclesiastes 2:4–10, a passage also demonstrating that the joys of the world are worthless. The poem reflects the aureate language which came into vogue very late in the Middle English period, and it also bears some relationship to the morality play tradition. The *Part Sensitive and Part Intellective* is recorded in British Library MS Royal 18 D ii.

---

1) Base Text: Brit. Lib. Royal 18 D ii, fols. 195v–197v

2) Other mss: none

3) Printed Text: E. Flügel, *Anglia* 14 (1892), 473–6

4) *Index of Middle English Verse* 3482

[*Dialogue between the Part Sensitive and the Part Intellective*]

[S]   "The sermountynge pleasure, who can expresse,
        Whiche is in armony of songe, & the swetnes;
        All pensyuenes it puttithe away
        And withe myrthe and solas dryuethe furthe the day."   4

[I]   "On suche momentary pleasure yf thou sett thy mynde,
        The Joy that is euyrlastinge thou may neuer fynde;
        Joy here and in heuyn thou canst not optayne:
        "*Vanitas vanitatum*, all that is but vayne."   8

[S]   "Of all erthly substance better is none
        Then syluer, golde, and precius stone;

---

1. The rubrics "The parte sensatyue" and "The parte intellectyue" precede each of their speeches throughout the ms text.
1–4. This lyrical opening, in its praise of song and the power of song to banish "pensiveness," seems to anticipate an attitude especially common in the Renaissance (cf., for example, Milton's "L'Allegro" ll. 135 ff).
7. Earthly joy and heavenly joy, according to this view, are mutually exclusive.
8. Elliptical references to well-known passages of scripture (here to Ecclesiastes 1:2) are fairly common; cf. *P3A* 639 ff.
9–12. Cf. Eccles. 2:8

For he that hathe haboundaunce of suche treasure,
In this worlde can want non of his pleasure." 12

[I]   "*Vanitas vanitatum*, beholde and see,
In worldly gyftis is mutabilite;
Gyftis of grace gett the,
For they be of suerte; 16
Erthly thingis be fletynge and vanite,
And as transitory they passe:
Vanitas vanitatum, et omnia vanitas."

[S]   "Riche apparell, costly and precius, 20
Makithe a man lusty, cumly, and gloryus;
Vestueris of estate wrought preciusly
Causithe men to be honowrede & muche sett by."

[I]   "In suche apparell yf thou sett thyne affeccioun, 24
In thy soule it will cause synfull infexioun;
It will not excuse the, I tell the playne,
Vanitas vanitatum, all this is but vayne."

[S]   "To walke in gardyngges all garnysshede with floures, 28
What pleasure is it bycause of the swete odowres;
And in the arburis to here the byrdis synge
Whiche to mans hart grete comforth dothe brynge."

[I]   "For the soule thou shalt fynde more quyetnes 32
Of repentaunce to walke in the wilderness;
Amonge thornes of aduersite yf thou take payne,

13-8. This concept of earthly mutability, in contrast to heavenly permanence, so fre-
quently encountered in morality plays and in Renaissance literature, probably stems
from Matthew 6:19-20; for a vivid visual portrayal of the mutability of worldly treas-
ures, see Bosch's painting "Death and the Miser."

20-4. The Body and Soul poems and mortality lyrics frequently call this point of view
into question (cf. *In a pestri*, l. 34).

22. *Vestueris of estate*: i.e., clothing indicative of high social rank

28-31. Similar sentiments are reflected in the opening verses of poems such as the *Parliament
of Birds* in this volume, and Chaucer's *Legend of Good Women*.

> To swete flowres of paciens thou maist attayne;
> *Vanitas vanitatum*, all other is but vayne." 36

[S] "Highe wisdome and prudens is to me lent,
>   My reason rewlithe all thynge after myne entent;
>   All other to be folis, myne opynyon dothe say,
>   Therfore to my pleasure they shall obey." 40

[I] "If in witt and reason thou other excell,
>   To the pleasure of God ordure it well;
>   For accompte thou must gyue, I tell the playne,
>   *Vanitas vanitatum*, all is but vayne." 44

[S] "I passe all other and am principall
>   In fauoure and frendship of men terrestriall;
>   By my wysdome I haue goten on euery syde
>   Faithfull frendis whiche withe me will abyde." 48

[I] "Frendis be but lent the, vse them wysly;
>   As God will inclyne them, trust it surely,
>   So shalt thou haue them in loue and disdayne:
>   *Vanitas vanitatum*, all that is but vayne." 52

[S] "God and Nature to me most frendly be,
>   For right gracius ysshew they haue sent me,
>   Whiche ar inclynede to vertu and grace,
>   Nedis must greate comfort my hart embrace." 56

[I] "If suche gracis of God towarde the rebownde,
>   To his bounteus goodnes thou art the more bounde;

---

38. "My reason ruleth all things according to my desire"; i.e. desire is ruling over reason.
39. "Any other course would be foolish, in my opinion."
40. *they* refers to wisdom, prudence, and reason.
41-3. Probably a reference to the parable of the talents (Matt. 25:14-30)
43. Cf. Death's message in *Everyman* that God requires a reckoning from every person.
49. This point is also made in *Everyman*.
54. *ysshew*: "issue"; i.e., "off-spring"

Yet sett not in them to muche thyne affexion
For God may take them awey for they correccion;   60
Corporall lyf here is not certayne:
Vanitas Vanitatum, all that is but vayne."

[S]   "I haue neighboures kynde and benyuolent,
And my seruauntes to me be fast and obedient;   64
What-so-euyr I commaunde or call,
It is accomplisshede furth with all."

[I]   "To presume of this is not moste profitable;
Kyndenes amonge neighboures is not allways stabill,   68
And yf seruauntes to the be obedient and kynde,
It cummythe of God, therfore sett not thy mynde
To muche on them, but thy wysdome refrayne:
Vanitas vanitatum, all that is but vayne."   72

[S]   "Of possessiones a greate lorde am I,
Honourede and regardede moste specially;
Of erthly thynges I haue haboundaunce,
To my joy and comfort & hartis pleasaunce."   76

[I]   "In erthly thynges there is no surete,
For vnstabill and transitory they be;
But for a tyme to the they ar lent,
To forsake them thou must be content,   80
For here thou may not allway remayne:
Vanitas vanitatum, all that is but vayne."

[S]   "I am yonge, lusty, and of high corage,

59-60. For this commonplace attitude compare, for example, the Book of Job, the gourd
    episode in *Patience* (from the Book of Jonah), and Chaucer's *Clerk's Tale*.
69-70. The Part Intellective firmly denies giving credit to the Part Sensitive for his worldly
    successes; if one achieves such successes, he argues, they come from God.
73. The character of the Part Sensitive seems to shift from being an aristocrat, as here
    (l. 73), to a royal prince (ll. 83-4), and finally to a successful merchant (ll. 121-4);
    clearly, the didactic purposes of the poem are outweighing consistency or literal plau-
    sibility.

Desscendid of ryall blode & noble parentage;   84
If in erthe ther can be any blis,
I haue it as I wolde or can wyshe."

[I]   "If in erthe ye haue suche felicite,
Put not thy mynde on it for it hath no surete;   88
In no wyse it can not agree,
In this worlde here to haue prosperite
And the joyes of heuyn afterwarde optayne:
Vanitas vanitatum, all that is but vayne."   92

[S]   "My causes must prosper an nedis procede,
For I haue assuride councell to helpe in nede;
On there sentence my mynde shall rest,
For they will councell me for the best."   96

[I]   "For all thy councell, for thy self take care;
In councell may be confusyon, therfore beware;
Amonge councell myche dissymylynge is
And of thy purpos thou mayst mys;   100
Many one of councell be not playne:
Vanitas vanitatum, all that is bot vayne."

[S]   "Myne enemys agaynst me may not preuayle,
So grete is my strenght them to assaile;   104
By strength of men and treasure of golde
I can subdew myne enemes, be they neuyr so bolde."

[I]   "To presume of it I compt it foly,
For of God commyth tryumphe and victory;   108

---

97. take *added*

89-91. This view may indirectly reflect scriptures such as Mark 10:21-5.

He that in strenght or riches puttithe his trust,
Many tymes, for all that, lyethe in the dust;
All erthly pouer is vncertayne:
Vanitas vanitatum, all that is bot vayne."   112

[S]   "Curyusly and connyngly I can kerue,
And withe assurede maner at the table serue,
So that no thinge shall pas me
Bot it shall haue his formall properte."   116

[I]   "Withoute excersyse and contenaunce
Suche connynge fallithe from remembraunce;
To know thy self is a connynge souerayne:
Vanitas vanitatum, all that is but vayne."   120

[S]   "My ship is fraught withe marchandyse,
Of substanciall riches and grete price;
When it is arryuede, yf I do my dever,
Doutles I am made a man for euyr."   124

[I]   "If fortune be fauourable, extoll not thy mynde;
A sodeyne pyrry or a great blast of wynde
By myschaunce may all confounde;
Where is thy goode when they ship is drowned?   128
It bootis not afterwarde to complayne:
Vanitas vanitatum, all that is but vayne."

[S]   "I floure in youthe, delyght, and pleasure,
To fede all my fantasys I want no treasure;   132

113–4. Cf. Chaucer's Squire *CT* I 99–100.

117–9. The Part Intellective, in response to the Part Sensitive's claim of having mastered the social graces, points out that such knowledge is fleeting and superficial and that knowledge of one's inner self is wisdom of a far superior kind.

121. The characterization of the Part Sensitive here shifts to that of a merchant, another conventional figure of worldliness.

124. *made a man*: i.e., "a made man"

126. *sodeyne pyrry*: "a sudden squall"

131–4. The Part Sensitive now embodies characteristics which reflect typical portraits of Youth; cf. *P3A* 246–56.

I synge and daunce, I reuell and play,
I am so louede of ladyes I nede not to pray."

[I] "Suche corporall pleasure is bot momentary,
ffastinge and prayer for thy soule more necessary; 136
All worldely pleasures vanysshethe away,
To-day a man in golde, to-morow closyde in clay;
Repres vice, let vertu optayne:
Vanitas vanitatum, all that is but vayne."   140

[S] "So greate is my pusiaunce, so muche is my myght,
That I am moste dredfull to euery wight.
Euery man afforsyth to content me and please,
Who that dothe contrary shall not leue in ease." 144

[I] "Cast thy sight vpwarde and thou shall see
One myghtier than thou a thousande degree;
Compare thy myght to his and thy myght is none;
Drede hym that is moste myghty whan thy myght is gone; 148
Loue and dreade hym and in heuyn thou shalt reigne:
When all other thynge is vanite, that is not vayne."

Finis

146-7. Man's might, when compared to God's, is of course completely inconsequential;
 cf. the description in *St. Erkenwald*, ll. 163-7, in which the collective might of mankind
 is said to be less than that of God's finger.

The Debate between Mercy and Righteousness

The Debate between Mercy and Righteousness belongs to the extensive body of penitential literature which flourished in England particularly in the fourteenth and fifteenth centuries, and the poet's specific purpose is to address the dangers implicit in the sin of wanhope. He does this by depicting a confrontation between the personification of Righteousness, a despairing sinner who refuses to believe that he can atone for his sinful deeds, and the personification of Mercy, who espouses the view that God's forgiveness will be granted to all who sincerely seek it and are willing to undergo penance. Throughout much of the poem Righteousness clings to his belief that he must receive a punishment appropriate to his sins; finally, however, he accepts the fact that God's mercy may extend even to such a sinner as he. The conflict in the poem is essentially between the New Testament code of compassion and forgiveness and the Old Testament code of retribution — the conflict between Church and Synagogue found elsewhere in the Middle English debate tradition in poems such as the *Disputation Between a Christian and a Jew* and the *Disputation Between Child Jesus and the Masters of the Laws of the Jews*. This debate between the personified figures of Mercy and Righteousness is also related to the conflict between the Four Daughters of God, in which Mercy and Peace are set in opposition to Truth and Righteousness, a concept derived from Psalm 84:11 (Vulgate).

Although *Mercy and Righteousness* may not seem to us as compelling or as artful as some other poems in the Middle English debate tradition, its popularity in the later Middle Ages is attested by the poem's four surviving manuscript texts. These texts are notable for their considerable divergences, and it is difficult to determine how each relates to the others. These divergences, however, make the four versions of *Mercy and Righteousness* of particular interest for the study of the transmission and dissemination of manuscript texts in the later Middle Ages. (For a study of the texts in relationship to the Cowfold text, see Joyce Bazire, "Mercy and Justice," *Neuphilologische Mitteilungen* 83 [1982], 178–9). It is also worth noting that the Thornton text of *Mercy and Righteousness* is incorporated into a sequence of poems which have God's mercy as their common focus. In this sequence *Mercy and Righteousness* occupies the penultimate position, with "Mercy passeth all things" (*Index* 583) occupying the climactic position. In form and content, *Mercy and Righteousness* is similar to the Middle English debates between *Meed and Much Thanks* and *Nurture and Kind*. Moreover, *Mercy and Righteousness* and *Nurture and Kind* employ the same stanzaic form and rhyme scheme, as well as similar sets of paired refrains.

---

1)   Base Text: Lambeth MS 853, pp. 66–73

2)   Other mss: British Library Addit. MS 31042 (Thornton MS), fols. 122v–123r
Nat. Lib. of Wales MS Porkington 10 (Harlech 10), fols. 203r–207v
Cowfold Parish Account Book (West Sussex Public Record Office), fols. 18r–19v

3)   Printed Texts: F. J. Furnivall, EETS 24 (1867), 95–100 (Lambeth)
K. Brunner, *Archiv* 132 (1914), 319–21 (Thornton)
A. Kurvinen, *NM* 73 (1972), 181–91 (Porkington)
J. Bazire, *NM* 83 (1982), 178–91 (Cowfold)

4)   *Index of Middle English Verse* 560

Merci Passith Riȝtwisnes

Bi a forest as y gan walke
With-out a paleys in a leye,

1–3. The poem begins with the conventional *chanson d'aventure* opening: "By a forest as I did walk, outside a palisaded enclosure in a meadow, I heard . . . ."

I herde two men togidre talke,
I þouȝte to wite what þei wolde seie.   4
Þat oon stood in a doolful aray,
Hise deedli synnis he gan to defie,

[Right.]   "Alas," he seide, "me dreediþ to-day
Þat riȝt wole forþ & no mercye."   8

Þanne answeride merci with sobir cheer,
[Mercy]   "Man, me þinkiþ þi witt is bare;
If þou wolt y schal þee leer,
Þee nediþ not to moorne so sare.   12
I rede þee to foonde to ameende þi fare;
Go euery day & heere a messe
And schryue þee cleene & haue noo care,
For mercy passiþ riȝtwisnes."   16

Þanne seide þe synner with angri mood,
[Right.]   "Man, me þenkist þou doost raue;
I woot weel þou canst no good,
Þou barist neuere staat but as a knawe.   20
As y deserue so schal y haue,
Weel bittirli y schal a-bie;
I knowe noon helpe þat me schulde haue,
But þat riȝt schal forþ and no mercie."   24

Þanne seide mercye meeke & mylde,
[Mercy]   "If þou wolt fro þi synnes drawe,
Þouȝ þou speke þese wordis wilde,
To helpe þee ȝit I wolde be fawe.   28

---

5. *doolful aray*: "sorrowful condition"
6. *defie*: "declare"
8. "that justice will prevail, with no mercy"
10–16. The reclamation of the despairing soul must begin with the knowledge of God's
grace, the initial stage in regaining one's faith.
20. "You've never held any rank but that of a servant."
25. Note the reasonable and only mildly reproving tone adopted by Mercy. Mercy's
tactics throughout the poem bring to mind the Pearl-maiden's instructing of the nar-
rator in *Pearl*.

                Loue weel God, þat is my sawe,
                Repente þee blyue of al þi mys;
                Almyȝti God is ouer þe lawe,
                His merci þassiþ his riȝtwisnes."   32

[Right.]   ["Tell," quod Ryȝt, "þat I nevyr knewe,
                Thow wold speke fayne, yf þou had lyȝte.
                God hathe euyr mor byn trewe,
                For he dede neuyr but þat was ryȝte,   36
                And I have byn a synfull wyȝte;
                Therfor I drede when I schall dy,
                Lest he þat is so full of myȝte
                Wyll don ryȝt and no mercy."   40

[Mercy]   Mercy lokod in his face;
                He sayd, "Ryȝt, þou art a dolfull goste;
                Thow hast myche wytt wyttouttyn grace,
                But ȝette be meke & leyfe thy boste;   44
                For God ys gracyus, full well þou wost,
                He boȝt vs all to dwell in blys.
                Thorow prayer of þe Holly Goste,
                His mercy passythe ryȝttusnys."   48

[Right.]   "Iwyse," quod Ryȝt, "I may no mor.
                Sum tyme I wend to have schowyd my face;
                Wherto schuld I nowe lern thy lor,
                That says I am wyttouttyn grace?   52
                Alas, þis is a sylly case

33–64. *These verses, which are missing from the Lambeth text, have been supplied from the Porkington MS.*
34. speke *supplied*

31–2. Cf. *Pearl* 665–70.
34. *lyȝte*: i.e., "understanding" (illumination)
51–4. Puzzling lines; perhaps the text is flawed, but it could be that they reflect Right-
    eousness's misunderstanding of Mercy.

That I myȝt neuyr grace by;
I am adred to com in þat place
Ther ryȝt schall forthe & no mercy."   56

[Mercy]   "Nowe myȝtty God," quod Mercy tho,
"Thow trowyst no resson þat I þe say.
Of thy beleue, I rede þe, whoo,
And fond to serfe thy God to pay;   60
Beseche our Lady, þat best may,
To be thy helpe to rede & wyse.
My soule for thyn þen dar I lay
That mercy schall pase ryȝttusnis."]   64

[Right.]   "Seie me," quod þe synner, "þou foonued clerk.
Þou coudist neuere rede in no spel;
I wrouȝte wilfulli neuere good werk;
What riȝt haue y in heuen to dwelle?   68
I haue deserued to go to helle,
And þerfore ofte sore sike y;
My wickid dedis wole me quelle,
Pere riȝt schal forþ and no mercye."   72

[Mercy]   Merci seide, "Þou canst no good.
God schewiþ þee kyndenes many foolde,

---

61. Beseche *ms*: Besche
63. lay *ms*: ay

---

55. *þat place*: "that place" where the Last Judgment will occur
56. *Ther*: "where"
59. *whoo*: "stop" or "cease"
60. "and try to serve (in a manner) pleasing to God"
61-2. Mercy counsels Righteousness to pray to the Virgin, in the hope that she will serve as intercessor for sinful man.
63. The line reflects Mercy's absolute confidence in God's compassion for reformed sinners.
65. *foonued clerk*: "foolish clerk"; Mercy is viewed by Righteousness as an ignorant cleric.
66. I.e., "you can't even read a book"; the Lambeth ms deviates from the other three mss which read: "þow canst noþer rede nor spelle" (Cowfold ms).

For þee & me he schedde his blood
And suffride woundis bittir & colde.   76
His fair body to þe iewis was solde
To bie oure synful soulis to blis;
Þi soule is his, y myȝt be bolde,
His merci passiþ his ryȝtwisnes."   80

[Right.]   "Forsoþe," quod þe synner, "þat leue y weel
Þat he is boþe good & kynde
And þerto trewer þan ony steel;
Þat he loueþ truþe weel schal y fynde.   84
How myȝt God me of care vnbinde,
Siþen God loueþ trouþe so verrili?
Do way, mercy, þou spillist myche winde,
For riȝt schal forþ & no mercy."   88

[Mercy]   Merci seide, "Woldist þou God knowe,
And wiþ good entent mercy calle,
And to Him meekeli þee abowe,
Þan schal neuere myscheef in þee falle.   92
Þouȝ þou haddist do þe synnis alle,
And þou crie mercy for al þi mys,
And with good herte on him to calle,
Þan wole his mercy passe riȝtwisnes."   96

---

87. "Go away, Mercy, you're full of hot air."
91. "and meekly humble yourself to Him"; *abowe*: "bow"
93-6. The sinner must be genuinely contrite to receive God's mercy.
94. *And*: "if"; *mys*: "misdeeds"
96. The following unique stanza occurs at this point in the Porkington text:

> Yfe ȝe woll her þis songe to ennde,
> Howe they endyde longe in fere,
> I schall yowe tell, or I wende,
> Howe mercy ys all & hase no pere.
> Of Goddys grace, I rede yowe, lere;
> The ner þe ende þe sonnge ys beste;
> Geyfe me drenke, & ȝe schall her.
> Her ys a fette, nowe wyll I reste.

Although "minstrel calls" of this sort are not unusual in romances and other popular texts (cf. *WW* 216-7, 366-7), *MR* seems an unlikely text in which to encounter such sentiments.

[Right.]   "What," quod þe synner, "Y trowe þou raue!
              Canst þou neuere of þi pletinge blynne?
              Pe deuel bad me neuere mercy craue,
              And he can more clergie þan al þi kynne;   100
              And he him-silf is ful of synne,
              And ʒit wole he neuere mercy crie:
              I coueite neuere heuen to wynne
              While riʒt schal forþ & no mercie."   104

[Mercy]   Merci seide, "Y preue bi skile
              Witt is nouʒt worþ but grace be souʒt;
              Pe deuel haþ clergie & witt at wille,
              And euere he settiþ it foule at nouʒt: 108
              He fil in wanhope as him neuere rouʒte,
              Poruʒ pride in heuen he loste his blis;
              Hadde he oonys grace bisouʒte,
              Merci hadde passid riʒtwijsnes."   112

[Right.]   Whanne þe synner herd þis he siʒed sore,
              With rewful cheer greet dool he made,
              And seide, "Of þee wole y lerne more;
              Pan is the deuel fals and bad,   116

---

98. *pletinge*: "pleading," a term commonly applied to a legal debate or lawsuit; cf. *O & N* 12.
100. "And he knows more theological doctrine than all your kind."
106–9. "Knowledge is worthless unless grace is obtained; the devil has doctrinal knowledge
    in abundance, yet he considers it worthless: he fell into wanhope like one who no
    longer cares."
109. *Wanhope*. Chaucer's Parson describes wanhope as follows: "*Wanhope* is in two ma-
    neres: the firste wanhope is in the mercy of Crist; that oother is that they thynken
    that they ne myghte nat longe persevere in goodnesse./ The firste wanhope comth
    of that he demeth that he hath synned so greetly and so ofte, and so longe leyn in
    synne, that he shal nat be saued./ Certes, agayns that cursed wanhope sholde he thynke
    that the passion of Jhesu Crist is moore strong for to unbynde than synne is strong
    for to bynde./ Agayns the seconde wanhope he shal thynke that as ofte as he falleth
    he may arise agayn by penitence. And though he never so longe have leyn in synne,
    the mercy of Crist is alwey redy to receiuen hym to mercy" (*Cant. Tales X*, 1070–3).
    The figure of Righteousness in *MR* seems to be experiencing the first of these two
    kinds of wanhope more than the second.
115. Righteousness has now come to accept the potential value of Mercy's instruction.

             For if he myȝte merci haue had,
             A þousand siþis y him defie;
             He may be sory & no-þing glad
             Þat schal haue riȝtwisnes & no mercy."   120

             Mercy biheeld þat semeli goost
[Mercy]   And seide, "Leue broþer, forsake þe feend,
             For he wolde fayn þi soule were lost,
             To dwelle in helle without eend.   124
             Biseche now grace & God wole sende,
             And þou wolt do as y þee wijs,
             And þan þi soule to heuen schal wende,
             Þere merci passiþ riȝtwisnes."   128

[Right.]   "Alas," quod þe synner, "Al my lijf y rue,
             For it is no þing as y wende;
             To serue God y wole be trewe,
             If ony grace he wole me sende.   132
             Of al wickidnes he me defende;
             Þe fals feend, y him defie;
             He wolde no þing þat y dide meende,
             Þat biheet me riȝt & no mercie."   136

[Mercy]   Merci seide, "If þou wolt so,
             Þou myȝt be glad al þi lijf,
             And for þi synne þou maist be woo,
             And to a preest cleene þee schriue,   140
             And take penaunce without strijf,
             Repentynge þee of al þi mys,

---

120. riȝtwisnes *and* mercy *are transposed in the ms*

135–6. "He was not at all concerned with my well-being, he who promised me right-
    eousness and no mercy."
139–44. Mercy instructs Righteousness in the way to spiritual regeneration — through
    contrition, confession, penance, repentance, and a belief in God's infinite forgiveness.

Þan bi þi witt þou maist knowe rijf
Þat merci passiþ riȝtwisnes."   144

[Right.]   "Alas," quod the synner, "Y haue lyued wrong.
           What penaunce were y worþi to haue?
           Þer may no man sette me to strong,
           Þouȝ y were quicke doluen on graue.   148
           A! Almiȝty God, mercy I craue,
           Now lete my flesche my synnis abie;
           Graciose Crist, my soule þou haue,
           For riȝt is nouȝt wiþout mercie."   152

[Mercy]   Mercy seide, "Ful weel þou woost,
           As þou hast often herd sayen,
           What man is founde þat was lost,
           Wiþ him is Crist plesid & fayn.   156
           What nede had Crist to suffre payne
           But for to bie oure soulis to blis?
           Telle me þi lijf heere al playn,
           Þat mercy may passe riȝtwisnes."   160

[Right.]   "My fyue wittis y haue mys-spende
           Þoruȝ pride, enuie, & leccherie;
           To þe ten heestis y haue not tende,
           Þoruȝ slouþe, wraþþe, & glotenie.   164
           In coueitise lyued haue y,
           And neuere dide werkis of mercyes;
           God ȝeue me grace or þat y die,
           Þi merci may passe riȝtwisnes."   168

147–8. "No man might create too great a penance for me, even if I were buried alive
     in my grave."
153–6. Cf. Luke 15:4–7
159. Mercy, in the role of Father Confessor, invites Righteousness to recount his sinful life.
161. *fyue wittis*: the five physical senses of the body, which Righteousness has abused by
     indulging in the Seven Sins, as indicated in ll. 162, 164, and 165.
163. *ten heestis*: "ten behests," the Ten Commandments
166. The importance of doing merciful deeds is stressed; cf. *Als I lay* 61–4.

[Mercy]   Merci ȝaf him penaunce stronge,
And seide, "Man, wolt þou þis take?
Þou muste suffre boþe riȝt and wrong
If þou þi synne wolt forsake;   172
In good praiers þou muste wake,
And neuere wilne to do a-mys;
And for þi sorewe þat þou doost make,
Merci schal passe riȝtwisnes."   176

Þe synner took penaunce wiþ good entent,
And lefte al his wickid synne;
Whanne he hadde leeue, away he went
From alle his freendis, kiþ & kynne.   180
In greet penaunce he putte him inne,
And neuere aftir wilfulli dide mys;
He truste on God heuen to wynne,
Þere mercy passiþ riȝtwijsnes.   184

Almiȝti God, now make us stable,
And ȝeue us grace weel to spede,
And to us alle bee merciable,
And forȝeue us alle oure mysdede.   188
And helpe us, ladi, att oure moost nede,
To þi sone oure soulis þou wys,
And with his mercy fulli us fede,
Þere mercy passiþ riȝtwijsnes. A-M-E-N.   192

169–76. Mercy assigns Righteousness his penance.
185–92. The poet's benediction; there is no return to the opening narrative frame.
188. Matthew 6:12, Luke 11:4
189. Again (cf. ll. 61–2) an appeal to Mary to intercede on behalf of sinful man.

Mede & moche thank:
A Dialogue between a Courtier and a Soldier

The brief debate entitled *Mede & moche thank*, ostensibly a satiric attack on court flatterers, uses the common devices of the *chanson d'aventure* opening, a first-person observer-narrator, and a pair of debaters with antithetical values and personalities — stock character types of the impoverished soldier and the amply rewarded, sycophantic courtier. The poem is concerned with exploring the fundamental motivations which underlie human choices and actions. It may be read on the one hand as a straight-forward denunciation of do-nothing flatterers, but it may also be read as suggesting that, for all their apparent differences, the soldier and the courtier are not really so very different. These two plausible but contrastive interpretations result from the fact that the speeches in the final stanzas may be assigned in various ways (see note to ll. 65–88). Since the manuscript provides no indication of who is speaking, the reader must make this determination strictly on the basis of internal evidence.

Mede & moche thank is recorded in MS Digby 102, a late fourteenth-century miscellany consisting chiefly of poems on political subjects. The poem has the metrical form of a ballade with a refrain, rhyming ababbcbc, and many of its verses alliterate.

---

1) Base Text: Bodl. Lib. MS Digby 102 (Bodl. 1703), fol. 99v

2) Other mss: none

3)   Printed Texts: J. Kail, EETS 124 (1904), 6–9

4)   *Index of Middle English Verse* 1475

Mede & moche thank

In blossemed buske I bode boote,
In ryche array with ryches rank,
ffaire floures vnder foote,
Sauour to myn herte sank;   4
I sawe two buyrnes on a bank,
To here talkyng I tok hede:
That on preysede moche thank,
That other held al with mede.   8

That on a trauaylyng man had ben,
He was but in mene array;
That other clothed in gawdy gren,
Blasande briȝt, embrowdid gay.   12

1–6. The use of alliteration, obviously intentional here at the outset, occurs only in-
    cidentally through the remainder of the poem. Heavy alliteration in the opening stan-
    zas of non-alliterative poems is fairly common (cf. *Jesus and the Masters*).
1. "Through blossoming woods I wandered about"; a typical *chanson d'aventure* opening.
    The poet does not return to this framing device at the end of the poem.
2. The line refers to the beauty of the natural setting, not to the "array" of the speaker.
3–4. In dream-vision poems using the *chanson d'aventure* device, the fragrance of the flow-
    ers contributes to the narrator's drowsiness; but there is nothing here to indicate that
    the debate the narrator overhears actually occurs within a dream.
5. *buryne* (often spelled *burne*) is one of several synonyms for "man" found especially in
    alliterative poems such as *WW* (others include *freke, gome, hathell, renke, segge*, etc.).
6. *Here*: "their"
7. "That one praised 'much thanks' "; i.e. mere words of appreciation, e.g. "many thanks"
8. *mede*: tangible rewards such as pay, gifts, or bribes; the corrupting influence of money
    is vividly rendered in the Lady Meed episode in Passus 2–4 of *Piers Plowman*.
9. *trauaylyng man*: "soldier"
10–12. The *mene array* ("modest garb") of the soldier contrasts sharply with the brightly
    blazing *gawdy gren* ("yellowish-green") apparel of the courtier; the courtier's dress resem-
    bles that of Chaucer's Squire in the Ellesmere MS portrait, whose fashionable green
    coat is "embrouded . . . as it were a meede" (*CT* I 90); cf. also the description of Youth
    in *P3A* 122–3.

[Courtier]   "Loo, felow, chese Y may
                To ryde on palfray or on stede;
                Shewe forth moche thonk, Y the pray,
                Loo, here Y shewe sumwhat of mede."   16

[Soldier]   "Syre, Y see thou hast richesse;
                How thou hit get, whiche is thy fame
                In corage & prowesse,
                After thy dede resceyue thy name,   20
                Other in worshipe or in shame.
                Men wol the deme after thy dede,
                Thy fer trauayle or cochour at hame.
                How serued thou to haue that mede?"   24

[Courtier]   "I plese my lord at bed & bord,
                Þoyʒ Y do but strype a stre,
                And florische fayre my lordis word,
                And fede hem forth with nay & ʒee.   28
                Whan trauaylyng men fare euele on see,
                In fight, in preson, in storme & drede,
                With moche thonk than mery ʒe be,
                And Y wole make me mery with mede!"   32

[Soldier]   "fflateryng is the fendis scoles!

---

13. *Loo*: "Ah" or "Behold," an attention-getting interjection; *chese*: "choose"
14. A *palfray* is a fine riding horse, a *stede* a war horse suitable for use in battle or for jousting; cf. *Als I lay* 35.
15. *shewe forth*: i.e. "explain the virtues of"
17. *Syre*: "Sir" or "sire"; in either case suggesting the soldier's deferential attitude.
18–21. "Men will honor you or blame you according to how you got your riches."
20–3. These sentiments, that one should be judged strictly by his deeds, are common-place; cf., for example, the *Wife of Bath's Tale* (*CT* III 1158 and 1170).
21. *other*: "either"
23. *cochour at hame*: "malingering at home"
26. *þoyʒ*: "though"; *strype a stre*: "strip a straw," i.e., "do nothing but trifles"
27. *florische fayre*: "embellish attractively"
29. *euele*: i.e., "painfully"
30. *drede*: "peril"
33. *fendis scoles*: i.e., "the fiend's method"

ſoure awen werkys preueth ſow nys;
ſe skorne lordes and make hem ſoure foles,
To playe & lawhe at ſoure delys.   36
Do for a lord and he be wys,
Trewe trauayle shal not lese his dede.
To vertuous lord al worship lys;
The trewe seruant is worthy hys mede."   40

[Courtier]   "Say, felowe, what doth the greue
My glosyng, flateryng, play & daunce?
Shulde my souerayn aske the leue
Whom hym list to auaunce?   44
Thou getest the thonke with spere & launce,
Therwith thou myght the clothe & fede;
I, gloser, wil stonde to my chaunce
And mayntene my men al with mede.   48

My flateryng, glosyng, not me harmes;
I gete loue & moche richesse
When wel-faryng men of armes
In fight, in presoun, and distresse.   52
When thou art old & feble, Y gesse,
Who wole the fynde fode or wede?
Lete moche thonk than thy mete dresse,
And Y wole make me mery with mede."   56

[Soldier]   "I likne a gloser in eche weder
To folwe the wynd as doth the fane.

---

34. *awen*: "own"
37-8. "If one works for a lord and he is wise, (then) true labors will not go unrecognized."
40. Cf. I Tim. 5:18 (and Luke 10:7): ". . .the labourer is worthy of his reward"; cf. also the *Summoner's Tale* (*CT* III 1972-3).
41. *what doth*: i.e., "why does"
43. *aske the leue*: "ask your permission"
51-2. Cf. 29-30; here the verb must be supplied.
54. "Who will find you food or clothing?"
55. *thy mete dresse*: "your food prepare"
55-6. Cf. 31-2.
58. *fane*: "weather vane"

3e begeten hony togedere —
To stroy3e that cometh the drane!   60
Me thenkeþ þere wit is wane
To stroi3e the hony and foule it shede.
Gloser hath brought faytour lane
To halle & chambre, to lordes, for mede."   64

[Courtier?]   "Thy wikked speche come fro ferre;
Euel thou spekest, worse dost mene;
Thou woldest euere-more were werre,
ffor profyt & pilage thou myght glene;   68
Cristen blod destroyed clene
And townes brent on a glede.
Thy conscience is ful lene —
Thou noldest not come ther but for mede."   72

[Soldier]   "In wikked lyuer no good counsayle
Is coward of kynde, ny3t & day;
Good lyuere dar fende & assayle,
And hardly in dede brou3t to bay.   76
I wolde thou were brou3t to assay

59–60. "You gather honey together — which the drone (then) comes to destroy"; for a
more elaborate account of drones as symbolic social parasites, cf. *Mum and Sothsegger*,
EETS 199, p. 55, ll. 966 ff.

61. *is wane*: "is gone" (has waned)

62. *shede*: "distribute"

63. *faytour lane*: "impostors' lane"; probably a metaphor, meaning something like "beg-
gars' alley."

65–88. Kail, the only previous editor of the poem, assigned the last four stanzas to the
soldier. Such a reading is entirely defensible, even though it represents a departure
from the regular pattern of alternation followed up to this point (no more than two
stanzas are spoken consecutively by one speaker elsewhere in the poem). However,
it is also conceivable that ll. 65–72 and ll. 81–8 are spoken by the courtier, not the
soldier. Lines 65–72 seem to be a direct response to the soldier's extreme indictment
of the courtier in the previous stanza, and the activities described in ll. 67–70 clearly
apply to one engaged in soldiering. Furthermore, unexpected reversals of this kind
are not unusual in debate poetry, a poetic strategy sometimes referred to as "wrong-
footing" the audience.

65. *come fro ferre*: "goes too far" (?) or "stems from fear" (?)

73. *lyuere*: "liver" (i.e., a wicked living person); cf. 75

77–8. "I think that if you were tested by real need, you would then follow a wise course."

At nede, a wys counseil to rede.
Were thou as hardy as thou art gay,
ȝe were wel worthy to haue good mede.   80

[Courtier?] "Thenketh the not it doth the good,
Whan thou out of thy bed dost swerue?
ȝe clothe ȝow & do on ȝoure hod,
At tyme of day thy mete dost kerue.   84
Why dost thou thy seluen serue?
I trowe thou do it for gret nede,
ffor hunger & cold, elles myghtest thou sterue;
This preueth thou seruest al for mede!"   88

81-8. If the speaker here is the courtier, he is suggesting that the soldier's actions are, at bottom, just as self-serving as his own.
82. *swerue*: i.e., "move"

The Debate between Nurture and Kynd

The Debate between Nurture and Kynd, or nurture and nature, illustrates the medieval truism that a creature's basic nature will eventually surface, regardless of the training or education it has received. The belief that one's inborn traits can never be entirely eradicated was often expressed in proverbs and gnomic tags—"Nature will have its course," "Nature passes Nurture"—and in works such as Boethius' *Consolation*: ". . . alle thynges rejoysen hem of his retornynge ayen to his nature" (Bk. III Meter 2), the *Roman de la Rose* (ll. 14037 ff.), and Chaucer's *Squire's Tale* (V 608–9) and *Manciple's Tale*: ". . . ther may no man embrace / As to destreyne a thyng which that nature / Hath natureely set in a creature" (IX 160–2). In *Nurture and Kynd* the interest lies more in the exemplum involving the cat, the candle, and the mouse than in the debaters' arguments. In this exemplum Nurture invites Kynd to dinner, with the intention of demonstrating the superiority of education by means of his cat, which he has trained to sit at the table holding a lighted candle on its head. But Kynd outsmarts Nurture by arriving at the dinner with a mouse hidden in his glove; when he releases the mouse before the cat, the cat's instincts overcome its training, and all of Nurture's work is undone in a flash. Versions of this fable have been traced back to classical antiquity, including a version attributed to Aesop (see E. Cosquin, *Romania* 40 [1911], 371–430 and 481–531). In some versions of the fable Nature comes to Nurture's dinner with three mice hidden in his sleeve. Upon the release of the first mouse, the cat remains firm, although its eyes betray its interest; upon the release of the second mouse, the cat still maintains its position, but its tail twitches and the candle on its head wavers; but upon release of the third mouse the cat's instincts get the better of it, and it abandons its candle-bearing role to take up the chase.

Although *Nurture and Kynd* is fragmentary at the outset, it is unlikely that many verses have been lost. Judging from the poem's concluding stanza, where there is a return to a first-person narrator, the opening portion of the narrative frame was probably similar to those in *Mede & moche thank* and *Mercy and Righteousness*, poems having much in common with *Nurture and Kynd*. In *Nurture and Kynd*, however, the debaters are actual personifications of the concepts they defend. *Nurture and Kynd* and *Mercy and Righteousness* also employ the same stanzaic form and rhyme scheme, and the two poems have similar kinds of alternating refrains. The debate between *Nurture and Kynd* is preserved only in British Library MS Harley 541, a fifteenth-century miscellany containing poems, songs, prayers, and prose works, in English and in Latin.

---

1)   Base Text: British Library MS Harley 541, fol. 212-3

2)   Other mss: none

3)   Printed Texts: W. L. Braekman and P. S. Macaulay, "The Story of the Cat and the Candle in Middle English Literature," *NM* 70 (1969), 690–702.
                                 V. J. Scattergood, "The Debate Between Nurture and Kynd—An Unpublished Middle English Poem," *Notes & Queries* 17 (1970), 244–6.

4)   *Supplement to the Index of Middle English Verse* 995.4

[The Debate between Nurture and Kynd]

[Nurture]   " . . . .
           Goddis grace is redy bothe erly & late;
           A vertuys man men may oft fynd

---

1. Although the text is initially imperfect, only a few verses appear to be lacking. The missing material no doubt provided a brief narrative frame akin to those in *Mercy and Righteousness* and *Mede & moche thank*, which establish the circumstances of the narrator's overhearing the debaters. The surviving portion of Nurture's speech seems to reflect the view that one's education provides a key to his social standing.

Þat moche worship wynnes in many a place:
I preue þat nurture passis kynd."   4

[Kynd]   "In fayth," said kynd, "I shalle not lye:
To þis mater þou may not appere.
It were fulle hard semyng to the
To make a crab preve lyke a blaundrere,   8
By word, by countenaunce, or oþer by chere.
ffor alle thy helpe and socoure,
Yet þou wille shew sum touch from whens þou come yn a gere:
I preve that kynd passis nurture."   12

[Nurture]   "Now, yn faith," said nurture, "& þou were myn
And were but ij yere old we shuld se game.
I wold make þe by nurture gront as a swyne,
And go on alle iiij as þou were lame,   16
And ete draf and thynk no shame,
And drynk dregges, have þis yn þi mynd,
And nother to know þi sire ne dame:
I preve þat nurture passis kynd."   20

[Kynd]   "ffor sothe," said kynd, "I wil not lye,
This mater þou may not honoure.

---

4. Cf. the refrains in *Mercy and Righteousness*, especially the one spoken by Mercy: ". . .
mercy passes rightwisness."
6. "You may not be equal to your proposition" (as stated by Nurture in l. 4, that a thing's
nature can be controlled by training or education).
7–8. These lines are surely proverbial, though this exact expression is unrecorded else-
where. Scattergood has called attention to the later proverb cited in the *Oxford Dic-
tionary of English Proverbs* (p. 117): "Plant the crab-tree where you will, it will never bear
pippins"; cf. also *Piers* C.10.206–7: ". . . Shal neuere goed appel / Thorw no sotil sciense
on sour stok growe," a paraphrase of Matt. 7:18.
11. *yn a gere*: i.e., "through your conduct"; Braekman and Macaulay read *agere*, a word
unrecorded in the *MED*.
14. *ij*: "two"
15–17. Also probably proverbial; cf. "Draff is good enough for swine" (Whiting D372).
16. *on alle iiij*: "on all fours"
21–8. Kynd's second speech is little more than a re-statement of his first; ll. 21–2 parallel
5–6, 27–8 parallel 11–12, and 23–4 offer a proverb analogous to the one stated in
7–8. The proverb cited in 23–4 is a version of the adage, "You can't teach an old
dog new tricks"; Whiting records several variations on this proverb: e.g., ". . . it is

It were fulle hard semand to the
To make an old hound for to cowre.   24
If þou were bred yn halle or boure,
Among ladyes & lordes þat ar sure,
Yet wylle þou shew from whens þou come some houre:
I preve that kynde passis nurture."   28

[Nurture]   "Now I pray þe," said nurture, "Come soupe with me;
Thus to stryve alle day I hold vs not wise.
Thow shalt see alle with thyne iye,
Bothe of nurture & of exercise.   32
I haue a catte, I calle her Nyce,
An vnresonabulle best, haue þis yn mynd;
I haue taught her by nurture to do me gode seruyce:
Come see how nurture passis kynd."   36

[Kynd]   "Now, yn faith," said kynd, "if it be so,
That shal I wete or I blynne.
I wille yn to my chaumbur goo,
Mi dores to lokke my tresure withynne."   40

---

27. whens *ms*: when

---

harde to make an olde dog stoupe" (D313), and "It is to late an olde hounde in a
bande to lede" (H570).
24. Braekman and Macaulay read *henne* for *hound*, producing the dubious reading, "it
would seem to be very hard to make a hen crow."
25-7. The sense of these lines is neatly summed up in a proverb cited in the *Owl and
the Nightingale*, 135-8: "Peȝ appel trendli fron þon trowe / Par he & oþer mid growe,
/ Peȝ he bo þarfrom bicume / He cuþ wel whonene he is icume"; i.e., "Though the
apple trendles never so far, it shows whence it came" (Whiting A169).
29. *said*. Previous editors have misread the ms abbreviation for *said*; Scattergood expands
the abbreviation to *þer*, Braekman and Macaulay to *quoth*.
32. *of nurture & of exercise*: i.e., "(the results) of both teaching and of practice"
33. *Nyce* (i.e., Fool) is apparently the name Nurture has given his cat (cf. l. 58); the cat's
later behavior makes Nurture's choice ironic.
38. *or I blynne*: "before I stop (arguing)"
39-40. Kynd excuses himself and goes to his room, ostensibly to lock up his valuables
but actually to catch a mouse, before returning to sup with Nurture.

He caught a mows yn a gynne
And closed her yn his glove ful sure.
Thider agayn with hast did he wynne
To se whether kynd shuld passe nurture.   44

Now kynd come yn & spake no worde,
But fast drewe hym to the light.
He sawe sittyng vpon a borde
A catte held up a candylle light.   48
Nurture came ynne with metes ryally dight
[Nurture]   And said, "Kynd neybor, welcome, tru þou may me fynd.
How likis þou now þis good sight?
I preve þat nurture passys kynd."   52

Now kynd poled out his glove anon —
It was no nede to bydde the mous renne out.
As sone as the catte sawe þe mous gon,
She lepte and lete þe candylle falle oute;   56
Thay ran the chaumbyr round aboute.
[Nurture]   "What, Nyce," said nurture, "Come do thi cure."
By þat the cat had geven þe mous a cloute.
She dud her kynd & left nurture.   60

I left hem sittyng bothe me behynd
And went forthe vpon my way;

41–60. These lines relate the story of the "Cat and the Candle," an anecdote widely record-
ed in Eastern and European literatures (see E. Cosquin, 371–430 and 481–531). The
story occurs both as a self-contained entity and as an episode in longer tales about
notable wisemen — e.g. in the dispute between King Solomon and the clever peasant
Marcophus (see W. Benary, *Salomon et Marcolfus*).

50. Puns such as this on the two meanings of *kynd* ("kind" and "nature" or "natural")
are commonplace in Middle English literature.

53. Kynd is using his glove as a pouch.

54. An effective use of understatement. Kynd doesn't need to instruct the mouse in what
to do.

58. *said*. See note to l. 29.

59. *by þat*: "by then" or "by that time"

60–1. The repetition of *left* may indicate the poet's intention to use a stanza-linking device
throughout the poem.

This mater stik soore yn my mynd.
I meruelid theron many a day,   64
Yet could I neuer declare, yn fay,
For alle my helpe & alle my socoure;
But nedes þai must togidre, yn fay,
Be closed yn on, kynd and nurture.   68

Explicit.

---

64. *theron*. Scattergood reads *thorou*.

64–8. Although Kynd has here emerged victorious, the narrator concludes that nature and nurture must co-exist with each other.

The Debate of the Carpenter's Tools

The Debate of the Carpenter's Tools depicts an altercation between two factions of personified tools who are portrayed as carpenter's apprentices. The tools in one group rebuke the carpenter for his drunkenness and irresponsibility while those in the other group stoutly defend him and urge all of the tools to work harder. Brief individual speeches are offered by twenty-five different tools, including five kinds of axes and four kinds of boring tools; on the whole, however, there is no real attempt at individual characterization, and the two opposing groups are differentiated primarily by their contrasting attitudes toward the carpenter. As a result the poem becomes rather repetitious, but the tools' heated and highly colloquial exchanges help to sustain interest until the poem's surprising finale, when the carpenter's wife enters and expresses her sentiments on the matter, and when the Draught Nail (i.e., nail puller) exposes the carpenter's erstwhile supporters as the very ones who have been leading him astray.

The *Carpenter's Tools* is fundamentally a *jeu d'esprit*, but the social satire found near the end of the poem is not entirely light-hearted. In a fashion reminiscent of the Wren in the *Owl and the Nightingale*, the Draught Nail brings reason to the poem as he exposes the corrupting influence of the wayward tools by recounting their activities in the ale house and their later pleas to the carpenter not to work them too hard. Thoroughly disillusioned, the Draught Nail expresses his intention to leave the trade altogether. The carpenter's wife, however, has no such option for she is constrained by her marriage vows to remain with her husband. For her there is neither escape nor respite, and she can only curse the priest who bound her to such a shiftless carpenter. The character of the carpenter's wife may reflect to some degree the medieval stereotype of a shrewish, nagging wife, but the sympathetic attitude toward women found in the *chanson de mal mariée* is also suggested (see Sandison, pp. 11–4, 50–6).

The Debate of the Carpenter's Tools, which is written in iambic tetrameter couplets, is preserved only in Bodleian Library MS Ashmole 61, a manuscript which may have served as a minstrel's storybook. This surmise is based on the long, narrow shape of the manuscript, as well as its varied but largely popular contents. It is, in fact, easy to envision the poem receiving a vigorous public performance before an audience including artisans and tradespeople. It is also conceivable that the idea of a rebellion of tools was suggested to the poet by Isaiah 10:15: "Shall the axe boast itself against him that heweth therewith? or shall the saw magnify itself against him that shaketh it?" The best source of information about medieval and renaissance tools is Joseph Moxon's *Mechanick Exercises*, first published in 1677. Volume One treats "smithing, joinery, house-carpentry, and turning." A reprint of the 1703 edition has been published by the Early American Industries Association (Scarsdale, NY).

---

1) Base Text: Bodl. Lib. MS Ashmole 61 (Bodl. 6922*), fols. 23r–6r

2) Other mss: none

3) Printed Texts: J. Halliwell, *Nugae Poeticae* (1844), 13–20
                         W. C. Hazlitt, *Remains* I (1864), 79–90

4) *Index of Middle English Verse* 3461

[The Debate of the Carpenter's Tools]

The shype ax seyd vnto þe wryght,
[Chip Ax]   "Mete & drynke I schalle þe plyght,

---

1. This poem is unusual among Middle English debates in having no introductory narrative; there is, however, a closing frame spoken by a first-person narrator. *Shype ax*: "chip ax," i.e., a hatchet or small one-handed ax used to smooth timbers; the chip ax is the first of the five varieties of axes among the carpenter's tools.
2–16. The comments of the first three tools (all axes) reflect three different viewpoints.

Clene hose & clene schone,
Gete þem wer as euer thou kane;   4
Bot fore all þat euer þou kane,
Thall neuer be thryfty man,
Ne none þat longes þe crafte vnto,
Fore no thyng þat thou kane do."   8

[Belt Ax]   "Wherefore," seyd þe belte,
"With grete strokes I schalle hym pelte;
My mayster schall full welle thene
Both to cloþe & fede his men."   12

[Twibill Ax]   "3e, 3e," seyd þe twybylle,
"Thou spekes euer ageyn skylle;
I-wys, i-wys, it wylle not bene,
Ne neuer, I thinke, þat he wyll thene."   16

[Wimble]   "3is, 3is," seyd þe wymbylle,
"I ame als rounde as a thymbyll;
My maysters werke I wylle remembyre;
Y schall crepe fast in-to þe tymbyre   20
And help my mayster within a stounde

---

8. thyng *ms*: thnyg
12. & *supplied*

The Chip Ax's remarks, which set the debate in motion, are a neutral comment on the economic prospects of carpenters: the Chip Ax believes that carpenters can expect to gain from their trade only the basic necessities of food and drink (l. 2) and clean clothing (ll. 3–4), but not the substantial wealth of a "thrifty man" (l. 6). The Belt Ax, however, expresses his belief that the carpenter *can* prosper if the tools will only apply themselves, but the Twibill Ax holds the opposite view. The remaining tools alternately support and attack the carpenter.

3. *schone*: "shoes"
6. *Thall*: "thou will"; *thryfty*: i.e., "prosperous"
9. *wherefore*: the meaning seems to be "on the contrary"; *belte*: "belt-ax," a large tree-felling ax
10. "I will work hard for him by striking great strokes."
13. *twybylle*: a narrow-bladed ax (Hazlitt incorrectly glosses it as a "large mallet") used to make mortises; its two blades are set at right angles to one another.
14. *skylle*: "reason"
17. *wymbylle*: a gimlet, an implement for boring small holes which could then be enlarged by an auger

To store his cofere with xx pounde."

[Compass]   "Ʒe, ʒe," seyd þe compas,

"Thou arte a fole in þat case,   24

For þou spekes without vysment;

Therefore þou getyst not þi entent;

Wyte þou wele it schall be so

That lyghtly cum schall lyghtly go;   28

An þou gete more than oþer fyue,

Ʒit schall þi mayster neuer thryue."

[Groping Iron]   The groping iren than spake he,

"Compas, who hath grevyd þe?   32

My mayster ʒit may thryue full wele;

How he schall I wylle þe telle:

I ame his seruant, trew & gode,

Y suere þe, compas, by þe rode;   36

Wyrke I schalle boþe nyght & dey

To gete hym gode I schall assey."

[Saw]   "Ʒe, ʒe," seys þe saw,

"Yt is bote bost þat þou doyst blow,   40

Fore thofe þou wyrke bothe dey & nyght

---

41. & *supplied*

---

22. *xx pounde*: "twenty pounds"

23. *ʒe, ʒe*: i.e., "yeah, yeah," implying disagreement; medieval carpenters used small iron compasses to make circles in a process known as "scribing."

28. A common proverb; Whiting cites several examples for medieval literature (C384). The modern equivalent is "easy come, easy go."

29. "even if you earn more than five others (put together). . ."

31. *groping iron*: an implement for grooving or carving, probably related to a cooper's "croze." It was used to cut vertical grooves in boards so that they could be fitted together by means of tongue and groove.

36. *suere*: "swear"

38. *gode*: "goods," i.e., "wealth"

39. According to medieval legend, the saw was invented by Perdix, the nephew of Daedalus.

41. *thofe*: "though"

43. Although Whiting doesn't record this expression, it is clearly a colloquialism indicating overfondness for the tavern (cf. l. 88).

He wyll not the, I sey þe ryght;
He wones to nyӡe þe ale wyffe
And he thouht euer fore to thryffe."   44

[Whetstone]   Than seyd þe whetstone:
"Thoff my mayster thryft be gone,
Y schall hym helpe within þis ӡere
To gete hym xxti merke clere;   48
Hys axes schall I make fulle scharþe
That þei may lyӡhtly do þer werke;
To make my master a ryche mane
I schall asey, if þat I canne."   52

[Adz]   To hym þan seyd þe adys
And seyd, "Ӡe, ser, God glades,
To speke of thryfft it wyll not be
Ne neuer, I thinke, þat he schall the;   56
Fore he wylle drynke more on a dey
Than þou cane lyghtly arne in twey;
Therefore þi tonge I rede þou hold
And speke no more no wordes so bold."   60

To þe adys than seyd þe fyle,
[File]   "Thou schuldes not þi mayster reuyle,
Fore thoff he be vnhappy,
Ӡit fore his thryft þou schuldes se;   64
Fore I thinke or tomorow at none
To arne my mayster a pyre of schone;
Fore I schalle rube with all my myght
My mayster tolys forto dyght,   68

---

44. "if he ever expects to thrive"
46. "although my master is not (now) prospering . . ."
48. *xx^t merke*: "twenty marks"; a mark was thirteen shillings, four pence.
53. The adz, a tool intermediate in function between a chip ax and a plane, was used
to slice thin chips or strips off boards and timbers.
54. *god glades*: a mild oath, e.g., "God bless me."
62. Files, in contrast to rasps, were used for working on metals, not on wood; ll. 67–8
indicate the file was used to sharpen or clean the carpenter's other tools.
63. *vnhappy*: "misfortunate"
65. *Fore*: "therefore"; *or*: "ere"
68. "to prepare my master's tools"

	So þat with-in a lytell space	
	My mayster purce I schall encrece."	
	Than seyd þe chesyll,	
[Chisel]	"And euer he thryue, he berys hym wele;	72
	Fore tho þou rube to þi hede ake,	
	His thryfte fro hym it wyll be take;	
	Fore he loues gode ale so wele	
	That he þerfore his hod wyll selle;	76
	Fore some dey he wyll vij^d drynke;	
	How he schall thryue I canne not thinke."	
[Chalk line]	"Ʒe, ʒe," seyd þe lyne & þe chalke,	
	"My mayster is lyke to many folke;	80
	Tho he lufe ale neuer so wele,	
	To thryu & the I schall hym telle;	
	Y schall merke well vpone þe wode	
	And kepe his mesures trew & gode;	84
	And so by my mesures all	
	To the full wele my mayster schall."	
[Pricking knife]	Than bespake þe pryking knyfe,	
	"He duellys to nyʒe þe ale wyfe;	88
	Sche makes oft-tyme his purse full thynn;	
	No peny some tyme sche leuye þerin;	
	Tho þou gete more than oþer thre,	
	Thryfty man he canne not be."	92
[Piercing iron]	"Ʒe, ʒe," seyd þe persore,	

---

71. The chisel was essential for cutting mortice and tenon joints, which are basic to timber frame construction.

72. *berys*: "bears"

76. Cf. the similar reference to the selling of a hood to raise cash in the graphic tavern scene depicted within Gluttony's confession in *Piers Plowman* (B.5.327–32).

77. vij^d: "seven pence"; presumably a large bar bill for one day; it is a full day's wage for an apprentice; see l. 242 and its note.

79. The chalk line was made of spun linen; English undersoil (as in the white cliffs of Dover) provided the chalk.

87. The pricking knife was used to make dotted guidelines on wood and also to make small guide holes for screws and nails.

88. Cf. l. 43

93. The piecing iron or piecer, one of the four boring tools in the poem, is today's brace and bit. It didn't appear in Europe until the fifteenth century, and it may have come into use as a result of technology brought back to Europe by the crusaders.

"That þat I sey it schall be sure;
Whi chyd ȝe iche one with oþer?
Wote ȝe not wele I ame ȝour broþer?   96
Therefore none contrary me,
Fore as I sey so schall it be;
My mayster ȝit schall be full ryche,
Als fere as I may stret & streche;   100
Y wyll helpe with all my myght
Both by dey & by nyght,
Fast to runne in to þe wode
And byte I schall with moth full gode;   104
And þus I trow be my crowne
To make hym schyreff of þe tounne."

[Scantillion]   "Sof, ser," seyd þe skantyllȝon,
"Y trow ȝour thryft be wele ny done;   108
Euer to crewyll þou arte in word;
And ȝet þou arte not worth a tord!
Fore all þe gode þat þou gete myght,
He wyll spend it on a nyght."   112
Than þe crow bygane to speke
Fore-why is herte was lyke to breke,
To here his broþer so reuyld
[Crowbar]   And seyd, "Þou spekes lyke a chyld!   116
Tho my mayster spend neuer so faste,
Y-nouȝe he schall haue at þe laste
May forteyne as mych as euer shall he

---

94. That þat *ms*: That at

---

105. *crowne*: "head" of the piercing iron; possibly a play on words
107. The scantillion is the equivalent of the modern gauge, used to scribe a line parallel to an opposing surface.
112. *on a nyght*: "(all) in one night"
113. Early crows (or crowbars) were used for prying and lifting but not for pulling nails.
114–5. Although few of the tools are rendered as distinctive individuals, the soft-hearted Crowbar stands out.
119. *forteyne*: "retain"

	That drynke neuer peny to þat he dyȝe."	120
[Rule]	"Ȝe, ȝe," syed þe rewle,	
	"Y-feyth þou arte bot a fole!	
	Fore & he dyȝe & haue ryght nouȝht,	
	Who trowys þou wyll gyfe hym owght?	124
	Thus schall he ly vpone þe grownd	
	And be beryd lyke an hund;	
	Fore & a man haue ought before,	
	When he has nede it is gode store."	128
[Plane]	"What, ser reule," seyd þe pleyn,	
	"Anoþer reson I wyll þe seyne;	
	Thoff my mayster haue no happe,	
	Ȝit þi mayster þou schudyst not lake;	132
	Fore ȝit a mene I schall se	
	That my mayster schall wele the;	
	Y schall hym helpe both dey & nyght	
	To gete hym gode with all my myght;	136
	Y schalle clens on euery syde	
	To helpe my mayster in his pride."	
	The brode ax seyd, withouten mysse,	
[Broad ax]	He seyde, "Þe pleyn my broþer is;	140
	We two schall clence & make full pleyne,	
	That no man schall vs geyne-seyne;	
	And gete oure mayster in a ȝere	
	More syluer than a man may bere."	144
[Twivell]	"Ȝe, ȝe," seyd þe twyuete,	
	"Thryft I trow be fro ȝou fette	
	To kepe my mayster in his pride;	

---

120. "that never [spent] a penny on drink till he died"
121. The rule might be either an ungraduated straight edge of some length, or a folding "carpenter's rule," as short as a foot.
125–6. This prediction of the carpenter's humiliating treatment upon his death is a variation on the expression "to die like a dog" (Whiting D321).
132. *lake*: "lack," i.e., "find fault with"
139. *withouten mysse*: "without fail"; a filler phrase
142. *geyne-seyne*: "gainsay"
145. The *twyvette*, or twivell, is a two-headed morticing knife; it should not be confused with the twibill in l. 13.

Yn þe contre ȝe canne not byde   148
Without ȝe stele & be thefys
And put meny men to greffys;
Fore he wylle drynke more in a houre
Than two men may gete in fowre;   152
When ȝe haue wrouȝht alle þat ȝe canne,
Yit schalle he neuer be thryfty mane."
Than bespake þe polyff
With gret strong wordes & styffe: 156

[Pulley]   "How, ser twyuet, me thinke ȝou greuyd;
What deuylle, who hath ȝou þus meuyd?
Thof he spend more in a ȝere
Off gold & syluer than þou may bere,   160
Y schall hym helpe with all my myght;
I trow to make hym ȝet a knyght."

[Windlass]   "What, ser," seyd þe wyndas rewle,
"Me thynke þou arte bot a fole,   164
Fore þou spekes oute of sesone;
He may not the þerfore by resone;
A carpenter to be a knyght?
That was euer ageyne ryght.   168
Therefore I schall telle þe a saw:
'Who-so wold be hyȝe he schall be law!'"

[Rule stone]   "ȝe," than seyd þe rewle stone,
"Mayster hath many fone;   172
And ȝe wold helpe hym at his nede
My mayster schuld þe better spede;

---

173. hym *supplied*

---

157. *How:* "stop" or "hold on"; an interjection
163. A windlass is a lever acting on a rope; in conjunction with a block and tackle, it could exert great force; cf. Chaucer's *Squire's Tale, CT* V 184).
170. This proverb may have a biblical origin, e.g., Luke 18:14; see Whiting D321 (and cf. Whiting M216).
171. A *reule stone* may be a plummet (or plumb bob), a heavy bob needed for vertical truing; this important tool is otherwise absent from the debate.

	Bot what-so-euer ȝe brage ore boste,	
	My master ȝet schall reule þe roste;	176
	Fore as I ame a trew mane	
	I schalle hym helpe all þat I canne."	
[Gouge]	The gowge seyd, "Þe deuyles dyrte	
	Fore any thyng þat thow canne wyrke!	180
	Fore all þat euer þou canne do,	
	Yt is not worthe an old scho!	
	Thow hast be prentys þis vij ȝere	
	And ȝit thy crafte is forto lere;	184
	And þou couthe wyrke als wele as he,	
	ȝet schall þi mayster neuer the!"	
[Cable]	"Softe, ser," seyde þe gabulle rope,	
	"Me thinke gode ale is in ȝour tope;	188
	Fore þou spekes as þou wold fyght,	
	There-to & þou hade any myght;	
	Y schall telle þe an oþer tale	
	My mayster how I schall aveyle:	192
	Hayle & pulle I schall fulle faste	
	To reyse housys whyle I may laste,	
	And so within a lytell throw	
	My mayster gode schall not be know."	196
	Than spake þe wryghtes wyfe:	
[Carpenter's Wife]	"Noþer of ȝou schall neuer thryfe,	
	Noþer þe mayster ne þe mane,	
	Fore nothinge þat ȝe do canne;	200
	Fore ȝe wyll spend in a moneth	

---

176. *reule þe roste*: "rule the roost"; the earliest recorded use of this popular phrase (Whiting R152).

179. The gouge is a chisell with a round edge, for use on wood to be rounded or hollowed, as in decorative mouldings.

179. *deuyles dyrte*: "devil's dirt," a phrase not recorded in the MED, but its meaning ("excrement") is fairly obvious; cf. the phrase *cattes dyrt* ("cat's dirt") in "Satire on the Retinues of the Great" (*Index* 2649), l. 31.

183–4. Seven years was the usual term of apprenticeship, so one who has been an apprentice for seven years should be close to mastering his craft.

190. "if you had the strength"

195. *lytell throw*: "short time"

	More gode than iij men hath."	
[Square]	The squyre seyd, "What sey ȝe dame?	
	Ȝe schuld not speke my mayster schame!"	204
[Carpenter's Wife]	"Squyre, I haue none oþer cause,	
	I suere þe by Seynt Eustase;	
	Fore alle þe ȝerne þat I may spynne	
	To spend at ale he thinkes no synne;	208
	He wylle spend more in an owre	
	Than þou & I canne gete in a fowre!"	
[Square]	"Ȝit me thinke ȝe be to blame	
	To gyffe my master syche a name;	212
	For thoff he spend more than ȝe haue	
	Yit his worschype ȝe schuld save."	
[Carpenter's Wife]	"Mary, I schrew hym & þe to	
	And alle them þat so canne do!	216
	Fore hys seruaunt i trow þou be;	
	Therefore þou schalle neuer the;	
	Fore and þou lerne þat craft at hym,	
	Thy thryft I trow schall be fulle thine."	220
	The draught nayle þan spake he	
[Nail Puller]	And seyd, "Dame, þat is no le;	
	Ȝe hafe þe maner of þes frekes	
	That þus fore my mayster spekes;	224

---

218. Therefore *ms*: there

---

203. This guide to right angles is perhaps the carpenter's most essential tool, and one which has been used to symbolize his craft from ancient times.

206. *Seynt Eustase*: St. Eustace; used only to supply the rhyme.

207. Medieval women often practiced the trade of yarn-making, spinning it from wool or flax. Chaucer's Wife of Bath, for example, is also a cloth-maker.

215. *schrew*: "beshrew," i.e., "curse"

216. *so canne do*: i.e., "do as you do"

221. The *draught nail* (nail "drawer") is an implement for pulling nails, its exclusive function. (The claw hammer wasn't used in the Middle Ages.) It is interesting to observe that the nail puller is used here to "correct" the mistakes of the others, just as it functions in the hands of a builder.

223. "You understand the kind of fellows these are."

Bot lythe to me a lytelle space,
Y schall ȝow telle all þe case
How þat they wyrke fore þer gode;
I wylle not lye, be þe rode.   228
When þei haue wroght an oure or two,
Anone to þe ale þei wylle go
And drinke þer whyle þei may dre,
'Thou to me' & 'I to the!'   232
And seys, 'Þe ax schall pay fore þis;
Therefore þe cope ons I wylle kys';
And when þei comme to werke ageyne
The belte to hys mayster wylle seyne,   236
'Mayster, wyrke no oute off resone;
The dey is vary longe of seson;
Smale strokes late vs hake
And sumtyme late vs es oure bake.'   240
The wymbull spekes lyte: 'A, syre,
Seuyne pens off a dey is smale hyre
Fore wryghtes þat wyrke so faste,
And in owre werke haue grete haste.'   244
The groping iren seys full sone,
'Mayster, wylle ȝe wele done?
Late vs not wyrke to we suete
Fore cachyng of ouer gret hete;   248
Fore we may after cold to take,
Than on stroke may we no hake.'
Than bespake þe whetstone
And seyd, 'Mayster, we wylle go home   252

---

234. *cope ons*: "cup once"
238. In the summer a carpenter's "day" might begin about 5 a.m. and last until 7 p.m., with breaks for breakfast, mid-day dinner, and possibly a nap.
239–40. "Small strokes let us hack / And sometime(s) ease our back(s)."
241. *lyte*: i.e., "softly"; the wimble is a small tool and has a voice to match.
242. Cf. l. 77; seven pence is actually a very good wage, even for summer, when the working day was much longer and the pay proportionally higher.
246. "Master, do you wish to have us do a good job?"
246–50. Compare the groping iron's earlier pledge to work night and day without stopping (l. 37).

For faste it draw vnto þe nyght;
Oure soper by þis I wote is dyght.'
The lyne & stone, þe persere, & fyle
Seys, 'Þat is a gode counesylle.'   256
The crow, þe pleyn, & þe squyre
Seys, 'We haue arnyd wele oure hyre.'
And þus with fraudes & falsyd
Ys many trew man deseyuid.   260
Therefore by ought þat I canne se
They schall neuer thryue ne the;
Therefore þe craft I wylle go froo
And to an oþer wylle I goo."   264
Than ansuerd þe wyfe in hye:

[Carpenter's Wife]   "And I myght, so wold I;
Bot I ame to hym bounde sa faste
That of my halter I may not caste;   268
Therefore þe preste þat bounde me prentys,
He schall treuly haue my curse
And ever schall haue to þat I dyȝe,
In what contre þat euer he be!"   272

[Narrator]   Therefore, wryȝtes, take hede of þis
That ȝe may mend þat is amysse,
And treuly þat ȝe do ȝour labore
Fore þat wylle be to ȝour honour.   276
And greue ȝou no-thinge at þis songe
Bot euer make mery ȝour-selue amonge;
Ne ȝet at hym þat it dud make,
Ne envy at hym ȝe take,   280

---

254. "Our supper by this (time), I'm sure, has been prepared."

265. *in hye*: "quickly"

268. The wife's comment on her inability to cast off her halter recalls several antifeminist lyrics in which a husband or lover is advised to end his association with a woman by releasing her from her halter; cf. *Index* 1338 and *Index* 1938; cf. also the little debate between the *Clerk and Husbandman* (*Index* 344) l. 16.

269. The wife, appropriately, characterizes her relationship to the carpenter as that of a bound apprentice also.

273–83. These verses contribute to the impression that the poem was intended for public performance.

Ne none of ȝou do hym blame,
Fore-why the craft hath do hym schame
By mo weys than two or thre;
Thus seys þe boke, serteynlye.   284
God þat is both gode & hend,
Gyff ȝou grace þat ȝe may mend
And bryng vs alle vnto his blysse,
That neuer fro vs schall mysse.   288
       Amen qd Rate

---

284. Medieval poets often suggested that their work was based upon a previous "book," a book which many times existed only in the writer's imagination. Here the remark may be designed to ward off reprisals by offended or incensed carpenters (such as Chaucer's thin-skinned Reeve).

289. *Amen qd Rate*: " 'Amen' said Rate"; Rate is probably the name of the scribe of Ashmole 61 (as well as that of MS Camb. Univ. Lib. Kk.1.5). It has been suggested, however, that he is the author of this poem and others in these mss., and the author of *Ratis Raving* (*Index* 2235 and 3154); see J. T. T. Brown, "The Author of Ratis Raving," *Bonner Beiträge zur Anglistik* 5, p. 145.

The Thrush and the Nightingale

The Thrush and the Nightingale is the second of the surviving Middle English bird-debates, coming not long after the *Owl and the Nightingale* in the second half of the thirteenth century, and it is natural to assume that the poet is writing in imitation of that much greater work. In fact, aside from their use of birds as disputants, the two poems have little in common. Compared to the erudition, humor, vivid characterization, and structural sophistication of the earlier poem, the *Thrush and the Nightingale* seems a meager performance. It reflects the form and style commonly found in Latin and French debate poems: in its brevity, in the absence of connecting narrative, in the use of equal and alternating speeches that are contained within the stanza, and in its focus on a single, rather conventional topic. Unlike the *Owl and the Nightingale*, which addresses a great number of issues (but primarily which of the two birds is the superior creature), the *Thrush and the Nightingale* concentrates on a single issue, in this case the worth of women. The Nightingale's principal argument is that women comfort men by means of their physical charms and their gentility. The Thrush asserts that women are simply masters of deceit and that the man who is foolish enough to trust a woman will suffer the fate of Adam, Samson, Gawain, and other heroes who were betrayed by women. Throughout most of the debate the Nightingale seems ill-equipped to withstand the Thrush's anti-feministic onslaught. But when the Thrush challenges the Nightingale to name five good women, he inadvertently prepares the way for his own defeat. For although the Nightingale is apparently unable to name five good women, the one she proposes, the Virgin Mary, proves to be sufficient. The Thrush, in an unexpected about-face, admits the error of his previous beliefs and voluntarily exiles himself from the woodland scene of their debate. But the poet — although

exonerating women from the criticisms of misogynists — probably intends
to venerate the Blessed Virgin more than to praise the goodness of women
in general.

The *Thrush and the Nightingale* was probably composed during the second
half of the thirteenth century, and the only complete text is preserved in
Bodleian Library MS Digby 86, a trilingual miscellany which also includes
such works as the *Lai du cor, Dame Sirith,* and the Middle English debate
In a pestri. Digby 86 is the handiwork of the Dominican friars of Worcester-
shire; it contains more works in French than in English, and more secular
works than religious ones. The first seventy-five verses of the *Thrush and the
Nightingale* also appear in the Auchinleck manuscript, but with considera-
ble departures from the Digby text. In the Digby manuscript the *Thrush
and the Nightingale* consists of 192 verses, written in tail-rhyme stanzas rhym-
ing aabccbddbeeb.

---

1)   Base Text: Bodleian Lib. MS Digby 86 (Bodl. 1687), fols. 136r (col. ii)–138v (col. ii)

2)   Other mss: National Libr. of Scotland, Advocates 19.2.1 (Auchinleck MS), fol. 279r
      (75 verses only).

3)   Selected Printed Texts: Wright and Halliwell, *Reliquiae Antiquae* I, p. 241
                              Hazlitt, *Remains of the Early Popular Poetry of England* I,
                                  (1864), 50
                              C. Brown, *English Lyrics of the Thirteenth Century* (1932),
                                  101
                              Dickins and Wilson, *Early Middle English Texts,* 2nd ed.
                                  (1952), 71
                              Owen and Owen, *Middle English Poetry* (1971), 272
                              Varnhagen, *Anglia* 4 (the Auchinleck text)

4)   *Index of Middle English Verse* 3222

Ci commence la cuntent parente

le Mauuis & la russinole

Somer is comen wiþ loue to toune,
Wiþ blostme and wiþ brides roune,
Þe note of hasel springeþ,
Þe dewes darkneþ in þe dale.   4
For longing of þe niȝttegale
Þis foweles murie singeþ.
Hic herde a strif bitweies two,
Þat on of wele, þat oþer of wo,   8
Bitwene two i-fere;

Title. "Here begins the contention between the Mavis and the Nightingale." French ti-
tles are commonly assigned to English works in Digby 86, though some scholars see
this title as suggesting that the *Thrush and the Nightingale* is a translation of an Old
French poem.

1–8. Cf. this conventional spring-time opening with the opening verses of the well-known
Harley lyric "Lenten is come with love to town":

> Lenten ys come with love to toune,
> With blosmen ant with briddes roune,
> That al this blisse bryngeth.
> Dayeseȝes in this dales,
> Notes suete of nyhtegales,
> Vch foul song singeth.
> The threstelcoc him threteth oo;
> Away is huere wynter wo
> When woderoue springeth.

It is possible that the notion of a debate between birds stems from lines 5–7 of the
Harley lyric, which portray the thrush's song as a response to the nightingale's sing-
ing. MS Harley 2253 was written after Digby 86, but the poem could have existed
prior to its being recorded in the Harley manuscript.

3. "The notes of the birds' song (*roune*) spring from the hazel trees"; or possibly "hazel
nuts begin to appear."

4. Cf. Dunbar's *Tretis of the Tua Mariit Wemen*, l. 4.

5–6. "Because of the love-longing of the nightingale, these birds (are inspired to) sing
merrily."

7. *Hic:* "I"; this is the only reference to the first-person narrator, and this brief opening
frame has no counterpart at the end of the poem.

7. *strif:* "debate"; the Old French term *estrif* was one of several terms commonly applied
to debate poems.

Þat on hereþ wimmen þat hoe beþ hende,
Þat oþer hem wole wiþ miȝte shende.
    Þat strif ȝe mowen i-here.   12

Þe niȝtingale is on bi nome
Þat wol shilden hem from shome,
    Of skaþe hoe wole hem skere;
Þe þrestelcok hem kepeþ ay,   16
He seiþ bi niȝte and eke bi day
    Þat hy beþ fendes i-fere:
[Thrush]   "For hy biswikeþ euchan mon
Þat mest bileueþ hem ouppon.   20
    Þey hy ben milde of chere,
Hoe beþ fikele and ffals to fonde,
Hoe wercheþ wo in euchan londe;
    Hit were betere þat hy nere."   24

[Nightingale]   "Hit is shome to blame leuedy,
For hy beth hende of corteisy;

_____

22. ffals _ms_: fflls

_____

10-1. "That one praises women for their gentility, that other wishes with (all his) might to shame them."
15. "From blame she wants to keep them."
16. "The thrustlecock always maintains his guard against them."
18. "that they are all fiends"
19-24. These lines may be assigned to the Thrush, or they may be viewed as the narrator's paraphrase of the Thrush's sentiments. One reason for preferring their assignment to the Thrush is that it seems to be these very words the Nightingale is responding to in ll. 25-36.
19-20. "For they deceive every man who believes in them."
21. _þey_: "though"
22. _fals to fonde_: "false when put to the test"
24. "It would have been better if they had never been created."
25-36. In this poem, as in the _Owl and the Nightingale_ and the _Cuckoo and the Nightingale_, it is the Nightingale whose verbal attack actually initiates the debate — though here, perhaps, she has greater provocation than in the _Owl and the Nightingale_.

Ich rede þat þou lete.
Ne wes neuere bruche so strong   28
I-broke wiþ riȝte ne wiþ wrong,
   Þat mon ne miȝte bete.
Hy gladieþ hem þat beþ wroþe,
Boþe þe heye and þe lowe,   32
   Mid gome hy cunne hem grete.
Þis world nere nout ȝif wimen nere;
I-maked hoe wes to mones fere,
   Nis no þing al so swete."   36

[Thrush]   "I ne may wimen herien nohut,
ffor hy beþ swikele and false of þohut,
   Also ich am ounderstonde.
Hy beþ feire and briȝt on hewe,   40
Here þout is fals and ountrewe;
   Ful ȝare ich haue hem fonde.
Alisaundre þe king meneþ of hem —
In þe world nes non so crafti mon,   44
   Ne non so riche of londe.
I take witnesse of monie and fele
Þat riche weren of worldes wele —
   Muche wes hem þe shonde."   48

---

27. "I advise that you cease."
28–30. "Nor was there every any breach committed, either rightly or wrongly, that one
   (i.e., a woman) might not make better."
33. "They know how to greet (i.e., divert) them with (love) games."
34. "This world would not exist at all if it weren't for women."
42. "Full yore have I found them to be (i.e., deceitful)."
43. *meneþ*: "says" or "complains"; the allusion in ll. 43–5 may be to the story in the Mid-
   dle English romance *Kyng Alisaunder* in which Alexander is deceived (somewhat) by
   Candace (see G. V. Smithers, EETS es 227, ll. 7578–769). The specific lines alluded
   to here may be 7698–9 in which Alexander remarks: *Ac noman ne may hym waite / From
   thise wymmens dissaite* (i.e., "but no man can guard himself from these women's deceits").
44. "In (all) the world there is no one so cunning (as women)."
46. *monie and fele*: "many and sundry"
48. "Great was their disgrace."

[Night.]

Þe niȝtingale hoe wes wroþ:
"Fowel, me þinkeþ þou art me loþ,
   Sweche tales for to showe.
Among a þousent leuedies i-tolde   52
Þer nis non wickede, I holde,
   Þer hy sitteþ on rowe.
Hy beth of herte meke and milde,
Hem-self hy cunne from shome shilde   56
   Wiþinne boures wowe,
And swettoust þing in armes to wre
Þe mon þat holdeþ hem in gle.
   Fowel, wi ne art þou hit i-cnowe?"   60

[Thrush]

"Gentil fowel, seist þou hit me?
Ich habbe wiþ hem in boure i-be,
   I haued al mine wille.
Hy willeþ for a luitel mede   64
Don a sunfoul derne dede,
   Here soule for to spille.
ffowel, me þinkeþ þou art les;
Þey þou be milde and softe of pes,   68
   Þou seyst þine wille.
I take witnesse of Adam,
Þat wes oure furste man,
   Þat fond hem wycke and ille."   72

---

72. wycke *ms*: wycle

---

60. "Bird, why don't you realize this?"
62-3. The Thrush, who is male, claims to have had extensive experience with the opposite sex.
65. "do a sinful secret deed"; cf. *Clerk and Nightingale* I, 101–4.
67. *art les*: "are lying"
68-9. "Although you appear to be gentle and soft-spoken, you are behaving willfully."

[Night.]   "Þrestelcok, þou art wod,
                 Oþer þou const to luitel goed
                     Þis wimmen for to shende.
                 Hit is þe swetteste driwerie,   76
                 And mest hoe counnen of curteisie.
                     Nis noþing also hende.
                 Þe mest murþ þat mon haueþ here,
                 Wenne hoe is maked to his fere   80
                     In armes for to wende.
                 Hit is shome to blame leuedi,
                 For hem þou shalt gon sori —
                     Of londe ich wille þe sende!"   84

[Thrush]   "Niʒttingale, þou hauest wrong!
                 Wolt þou me senden of þis lond
                     ffor ich holde wiþ þe riʒtte?
                 I take witnesse of Sire Wawain,   88
                 Þat Jesu Crist ʒaf miʒt and main
                     And strengþe for to fiʒtte;
                 So wide so he heuede i-gon,

74–7. "Or you know too little good (i.e., are ignorant) to shame women this way. Theirs
    is the sweetest love-making, and they are masters of courtesy."
84. The threat of expelling or exiling an opponent occurs often in the bird debates.
87. *For*: "because"
88. *Sire Wawain*: "Sir Gawain"
85–120. Editors of the poem disagree about the assignment of these lines. Wright as-
    signed all thirty-five of them to the Thrush, though nowhere else in the poem does
    one bird speak more than twelve lines consecutively. Hazlitt divided the lines into
    five speeches, assigning the Thrush 85–93, 106–8, and 112–20, and the Nightingale
    94–105 and 109–11. Brown, and Dickins and Wilson, divided the lines into three
    speeches, assigning the Thrush 85–93 and 109–20, the Nightingale 94–108. Owen
    and Owen shifted 94–6 to the Thrush, giving the Thrush 85–96 and 109–20, and
    the Nightingale 97–108. I have followed their division since it is the only one which
    doesn't violate the correspondence of one stanza to one speech, a pattern which is
    consistent throughout the poem.
91–2. "As widely as he had traveled, he never found a true one"; although Gawain was
    deceived by women in several of his adventures, the Thrush is surely exaggerating.
    But cf. Gawain's sentiments in ll. 2414 ff. of *Sir Gawain and the Green Knight*:

            Bot hit is no ferly þaʒ a fole madde,
            And þurʒ wyles of wymmen be wonen to sorʒe,
            For so watʒ Adam in erde with one bygyled . . .

Trewe ne founde he neuere non   92
   Bi daye ne bi niȝtte
Fowel, for þi false mouþ
Þi sawe shal ben wide couþ;
   I rede þe fle wiþ miȝtte."   96

[Night.]   "Ich habbe leue to ben here,
In orchard and in erbere
   Mine songes for to singe.
Herd I neuere bi no leuedi   100
Bote hendiness and curteysi,
   And ioye hy gunnen me bringe.
Of muchele murþe hy telleþ me.
ffere, also I telle þe,   104
   Hy liuieþ in longinge.
Fowel, þou sitest on hasel bou,
Þou lastest hem, þou hauest wou—
   Þi word shal wide springe!"   108

[Thrush]   "Hit springeþ wide, wel ich wot—
Þou tel hit him þat hit not!
   Þis sawes ne beþ nout newe.
Fowel, herkne to mi sawe,   112
Ich wile þe telle of here lawe—
   Þou ne kepest nout hem i-knowe.

---

105. longinge *ms*: longinginge

---

95. *wide couþ*: "widely known"
96. Now the Thrush is advising the Nightingale to fly away, a rejoinder to l. 84.
107. *lastest*: "slanders"; *hauest wou*: "are wrong"
108. *wide springe*: "spread abroad"
110. "(For) you tell it to anyone that doesn't know it."
114. "You do not care to acknowledge (or understand) them."

Þenk on Costantines quene—
Foul wel hire semede fow and grene—   116
   Hou sore hit gon hire rewe.
Hoe fedde a crupel in hire bour
And helede him wiþ couertour:
   Loke war wimmen ben trewe!"   120

[Night.]   "Þrestelkok, þou hauest wrong!
Also I sugge one mi song,
   And þat men witeþ wide,
Hy beþ briʒttore ounder shawe   124
Þen þe day wenne hit dawe
   In longe someres tide.
Come þou heuere in here londe,
Hy shulen don þe in prisoun stronge,   128
   And þer þou shalt abide.
Þe lesinges þat þou hauest maked,
Þer þou shalt hem forsake,
   And shome þe shal bitide."   132

[Thrush]   "Niʒttingale, þou seist þine wille;
Þou seist þat wimmen shulen me spille.
   Daþeit wo hit wolde!
In holibok hit is i-founde,   136

115–9. Medieval tales concerning queens who have love affairs with physically deformed persons are common, with such affairs attesting to the woman's sexual depravity. Several Old French poems (e.g., *Auberi le Bourguignon*) portray Constantine's wife as such a woman.

116–7. "Full well she liked green and particolored furs (i.e., she liked rich apparel)—how sorely she regretted it." The phrase *fow and grene* is a variation on the more common expression *fowe and grai*, here altered for the sake of the rhyme.

118. *crupel*: "cripple"

119. "and healed him with a bedspread" (i.e., "went to bed with him")

120. "Look how true women are!"

124–5. "They (women) are brighter under a (shady) grove than the day when it dawns."

12~. *heuere*: "ever"

128. *shulen don*: "shall put"

135. "A curse on whoever wishes it (that women should destroy me)."

Hy bringeþ moni mon to grounde
   Þat proude weren and bolde.
Þenk oupon Saumsum þe stronge,
Hou muchel is wif him dude to wronge;   140
   Ich wot þat hoe him solde.
Hit is þat worste hord of pris
Þat Jesu makede in Parais
   In tresour for to holde."

                144

Þo seide þe niȝttingale:

[Night.]   "Fowel, wel redi is þi tale;
   Herkne to mi lore!
Hit is flour þat lasteþ longe,   148
And mest i-herd in eueri londe,
   And louelich ounder gore.
In þe worlde nis non so goed lech,
So milde of þoute, so feir of speche,   152
   To hele monnes sore.
ffowel, þou rewest al mi þohut;
Þou dost euele, ne geineþ þe nohut,
   Ne do þou so nammore!"   156

[Thrush]   "Niȝtingale, þou art ounwis
On hem to leggen so michel pris —

---

138. prude *ms*: pude

---

137. *to grounde*: i.e., "to their downfall"
140. *is*: "his"
142-4. "It (i.e., a woman, especially one such as Delilah) is the worst hoard of great value that Jesus created in Paradise to be held as a treasure." There is possibly a pun on *hoard* and *whore*.
149. *mest i-herd*: "most praised"
150. *louelich ounder gore*: "lovely in her garments"; a common idiom.
151. "In (all) the world there is not so good a physician."
154. "Bird, you make me very sad."

Þi mede shal ben lene.
Among on houndret ne beþ fiue,   160
Nouþer of maidnes ne of wive,
   Þat holdeþ hem al clene,
Þat hy ne wercheþ wo in londe,
Oþer bringeþ men to shonde,   164
   And þat is wel i-seene.
And þey we sitten þerfore to striuen,
Boþe of maidnes and of wiue,
   Soþ ne seist þou ene."   168

[Night.]   "O fowel, þi mouþ þe haueþ i-shend!
Þoru wam wes al þis world i-wend?
   Of a maide meke and milde;
Of hire sprong þat holi bern   172
Þat boren wes in Bedlehem,
   And temeþ al þat is wilde.
Hoe ne weste of sunne ne of shame;
Marie wes ire riȝte name,   176
   Crist hire i-shilde!
ffowel, for þi false sawe
fforbedd I þe þis wode shawe,
   Þou fare into þe filde!"   180

---

170. wes *ms*: wel
179. Forbedd I *ms*: fforbeddi

---

159. "Your reward will be small."
160. "Among one hundred there are not five."
166. *þey*: "though"; *to striuen*: "to debate"
168. "The truth you don't speak at all."
169. "Oh bird, (by) your (own) mouth you have destroyed (yourself)."
170. "Through whom was all this world changed?"
175. "She knew neither sin nor shame."

[Thrush]
> "Niȝttingale, I wes woed,
> Oþer I couþe to luitel goed,
>   Wiþ þe for to striue.
> I suge þat ich am ouercome   184
> Þoru hire þat bar þat holi sone
>   Þat soffrede woundes fiue.
> Hi swerie bi his holi name
> Ne shal I neuere suggen shame   188
>   Bi maidnes ne bi wiue.
> Hout of þis londe will I te,
> Ne rech I neuere weder I fle;
>   A-wai ich wille driue."   192

---

182. "Or I knew too little good," i.e., "was ill-informed"; cf. l. 74.
186. *woundes fiue*: the five wounds of Christ on the cross
190. "Out of this land I will go"; the defeated Thrush willingly accepts his banishment from the wood.
192. The poem lacks any concluding framework.

The Cuckoo and the Nightingale

The Cuckoo and the Nightingale (or *The Book of Cupid, God of Love*) is perhaps the most impressive of the pseudo-Chaucerian poems that make up the "Chaucer Apocrypha." In fact, it wasn't until late in the nineteenth century that scholars decided to exclude the *Cuckoo and Nightingale* from the official canon of Chaucer's works. But the poem's long-standing attribution to Chaucer is not at all surprising, for it is recorded in several of the best manuscripts containing Chaucer's earlier works, it contains a number of devices and elements that are typically found in Chaucer's poetry, and its wryly comic treatment of love and lovers creates tonal qualities which are strikingly similar to those found in Chaucer's own poems.

Evidence occurs in only one manuscript—Camb. Univ. Lib. MS Ff.1.6, which concludes with the phrase "Explicit Clanvowe"—as to the authorship of the *Cuckoo and the Nightingale*. This "Clanvowe" was Sir John Clanvowe, in all probability, a close friend of Chaucer's and one of an important group of knights at the court of Richard II who shared literary and intellectual interests (this group also included such notable figures as Lewis Clifford, Richard Sturry, Thomas Latimer, and William Nevill, among others). Sir John Clanvowe died in 1391. Some scholars favor assigning the poem to Thomas Clanvowe (probably Sir John's son) and favor an early fifteenth-century date of composition, but it seems more likely that the poem was written by John Clanvowe during the late 1380s, the period when Chaucer's *Legend of Good Women*—to which the *Cuckoo and the Nightingale* apparently alludes—would have become known to members of the court. It is Chaucer's *Parliament of Fowls*, however, which provides the primary inspiration. Both poems are debates set within dream-vision frameworks; both refer to the pairing of birds on St. Valentine's Day; both depict a narrator who is an unlikely lover and who is confronted in his visionary world with conflicting views about the nature of love; and both end abruptly and without clear resolutions when the dreamer is awakened by the singing of the birds. The poet's literary sources also include a version of Chaucer's *Knight's Tale* (from which he fashioned his opening verses), the *Roman de la Rose*, and French love-visions of the fourteenth century generally. It is quite possible that the poet was familiar with the earlier Middle English debate between the *Thrush and the Nightingale*, and it is also possible that he had at least some knowledge of the *Owl and the Nightingale*.

The *Cuckoo and the Nightingale* is written in five-verse stanzas, rhyming aabba, a stanza form which Chaucer uses only in the single stanza of the envoy to "The Complaint of Chaucer to his Purse," a stanza which may not be integral to Chaucer's poem. This stanza form is common, however, among the poems of Deschamps, Froissart, and Chartier, and it was used later by William Dunbar in several poems. The text of the *Cuckoo and the Nightingale* survives in five manuscripts, the best of which is Fairfax 16 of the Bodleian Library. Because that text is now available in the Scattergood edition, the text of the Tanner MS has been here used as the base in order to make this important but less well-known version of the poem also available.

---

1)   Base Text: Bodl. Library MS Tanner 346 (Bodl. 10173), fols. 97r–101v

2)   Other mss: Bodl. Library MS Fairfax 16 (Bodl. 3896)
                                    Bodl. Library MS Arch Selden B 24 (Bodl. 3354)
                                      Bodl. Library MS Bodley 638 (Bodl. 2078)
                                      Cambridge Univ. Library MS Ff. 1.6

3)   Selected Printed Texts: W. W. Skeat, *Chaucerian and Other Pieces* (1897), 347–58
                                      E. Vollmer, *Berliner Beiträge zur germanischen und romanischen Philologie* 17 (1898), 28
                                      V. J. Scattergood, "*The Boke of Cupide*—An Edition," *English Philological Studies* 9 (1965), 47–83
                                      V. J. Scattergood, *The Works of Sir John Clanvowe* (1975), 35–53
                                      Thomas J. Garbáty, *Medieval English Literature* (1984), 620–9

4)   *Index of Middle English Verse* 3361

Of þe Cuckow & þe Nightingale

The god of loue, a, benedicite!
Hov myȝti and hou gret a lord is he!
ffor he can make of lowe hertis heiȝe,
And of hie lowe and like forto deie,
And hard hertes he can maken fre.   5

He can make, within a litel stound,
Of seke folk hole, fressh, and sound,
And of hole he can make seke;
He can bynd & vnbynde eke
That he wil haue boundin or vnbound.   10

To tel his myȝt my wit may not suffise,
ffor he may do al þat he wil deuyse;
ffor he can make of wise folk ful nice,
And leþi folk to destroien vice,
And proude hertes he can makin agrise.   15

12–3. *These lines are transposed in the* ms.

1–5. Skeat suggested that this five-verse stanza form might stem from the Envoy to Chaucer's *The Complaint of Chaucer to his Purse*, but as Scattergood notes, this stanza was also used by Deschamps, Froissart, and Chartier; Dunbar employs the same form in several of his poems somewhat later.

1–20. By the final decades of the fourteenth century, descriptions such as this of the overwhelming power of love had become commonplace in courtly poetry.

1. *god of loue*: i.e., Cupid, portrayed in medieval literature as a handsome youth; *benedicite*: "bless you"

1–2. These lines are quoted from Chaucer's *Knight's Tale* (*CT* I 1785–6); Theseus' speech on the power of love, from which they are taken, may provide a clue as to the author's attitude toward love, which may differ from the attitude held by his narrative *persona*, and which may be an example of the "Chaucerian irony" to be found in the poem.

3. *For he can make*. This phrase, and the repetitions of it in lines 5, 6, 8, etc., also stems from the *Knight's Tale* (*CT* I 1789).

5. *fre*: usually means "generous" but here it implies "soft-hearted" or "generous of affection"

10. *that*: i.e., "those whom"

15. *makin agrise*: "cause to tremble"

Shortli, al þat euer he wil he may;
Agaynes him dar no wiȝt sei nay,
ffor he can glade & greue whome him liketh,
And who þat he wol he lauȝeth or sikeþ,
And most his myȝt he shedeþ euer in May.   20

ffor euere trwe gentil hert fre
Þat with him is, or þenkeþ forto be,
Agein May nov shal have some stering,
Or to joy or ellis to som mournyng,
In no ceson so mych, as þenkeþ me.   25

ffor when þai mai here þe briddes sing,
And þe floures se, and þe leues spring,
Þat bringeþ into her remembraunce
A maner ease, medled with greuaunce,
And lusti þouȝtes, ful of gret longing.   30

And of þat longing comeþ heuynes,
And þerof groweþ oft gret sekenes,
And for lak of þat þat þei desire;
And þus in Mai ben hertes set on fire
So þat þei brenne forþ in gret distres.   35

I speke þis of feling, truli;
If I be oold & vnlusti,

---

18. *whome him liketh*: i.e. "whomever it pleases him (to provide cheer to)"
19. "And whomever he wishes, he makes him laugh or sigh."
20. *shedeth*: "dispenses" or "distributes"; i.e. the power of love is most commonly and most strongly felt during the month of May.
21. *euere*: "every"
23. *Agein*: "during"; *some stering*: "some stirring up"
29. "a kind of pleasure, mingled with sorrow": the bitter-sweet state of being in love
30–3. The common characteristics of lovesickness; cf. ll. 38–9.
37–42. The narrator in this pseudo-Chaucerian poem has much in common with the narrators in Chaucer's earlier works and perhaps also with Pandarus. In *Lenvoy de Chaucer a Scogan* Chaucer portrays also himself as an old and unsuccessful lover (ll. 29–36), as does Gower in the *Confessio Amantis* (VIII, 2403). It is often the case in

3it I haue felt of þat sekenes, þuru3 May,
Boþ hote and cold, an accesse euereday,
Hov sore, i-wis, þer wot no wi3t but I. 40

I am so shaken with þe feuers white,
Of al þis May slepe I but a lite;
And also it is not like to me
That eny hert shuld slepi be
In whom þat loue his fire dart wil smyte. 45

But as I lay þis oþir ny3t waking,
I thou3t hou louers had a tokenyng,
And among hem it was a comen tale
That it were good to here þe ny3tyngale
Rather þen þe lewde kukko syng. 50

And þen I þou3t, anone as it was day,
I would go sum whider to assay

---

39. An accesse *ms*: and anesse

---

dream-visions that the narrator's fears and desires become personified in the figures
that he sees in his vision.
37. *If*: i.e. "though"
39. *accesse*: "fever" or "attack"; the line describes the fevers and chills of the "lover's mala-
dy," a condition which is more fully shown in Chaucer's Arcite in the second part
of the *Knight's Tale* (*CT* I 1359–79).
41. *feuers white*: i.e. the fevers of love that cause the lover to turn pale; cf. the expression
blaunche fevere in *Troilus and Criseyde* (I 916).
43. "It does not seem right to me."
47–50. It was apparently a common belief that if a lover heard the song of the nightin-
gale before the song of the cuckoo, he would be successful in love; if he heard the
cuckoo first, he would be unsuccessful. The value of the nightingale's song to lovers
is also referred to in *The Floure and the Leafe*, ll. 39–42, and in Milton's sonnet on the
nightingale.
48. *comen tale*: i.e. "commonly believed"
50. *lewde*: "lewd" usually means "ignorant" or "coarse" but in conjunction with the cuck-
oo sometimes means "wanton" (cf. *Parl. of Fowls* 616); in the *Parl. of Birds* the cuckoo's
lack of refinement is indicated by his inability to sing in French (ll. 74–80).

If þat I myȝt a nyȝtyngale here;
ffor ȝit herd I none of al þis ȝere,
And it was þo þe þridd nyȝt of May.   55

And anon as I þe day aspied,
No lenger would I in my bed abide,
But vnto a wode þat was fast bi
I went forþe allone boldli,
And held me þe wai doun bi a broke side,   60

Til I came til a lavnde of white and grene;
So faire one hade I neuer in bene.
The grounde was grene, i-poudred with daise,
The floures & þe grenes like heigh,
Al grene and white, was noþing ellis sene.   65

There sate I doune among þe faire floures,
And sauȝ þe briddes trip oute of her boures,
Per as þei rested hem al the nyȝt;
Thei were so ioiful of the daies liȝt
Thei bigan of May forto done houres.   70

---

55. This date is another of the Chaucerian elements that abound in the poem, for the
third of May apparently held special significance for Chaucer: it is on this day that
Palamon escapes from prison, Pandarus first woos Criseyde for Troilus, and Chaun-
tecleer is carried off by the fox. It isn't known for certain what meaning this date
had for Chaucer, but most scholars believe May 3 was considered to be a day of
ill-fortune, something like Friday the 13th (for some suggestions about Chaucer and
May 3, see for example John P. McCall, *MLN*, 76 [1961], 201–5, and George R. Adams
and Bernard S. Levy, *ELN*, 3 [1966], 245–8). It does seem clear, in any case, that
on May 3 events of grave consequence take place, and these events all involve characters
whose romantic feelings are at flood tide. It is also possible that May 3 had some
personal significance for Chaucer and that Chaucer's friend Clanvowe was aware of
this fact.
61. *lavnde*: "meadow"
64. *like heigh*: "alike (were) high"
70. *forto done houres*: the singing of the birds is compared to the singing of the liturgical
hours of the Church, not an unusual comparison.
71. "They knew that service entirely by heart."
72–5. Cf. the variety of songs in *A Parl. of Birds*.

Thei koude þat service al bi rote;
Ther was many a loueli note;
Some song loude, as þei hade pleyned,
And some in oþer maner voice i-fayned,
And som al oute, with al þe ful throte.   75

Thei preyned hem & made hem riȝt gay,
And davnseden and lepen on þe spray;
And euermore two and two in fere,
Riȝt so as þey hade chosen hem to-ȝere
In feuirȝere, opon seint Valentynes day.   80

And þe riuer þat I sate opon,
It made such a noise as it ron,
Acordant with þe briddes armonye,
Me þouȝt it was þe best melodie
Þat myȝt ben i-herd of eny man.   85

And for delite, I wot neuir hov,
I fil in such a slombre and swow —
Nouȝt al a-slepe, ne fulli wakyng —

---

71. þat *ms*: not
75. al *ms*: þe

---

76. *preyned hem*: "preened themselves"
78. *in fere*: "together in companionship"
79. *to-yere*: "this year"; cf. the current use of the word *today* (i.e., "this day").
80. *seint Valentynes day*. According to popular belief, the birds assembled on Valentine's Day to select their mates for the coming year, as they do in Chaucer's *Parliament of Fowls*, and as is referred to in Chaucer's poems the *Complaint of Mars* and the *Complaynt D'Amours*. Cf. also the statement in the *Paston Letters*: "And, cosyn, vppon Fryday is Sent Volentynes Day, and euery brydde chesyth hym a make . . ." (ed. N. Davis, 2:436).
81–8. The description of the narrator being lulled into a state of semi-consciousness by the singing of the birds and the babbling brook is a convention in dream-vision poetry (cf. *Death and Life* 32–6 and *Winner and Waster* 36–46). From l. 88 until the final line of the poem when the narrator is awakened, all the action takes place within his dream.

And in þat swow me þouȝt I herd syng
The sori brid, þe lewde cukko.   90

And þat was on a tre riȝt fast bie:
But who was þan euyl apaied but I?

[Narrator]   "Nov God," quod I, "þat deid on þe crois,
ȝeve sorou on þe and on þi lewde voys!
ffor litil ioy haue I nov of þi crie."   95

And as I with þe cukko þus gan chide,
I herd in þe next bussh biside
A nyȝtyngale so lustely syng
That wiþ hir clere vois she made ryng
Puruȝ al þe grene wode wide.   100

[Narrator]   "A! goode nyȝtyngale," quod I þanne,
"A litel hast þou be to long henne;
ffor here haþ bene þe leude cukko,
And songen songes raþer þen hast þou —
I prai to God euyl fire him brenne!"   105

But nov I wil ȝov tel a wondir þing:
As long as I lai in þat swownyng,
Me þouȝt I wist what þe briddes ment,
And what þey seide, and what was her entent,
And of her spech I hade goode knowyng.   110

---

89. þouȝt *ms*: þouȝ
103. leude *ms*: loude

---

92. *evyl apaied*: "displeased" (i.e., "angry"), a common idiom; cf. the phrase *right wel apaied*
    ("pleased") in l. 231.
101-2. The narrator, mindful of the "lover's tokening" described in ll. 47-50, is chagrined
    that the Nightingale did not sing sooner.
105. *him*. The Cuckoo is male, the Nightingale female.
106. Cf. *The Clerk and the Nightingale*, 7-8.

And þere herd I þe nyȝtingale say,
[Nightingale] "Nou, goode cukko, go somwhere a-way,
And let vs þat can singen dwellin here;
ffor euere wiȝt eschewiþ þe to here,
Ti songes ben so elenge, in goode fai."   115

[Cuckoo] "What!" quod he, "what mai þe aylen nov?
It þinkiþ me I sing as wel as þou;
ffor my song is boþ trwe & plein,
And þouȝ I cannot crakil so in vayne,
As þou dost in þi þrote, I wot not howe;   120

And euere wiȝt mai vnderstonde me;
But nyȝtingale, so mai þai not do þe,
ffor þou hast many a nyce queynt crye.
I haue þe herd seyn 'Ocy! Ocy!'
Hou myȝt I cnow what þat shuld be?"   125

[Nightingale] "A, foole," quod she, "wost þou not what it is
Whan þat I sai 'Oci! Oci!,' i-wis?

---

113. here *ms*: he

---

112. The desire of one bird to expel the rival bird from the area is frequently expressed in bird-debates, beginning with the *Owl and the Nightingale* (33) and continuing in the *Thrush and the Nightingale* (84, 97–8).

113–20. Dispute over the merits of the birds as singers is another point of contact between this poem and the *Owl and the Nightingale*. It is possible that the contrast in singing styles is here intended to suggest the differences between the monophonic and polyphonic music of the Middle Ages.

118. *plein*: carries both the meaning "plain" (i.e., "easily understood"—see l. 121) and "plain-song."

119. *crakil*: "trill," but meant pejoratively

123. *a nyce queynt crye*: "a silly, strange cry"

124. *Ocy! Ocy!* This is the cry of the nightingale as described in several Old French poems. In addition to the onomatopoeia, *oci* is the imperative form of the OF verb *ocire*, "to kill," and in 126–30 the Nightingale builds upon this meaning. Cf. the interpretation of the nightingale's cry that occurs in Lydgate's *A Seying of the Nightingale* (ed. Mac-Cracken, pp. 22 ff); cf. also l. 23 in a *Parl. of Birds*.

126. *A*: "oh"

Then mene I þat I would, wondir feyne,
That al þai were shamefulli slayn
That menen ouȝt again loue amys.   130

And also, I would þat al þoo hade þe dede,
That þink not in loue her life to lede;
ffor who þat wil not þe god of loue serue,
I dar wel sai, he is worþi to sterue;
And for þat skil 'Ocy! Oci!' I grede."   135

[Cuckoo]   "Fy," quod þe cukko, "þis is a queint lawe,
That euere wiȝt shal loue or be to-drawe!
But I forsake al such companye;
ffor myn entent is not forto deye,
Ne neþir, while I lyve, on loues yokke to drawe.   140

ffor louers ben þe folk þat bene on lyue
That most disease haue and most vnthryue,
And most endure sorow, wo, and care,
And lest felen of welfare;
What nediþ it ayens trouth to stryue?"   145

[Nightingale]   "What?" quod she, "þou art oute of þi mynde!
Hou myȝt þou, in þi clerenes, fynde

---

140. lyue *ms*: leve

---

130. "that say anything falsely against love"
131-2. "And I also wish that all those receive the death (penalty) that do not plan to
   lead their lives as lovers."
134. *worþi to sterue*: "deserves to die"
136. *queint*: "strange"
137. *to-drawe*: "torn apart" (i.e., "executed")
140. *on loves yokke to drawe*. This metaphor of subjugation is often used in a positive sense,
   in reference to the blissful bondage of marriage; cf. the *Clerk's Tale* (*CT* IV 113) and
   the *Merchant's Tale* (*CT* IV 1285), but the Cuckoo uses it to introduce the idea of the
   sufferings of lovers.

To speke of loues seruantis in þis wyse?
ffor in þis world is noon so goode seruyse
To euere wiȝt þat gentil is of kynde.   150

ffor þer-of, truli, cometh al goodnes,
Al honour, and al gentilles,
Wirship, ease, and al hertis lust,
Parfit ioy, and ful a-ssured trust,
Iolite, plesaunce, and fresshenes,   155

Lowlihed, larges, & curtesie,
Semelihed, and trwe companye,
Drede of shame forto done amys;
ffor he þat truli loues seruant is
Were loþer be shamed þen to dey.   160

And þat þis is soþe, þat I sey,
In þat bileue I wil lyue and deye;
And cukko, so I rede þat þou do, iwis."

[Cuckoo]   "Than," quod he, "let me neuer have blis
If euer I vnto þat counsel obey!   165

Nightingale, þou spekist wondir faire,
But, for al þat, is þe soþ contrarie;
ffor loue is in ȝung folk but rage,
And in old folk a gret dotage;
Who most it vseth, most shal empeire.   170

---

162. lyue *ms*: leve

151–60. The Nightingale here gives voice to the conventional wisdom of *fine amour*, which
    views love as ennobling and as inspiring refined behavior, in fact, as the source of
    all good (l. 151).
168–9. The Cuckoo's definition of "love"—in Youth mindless passion, in Old Age senile
    lusting; the narrator would belong to the latter category, according to the Cuckoo.
170. "Who practices it the most shall be harmed the most."

ffor þerof comeþ disease & heuynes,
Sorow and care, and many a gret sekenes,
Despite, debate, anger and envie,
Deprauyng, shame, vntrist & ielousye,
Pride, myschef, pouert, and woodnes.   175

Louying is an ofice of dispaire,
And oo þing is þerin þat is not faire:
ffor who þat getiþ of loue a litel blisse,
But if he be alwai þerwith, i-wisse,
He may ful sone of age haue his eyre.   180

And, nyȝtyngale, þerfore hold þe neigh;
ffor leue me wel, for al þi queynt crye,
If þou be ferre or long fro þi make,
Þou shalt ben as oþer þat ben forsake —
And þen þou shalt hoten as I do."   185

[Nightingale]   "ffy," quod she, "on þi name and on þe!
The god of loue ne let þe neuer þe!
ffor þou art worse a þousand fold þan wood;
ffor meny oon is ful worþi & ful goode
That hade be nouȝt, ne hade loue i-be.   190

ffor euermore loue his seruantes amendiþ,
And from al euel tacches hem defendiþ,
And makeþ hem to bren riȝt as a fire

171–5. These verses are intended to counter-balance ll. 151–60.

177. *faire*: "pleasant"

178–80. Skeat paraphrased these verses: "For he who gets a little bliss of love may very
soon find that his heir has come of age, unless he is always devoted to it"; but it is
more likely they mean: "For he who gets a little bliss of love may very soon find,
unless he is always near his lover, that he will have an heir (fathered by someone
else)." This train of thought is continued in the next stanza in ll. 183–5.

185. "And then you will be called what I am called," i.e., a cuckold; this *double entendre*
stems from the two meanings of the Old French word *coucou*: "cuckoo" and "cuckold."

190. "that would have been worthless, if it hadn't been for love"

In trouþe and in wirshipful desire,
And when hem likeþ, ioy inov hem sendeþ."   195

[Cuckoo]   "Thou nyȝtingale," he said, "hold þe stil!
ffor loue haþ no reson, but it is wil;
ffor oft tyme vntrwe folk he esiþ,
And trwe folk so bittirli he displesiþ
That for defaute of grace he let hem spil.   200

[With such a lorde wol I never be;
For he is blind alwey and may not see;
And whom he hit he not, or whom he fayleth;
And in his court ful selden trouthe avayleth,
So dyvers and so wilful is he."]   205

Than toke I of þe nyȝtingale kepe,
Hou she cast a sigh oute of her depe,
[Nightingale]   And said, "Allas þat euer I wos i-bore!
I can, for tene, nouȝt sey oo word more."
And riȝt with þat she barst oute forto wepe.   210

"Allas," quod she, "myn hert wil tobreke,
To herin þus þis fals brid speke
Of loue and of his wirshipful seruice.
Nou god of love, þou help me in som wise
That I may on þis cukko bene awreke."   215

201–5. *This stanza, omitted from the Tanner MS, is supplied from Cambridge University Library MS Ff. I. 6.*
208. i-bore *ms*: i-hore

---

197. "Love knows no reason, only caprice."
200. "that for lack of mercy he lets them die"
202. Proverbial (Whiting C 634)
203. "And he knows not whom he hits, or whom he fails (to hit)."
209. *for tene*: "because of (my) grief"; the Nightingale ends her participation in the dispute by bursting into tears.

Me þouȝt þen I stert vp anone,
[And to the broke I ran, and gat a stoon,
And at the Cukko hertely I cast;
And he, for dred, fley away ful faste;]
And glad was I þat he was agone.   220

[Cuckoo]

And euermore þe cukko as he flai
Said, "Farewel, farewel, popingay,"
As þouȝ he hade scorned, [thoughte me;
But ay I hunted him fro tree to tree
Til he was fer al out of sighte awey.]   225

[Nightingale]

And þen come þe nyȝtyngale to me,
And seid, "Firende, forsoþe I þank þe
Þat þou hast liked me to rescow;
And oon avow to loue make I now,
That al þis Mai I wil þi singer be."   230

[Nightingale]

I þankid hir and was riȝt wel apaied.
"Ȝe," quod she, "and be þou not dismaied,
Þouȝ þou haue herd þe cukko syng erst þan me;

216–25. *These two stanzas have been combined into a single stanza in the Tanner MS; the lines supplied are from MS Ff. I. 6.*

---

216. *Me þouȝt*: a reminder that the narrator is describing his own actions within his dream.
216–20. The narrator himself provides the answer to the Nightingale's prayer; ironically, it was bad luck to throw things at a cuckoo, according to proverbial lore (Whiting C 603): "He that throwyth stone or stycke at suche a byrde he is lycke To synge that byrdes songe" (quoted from Henry Medwall's *Fulgens and Lucres*).
222. *popingay*: i.e., "parrot"; in the *Parl. of Fowls* Chaucer describes the popinjay as "ful of delicasye" (l. 359), indicating that the bird was considered to be a voluptuary. Pliny describes the parrot in his *Natural History*: "in vino praecipue lasciva" (Bk. X, Chap. 58). The implication of the Cuckoo's gibe, then, is that in his opinion the narrator is a lecherous old fool.
232–5. The Nightingale's promise to give the narrator better assistance *next* year, qualified by two "if" clauses, can hardly be considered a certainty.

ffor, if I lyve, it shal amendid be
The next May, if I be not affraied.   235

And oo þing I wil rede þe also:
Ne leue þou not þe cukko, loves foo,
ffor al þat he haþe seyde is strong lesing."
[Narrator]   "Nay," quod I, "þis shal noþing me bring
ffro loue, but it haþ do me myche wo."   240

[Nightingale]   "3e vse," quod she, "þis medicyne
Euere day þis Mai or þou dyne:
To loke opon þe fressh daise.
And þou3 þou be for wo in poynt to dey,
That shal ful greetli lessin þe of þi peyn.   245

And loke alway þat þou be goode & trwe,
And I wil sing oon of the songis nwe,
ffor loue of þe, as loude as I mai crie."
And than she bigan þis song ful hey3:
"I shrew all hem þat bene of loue vntrwe."   250

---

234. lyue *ms*: leve
237. *The ms reads*: Ne love thou not the cukko ne his loyve foo
239. nothing *ms*: noman
240. Fro *ms*: for; but *ms*: and

---

237. *leue*: i.e. "believe"
239–40. " 'No,' I said, 'this won't cause me to leave the service of Love, but it has caused
    me much woe.' "
241–5. These lines may allude to a late fourteenth- and early fifteenth-century courtly
    phenomenon known as the cult of the daisy, which Chaucer also seems to be allud-
    ing to in verses 40–57, 182–7, 201–2, and 211 of the *F Prologue to the Legend of Good
    Women*. (For speculations about the cult of the daisy, see Derek Pearsall, *The Floure
    and the Leafe* [London, 1962], 22ff. and D. W. Robertson, Jr., *A Preface to Chaucer* [Prince-
    ton, 1963], 225–6, n. 138.) Because the daisy is able to withstand harsh weather and
    because it is a flower that follows the sun, it came to symbolize constancy in love.
249–50. The Nightingale's song is similar to those sung by the various birds in a *Parl.
    of Birds*.

                And whan she hade song hit to þe ende,

[Nightingale]   "Nou farewel," quod she, "for I mot wende;

                And gode of loue þat can right wel and may,

                As mykil ioy send þe þis day

                As eny ʒit louer he euer send!"   255

                Thus takeþ þe nyʒtyngale her leue of me.

                I prai to God alwai wiþ her be,

                And ioy of loue he send hir euermore,

                And shild vs fro þe cukko and his lore —

                ffor þer is not so fals a brid as is he!   260

                fforthe she fleuth, þe gentil nyʒtyngale,

                To al þe briddes þat were in þat dale,

                And gate hem al into a place in fere,

                And bisouʒten hem þat þei would her

                Her diseas, and þus bigan hir tale: 265

[Nightingale]   "ʒe witen wel, it is not fro yow hide,

                Hou þe cukko and I fast haue chide

                Euer siþen it was daies liʒt.

                I pray ʒow al þat ʒe do me riʒt

                Of þat foule, fals, vnkynd brid!"   270

                Than spake oon bryd for all bi oon assent:

[Bird]   "Þis mater askiþ good auisement;

---

257. he *supplied*

266. *The ms reads*: the cukko wel it is forto hide

---

264. *her*: "hear"

265. *Her diseas*: i.e., "her troubles"

270. *of*: i.e., "in regard to"

271–80. Bird parliaments became quite popular during the fifteenth century, when several
    poems were written in imitation of Chaucer's *Parliament of Fowls*, including a *Parl. of
    Birds*. The unnamed bird who speaks here seems to be a very rational creature, reminis-
    cent of the wren who is a voice of reason near the end of the *Owl and the Nightingale*.

ffor we ben few briddis here in fere,
And soþ it is þe cukko is not here;
And þerfore we wil haue a parlement;   275

And þerat shal þe egil be oure lord,
And oþer peris þat ben of record,
And þe cukko shal be after sent.
Ther shal be ȝeue þe iugement,
Or ellis we shal fynalli make acord.   280

And þis shal be, wiþouten nay,
The morov after seint valentynes day,
Vndir a mapul þat is faire & grene,
Bifore þe chavmber window of þe quene
At Wodstoke, opon the grene lay."   285

She thanked hem & þen hir leue tooke,
And fley into an hauthorne bi þat broke;
And þere she sate and song opon þat tre:
[Nightingale]   "Terme of life, love haþ withhold me,"
So loude þat I with þat song awoke.   290

287. fley *supplied*

285. If the poem is the work of John Clanvowe and was written during the late 1380s, then the reference to the Queen at Woodstock would be to Anne of Bohemia, the wife of Richard II. Commentators who give the poem a later date believe the Queen to be Joan of Navarre, the second wife of Henry IV.
287. The hawthorn, like the daisy, is associated with constancy in love (cf. *The Temple of Glas* 510–22).
289. "All my life love has sustained me."
290. Cf. Chaucer's *Parl. of Fowls* 693–5. This abrupt and unresolved ending is similar to the brief and ambiguous conclusions of Chaucer's dream-vision poems.

The Clerk and the Nightingale I and II

The Clerk and the Nightingale I and *The Clerk and the Nightingale II* are here considered one poem even though they survive as two separate fragments, one in Cambridge MS Ff.5.48, the other in Bodleian MS Rawlinson Poetry 34. The Cambridge text preserves the opening 106 verses of a poem from which the concluding verses have been lost, while the Oxford text preserves only the final 86 verses of a very similar poem; and although these two manuscript fragments are not written in the same hand, it seems probable that together they constitute the greater part of a single poem from which a small number of verses have been lost. In the strictest sense *The Clerk and the Nightingale* is not a true bird debate since one debater is human, but the poem has close affinities to the bird-debate poems as a group. Both *The Clerk and the Nightingale* and the *Thrush and the Nightingale* focus on the same issues — the worth of women and the fidelity of women — and in both poems an idealistic and sentimental lover of women is confronted by a disillusioned and embittered woman-hater. In both poems the misogynist cites examples of illustrious men who were brought to grief by their faithless wives or lovers, and in both the advocate of women introduces the Virgin Mary as the supreme example of womanly goodness. *The Clerk and the Nightingale* provides no explicit answer to the question of women's worth. But the final lines of the poem suggest that the poet's sympathies reside with the Nightingale, whose final admonition to the Clerk as she flies away is one that the reader would do well to heed also. It is reasonable, therefore, to view *The Clerk and the Nightingale I and II* as providing a clear response to the *Thrush and the Nightingale* and as attempting to turn the earlier poem on its head. *The Clerk and the Nightingale* is written in quatrains rhyming abab (which in the Rawlinson text are recorded as septenary couplets), and both manuscripts date to the second half of the fifteenth century.

---

1) Base Text: Cambridge University MS Ff.5.48, fols. 57r–57v
(*Clerk & Night. I*)
Bodleian Lib. MS Rawlinson Poetry 34 (Bodl.
14528), fols. 5r–5v (*Clerk & Night. II*)

2) Other mss: none

3) Printed Texts: J. O. Halliwell, *Nugae Poeticae* (1844), 37–9 (*Clerk & Night. I* only)
R. H. Robbins, *Secular Lyrics of the XIV and XV Centuries* (1952), 172–9

4) *Index of Middle English Verse* 1452 (*Clerk & Night. I*)
Supplement to the Index of Middle English Verse 295.5 (*Clerk & Night. II*)

[The Clerk and the Nightingale I]

In a mornyng of May,
   As I lay on slepyng,
To here a song of a fowle
   I had gret likyng.   4

I herd a ny3tyngale syng,
   I likyd hir full welle;
She seid to me a wonder thyng,
   I shall tell þe euery delle.   8

1–5. The usual spring-time setting is here described in very abbreviated fashion, and the narrator, a conventional love-sufferer, becomes a participant in the debate rather than a mere observer. His pleasure at hearing the Nightingale sing (compare the narrator in the *Cuckoo and the Nightingale* and his displeasure at hearing the Cuckoo rather than the Nightingale) turns to dismay at the views this unconventional Nightingale expresses.

2. This line may suggest that the debate occurs while the narrator is in a semi-conscious or dream-like state, though more likely the singing of the bird has simply awakened him.

[Nightingale]   "Thynk, man, for þi curtesy
                    & for þine owne gode;
                 Stonde a while and sey me
                    Why þou mornyst in þi mode?"   12

[Clerk]   "Niȝtyngale, wel I may
                    & wele I wot and wene;
                 I morne nyȝt and day
                    For on þat is so schene."   16

[Night.]   "Now, clerk, for-soth þou art a fole
                    Þat þou mournys so depe:
                 Þat now is hot shalbe colde,
                    Þat now lawȝgh oft may wepe."   20

[Clerk]   "Nyghtyngale, she is so gode
                    Þat no thyng may telle,
                 Fayre and trwe, mylde of mode—
                    She may me gif and sell!"   24

[Night.]   "Be-warre, clerk, I warne þe:
                    Luf þou not so depe;
                 When þou levyst in luf to be,
                    Nede þou hase to wepe.   28

                 A woman is a wonder thyng,
                    Þow sho be fayre and stille;

---

14. "and well I know and think"
16. a cliché often expressed by lovers; cf. *Parl. of Birds*, 61.
19–20. common proverbs (Whiting S19 and Whiting L92)
22. "that words can't express it"
23. *mylde of mode*: "gentle in temperament"; cf. *Clerk & Night.* II, 15 and more generally, *Thrush & Night.* 55 and 152.
24. "She may me give or sell"; i.e., "(I am hers so completely) she can do with me as she likes."
27. "when you believe yourself to be in love"

She nys trwe to knyȝt nor kyng;
    Clerke, to þe she nylle."   32

[Clerk]   "Nyȝtyngale, why seyst þou so?
    Þou gabbust in þi tale.
    Wymmen bryng men owt of woo,
      She is bote of alle bale."   36

[Night.]   "Ne art þou not to lore sete,
      And wist of olde and newe.
    Treue þi luf and lockyt boþe?
      Þat werk is not trwe!   40

    Alle woo a woman began,
      She was begynyng;
    Wyttenesse Adam, þe formast man—
      Þat is no lesyng."   44

[Clerk]   "Nyȝtyngale, þat wot I wele:
      A woman wroȝt a shame.
    A-noþer, I telle þe euery dell,
      Broȝt vs alle to game."   48

---

31. knyght nor kyng *ms*: kyng nor knyght
35. of *supplied*

---

34. I.e., "you are talking nonsense."
36. *bote of . . . bale*: "a remedy for suffering," an expression commonly associated with the Virgin (cf. the lyric "At a sprynge wel under a thorn," *Index* 420) and thus anticipating the Clerk's next point. The suggestion that women provide comfort for men is the first argument offered by the Nightingale in the *Thrush & Night*.
37–40. "You are not well-schooled in lore, either old or new. Your love be both true and secure? That notion is not true!"
40. *werk*. Robbins reads *wors*, which he emends to *word*.
41–4. These verses echo *Thrush & Night*. 70–2.
45–8. Cf. *Thrush & Night*. 28–33

[Night.]　　　"Be stille, clerk, þou art vn-wyse;
　　　　　　　　Þou spekist of a mayde
　　　　　　　Þat bare þe Lord of Paradyse,
　　　　　　　　Þat oure foo-men frayed.　　　　　　　52

　　　　　　　Name hir to no woman,
　　　　　　　　To mayden nor to wyfe,
　　　　　　　For þou knowist, nor I ne kan,
　　　　　　　　Non so trwe of life.　　　　　　　　56

　　　　　　　I take wyttenesse of Dauyd Kyng,
　　　　　　　　And at Salomon þe wyse,
　　　　　　　Þat a woman for a litull thyng
　　　　　　　　Ofte change hir seruyse.　　　　　　60

　　　　　　　Luf a woman as þi lyfe,
　　　　　　　　And kepe hir all with wynne,
　　　　　　　For a purse or for a knyfe,
　　　　　　　　When on is owt anoþer is in."　　　64

[Clerk]　　　"Niȝtyngale, þou gabbist me!
　　　　　　　　Wymmen be fayre and hende,
　　　　　　　Ful of game and of glee
　　　　　　　　Wher-so þei wende.　　　　　　　　68

　　　　　　　Were a mon in sorow broȝt,
　　　　　　　　Wymmen myȝt out hym bryng;

---

51. Lord *supplied*

49-56. The Nightingale here rejects the argument which the Thrush so quickly accepts in *Thrush & Night.*
57-8. The Old Testament figure included in the list of betrayed men in *Thrush & Night.* is Samson (in addition to the earlier reference to Adam).
64. Cf. Cassandra's comments to Troilus: "This Diomede is inne, and thow arte oute" (*Troilus & Criseyde* V 1519).
69-72. Cf. *Thrush & Night.* 28-33

          With a lokyng turne his thoȝt,
            And with a kysse turne his mournyng."   72

[Night.]   "Clerke, if þou wil riȝt begynne,
            Rede and vndurstonde,
          Mannes thoȝt chaungis with synne,
            Wel oft þou turnyd fonde;   76

          Kysse of women wyrkyth wo
            With synne mony folde;
          Iudas kissed God also,
            And to þe Iewes he hym solde.   80

          Clerk, as þou art wyse,
            Þou louyst wel hir lokyng;
          When þi purse shakyn is,
            Fare-wel, clerk, þi cossyng!"   84

[Clerk]   "Nyȝtyngale, þou spekist noȝt,
            Late be alle þi fare.
          How sholde men be forth broȝt
            Ne wymmen ware?"   88

[Night.]   "Ther-to onswer I can
            With-out any stodying:
          Wymmen was for man-
            Kynd forth to bryng.   92

91–2. man- / Kynd *ms*: mankynd

---

76. "Very often you (men are) turned into fond (fools)."
78. *mony folde*: "manifold," i.e. "on many occasions"
85–6. "Nightingale, you say nothing (of any value), stop all your carrying on."
87–8. Cf. the Wife of Bath's somewhat similar argument: "And certes, if ther were no
    seed ysowe, / Virginitee, thanne wherof sholde it growe?" (*Cant. Tales* III 71–2).

She was made to helpe man,
   And no-thyng for to leve.
Þou myʒtes þat wete at Adam,
   But þou ne wilt me leve.   96

I sey alle wymmen ar mysse-went,
   On gode is not in londe.
Men thruʒ wymmen be shent
   And ofte broʒt in bonde;   100

For I fynde non so gode,
   Be way nor be strete,
But a man may change hir mote
   If his purse wey grete."   104

[Clerk]   "Nyʒtyngale, þou gabbist me,
        And þat is shame thym . . . ."

[The Clerk and the Nightingale II]

Philomena   ". . . . .
      And a woman off hauntyng moode,
      Blythly sche wyll be swyuyd.   2

---

97. mysse-went *ms*: mysse-gon

---

93. Gen. 2:18
94. "and not to desert him"
103. *mote*: "mind" (i.e., "mood")
1–10. Just before the point at which the *Clerk & Night. I* fragment breaks off, the Nightingale has raised the issue of woman's fickleness and the ease with which one man may entice a woman away from another man. In these first verses of the *Clerk & Night. II* fragment, the Nightingale is also addressing the subject of woman's lack of steadfastness. (The speaker rubrics *Philomena* and *Clericus* occur in the ms.)
1. *hauntyng moode*: i.e., "haughty mood"

Butt in a lytyll whyle
Hur wyll wyll a-way wende.
Be thow i-ware off gyle
Euer at the last ende; 6

For whan a woman wepyt most
And sorowyth all her fyl,
Than myght þou be soryst a-gast,
Leste þat sche be-gyle the wyl." 10

Clericus   "Doe wey, fole, thi blamyng,
And ffle a-way owt of þis lond.
For a woman ys a wel fayre thyng
And trew for to fond; 14

Bryght & schene, myld of mode,
Off dedys good and hend.
Nyʒtyngale, I telle the, my fode,
That þou darst women a-schend." 18

Philomena   "Be styl, clerk, and hold thi mowth,
And let gabbyng a throwe;
This lesyng ys wel wyde cowde,
That may al folk know. 22

---

5. i-ware *ms*: I-ware
10. wyl *supplied*

---

4. "Her desires will follow a new course."
9–10. "Then you should be most sorely afraid, lest that she will beguile you."
11. *fole*: "fool" rather than "fowl," cf. note to *Merle & Night*. 29
12. Cf. *Thrush & Night*. 191–2
14. *fond*: "prove"; cf. *Thrush & Night*. 42
17. *my fode*: "my young friend"
20. "and stop arguing for a moment"
21. *wyde cowde*: "widely known"; cf. *Thrush & Night*. 95

Clerk, be a appyl þou myght se:
  Sownd with-owtte and grene,
And in the core rotyd be.
  So faryth a woman, I wene.   26

Þou seyth þei be all hend & good,
  To doe al mannes wyll,
. . . .
  An þerfor, clerke, be styl."   30

Clericus   "Whan þou wylt al master be,
                And thy wyl al-wey haue,
              O thyng I be-seche þe,
                As I schall be thy knaue,   34

              And as þou art hend and ffre,
                And comyn off good blode —
              How schall I, tell thow me,
                To know the trew and the good?"   38

Philomena   "Clerk, ylk trew woman hath vpon,
                With-owt any lesyng,
              A robbe of grey marbyl ston,
                And of gret cumpasyng.   42

---

27. seyth *ms*: seyths
29. *This verse is lacking in the ms.*
36. comyn *ms*: Comyn

31-8. In this *master* and *knaue* (i.e., "teacher" and "pupil") section, the Clerk asks the Night-
    ingale to instruct him on identifying "true and good" women. The Nightingale responds
    by posing an elaborate enigma incorporating a series of impossible occurrences (*im-
    possibilia*) — implying that "true and good" women do not exist.
41-6. The woman's gray marble robe (ll. 41-2) is probably a tomb, which is also the
    "foot" with which she reaches the sky in l. 45. The implication is that she is "good"
    only when she is dead.

Ylk a woman þat ys good
   May doe gret merveyle —
A-reche þe sky with hur fote
   With-owtyn any fayle.   46

And ȝyf sche do, þe lady good,
   With her rokkes gore
Sche may spred all Ynglonde —
   Schyp, sayle, and eke ore.   50

They schul be god wan god ys dede,
   And afterward maad all new.
Now take, clerk, thi best rede,
   For woman schul neuer be trewe."   54

Clericus   "Alas, nyȝtyngale, alas,
   Me rewyth þat ilke stownde!
Thowe hast i-broght me on a cas;
   I wene I fal to grownde!   58

My hert wyll to-berst;
   Alas, my lyf ys to long.
The to smyte I ame prest,
   Hens but þat thow be goyng.   62

---

47. ȝyf *ms*: ȝyt

---

47. "and if she does (perform this marvel)"
48. *rokkes gore*: "the skirt of her dress"
48–9. The skirt spreading over all of England may be the grass which grows on the woman's grave.
50. "entirely"
51. "They shall be good when God is dead" (?), i.e., never.
52. The suggestion here is that women might be good if they could be created anew.
55–62. Cf. the *Cuckoo & Night.*, 208–15
56. "It saddens me to think of that time (when women shall be dead)."

                    Ne blame þou women ne more,
                        For-soth I rede the;
                    Thow schalt aby yt fful dere,
                        Hennys but þat thow ffle!"   66

Philomena   "Nay, clerk, for thi curtesy,
                        Mys-doe thow me ryght noght.
                    I wole theym preyse by and by,
                        Y wyle chaunge my thoght.   70

                    I preyse women þat be good,
                        What afterward be-fall;
                    They be full of curtesy and mood,
                        In bowre or eke in hall.   74

                    Haue good day, clerk ffre,
                        Fro the wyll Y wende;
                    Take hede what þat I haue seyde þe,
                        Fro the bygynnyng to the ende.   78

                    Loue wher thy ert may be-happe,
                        What-so-euer sche be;
                    And sche schal make a glasyn cappe,
                        And to skorn lawth the.   82

                    Fare-wel, clerk, and haue goodday,
                        No more wyl I spute.

69–74. The Nightingale's apparent change of heart is only an ironic response to the
    Clerk's threat of violence.
79. "Love wherever your heart may lead you."
81. *glasyn cappe*: "a glazed cap" or a "cap of glass"; there are several references in Middle
    English literature to glassy caps or hoods, and in most cases they indicate the self-
    deception of the wearer, who believes himself to be protected. Cf., for example, ll.
    246–7 in *Als I lay*, as well as *Troilus and Criseyde* (II 867 and V 469), the *Monk's Tale*
    (*CT* VII 2372), and *Piers Plowman* (B.20.171).
82. "and laugh at you in scorn"

Now wyl I fare in my way:
I rede þou to my wordys tak hede." 86

Explicit disputacio
inter clericum et
philomenam / etc.

The Merle and the Nightingale

The Merle and the Nightingale, composed near the close of the fifteenth century, is attributed to William Dunbar in both the Maitland folio and the Bannatyne manuscript. While the poem reflects the difficulty in categorizing Dunbar's poetry—it is a religious allegory, "a fable, a debate, an example of aureation, a love poem, and uses the device of the double *ballade*" (Tom Scott, *Dunbar: A Critical Exposition of the Poems* [Edinburgh, 1966], p. 280)—the *Merle and the Nightingale* is also the culminating work in the Middle English bird-debate tradition. As in the earlier bird-debates, the concern is once again with love, but here the contrast is between romantic love, advocated by the Merle (the European blackbird), and the love of God, advocated by the Nightingale. In her support of earthly, romantic love, the Merle recapitulates many of the arguments voiced in the earlier bird-debates: love between human beings can be ennobling; earthly love is necessitated by the Law of Kind; women were created by God for the purpose of being loved; and, with an ingenuity reminiscent of the Wife of Bath, the biblical admonition to "love your neighbor" may be interpreted to include the women in one's neighborhood. Responding from across an obviously symbolic river, the Nightingale cautions the Merle against the pursuit of earthly love in sentiments that recall the final stanzas of Chaucer's *Troilus and Criseyde*: earthly love is a form of vanity and is unstable, in contrast to the permanence of divine love; and therefore, all love is lost that isn't directed toward God. It is notable that the mood of the *Merle and the Nightingale* is sedate and that the birds are given temperate dispositions; they do not revile each other, and there is little of the rancor and suppressed violence of the earlier poems. Here the Nightingale is neither a cynic nor a woman-hater but a gentle, patient, speaker of truth. The Merle presents her arguments as earnestly as she can, but when she is finally won over through the Nightingale's exposure of her ignorance, she happily blends her voice with the Nightingale's in praising love of God. This blending together of the birds' two voices reflects the achievement of spiritual harmony, and it may also suggest a resolution through Christian marriage, in which the love of woman and the love of God flow from one to the other. In any case, there is in this final bird-debate a clear resolution and one that provides a genial conclusion to this entire group of poems.

The Merle and the Nightingale reflects the influence of Lydgate, in particular *The Churl and the Bird, A Saying of the Nightingale*, and *The Nightingale* (a poem no longer attributed to Lydgate), as well as the influence of Chaucer. A few scholars have questioned assigning the poem to Dunbar, but the poetic language of the poem is very similar to that found in many of his poems. The form of the poem — ten-syllable octaves rhyming ababbcbc, with alternating refrains — is one especially favored by Dunbar.

---

1)   Base Text: National Library of Scotland MS 1.1.6 (Bannatyne)

2)   Other mss: Magdalene Coll. Camb. 2553 (Pepysian Libr. Maitland Folio)

3)   Selected Printed Texts: *John Small, The Poems of William Dunbar* STS 2 (Edinburgh, 1898), 174–78
W. Mackay Mackenzie, *The Poems of William Dunbar* (London, 1932), 134–7

4)   *Supplement to the Index of Middle English Verse* 1503.5

The Merle and the Nightingale

In May as that Aurora did vpspring,
With cristall ene chasing þe cluddis sable,

1-2. Cf. *The Thistle and the Rose* 9; in both poems there is heavy use of aureate diction.

I hard a merle with mirry notis sing
A sang of lufe, with voce rycht comfortable,   4
Agane the orient bemis amiable,
Vpone a blisfull brenche of lawryr grene;
This wes hir sentens sueit and delectable:
[Merle]   "A lusty lyfe in Luves seruice bene."   8

Vnder this brench ran doun a revir bricht
Of balmy liquour, cristallyne of hew,
Agane the hevinly aisur skyis licht,
Quhair did, vpone þe toþer syd, persew   12
A nychtingall, with suggurit notis new,
Quhois angell fedderis as the pacok schone;
This wes hir song, and of a sentens trew:
[Nightingale]   "All luve is lost bot vpone God allone."   16

With notis glaid and glorious armony
This ioyfull merle so salust scho the day,

---

18. ioyfull *ms*: Ioyfull

---

3. The merle is the European blackbird. Like all of the birds in the Middle English bird-debates — except for the owl — it is a spring- time song bird. (As is true for "mavis," which is also a kind of bird, "merle" became a common given name, though the name could be either masculine or feminine.)
5. *agane*: "against," i.e., "in response to"
6. *lawryr*: "laurel"; cf. Lydgate's *The Churl and the Bird* 25, and also l. 63 in *The Nightingale* (*Index* 931), formerly attributed to Lydgate.
8. The Merle's refrain expresses the usual sentiments of the "courtly lover," which was the view of the Nightingale in the *Cuckoo and the Nightingale*. Love is treated in the poem both as an abstraction and as the personification of that abstraction into Cupid, the god of love. Here "Love's service" probably means "serving Cupid."
9-11. Cf. *The Golden Targe* 28–31
10. *liquour*: i.e., "liquid"; cf. *Gen. Prol.* of *Cant. Tales* l. 3.
12. *toþer sid*: "the other side"; *persew*: "carried on," i.e., "sang"
12-3. Cf. the *Treatise of the Two Married Women and the Widow* 5–7
14. The poet indulges his license here to depict the "divine" qualities of the Nightingale; in fact, nightingales are not especially attractive birds.
16. The Nightingale's refrain, in contrast to the Merle's, expresses the Augustinian principle that no love is of value unless it is a reflection of man's love of God.

	Quhill rong the widdis of hir melody,	
[Merle]	Saying, "Awalk ʒe luvaris O this May.	20

Lo, fresche Flora hes flurest every spray
As Natur hes hir taucht, þe noble quene;
The feild bene clothit in a new array:
A lusty lyfe in Luvis seruice bene."   24

Nevir suetar noys wes hard with levand man,
Na maid this mirry gentill nychtingaill;
Hir sound went with the rever as it ran,
Outthrow the fresche and flureist lusty vaill.   28

[Nightingale] "O merle," quod scho, "O fule, stynt of thy taill,
For in thy song gud sentens is þair none,
For boith is tynt the tyme and the travaill
Of every luve bot vpone God allone."   32

[Merle] "Seiss," quod the merle, "thy preching, nychtingale;
Sall folk thair ʒewth spend into holiness?
Of ʒung sanctis growis auld feyndis but fable;
Fy, ypocreit, in ʒeiris tendirness   36
Agane the law of kynd thow gois express,
That crukit aige makis on with ʒewth serene,
Quhome Natur of conditionis maid dyverss:
A lusty lyfe in Luves seruice bene."   40

---

19. *widdis*: "woods"; cf. *Cuck. & Night.* 99–100
20. From the French poetry of the thirteenth century onward, lovers are awakened in May by the singing of birds; in Dunbar's *The Thistle and the Rose* (12–14) it is a lark, perched on Aurora's hand, that urges the lover to awake.
21. *Flora.* The goddess of plant life and a principal assistant to the goddess Natura (1.22).
25. *with levand*: "by living"
26. *na*: "than"
28. *flureist lusty vaill*: "flower-covered, pleasant vale"
29. *O fule*: "oh bird"; there is always some ambiguity with *fule* ("fowl" or "fool"), but name-calling would be uncharacteristic of *this* nightingale — in contrast to the nightingales in the previous poems.
35. "From young saints grow old fiends, without a doubt"; proverbial (Whiting S19).
37. *law of kynd*: "law of nature"
38-9. "that crooked Age should be no different from pleasant Youth [two conditions of Man], which Nature made quite diverse"

[Nightingale]   The nychtingaill said, "Fule, remembir the,
                   That both in ʒewth and eild, and every hour,
                   The luve of God most deir to man suld be,
                   That him of nocht wrocht lyk his awin figour,   44
                   And deit him-self fro deid him to succour.
                   O, quhithir wes kythit þair trew lufe or none?
                   He is most trew & steidfast paramour:
                   All luve is lost bot vpone him allone."   48

[Merle]   The merle said, "Quhy put God so grit bewte
                   In ladeis, with sic womanly having,
                   Bot gife He wald þat thay suld luvit be?
                   To luve eik Natur gaif thame inclynnyng;   52
                   And He, of Natur þat wirker wes and king,
                   Wald no thing frustir put nor lat be sene
                   In-to his creaturis of his awin making:
                   A lusty lyfe in Luves seruice bene."   56

[Nightingale]   The nychtingall said, "Nocht to þat behufe
                   Put God sic bewty in a ladeis face,

---

55. creaturis *ms*: creature

41-5. The Nightingale reminds the Merle of the biblical injunction (Eccles. 12:1) to
     "Remember now thy Creator in the days of thy youth"; cf. *Troilus & Criseyde* V 1838-40.
42. *eild*: "elde," i.e., "old age"
44. "that made him from nothing in his own image"; Gen. 1:26.
45. "and died Himself to rescue (Man) from death"
46. *kythit*: "shown"; the question is rhetorical.
47. Cf. *Troilus & Criseyde* V 1845-8
50-1. "in ladies such femininity, unless He wished that they should be loved"
53. *wirker*: "creator"; this view of God as Creator and Natura as God's deputy was a
     medieval commonplace; for a concise statement of it, see Chaucer's *Physician's Tale*
     (*CT* VI 19-25).
54. *frustir*: "worthless"; an important term for the poem; cf. the phrase *frustir luve* in l.
     90 and l. 98.
57-64. These verses on the God-given attributes of women prove that the Nightingale
     is no misogynist.

That scho suld haif the thank þairfoir, or Lufe,
Bot He, the wirker, þat put in hir sic grace   60
Off bewty, bontie, richess, tyme or space,
And every gudness þat bene to cum or gone,
The thank redounis to him in every place:
All luve is lost bot vpone God allone."   64

[Merle]   "O nychtingall, it wer a story nyce,
That luve suld nocht depend on cherite;
And gife þat vertew contrair be to vyce,
Than lufe mon be a vertew, as thinkis me;   68
For ay to lufe invy mone contrair be:
God bad eik lufe thy nychtbour fro the splene,
And quho than ladeis suetar nychbouris be?
A lusty lyfe in Lufes seruice bene."   72

[Nightingale]   The nychtingaill said, "Bird, quhy dois thow raif?
Man may tak in his lady sic delyt
Him to forȝet þat hir sic vertew gaif,
And for his hevin rassif hir cullour quhyt;   76

---

64. bot *ms*: Bot
72. Lufes *ms*: lufe

---

59. "so that she should have the thanks therefore, or (that) Love (should)"
61. *tyme or space*: i.e., "whenever or wherever (they may occur)"
62. "and every virtue (in woman) that will be found or has been found"
66. "That (form of) love (which I have been describing) should not depend on *caritas*";
    the Merle is opposed to the Nightingale's implied suggestion, in her refrain line and
    in the preceding stanza, that love between human beings is of value only when it
    is a form of *caritas*—love derived from one's love of God.
67–9. "And if virtue is contrary to vice, then love must be a virtue, it seems to me; for
    always love must be contrary to envy."
70. *splene*: i.e. "heart"; cf. *Thistle & Rose* 12.
70–1. The Merle's appropriation of Christ's second great commandment (Mark 12:31)
    recalls the manipulation of the scriptures by the Wife of Bath in her *Prologue*.
75–6. "that he forgets Him who gave her such virtue, and exchanges for His heaven
    her white color (i.e. of her skin)"

Hir goldin tressit hairis redomyt,
Lyk to Appollois bemis thocht thay schone,
Suld nocht him blind fro lufe þat is perfyt:
All lufe is lost bot vpone God allone."   80

[Merle]   The merle said, "Lufe is causs of honour ay,
Luve makis cowardis manheid to purchass,
Luve makis knychtis hardy at assey,
Luve makis wrechis full of lergeness,   84
Luve makis sueir folkis full of bissines,
Luve makis sluggirdis fresche and weill besene,
Luve changis vyce in vertewis nobilness:
A lusty lyfe in Luvis seruice bene."   88

[Nightingale]   The nychtingaill said, "Trew is þe contrary;
Sic frustir luve, it blindis men so far,
In to þair myndis it makis thame to vary;
In fals vane glory þai so drunkin ar   92
Thair wit is went, of wo þai ar nocht war,
Quhill þat all wirchip away be fro thame gone,
Fame, guddis, and strenth; quhairfoir weill say i dar:
All luve is lost bot vpone God allone."   96

[Merle]   Than said the merle, "Myn errour I confess,
This frustir luve all is bot vanite;
Blind ignorance me gaif sic hardiness
To argone so agane the varite;   100

---

90. sic *ms*: sie

81-7. Such descriptions of the ennobling power of love are common; see, for example, the *Cuck. and Night.* 151-60 and 189-92.

85-6. "Love makes lazy folks full of activity, Love makes sluggards (appear) fresh and attractive."

92. In most treatments of the sins Vain Glory was considered a sub- variety of Pride, but it could also be viewed as a separate sin equal in seriousness to Pride or Envy, the most serious sins of the spirit.

97. The Merle's sudden and rather tame capitulation recalls the behavior of the Thrush in the *Thrush and the Nightingale*, as well as that of many a maiden in the *pastourelles*.

100. "to argue so against the truth"

Quhairfoir I counsall every man that he
With lufe nocht in þe feindis net be tone,
Bot luve þe luve þat did for his lufe de:
All lufe is lost bot vpone God allone." 104

Than sang thay both with vocis lowd and cleir;
[Merle] The merle sang, "Man, lufe God þat hes the wrocht";
[Nightingale] The nychtingall sang, "Man, lufe the Lord most deir,
That the and all this warld maid of nocht." 108
[Merle] The merle said, "Luve him þat thy lufe hes socht
Fra hevin to erd, and heir tuk flesche and bone."
[Nightingale] The nychtingall sang, "And with his deid the bocht:
All luve is lost bot vpone Him allone." 112

Thane flaw thir birdis our the bewis schene,
Singing of lufe amang the levis small,
Quhois ythand pleid ʒit maid my thochtis grene,
Bothe sleping, walking, in rest and in travall; 116
Me to reconfort most it dois awaill
Agane for lufe, quhen lufe I can find none,
To think how song this merle and nychtingaill:
All lufe is lost bot vpone God allone. 120

ffinis q dumbar

116. in rest and: *the ms has been altered so that* in *is deleted, and* rest *is joined to* and *making* restand.

102. "not to be taken in the fiend's net because of love"
103. "But love the Love (i.e., Christ) who, because of His love (for man), died"; this word-play on "love" no doubt stems from the biblical adage that "God is Love (I John 4:8, 16)"; and it also portrays Christ as the true God of love, in place of Cupid, so portrayed in the Merle's previous refrains.
105–12. The antiphonal singing of the two birds links the poem with several fifteenth century poems, such as the *Birds' Devotions* (*Index* 357), which depict the singing of the birds as a kind of religious observance; cf. also the birds' paraphrase of matins for Trinity Sunday that occurs in 1352–1442 of the *Court of Love* (*Index* 4205).
113. *thir*: "these"
115. "whose sustained dispute restored my spirits"
117. *awaill*: "avail"

A Parliament of Birds

A Parliament of Birds, or the *Birds' Praise of Love*, is one of the most effective shorter pieces among the pseudo-Chaucerian poems of the "Chaucer Apocrypha." It is recorded only in Camb. Univ. MS Gg.4.27, a manuscript also containing the three works which exerted the greatest influence on the *Parliament of Birds*, namely, Chaucer's *Parliament of Fowls*, *Troilus and Criseyde*, and the *Legend of Good Women*. A *Parliament of Birds* is an extremely conventional poem, yet it succeeds in creating a delightful context for the further exploration of human attitudes toward romantic love. As in the *Cuckoo and the Nightingale*, the narrator is prompted by his May-time love-longing to seek solace in a secluded natural setting. There he overhears the love songs of a great number of birds, songs which express varying attitudes toward love. Most of the birds sing in praise of love, but because they are also love-sufferers, like the narrator, their songs reflect the bitter-sweet qualities of romantic love. Dissenting views, however, are provided by the jay, pie, cuckoo, fieldfare, and starling, who are to various degrees love-scorners. Thus arises a conflict between those birds which subscribe to the more elevated concept of *fine amour* and those which adhere to more mundane views. The final speech in the poem, assigned to the throstle-cock, seems to mark a return to the sentiments initially expressed by the turtle dove, that one should choose a lover who will be forever faithful; yet a note of ambiguity may be intended through a possible allusion to the concluding verses of Chaucer's *Troilus and Criseyde*, where lovers are urged to direct their love toward Christ rather than toward earthly lovers. If this reading is credible, then the poem may also be linked with the *Merle and the Nightingale*, where such sentiments are more explicitly stated.

A Parliament of Birds consists of fifteen eight-verse stanzas, in tetrameters rhyming ababbccb, a rhyme scheme obviously adapted from rhyme royal. In most stanzas the final verse is written in French, skillfully blended with the Middle English, but the more "lewed" birds such as the cuckoo and starling are unable or unwilling to express their attitudes in French, suggesting the lowness of their views and their general lack of refinement. Some of the verses in French may be quotations from French lyrics (see note to 1. 32.), an aspect of the poem deserving further study.

1) Base Text: Cambridge University MS Gg.4.27, fols. 8r–10r

2) Other mss: none

3) Printed Texts: E. Hammond, *JEGP* 7 (1908), 105–9

4) *Index of Middle English Verse* 1506

A Parliament of Birds

In May whan euery herte is ly3t,
And flourys frosschely sprede & sprynge,
And Phebus with hise bemys bry3te
Was in þe Bole so cler schynynge,   4
Þat sesyn in a morwenynge,
Myn sor for syghte to don socour,
Withinne a wode was myn walkynge,
Pur moy ouhter hors de dolour.   8

1–8. This extremely conventional opening bears similarities to many Chaucerian and pseudo-Chaucerian poems; cf. *T & C* II 50–6; *LGW* (F) 36–8; *Floure & the Leafe* 1–3; etc.
4. *Bole*: "Bull," i.e. the sign of Taurus
6–7. The narrator's situation is much the same as that experienced by the narrator in *LGW* (F) 45–50, who also rises in May and seeks a "sight" in a secluded arcadian setting to relieve his suffering.
8. "to deliver myself from suffering;" cf. *LGW* (F) 50.

And in an erber sote & grene
Þat benchede was with clourys newe,
A-doun I sat me to bemene,
For verray seyk, ful pal of hewe,   12
And say be-syde a turtil trewe,
For leue gan syngyn of hire fere;
In frensch ho so þe roundele knewe:
[turtle dove]   "Amour me fait souent pensere."   16

Cupidis brid, þe nyȝtyngale,
With streynede þrote be melody,
Sat on a sidre be-syde a vale,
And angelly be-gan to cry   20
Þat euere in loue is melody
And brestis brede, with-outyn debat;
[nightingale]   And euere sche song "Ocy, ocy:
Ner esperaunce mon cuer senbat."   24

---

14. loue *ms*: leue
21. loue *ms*: leue
22. -outyn *added*

9-11. Cf. *LGW* (F) 203-4; *LGW* (G) 97-8. Fifteenth-century gardens customarily con-
tained an arbor, a shady bower tucked away in a corner of the garden where a lover
could meditate upon his beloved in relative seclusion. Turf-topped benches were com-
monly found in such arbors; cf. *LGW* (G) 97 ff.; *T & C* II 822, 1705; *F & L* 49-53;
etc. (See Frank Crisp, *Medieval Gardens* [London, 1924] Vol. I, 73-5, 81-3, and Vol.
II, figs. 114-32, 149-62.)
13. *a turtil trewe*. The turtle dove, one of the few birds that mates for life rather than
annually, was a common symbol of faithful, wedded love. Cf. *Parl. of Fowls* 355: "The
wedded turtil with hire herte trewe."
16. Literally the verse says, "Love often causes me to be pensive"; perhaps it could be
rendered, "My thoughts are always on the one I love"; however, the "pensiveness"
indicated here may anticipate the philosophical outlook suggested at the poem's close.
17. The nightingale is mentioned in *PF* (351-2) in conjunction with the sparrow, who
is identified as "venus's son."
22. *brestis brede*: "breast's bread," i.e., "heart's sustenance"
23. *ocy, ocy*. This imitation of the nightingale's cry, which occurs in the poetry of Frois-
sart and Deschamps as well as in the *Cuckoo & Nightingale* (124-35), is thought to stem
from the imperative form of the OF verb *occire*, meaning "kill" (cf. the note to l. 124
of *C & N*).
24. "Black hope swoops down upon my heart."

With dyuerse tunys þat were so sote,
Plesaunce to don onto Nature,
As I lenede vp-on a rote,
With werbelys tunede be mesure,   28
I herde a mauys don hire cure
To synge mercy be ermony,
And tauȝte trewely, I ȝow ensure:
[mavis]   "Qui bien ayme tard oublye."   32

Ȝit in þe wode þere was discord
Þoru rusti chateryng of þe jay,
Of musik he coude non acord,
Ek pyis vnplesaunt to myn pay;   36
Þey iangeledyn & made gret difray
Þat foly kyndelyth loue fere;
Þus watte gan syngyn in his lay:
[jay]   "Que je ne facece fors de bien aymmyer."   40

Robert redbrest & þe wrenne,
From bow to bow as þey gunne sterte,

---

27. *up-on a rote*: i.e., "against a tree trunk"
29. "I heard a mavis work at her occupation," i.e., do what mavises do, sing; a mavis
    is a variety of song thrush.
32. "He who loves well is slow to forget"; in several mss of Chaucer's *Parl. of Fowls* these
    words are inscribed in French above line 677; some scholars believe they indicate
    the tune of the roundel sung by Chaucer's birds; but Brewer and others question
    this suggestion. In any event, they reflect a well-known medieval French proverb,
    and they also occur in the first verse of a poem by Machaut and in the burden of
    a ballade by Deschamps. (See Brewer's note to l. 677 in his edition of Chaucer's *Parl.
    of Fowls*.)
32-7. The discordant sounds of the jay and pies introduce a conflicting attitude toward
    love, one in opposition to that expressed thus far by the love-sufferers who sing love's
    praises. These birds lack the refined sensibilities of those who espouse *fine amour*, as
    line 38 reveals, which is a clear response to line 32.
35. Either "he was not suited for making music," or "he had no sympathy with such
    music," or both.
38. *loue fere*: "love's fire"
39. *watte*: a common medieval nickname for the jay, deriving from the cry they were
    taught by men to make; cf. lines 642-3 in the *Gen. Prol.* to the *Canterbury Tales*.
40. "that I do not care (at all) about loving well"

[robin & wren]   Þey seyde, "Alas, it is gret synne
To hyndere ony trewe herte;   44
And in good feyth, for ioye or smerte,
We wele not lettyn in no weye;
To loue þyn song schal vs not lette:
Biele a biels yeulx on ge ie soye."   48

Þe fesaunt, scornere of þe cok,
Be nihyter tyme in frostis colde
Þat nestelyth lowe be sum blok,
Or be sum rote of bosschis olde,   52
With brest vp born sche gan hire bolde,
And with dym voys þus sche crew,
Hire hertis sentens to vnfolde:

[pheasant]   "Ma esperaunce mad deceu."   56

Þe larke, longe er it was day,
Gan mountyn hye in þe eyr,
And drerilyche song þis lay,
In compleynynge be dispeyr: 60

[lark]   "Allas, for on þat is so fayr,
Fortune, I fayle þoru þyn sort;

---

43. alas *ms*: agas

46-8. "We will not hinder (lovers) in any fashion; in regard to love, your song won't affect us: wherever I may be, (my song shall praise) a beauty with beautiful eyes."
49. Cf. *PF* 357.
56. "My hope has deceived me"; the pheasant and the goldfinch (ll. 65-72) seem to reflect the attitudes of lovers whose love has begun to turn in the direction of despair; the lark, in ll. 57-64, epitomizes the despairing lover who, like the deceived and disillusioned Troilus, seeks his own death as a respite.
61. *For on þat is so fayr*: a common formula; cf. *Clerk & Night. I* 16, and the lyric in praise of the Virgin Mary, "Of oon that is so faire and bright" (*Index* 2645).
62. "My plight stems from Fortune's capriciousness."

Troylus, in loue I am þyn eyr:
Car vene me ad purchace la mort."   64

A joly gold fynch, frosch & gay,
With sunny federys bry3te & schene,
Song as sche sat vp on þe spray:
[goldfinch]   "Þe dart of loue haþ cut so kene   68
Þoruout myn herte þat alwey grene,
Myn wounde abidyth for penaunce,
Vnmerci causith al myn tene:
De iour en iour par languisaunce."   72

Þe vncurteys coukkow, most vnkynde,
Seyde it was foly so to pleyne,
[cuckoo]   "Sithe alday in loue men may fynde
If on be lost whe oþere tweyne.   76
I can no french, soþ for to seyne,
Ne oþer langage withoutyn oth;
Þus am I lasyd in Venus cheyne:
I seye as good loue comyth as goþ."   80

---

67. þe *ms*: de
68. dart *ms*: date

63-4. "Troilus, in loving I am your heir: Oh, may I succeed in obtaining death." It is
curious that the lark, which in Renaissance literature often symbolizes fresh hope
(as in Shakespeare's Sonnet 29) is here an emblem of black despair.
65-72. The appearance and demeanor of the jolly goldfinch is in sharp contrast to her
sorrowful song; normally in medieval literature the goldfinch symbolizes sensuous-
ness and self-indulgence, but that does not appear to be the case here, where she
is aligned with the birds of refined sensibilities.
72. "from day to day through languishing"
73. Cf. *PF* 357; for a discussion of the cuckoo, see the headnote to the *Cuckoo & the Night-
ingale*.
76. *whe*: probably an interjection, perhaps equivalent to "why"; in any case the cuckoo's
sentiments are clear enough: i.e., "if one (lover) is lost, why (there are) two others
(to take her place)." Cf. Pandarus' remark to Troilus (*T & C* IV 406): "If she be lost,
we shal recovere another." It should be noted, however, that in Chaucer's *Parl. of Fowls*
(ll. 593-5) this attitude is expressed by the duck, not the cuckoo.
80. Proverbial (Whiting L479, *Oxford* 389). In Henryson's fable of the "Cock and the

[popinjay]

Þe popyniay gan to pikyn mod
And seyde, "Coukkow, lat be, lat be!
I trowe þu maddyst or þu art wod!
For schame to speke swich dyuerste!   84
For I loue on so fayre & fre
And for hire synge most verteuous,
Erly in morwe whan I hire se:
Estreyneȝ moy de cuer joyous."   88

Þanne spak þe frosty feldefare
And seyde þat loue is dere abouȝt,
A man to leuyn euere in care
For hire þat hym recheþ not;   92

[fieldfare]

"Þerfore put hire out of þyn þouȝt,
Sythn on þynne peynys sche wele not rewe;
And let hire grace no more be souȝt,
But synge for hyre 'adew, adew'."   96

[titmouse]

"Now certys," quod þe tetemose,
"Now is þis a wondyr þyng;
For he þat coueytyþ to han a rose,
Hym muste a-byde þe growyng.   100

---

97. tetmose *ms*: tetnose

Fox," when Chanteclere's three wives offer successive and contrastive comments on
his apparent demise, Sprowtok remarks, "As guid luif cumis as gaiss" (Kinghorn,
The Middle Scots Poets, p. 82).
81. *gan to pikyn mod*: an idiom meaning "to change one's tune" or "to sing a different tune";
here the popinjay sings a different tune from that just sung by the cuckoo, i.e., it
challenges the cuckoo's point of view.
88. "Embrace me with a joyous heart."
89. Cf. *PF* 364
92-6. The attitude of the fieldfare approximates that of the goose in Chaucer's *PF*: "'But
she wol love hym, let hym love another'" (l. 567). The fieldfare, like the other un-
couth birds before her, also fails to encapsulate her sentiments in a French expression.
99-100. Probably proverbial.

Ry3t so þat loue is so gladynge
Pat halt vp hertis par esperaunce;
Wherfore of on þus wele I synge,
Je ay en vous tut maffyaunce." 104

[starling]

Pe starlyng gan to sterte & stare
And seyde, "Pese songis ben so quenynte,
I can no skille of swich french fare,
To speke in engelych I haue more deynte, 108
For loue now so sore I feynte;
Pow womennes hertis were made of stel,
For hem oueral I wryte & peynte:
I loue hem alle a-lyche wel." 112

[throstle-cock]

Pe throstilcok song last of alle,
And seyde it was no stedefastnesse
In loue to turne as a bal,
Ne no tokene of gentillesse. 116
"Wherfore I rede 3ow alle to dresse
Of on to synge with herte entyre,
Pat wele not fayle in non distresse:
En dieu maffie san3 departer." Amen. 120

101–2. "Similarly, (just as one who wishes a rose must abide its growing), love is so pleasing that one's heart should be sustained by hope (until it is achieved)."
104. "I have (placed) all my confidence in you."
108. *deynte*: "delight"
111–2. "For women in general I write (songs) and paint (pictures): I love them all equally well"; the starling's indiscriminate love of women relates back to the attitude of the cuckoo, and like the cuckoo the starling is limited to the use of English.
113–20. Although there is no resolution to the question which has come before this informal parliament of birds, by giving the last word to the throstle-cock, who sides with the birds who have expressed an elevated, courtly attitude toward love, the poet's own position may be revealed. But there is also a likely echo here from the palinode of Chaucer's *Troilus* (V. 1842–8) — e.g. "For he nyl falsen no wight, dar I seye, / That wole his herte al holly on hym leye" — which creates yet a further ambiguity about the conclusion of the poem, and which may also provide a point of contact with the *Merle and the Nightingale*.
120. "In God I trust without ceasing."

In a fryht: The Meeting in the Wood

In a fryht as y con fare fremede ("The Meeting in the Wood"), the one true *pastourelle* among the lyrics of MS Harley 2253, is in many respects the most impressive poem from among the small group of *pastourelles* which survive in Middle English and Middle Scots literature. In comparison to many other "Harley lyrics," however, *In a fryht* has not received a great deal of critical attention or acclaim. This may be because the poem is quite difficult linguistically, and because the assignment of some verses to their proper speaker is uncertain. But these difficulties notwithstanding, *In a fryht* generates far greater emotional power than any of the other *pastourelles*, through its complex and poignant psychological portrait of the maiden, and through its sobering reflection of social realities.

Through the first thirty-two verses, *In a fryht* follows the usual *pastourelle* pattern: a young courtier chances upon an attractive lower-class maiden; he makes amorous overtures to her but is rebuffed; he offers her gifts which she scornfully refuses; he pledges his fidelity to her which she doubts. But beginning at l. 33 the poem takes on another character, for the final sixteen verses appear to be a monologue in which the maiden expresses her innermost thoughts. (Some commentators, it should be noted, assign ll. 37–44 to the courtier, not the maiden.) In this speech the maiden reflects upon her dilemma, weighing her choices and their probable consequences. She is well aware of what happens to young girls who have been abandoned by their lovers, pregnant but unwed. On the other hand, she is also well aware of what is likely to be her lot should she marry a member of her own social class. (Her sentiments in these verses recall those of the disillusioned wife of the *chanson de mal mariée*.)

The chief fascination in the poem, certainly, is to be found in the maiden's psychological conflict. As she reflects on her plight, her initial moral resolve yields to her pragmatism. Perhaps her own sensual impulses also contribute to her final decision. But questions remain. Has she been seeking reasons to do what she has wanted to do all along? If so, she is not unlike the young women in other *pastourelles* who suddenly change their minds (though in most instances more inexplicably than is the case here). Or is she genuinely resigning herself to a fate which she believes to be unavoidable, as well as the least unattractive of her options? The last two verses of the poem create additional ambiguities. Does l. 47 express her regret at having been born a woman, or her regret at still being a virgin? Does l. 48 imply that a good man is not only hard to find but well neigh impossible? However these final verses are interpreted, they cast her in a sympathetic light.

In a fryht is recorded only in BL MS Harley 2253, a Middle English manuscript anthology unrivaled in the excellence and variety of its lyric poetry—secular love lyrics, devotional and penitential lyrics, songs of political satire and social complaint. *In a fryht* is written in an unconventional meter, in stanzas of eight and sometimes four verses. It is one of the Harley poems characterized by a high degree of alliteration.

---

1) Base Text: Brit. Lib. MS Harley 2253, fols. 66v–67r

2) Other mss: none

3) Selected Printed Texts: Wright, *Specimens*, Percy Society 4 (1842), 36–8
Böddeker, *Altenglischen Dichtungen des MS Harl. 2253* (1878), p. 158
Brook, *The Harley Lyrics* (1956), 39–40
Luria and Hoffman, *Middle English Lyrics* (1974), 27–8

4) *Index of Middle English Verse* 1449

[The Meeting in the Wood]

In a fryht as y con fare fremede,
Y founde a wel feyr fenge to fere;

1–8. "As I was traveling through an unfamiliar wood, I found a very fine prize to encounter; she glistened like gold when it gleamed; there was never a being so pleasing

Heo glystnede ase gold when hit glemede;
Nes ner gome so gladly on gere.   4
Y wolde wyte in world who hire kenede,
Þis burde bryht, ʒef hire wil were.
Heo me bed go my gates lest hire gremede;
Ne kepte heo non henyng here.   8

[He]   "Y-here þou me nou, hendest in helde,
Nau y þe none harmes to heþe.
Casten y wol þe from cares & kelde,
Comeliche y wol þe nou cleþe."   12

[She]   "Cloþes y haue on forte caste,
Such as y may weore wiþ wynne;
Betere is were þunne boute laste
Þen syde robes ant synke into synne.   16
Haue ʒe or wyl, ʒe waxeþ vnwraste;
Afterward or þonk be þynne;
Betre is make forewardes faste
Þen afterward to mene & mynne."   20

[He]   "Of munnyng ne munte þou namore;
Of menske þou were wurþe, by my myht;
Y take an hond to holde þat y hore

---

in appearance. I wished to know who had begotten her, this pretty maiden, if it was
her desire (to tell me). She told me to go away, lest I grieved her; she did not wish
to hear any insult."
9. *hendest in helde*: "fairest in favor"
10. "I have no intentions of abusing you."
13. *forte*: "for to"
15. "It is better to wear thin (clothing) without blame" (perhaps there is a play on *þunne
boute laste*: i.e., clothes that are "thin but lasting").
17–8. "When you have had your wishes, you will become untrustworthy; afterwards your
thanks will be thin"; the clothing metaphor of the previous verses is cleverly reversed
here.
19. *forwardes fastes*: i.e., "a binding agreement"
20. *mene ant mynne*: "pine and reminisce"
21. "Of remembering, think you no more."
23. "I promise to be true till I am old and gray."

Of al þat y þe haue byhyht.   24
Why ys þe loþ to leuen on my lore
Lengore þen my loue were on þe lyht?
Anoþer myhte ȝerne þe so ȝore
Þat nolde þe noht rede so ryht."   28

[She]   "Such reed me myhte spaclyche reowe
When al my ro were me atraht;
Sone þou woldest vachen an newe,
Ant take anoþer wiþinne nyȝe naht.   32
Þenne miht I hongren on heowe,
In vch an hyrd ben hated & forhaht,
Ant ben y-cayred from alle þat y kneowe,
& bede cleuyen þer y hade claht.   36

Betere is taken a comeliche y cloþe
In armes to cusse ant to cluppe,

---

31. þou *ms*: þo
33. hongren *ms*: hengren

27-8. "Another lover might woo you for so long, (one) who would not be speaking to you sincerely"
29. Here all the remaining verses are assigned to the maiden; but a plausible case (involving a few minor emendations of the text) has been made for assigning 37-44 to the man (see Rosemary Woolf, *Medium Aevum* 38 (1969), 55-9). Since the concatenation seems to fail at lines 36-7, perhaps a case could also be made for a lost stanza.
30. *atraht*: "taken away"
31. *vachen*: "look for"; cf. ME *fecchen*, from which modern English *fetch* derives.
32. *nyȝe naht*: "nine nights"
33. "Then might I be starved within my (own) family."
34. *in vch an hyrd*: "in every household"; *forhaht*: "hated"
36. "And ordered to cling where I had clung (i.e., embraced)"; that is, her family will refuse to take her back and will order her to stay with the man she has chosen to give herself to.
37-44. As noted before, a case can be made for assigning this stanza to the courtier; but the maiden's abrupt about face is a common feature in the *pastourelle*; and the colloquialness of some of the expressions in these verses also seems better suited to the maiden than to the courtier.

Þen a wrecche y-wedded so wroþe;
Þah he me slowe, ne myht I him asluppe.   40
Þe beste red þat y con to vs boþe,
Þat þou me take ant y þe toward huppe;
Þah y swore by treuþe & oþe,
Þat God haþ shaped mey non atluppe.   44

Mid shupping ne mey hit me aschunche;
Nes y neuer wycche ne wyle;
Ych am a maide, þat me ofþunche;
Luef me were gome bout gyle."   48

---

40. "Though he killed me, I could not slip away from him."

42. *huppe*: "hop"

43-4. "Though I swore by truth and oath (to preserve my virtue), no one can escape what God has decreed"; line 44 may also provide an ironic echo of the phrase from the wedding ceremony, "What God has put together . . . ."

45-6. Difficult verses; "I cannot escape by shape-shifting; I am not a witch or sorceress" (R. Woolf's paraphrase).

47. The meaning of this verse is ambiguous: "I am a young woman, which displeases me"; or perhaps, "I am still a virgin, which I regret." The latter possibility is itself ambiguous.

48. "Dear to me would be a man without guile," either expressing her hope that she has found such a man, or expressing her recognition that such a hope is essentially futile.

As I stod on a day

As I stod on a day is one of the earliest Middle English *pastourelles* (late thirteenth or early fourteenth century). Like *In a fryht* and *Now sprinkes the sprai*, it exhibits the sophistication and formal complexity characteristic of the better Old French *pastourelles*. Here the poet uses alliteration and occasional internal rhyme to supplement a demanding pattern of end rhyme; and the initial verse, which stands by itself, may also serve as a burden, that is, a verse repeated at the beginning of each stanza. The chance encounter of young man and maiden depicted in *As I stod* largely adheres to the familiar pattern of the *pastourelle*, although in this instance it is the man who stands beneath a tree and the woman who chances upon him, an inversion of the usual convention. It also seems to be the case that the young man is a clerk rather than a courtier, and that the young woman belongs to a higher social class than is usual. What is especially noteworthy about this *pastourelle*, in contrast to the others in this volume, is that here the maiden remains firm in refusing her would-be lover and apparently thwarts his attempted seduction. The only text of *As I stod* occurs on the end leaf of MS College of Arms XXVII, at the College of Arms in London.

---

1) Base Text: College of Arms XXVII, fol. 130r

2) Other *mss*: none

3) Printed Texts: T. Wright, *Reliquiae Antiquae*, II (1845), 19–20
                    A. Brandl and O. Zippel, *Mittelenglische Sprach- und Literaturproben* (1917), 128

4) *Index of Middle English Verse* 371

As I stod on a day me-self vnder a tre,

I met in a morueninge a may in a medwe,
A semlier to min sithe saw I ner non:
Of a blak bornet al was hir wede,   4
Purfiled with pellour doun to þe teon;
A red hod on hir heued, shragid al of shridis,
With a riche riban gold-begon.
Þat birde bad on hir boke euere as sche зede.   8
Was non with hir but hir selue alon;
   With a cri gan sche me sey,
Sche wold a-wrenchin awey, but for I was so neye.

[He]   I sayd to þat semly þat Crist should hir saue,   12
             For þe fairest may þat I euer met.
[She]   "Sir, God зet þe grace god happis to haue
             And þe lyginges of loue," þus she me gret.
             Þat I mit becum hir man I began to craue,   16
             For noþing in hirde fondin wolde I let.
             Sche bar me fast on hond, þat I began to raue,

---

8. sche *ms*: he
18. me *written above line.*

---

3. "One ~~more~~ seemlier to my sight had I never seen before."
4–7. This description of the maiden's attire suggests a more elevated social status than
    is usually the case for the maiden in the *pastourelle*; it is also notable that she is not
    engaged in any rustic pursuit (i.e., tending cows or sheep), but is reading a book
    which she may own.
4–5. "She was dressed entirely in a rich brown fabric that was trimmed with fur right
    down to her toes."
6. *shrogid al of shridis*: "decorated with lace"
8. "The maiden looked upon her book as she walked"; the book is possibly a psalter,
    in which case it provides a tangible emblem of her moral resolve.
11. Apparently he has hemmed her in in some fashion.
14–5. "Sir, may God give you grace to have good fortune and (to receive?) the false-
    hoods of love . . ."
17. "For nothing on earth would I stop trying."
18. "She resisted me so firmly (?) that I began to rave."

And bad me fond ferþer, a fol for to feche:

[She]   "Quaer gospellis al þi speche?   20

Þu findis hir nout hire, þe sot þat þu seche."

For me þothe hir so fair, hir wil wold I tast,

And I freyned hir of loue, þerat she lowe:

[She]   "A! sire," she sayd, "hirt þow for non hast;   24

If it be your wille, ye an sayd innowe.

It is no mister your word for to wast.

Þer most a balder byrd billin on þe bow;

I wend be your semblant a-chese you for chast;   28

It is non ned to mak hit so tow.

    W. . .ri wet ye wat I rede?

Wend fort þer ye wenin bett for to spede."

---

32. *A few letters in* w. . .ri *are indecipherable.*

---

19. "and bade me search further in order to find a fool"
20. I.e., "why are you preaching at me?" There is surely irony in her use of the term *gospellis*, as well as a hint of his clerical status.
22. "Because she seemed so fair, I decided to test her resolve."
23. *lowe*: "laughed"
24. *hirt thow for non hast*: "don't hurt yourself out of haste"
26. "It isn't very wise to waste your words."
27. "There must be a bolder bird pecking on the bough," with word play on the two meanings of *byrd* ("bird" and "maiden").
28. "I thought by your appearance you had chosen to be chaste," a line which clearly suggests his status as a cleric.
29. "There is no need to be so flirtatious"; the idiom "make it tough" often occurs in Middle English literature in this sense.
31. *better for to spede*: "to have better success"

Throughe a forest as I can ryde: The Ballad of the Crow and Pie

Bodleian Library MS Rawlinson Poetry C 813, compiled during the first half of the sixteenth century, contains several lovers' dialogues. Poems such as *Throughe a forest as I can ryde* (R-C 3713.5), *Come Over the Woods Fair and Green* (R-C 642.5), and *When that Birds be Brought to Rest* (R-C 4020.3) preserve many of the conventional elements of the earlier *pastourelles* while also reflecting some of the characteristics of the ballad—especially in verse form and in the use of refrains and repetitive phrases. *Throughe a forest* is actually included in F. J. Child's collection where it is given the title "The Ballad of the Crow and Pie" (Child, no. 111), and it closely resembles the ballad of "The Baffled Knight" (Child, no. 112).

The confrontation between courtier and maiden which is depicted in *Throughe a forest* stands in contrast to those depicted in *In a fryht* (the Harley *pastourelle*) and *As I stod on a day*, especially in regard to tone. Here the typical *pastourelle* encounter is exploited for its comic potential. The language of the poem reflects a certain amount of wittiness, to be sure, in a fashion that recalls the Latin *pastourelles* of the *Carmina Burana*. But on the whole the poem is cynically comic rather than lighthearted; and the callousness with which the central events in *Throughe a forest* are handled may be offensive to some readers.

MS Rawlinson Poetry C 813, which has been specifically dated to 1530–40, contains fifty-one songs and lyrics; a few are free adaptations of Chaucerian poems, others represent the work of a variety of fifteenth-century poets (e.g. Lydgate and Richard Roos), and some date from the early Tudor period (e.g. poems from Stephen Hawes' *Pastime of Pleasure*). The manuscript also contains a poem extracted from *The Adulterous Squire of Falmouth*. The complete texts of all fifty-one poems are printed by Padelford and Benham in *Anglia* 31 (1908).

---

1) Base Text: MS Rawlinson Poetry C 813 (Bodl. 12654), 56v–58v

2) Other mss: none

3) Selected Printed Texts: J. O. Halliwell, *Nugae Poeticae* (1844), 42–4
   F. J. Child, *Popular Ballads*, Vol. II (1883–98) no. 111, 478–9
   Sargent and Kittredge, *Popular Ballads* (1904) 238–9
   Padelford and Benham, *Anglia* 31 (1908), 374–7

4) *Supplement to the Index of Middle English Verse* 3713.5

[The Ballad of the Crow and Pie]

Throughe a forest as I can ryde
To take my sporte yn on mornyng,
I cast my eye on euery syde,
I was ware of a bryde syngynge.   4
I sawe a fair mayde come rydyng;
I speke to hur of loue I trowe;
She answered me all yn scornyng
[She]   & sayd, "The crowe shall byte yow."   8

[He]   "I pray yow, damsell, scorne me nott,
            To wyn your loue ytt ys my wyll;

1–2. These verses suggest that the narrator who rides out in the morning to "take his sport" is a young courtier (cf. 61) whose ostensible purpose is hawking or hunting; as the poem develops, he comes to "take his sport" in quite another sense.

4. *bryde*: probably "bird" rather than "maiden" (in view of the fact that the maiden makes her appearance in l.5), though the term is ambiguous

8. He shall be food for crows, she says scornfully; such is literally the case for the slain knight in the Scottish ballad *The Twa Corbies*.

	For your loue I haue dere bought,	
	& I wyll take good hede ther-tyll."	12
[She]	"Nay, for God, sir, that I nyll;	
	I tell the, Jenken, as I trowe,	
	Thow shalt nott fynde me suche a gyll;	
	Therfore the crowe shall byte yow."	16

He toke then owt a good golde ryng,
A porse of velweytt that was soo fyne;

[He]
"Haue ye thys, my dere swetyng,
With that ye wyl be lemman myn." 20

[She]
"Be Cryst, I dare nott, for my dame,
To dele with hym þat I doo nott knowe,
For soo I myght dyspyse my name;
Therfore the crow shall byte yow." 24

He toke hur abowte the mydell small,
That was soo fair of hyde and hewe;
He kissed hur cheke as whyte as whall
And prayed hur þat she wolde vpon hym rewe. 28
She scornyd hym & called hym Hew,

11–2. *dere bought*: "paid dearly," i.e., suffered a great deal; this conventional expression of the lover's suffering is undercut by the fact that he has just met this maiden a moment earlier.

13. *for*: "before"; *nyll*: "will not"

14. *Jenken*: Jenkyn (or Jankyn) is a diminutive form of John; it is often the name given to an attractive young cleric (as in several ME lyrics) who is intent upon seduction; here the maiden is probably using it as a deliberate insult.

15. *gyll*: "gull," i.e., fool, though possibly the name Jill (cf. l. 39); if Jill is intended, there might be a connection between these two names (Jenkyn and Gyll) with the names "Jack and Jill" in the nursery rhyme.

17. Here the narrative slips out of first person and into third person.

17–20. The attempt to persuade (or bribe) the maiden through the offer of gifts occurs frequently in *pastourelles*.

21. *for my dame*: i.e., out of respect for my mother; or out of deference to her advice

23. *dyspyse*: "bring shame upon"

27. *as whyte as whall*: "as white as whale's bone," a conventional phrase for describing the fairness of a woman's skin (the actual "whale's bone" is the "ivory" tusk of the narwhal)

28. This common lover's plea is somewhat ironic, under the circumstances.

29. *Hew*: Hugh, like Jenkyn earlier, is surely meant to be insulting; perhaps the name carried implications of loutishness (related to its Welsh origin?).

His loue was as a-paynted blewe:

[She]   "To-day me, to-morowe a newe;

Therfore the crow shall byte yow."   32

He toke hur abowte the mydell small

& layd hur downe vpon the grene;

Twys or thrys he served hur soo with-all,

He wolde nott stynt yet, as I wene.   36

[She]   "But syth ye haue i-lyen me bye,

Ye wyll wedde me now, as I trow?"

[He]   "I wyll be aduysed, gyll," said he,

"For now the pye hathe peckyd yow."   40

[She]   "But sythe ye haue i-leyn me by

& brought my body vnto shame,

Some of your good ye wyll part with me

Or elles, be Cryst, ye be to blame."   44

[He]   "I wylbe aduysyd," he sayde,

"Þe wynd ys wast þat thow doyst blowe.

I haue anoder þat most be payde,

Therfore the pye hathe pecked yow."   48

[She]   "Now sythe ye haue i-leyn me bye,

A lyttle thyng ye wyll tell,

In case that I with chylde be,

What ys your name, wher doo ye dwell?"   52

[He]   "At Yorke, at London, at Clerken-Well,

---

30. I.e., his love isn't "true blue"; indeed, l. 47 will provide proof of what the maiden here asserts.

39. *be aduysed*: i.e., "advise you"

40. *pye*: i.e., magpie; the figurative use of a bird in this sense is fairly common; cf. the lyric in Rawlinson manuscript *When that Birds be Brought to Rest* (R-C 4020.3) which has the refrain, "Your bryde shall neuer hoppe yn my cage," and the ME lyric "I have a gentil cok" (*Index* 1299). The pie also provides a counterpoint to the crow of the earlier stanzas.

43. *good*: "goods," in reference to the gifts he had offered in 17–8; again she must realize that this is a faint hope.

53–6. These verses may be taken both as his refusal to make his identity known to her and as an indication that young men everywhere share the very same desires.

At Leycester, Cambryge, at myrye Brystowe;
Some call me Rychard, Robart, Jacke, & Wyll,
For now the pye hathe peckyd yow.   56

But all medons be-ware, be-rewe,
& lett no man downe yow throwe,
For & yow doo ye wyll ytt rewe,
For then þe pye wyll pecke yow."   60

[She]   "Fare-well, corteor, ouer the medoo;
Pluke vp your helys, I be-shrew yow;
Your trace wher-so-euer ye ryde or goo,
Crystes curse goo wythe yow!   64
Thoughe a knave hathe by me leyne,
Yet am I noder dede nor sleyne;
I trust to recouer my harte agayne;
& Crystes curse goo wythe yow."   68

57–60. It is possible that these verses should be assigned to the maiden, reflecting the
lesson she has now learned; but here they are considered as the courtier's parting
words of advice.

57. *medons*: "maidens"

61. *corteor*: "courtier," perhaps with sarcasm

62. "Lift up your heels, damn you," conveying her "go to hell" attitude

65–8. These verses portray the maiden's fundamental level-headedness and her emo-
tional resilience.

An Adventure on Wednesday:
A Middle Scots Pastourelle

Several lovers' dialogues appear among the works of the Middle Scots poets, of which Robert Henryson's *Robene and Makyne* and William Dunbar's *In Secreit Place* (or "A Brash of Wooing") are probably the best known. Less well-known is the poem which follows here and several others of a similar kind (see, for example, Dauney's *Ancient Scottish Melodies*, p. 49; Pinkerton's *Ancient Scottish Poems*, pp. 190–1; and the *Chronicle of Scottish Poetry*, III, pp. 201–2). *An Adventure on Wednesday* is preserved only in the Bannatyne manuscript of the National Library of Scotland. Like most of the other Middle Scots poems in this vein it is a comic variation on the *pastourelle*, with much of its humor stemming from the juxtaposition of courtly conventions with coarse behavior. The courtier encounters a maiden who appears to be innocent and devout (much like the maiden in *As I stod on a day*) and the poem seems to be headed toward an indirect condemnation of the illicit love so often depicted in the *pastourelle*. As it turns out, however, the maiden effects a dramatic about-face and proves to be a willing and enthusiastic lover, to the young courtier's abashment.

---

1) Base Text: The Bannatyne Manuscript, fol. 141

2) Other mss: none

3) Printed texts: J. Sibbald, *Chronicle of Scottish Poetry*, III (1802), 203–5
W. T. Ritchie, *The Bannatyne Manuscript*, Vol. III
(1928), 26–7

4)   *Index of Middle English Verse*: not listed

An Adventure on Wednesday

In somer quhen flouris sweitt smell,
As I fure ouir feildis and fell,
Allone I wanderit by ane well
    On Weddinsday,   4
I met a cleir vnder a kell,
    A weil faird may.

Scho had ane hatt vpoun hir heid
Off claver cleir, bayth quhyte & reid,   8
With catelukis strynklit in that steid
    And fynkill grene.
Wit ʒe weill, to weir þat weid
    Wald weill hir seme.   12

Ane pair of beidis abowt hir thrott,
Ane Agnus day with nobill nott,
Jyngland weill with mony joitt,
    War hingand doun.   16

---

1. With this conventional opening verse cf. *Index* 1533 and 1534.
2. *fure*: "fared"
3. The "well" is often associated with the Virgin (cf. the ME lyric "At a spring well," *Index* 420); here it contributes to the initial impression of this maiden's innocence.
4. Why Wednesday? Perhaps the poet, by having this "adventure" take place on this most ordinary of days, is making a wry comment about its "routineness." Certainly the maiden's actions in the aftermath of love-making suggest that for her this event has hardly been momentous.
5–6. "I met a fair maiden beneath a cap, a well-met maid."
8–10. The maiden's "hat" is an elaborate garland of white and red clover, entwined with cat's-claws (i.e., bird's-foot trefoil) and green fennel.
11–2. "You can be sure that wearing such an adornment would well become her."
13. *Ane pair of beidis*: two strands of beads(?)
14. *ane Agnus day*: "a lamb of God," i.e., an emblem in the form of a lamb, signifying Jesus; possibly worn more as a piece of jewelry than as a sign of her devout faith.

It wes full ill to fynd ane moit
　　Vpoun hir goun.

Als sone as I þat schene cowth se
I halsit hir with hart maist fre: 20

[He]　　"I luve ʒow leill, and nocht to le,
　　Wald ʒe me lane —"

[She]　　"Out hay!" quod scho, "My joy latt be;
　　ʒe speik in vane.   24

Quhat is the thing þat ʒe wald haif?"

[He]　　"Na thing bot a kiss I craif,
As I þat luvis ʒow our the laif,
　　Wald ʒe me trow."   28

[She]　　"ʒif þat ʒow may of sorrow saif,
　　Cum tak it now."

Than kissit I hir anis or twyiss,
And scho gan gruntill as a gryiss;   32

[She]　　"Allace!" quod scho, "I am vnwyiss
　　That is sa meit.
Tiss lyk þat ʒe had eiten pyiss,
　　ʒe are sa sweit.   36

---

17. I.e., "it was impossible to find a blemish."
22. "If you would me lend —"; the maiden hastily interrupts the courtier's address to her, before he has even had a chance to launch his opening appeal; she soon realizes herself that she has been over-hasty.
23. *Out hay*: I.e., "no more"
23–5. The maiden hardly allows the young man to speak before she silences him; perhaps she realizes that she has been premature, or else her curiosity gets the better of her, and so she poses her question in l. 26.
27. *our the laif*: "over the rest," i.e., above all others
29. "if that (i.e., a kiss) will save you from sorrow"
32. "And she began to snort like a young pig."
34. *sa meit*: "so meet," i.e., "so pleasurable"(?), in reference to his kissing
35. *pyiss*: "peas" (?); in any case, something which would make his breath sweet; "peas" suggests her countrified frame of reference.

My hatt is ȝouris of proper dett
And on my heid scho cowth it sett.
Than in my armes I cowth hir plett
   And scho to thraw.   40
[She]   "Allace!" quod scho, "ȝe gar me swett,
   3e wirk sa slaw."

Than doun we fell bayth in feir.
[She]   "Allace!" quod scho, "þat I cam heir;   44
I trow this labour I may ȝow leir,
   Thocht I be ȝing.
3it I feir I sall by full deir
   ȝour sweit kyssing."   48

Than to ly still scho wald nocht blin.
[She]   "Allace!" quod scho, "my awin sweit thing,
ȝour courtly fukking garis me fling,
   3e wirk sa weill;   52
I sall ȝow cuver quhen þat ȝe clyng;
   Sa haif I seill.

Sen ȝe stummer nocht for my skippis,
Bot hald ȝour taikill be my hippis;   56
I byd a quhasill of ȝour quhippis,
   Thocht it be mirk;
Bot and ȝe will, I schrew þe lippis,
   Þat first sall irk."   60

37–8. Giving him her garland signifies her willingness to become his lover.
39. *plett*: "embraced"
40. *thraw*: "twist" or "turn about"
41. *gar me swett*: "cause me to sweat"
43. *in feir*: "together"
45. "I think I may instruct you in this labor"; this surprising turn of events, in which the maiden takes the lead in the love-making, is not without precedent among the French *pastourelles*.
51. The phrase *courtly fukking* captures the ludicrousness of juxtaposing courtly elements with coarse ones; *garis me fling*: "causes me to dance."
55–60. "See that you don't stumble when I skip, but hold your tackle against my hips; I await the taste of your whip, though it be dark; and unless you do, I curse the lips that shall tire first."

Als sone as we our deid had done,
Scho reiss sone vp and askit hir schone,
Als tyrd as scho had weschin a spone.
　　To ȝow I say,   64
This aventur anis to me come
　　On Weddinsday.

62-3. "She rose up soon and fastened her shoes, as tired as if she had (merely) washed a spoon."

Glossary

The glossary is intended to serve only as a convenient aid to reading the texts, not as a philological tool, and an elementary knowledge of Middle English is assumed on the part of the reader. Words whose meanings should be obvious are not included. Since these texts reflect widely differing dialects and dates of composition, some words appear in several forms. Verbs are recorded in the glossary just as they appear in the texts; the variant forms and tenses of a particular verb have not always been listed in a single, inclusive entry, although some cross-referencing has been provided. The arrangement of the glossary is alphabetical, with þ following *t*, and ʒ following *y*; initial *ff* is treated as *f*.

GLOSSARY ABBREVIATIONS

Als	*Als I lay*
AW	*An Adventure on Wednesday*
BW	*A Disputation between the Body & the Worms*
CJ	*The Debate between a Christian & a Jew*
CNI	*The Clerk & the Nightingale I*
CNII	*The Clerk & the Nightingale II*
CN	*The Cuckoo & the Nightingale*
CT	*The Debate of the Carpenter's Tools*
D	*As I stod on a day*
DL	*Death & Life*
F	*In a fryht*
G	*The Grave*

---

abou3t v bought *PB* 90

abreidest v chides *Als* 146

aby3e, aby v pay for, atone for *Als* 327; *CNII* 65

ac *conj* but *Als* 218

accompte n account *SI* 43

aduencione n advent, coming *BW* 146

afforsyth v attempts *SI* 143

affrayede v frightened *P3A* 356

ai *adv* always, ever *Als* 224

aisur *a* azure *MN* 11

als *conj* as *Als* 1; *CT* 18, 100

also *adv* thus, so *TN* 39, 78

al-þayu3 *adv* although *JM* 172

ames v plans, resolves *P3A* 384, 394, 486, 493

and *conj* if *P3A* 106; *CT* 266

angarte *a* arrogant *WW* 267

apertly *adv* plainly, openly *CJ* 29, 82

apon *prep* over, above *BW* 143

appaire v impair *WW* 372

appere v be equal to *NK* 6

ar(e) *prep* ere, before *WW* 198, 409; *P3A* 283; *CJ* 50

ar(e)ste *a* first *P3A* 464, 586

as n ass *CJ* 43

assay, assey n test, attempt, try *CN* 52; *MM* 77; *MN* 83; *CT* 38

assentis v pursues *P3A* 63

asses n ashes *BW* 148

athell *a* noble *P3A* 345, 484, etc

athes v entreats *P3A* 499

atraht v taken away *F* 30

auaunce v advance, promote *MM* 44

aughte v possessed *WW* 1; *P3A* 392, 406, 465

aughtilde v intended *P3A* 483

auisement n consideration *CN* 272

aunterde v adventured (ventured) *P3A* 543

auntirs, auntoure, auntres n adventure(s), plight *P3A* 375, 543; *CJ* 204

avant n boast *DL* 366

aventure n fortune *BW* 120

avyse n judgment, advice *BW* 79

awreke v avenged *CN* 215

axles n shoulders *P3A* 113

babirlippede *a* thick-lipped (?) *P3A* 158

balder *a* bolder *D* 27

bale, ball; bales n evil, calamity, suffering; sorrows *Als* 42; *WW* 292, 357; *P3A* 453; *DL* 21, 234, 309, etc; *JM* 31, 128

balghe *a* rounded *P3A* 112

balkede v stumbled, bucked *P3A* 56

banely *adv* promptly *DL* 247

bareside *a* naked *Als* 23

baret *n* anguish, strife *CJ* 75

barme *n* lap *WW* 418

barne; barnes *n* child; children *WW* 418; *JM* 8

barnes (*see* beryne)

basilysk *n* basilisk *BW* 107

bate *v* abate *Als* 469

bearnes (*see* beryne)

bede(n); bid *v* ask, bid; commanded *WW* 437; *DL* 268; *JM* 103

bede(s) *n* prayer(s), petition *Als* 445; *BW* 7

bedis *n* prayer beads *P3A* 153

behufe *n* purpose *MN* 57

belde *v* built *P3A* 662

bemene *v* bemoan *PB* 11

bemis *n* beams *MN* 5; *PB* 3

benes *n* payments *P3A* 143

bent(s) *n* field *WW* 105, 143, 156, etc; *DL* 63, 149, etc

bere *n* bear(?), monster (?) *DL* 144

beres *n* beats *In* 30

berselett *n* hunting dog *P3A* 39, 69

beryn(e); bernes, bearnes *n* man, human being; men *In* 98; *TN* 172; *WW* 125, 131, etc; *P3A* 110, 153; *DL* 81, 90; *MM* 5

bet *n* redeemer *JM* 128

bete *v* remedy *In* 40

bewede *v* bowed *P3A* 490

bewes, bowes *v* turns, goes *P3A* 370, 395, 490

bewis *n* (*see* bow)

bid (*see* beden)

biddes *v* cares for *WW* 239

bigged(e) *v* built *WW* 1; *DL* 383

biglye *adv* strongly *DL* 418

bihiȝt, byhyht; bihete *v* promise(d) *Als* 252, 478, 529; *F* 24

bine *n* wickedness (?) *DL* 254

binimen *v* take away *In* 31

birdes (*see* buirde)

bireuen *v* deprive, take away *In* 62

birre *n* instant *WW* 292

bismere *n* criticism, scorn *Als* 356

biswikeþ *v* deceive, mislead *TN* 19

bithe *v* are *WW* 123

bitid, bitidde *v* happen(ed), occurr(ed) *In* 18, 20; *CJ* 3

blaundrere *n* a sweet-tasting apple *NK* 8

ble, blee *n* complexion, color *Als* 249; *WW* 93, 144; *DL* 65, 99

blenche(d) *v* avoid, turned *Als* 448; *DL* 32

blent *v* (spiritually) blinded *JM* 34, 135

blethely, bleþeliche, blythy *adv* gaily, gladly *P3A* 214; *CNII* 2; *CJ* 2

blin(ne), blynnes *v* cease, stop *Als* 368; *WW* 457; *DL* 254; *MR* 98; *NK* 38

bliþe *a* happy, glad, blissful *CJ* 1

blok *n* tree trunk *PB* 51

blonke *n* horse *P3A* 110

blostme *n* blossom *TN* 2

blushe(d) *v* turn(ed) *DL* 191, 388

blussche *n* shininess *WW* 187

blynnes (*see* blinne)

blynt *v* blinded *JM* 34

blyot *n* bleaunt, gown *P3A* 482

blythy (*see* blethely)

blyue *adv* quickly *MR* 30

bobaunce *n* pride *Als* 94

bodworde *n* message, request *P3A* 558

bold *n* house *G* 1

bole *n* bull (Taurus) *PB* 4

bone *n* prayer, boon *Als* 445

boolish *a* rounded (?) *DL* 58

bootis *v* helps *SI* 129

borde(s), burde *n* table *WW* 335, 342; *CJ* 209; *MM* 25; *NK* 47

borely *a* massive, strong *P3A* 26, 32

borowes *n* boroughs (cities) *P3A* 560

bot, boote *n* remedy, cure *Als* 319; *JM* 31, 188

bote *conj* but, unless *JM* 45; *CT* 40

boure(s) *n* chamber, bower *In* 47; *P3A* 608; *TN* 57; *NK* 25

boute *conj* without *F* 15, 48

bouwed *v* bowed, humbled himself *CJ* 39

bow, bowes, bewis *n* bough(s) *D* 27; *DL* 23; *MN* 113

bowes *v* (*see* bewes)

bown, bownne *a* ready, prepared, equipped *WW* 52, 110, etc; *P3A* 110, 153; *DL* 215

bown, bownnes; bownede, bownde *v* begin; prepared *BW* 117; *WW* 208; *P3A* 43, 265

bradd (*see* brayden)

brand, bronde, brandes *n* sword *WW* 239, 241, 431; *DL* 175, 288, 343

braste *v* burst *P3A* 55

brauden *v* woven, braided *WW* 113

brawders *n* borders (?), embroideries (?) *DL* 63

brayde *n* a moment, a short while *BW* 193

brayden, bradd *v* drew, unfurled *WW* 52, 163; *P3A* 69, 371; *DL* 175

brayed *v* jerked *P3A* 56

brede *n* breadth *P3A* 71

breemly, bremly *adv* noisily, vigorously *WW* 41; *DL* 364

breme *n* vigor *DL* 34

breme *a* lively, cheerful *DL* 74

brene, brenn; brend, brent *v* burn; burned *Als* 463; *WW* 292; *P3A* 560; *MM* 70

brente *a* burnished *P3A* 131

brerdes *n* borders *WW* 164

breues *v* tells *P3A* 424

briht *a* beautiful *CJ* 40

brod *n* goad *Als* 516

broiden *v* tore *Als* 557

brond *n* fire-brand *Als* 552

bronde (*see* brand)

broudered *v* embroidered *WW* 91, 96

bruche *n* breach *TN* 28

bryme *n* brim, water's edge *P3A* 7

bugge *v* redeem, save *JM* 122

buirde, buyrde, birdes *n* maiden *WW* 426; *CJ* 40; *JM* 128

bulches *n* humps *Als* 506

burgons *n* buds *P3A* 11

burlyest *a* loudest (?) *DL* 145

busked(e) *a* dressed *WW* 110; *P3A* 22

buyrnes (*see* beryne)

by-dene *a* together

by-hete *v* promise *P3A* 178

caitif, caytef(fe) *n* caitiff, wretch *Als* 594; *WW* 233, 425; *DL* 237, 246

calsydoynnes *n* chalcedonies *P3A* 124

can, canst *v* know *MR* 19, 49, 100; *PR* 77, 107

canker *n* canker worm *BW* 111

carpe(d), kerpede *v* said, spoke *WW* 218, 452, 452; *P3A* 462; *DL* 231, 362

carpynge *n* talking, conversation *P3A* 168

cas *n* predicament *CNII* 57

catel *n* property *Als* 285

cayre(n), kayre(n) *v* go, travel *WW* 210, 240, etc; *P3A* 246

caytef(fe) (*see* caitif)

cendels *n* rich cloths *Als* 30

certys *adv* indeed, certainly *WW* 221; *PB* 97

ceson *n* season *BW* 1

char *n* turn *Als* 294

charebocle *n* carbuncle *P3A* 246

chaules, chawylls *n* jaws *Als* 513; *P3A* 72

chaunched *v* changed *Als* 277

chefe-lere *n* head of hair *P3A* 118

chere *n* behavior, manner *In* 3; *TN* 21; *MR* 9; *NK* 9; *JM* 95

chynede *v* cut along the spine *P3A* 89

clef; cleuet *v* cleave; split, divided *Als* 244; *CJ* 147

cleie *n* clay *In* 51

clepen, clepien, clepeþ *v* cry, call *In* 40, 93; *WW* 355

clergye, clergys *n* learning, doctrine, theology *CJ* 21, 94; *JM* 95; *MR* 107

cleþe *v* clothe *F* 12

cleuet (*see* clef)

cliue (*see* clef)

cloches *n* clutches *Als* 502

closed *v* enclosed *NK* 42, 68

clourys *n* clover *PB* 10

cloute *n* blow, clout *NK* 59

clouȝt *n* clout, rag *Als* 414

cluppe, clyp *v* caress, embrace *P3A* 248; *F* 38

cochour *n* malingering *MM* 23

cokkatrys *n* cockatrice *BW* 107

coloppe *n* tasty morsel *P3A* 33

colter *n* plowshare *Als* 519

colour *n* collar *DL* 89

coluber *n* adder *BW* 108

comeli *adv* burdensome *BW* 165

compassed *v* devised *BW* 17

comper *n* peer, equal *BW* 162

condithe *n* aquaduct, conduit *P3A* 409

cone, const *v* know *Als* 348; *TN* 74

coniecture *n* conception *BW* 17

connyng *n* knowledge, understanding *JM* 98

contenaunce *n* continual maintenance *SI* 117

contre *n* country *CT* 148, 272

cope *n* cloak, mantle *Als* 531

core *a* excellent *JM* 82

cornelles *n* battlements *P3A* 411

cossyng *n* kissing *CNI* 84

courbede, cowrbed *v* bent *P3A* 154, 287

couertour(es) *n* bed coverings *Als* 29; *In* 46; *TN* 119

couthe *v* knew *P3A* 511

couthe, couþest *v* could *Als* 197; *CT* 185; *JM* 111

couthely *adv* knowingly *P3A* 462

cowchide *v* crouched, positioned *P3A* 39

cowltes *n* quilts *Als* 29

cowpe *v* contend *P3A* 203

cowrbed (*see* courbede)

cowre *v* hide, cower *NK* 24

cowschote *n* wood-pigeon *P3A* 12

crab *n* crabapple *NK* 8

crawpaude *n* crab *BW* 111

crupel *n* cripple *TN* 118

cunne *v* be able, know *TN* 33

cunnynge *a* learned, expert *JM* 209

cure *n* attention, heed, remedy *BW* 54; *JM* 67; *NK* 58

cusse; custe *v* kiss(ed) *F* 38

daderande *v* trembling *WW* 97

dadillyng *n* chattering *WW* 44

dang (*see* dongen)

dare *v* be dispirited *CJ* 111

dar(r) *v* dare *MM* 75

daþeit *v* a curse on *TN* 135

dawe *v* dawn *TN* 125

daynte (*see* deynte)

dede *n* effect, result *MM* 38

dees *n* dais *CJ* 169

del(e), delle *n* part, portion *Als* 576; *WW* 4; *CNI* 8, 47

delyn *v* deal with *WW* 5

delys *n* frivolous activities *MM* 36

deme, demeth, demeþ; dempt *v* judge, decide; condemned *Als* 197; *In* 6; *WW* 201, 220, 453; *JM* 99; *MM* 22

depycte *v* depicted *BW* 16

depynte *v* adorned *BW* 16

derffe *a* strong, bold *DL* 325, 380

derne *a* dark, secret *TN* 65; *WW* 413

derworþ *a* great, worthy *CJ* 199, 245

deueles, dueles *n* devils *JM* 99, 150

dever *n* duty *SI* 123

devyse *v* think about *BW* 67

deynte, daynte *n* delight, pleasure *DL* 281; *PB* 108

dight(e), diht, dyght *v* prepared, destined *WW* 330; *P3A* 125, 597; *CJ* 191, 122; *JM* 46; *NK* 49; *CT* 68, 254

dimme *a* dismal *G* 9; *In* 9

dint (*see* dynt)

disceyfyng *n* appearance *BW* 23

do, doo *v* cause, make *Als* 45; *WW* 478

dogh(e)ty, doughety *a* valiant, worthy *P3A* 181, 344, 442, etc; *DL* 53, 204

doghetynes *n* valor *P3A* 583, 631

dole, dool *n* sorrow, grief *P3A* 258, 344, 400, etc; *MR* 114

doluen *v* buried *P3A* 257

dom, dome(s) *n* judgment, sentence *In* 6, 26, 84

dongen, dung; dang *v* strike blows; dashed, knocked *Als* 546; *DL* 211, 325

dool (*see* dole)

dosers *n* ornamental cloths *CJ* 169

doussypers, dussypere *n* twelve peers *P3A* 348, 403, 521

douth *n* host *P3A* 348

draf *n* draff, chaff *NK* 17

drane *n* drone *MM* 60

drauȝt *n* labor *Als* 221

dre *v* drain a vessel *CT* 231

drede *n* jeopardy, dread *MM* 30; *CJ* 265

dree *v* endure *DL* 397

dreghe *a* long, heavy *P3A* 101

dreghe *v* try *P3A* 3

drepe; dreped, drepide, drepitt *v* slay; slew *P3A* 379, 456, etc

dreri *a* dreary *In* 3

drerilyche *adv* drearily *PB* 59

dresseth; dresse(d) *v* prepares, readies; prepare(d) myself *DL* 182, 189; *BW* 7; *MM* 55

dright *a* noble (?), heavy (?) *DL* 38

Drightyn, Dryghtyn *n* God *WW* 244; *P3A* 6, 442, 448

driwerie *n* love-making *TN* 76

droukening *n* a state of dejection or depression (?) *Als* 2

droupe *v* mourn *CJ* 111

druryes *n* treasures *DL* 87

drye *v* experience (?) *DL* 263

dueles (*see* deueles)

dunge (*see* dongen)

dure(s) *v* endures, lasts *BW* 142; *In* 73; *JM* 65

dwelle *n* delay *JM* 204

dyapre *n* textured cloth *CJ* 200

dyght (*see* dighte)

dynt, dynt; dynttis, dints *n* stroke; blows

Als 551; *WW* 103, 153, 167; *P3A* 447; *DL* 263, 275

dyvyne *v* worship *BW* 40

dyʒe *v* die *JM* 99

ede, edest *v* went *Als* 237, 264, 276

efte *adv* again *P3A* 436

egheliche *adv* wondrously *P3A* 28

eghne, ene, iye *n* eyes, eye *WW* 137, 215, 278; *P3A* 50, 549; *MN* 2; *NK* 31

eik, ek(e) *adv* also *TN* 17; *MN* 52, 70; *PB* 36

elenge *a* boring *CN* 115

emang(e) *prep* among *BW* 43, 61

encrampeschett *v* cramped up *P3A* 154

ene *n* (see *eghne*)

engine *v* ensnare *Als* 386

enowe *a* enough *DL* 457

enprise *n* enterprise, cleverness *Als* 423

ensure *v* assure *BW* 36

entyrvall *n* interval *BW* 155

erbere *n* arbor *PB* 9; *TN* 98

estres *n* inner places *WW* 403

euchan *a* each one, every one *TN* 19

euer(r)ichon *pron* everyone *JM* 116

euer(r)ous *a* eager for glory *P3A* 271, 306, 329, etc

evet *n* newt, salamander *BW* 112

eyr *n* heir *PB* 63

facounde *n* eloquence *JM* 196

fain (see fayne)

fange *v* receive *BW* 62

fare *n* behavior, commotion *P3A* 59; *DL* 22; *CNI* 86; *CJ* 109

fare, fareþ *v* go, travel *CJ* 50; *JM* 158, 206

ffarlye (see ferly)

fatills; fettled, fittilled *v* prepares; prepared *P3A* 20, 542; *DL* 30

ffawchyon *n* falchion, sword *DL* 274, 285

fawe *a* pleased, happy *MR* 28

fay *a* faith *NK* 65, 67

fayne *adv* gladly, happily *MR* 34

fayn(e), fain, feyne; ffainer, ffaynere *a* glad, fain; happier *Als* 601; *WW* 402; *P3A* 15; *DL* 274; *CN* 128; *MR* 156

faynt *a* poor, meager *BW* 52

fedderis *n* feathers *MN* 14

fee *n* reward *BW* 200

feere (see fere)

feete *a* comely *BW* 33

ffei *n* faith *JM* 4

feldefare *n* fieldfare, thrush *PB* 89

fele *a* many *Als* 592; *P3A* 1, 310, etc

felen *n* a feeling (of) *CN* 144

felle *n* skin *Als* 495; *P3A* 77

felle, ffell *a* evil, wicked *WW* 228; *DL* 432; *CJ* 138

felle *v* cast down *JM* 4, 206

fellys *n* moors *P3A* 59

fende *n* fiend (the Devil) *CJ* 78

fende *v* defend *MM* 75

fer(e) *a* far, distant *CT* 10; *MM* 23

ferde *n* company, host *P3A* 330, 480

ferde, ferdnes *n* fear *P3A* 97; *WW* 98

ferdede *v* were mustered *WW* 138

fere, feere; feris *n* companion; friends *Als* 273; *WW* 311; *P3A* 58, 564; *DL* 186; *CJ* 208; *PB* 14; *TN* 35, 80, 104

ferkes; ferkede *v* go quickly; went hurriedly *P3A* 20, 659

ferly, ferli, ffarlye *n* marvel, wonder *CJ* 151, 175; *DL* 49

ferly *a* wondrous *P3A* 310, 566

fet *n* feet *Als* 559

fet, fette *v* fetched, carried *Als* 558; *P3A* 378; *CT* 146

fettled (see fatills)

ffey *n* enchanted place *CJ* 184

feyndis *n* fiends *MN* 35

feyne (see fayne)

filmarte *n* polecat *P3A* 18

fittilled (see fatills)

flakerande *v* flapping *WW* 92

flayede *v* put to flight *P3A* 428

fleys *n* flesh *Als* 495

flyttynge *n* argument *WW* 154

fode *n* young man *CNII* 17

folde *n* battlefield *WW* 174

folde *n* fold of cloth *CJ* 175

folfellyd *v* satiated, glutted *MR* 101

folyes *n* follies *CJ* 2

fond(e), fondin, foondeþ *v* try, test, put to trial, prove (the better) *TN* 22; *CJ* 12; *MR* 13, 60; *D* 17

fonded *v* created *JM* 4

fon(e) *n* foes, enemies *CT* 172; *JM* 114

foned *a* foolish *MR* 65

fonge, fongen *v* seize, take *WW* 384; *P3A* 88, 572

foo-men *n* enemies *CNI* 52

foonde, foondeþ (*see* fonde)
foonued *a* foolish *MR*
forewardes *n* agreement *F* 19
fore-why *conj* because *CT* 114
forfrayede *v* frightened *P3A* 59
forgyd *v* constructed *BW* 16
forhaht *v* despised *F* 34
forhal *v* concealed *Als* 437
forlore(n) *v* lost *JM* 122
forme *a* first *In* 61
for-rad *v* deceived, seduced *Als* 398
fortalt *v* foretold *CJ* 98
forteyne *v* retain *CT* 119
for-thi *conj* therefore *WW* 439
foulene *n* birds' (gen. pl.) *CJ* 161
founde *v* seek *CJ* 143
founden, foundes *v* hasten, leap *P3A* 97, 222, 226, etc
founte *n* font *P3A* 549
fourch(e)s *n* haunches *P3A* 88, 92
fourme *n* lair, den *WW* 14; *P3A* 20
fow *n* particolored fur *TN* 116
ffraine (*see* freyned)
frawnchsyse *n* generosity, freedom *BW* 78
frayed *v* bruised *CNI* 52
fre *a* generous *PB* 85
freke, ffreake *n* man *WW* 287; *P3A* 108; *DL* 157, 161, etc
frete *n* food *Als* 44
fretynge *v* gnawing *BW* 26, 46
freyned; ffraine *v* questioned, inquired; ask *D* 23; *DL* 130
frith, frythe, ffryth, fryht *n* woodland *P3A* 15; *DL* 22, 72, 270; *F* 1
frouȝ *a* fickle *Als* 436
frustir *a* worthless *MN* 54
full *v* fill *WW* 217, 367
fulle *adv* very *NK* 7

gabbist, gabbust *v* speak untruthfully or foolishly *CNI* 34, 65, 105
gainest, gaynest *a* best, mightiest *DL* 208, 412
game, gome *n* joy, pleasure, sexual play, light amusement *TN* 33; *CNI* 48, 67; *NK* 14
garte *v* caused, made *P3A* 549, 561
gere *n* gear, things *CJ* 257
gere *n* behavior *NK* 11
gerede *a* adorned, dressed *WW* 63, 94; *P3A* 122

gesserante *n* mail-coat *P3A* 180
gille, gyll *n* knave, rascal, fool *JM* 43; *TF* 39
girde(s) *v* leap, strike *P3A* 318, 343
girdillis *n* belts *WW* 271
glayfe; gleyues *n* glaive, lance; swords *Als* 521; *P3A* 202
gle, glee *n* joy, delight *CNI* 67; *JM* 215
glede *n* coal, embers *MM* 70
glewe *v* entertain *Als* 49
glewemen *n* entertainers *Als* 49
gleyues (*see* glayfe)
glode *v* glided, moved *DL* 28
gloser *n* flatterer *MM* 47
glosyng *n* flattering *MM* 42
gnede *a* stingy *Als* 31
golyone *n* tunic *P3A* 138
gome (*see* game)
gome *n* man *WW* 118, 359, 391; *P3A* 169, 182, 475; *F* 48
gonen *v* gaze (?) *P3A* 17
gonne (*see* gunnen)
gore *n* garments *TN* 150; *CNII* 48
gram *n* anger, harm *Als* 71
grameful *a* irritating *JM* 43
grauen *v* buried *P3A* 629
gra(y)thede *v* prepare, array *P3A* 85, 339, etc
graythely *adv* ready, promptly, aptly *P3A* 202, 494, 644
greaten *v* increase, strengthen *DL* 17
greatlye *adv* completely, strongly *DL* 3, 126
grede *v* cries out; wept *Als* 37; *CN* 135; *JM* 158
gree *n* the highest award *P3A* 473
grefe *v* bring to grief *BW* 216
grete *n* gravel *CJ* 154
greue(þ); greuyd *v* speak angrily, insult; offended *CJ* 81; *CT* 32, 157, 277; *JM* 84, 89; *MM* 41
grewell *n* gruel *WW* 381
grille *n* argument *CJ* 298
grille *a* harsh, fierce *Als* 203
grise *v* suffer *Als* 328
grisliche *a* ghastly, grisly *Als* 539
griþ *n* peace *Als* 209
groome *n* servant, person *DL* 84, 86
grote *n* groat *Als* 544
grype *n* griffin *DL* 173
gunnen; gonne *v* begin; began *TN* 2; *JM* 158

gyle *n* guile *CNII* 5

gyll (*see* gille)

gynne *n* trap *NK* 41

gyse *n* fashion *BW* 22

hallede *v* hauled, pulled back *P3A* 53

halue *n* side *Als* 509

halse, haulse *n* neck *P3A* 90, 373

halsit *v* spoke to, addressed *AW* 20

hande-while *n* a little while *P3A* 106, 267

happe, happis *n* good fortune *CT* 131; *D* 14

happede *v* locked *WW* 298

haspes *n* clasps, hasps *Als* 533

haspede *v* buckled *P3A* 201

hathell(e) *n* man *WW* 68, 70; *P3A* 111, 170

hatt, hatten *v* is named *WW* 218, 222; *P3A* 405

haunt *n* place, space *DL* 55

hawes *n* hedges *P3A* 19

hawtayne; hawteste *a* proud; proudest *P3A* 209, 213

healice *adv* highly *G* 7

hechele *n* flax comb, hackle *Als* 543

hedde *v* held *CJ* 27

helys *n* heels *WW* 450; *TF* 62

hend(e), hynde *a* gentle, gracious *WW* 419; *DL* 80, 340; *TN* 10, 26, 78; CNI 66; *CT* 285

hendely, hendlye *adv* gently, kindly *P3A* 267; *DL* 213

henne, hens, hennys *adv* hence, away *In* 103; *CN* 102; *CNII* 62, 66

henppe *n* hemp *WW* 145

hent *v* arrived *BW* 11

henttis; hent *v* seize, take; took *WW* 211, 447; *P3A* 60, 66, 236; *BW* 130; *JM* 32

heo, hoe, hy *pron* they *In* 12, 36; *TN* 19, 22, 23; *CJ* 145; *JM* 65

heowe *n* servitude *F* 33

here *n* hair *P3A* 117

here *n* army *WW* 50, 58, 196

herest, hereþ; herede *v* praise; praised *In* 68; *TN* 10, 37

here-wedys *n* armor *P3A* 201

heryet(t) *v* dragged, carried *P3A* 66, 427

heste *n* promise *P3A* 178

hete, hetys *v* order, ask, promise *WW* 211, 279; *P3A* 643

hethyng *n* shame, scorn *WW* 68

heuele *adv* evilly *In* 20; *BW* 3, 73

hic *pron* I *TN* 7

highte, hiht *v* promised *P3A* 204; *CJ* 123

hil(l)ede *v* concealed, covered *WW* 76; *P3A* 93

hod *n* hood *CT* 77; *MM* 83

hoe (*see* heo)

hokes *n* hooks *P3A* 53

holt(e) *n* woodland *WW* 50, 70, 404; *P3A* 57; *DL* 55

homelyde *v* cut *P3A* 90

hon *prep* in, on *In* 1

hongren *v* starve, be hungry *F* 33

hontin *v* hunt *Als* 561

hore *n* sin *JM* 124

hore *a* white *DL* 31

houen, houes *v* approach, move *WW* 105, 123, 143; *P3A* 215

houpbreide *v* upbraid *Als* 42

howes *n* hoods *WW* 150, 314

hud *v* hidden, concealed *In* 19

hul, hulle *n* hill *In* 79; *CJ* 146, 271

hurcle, hurkles *v* crouch(es) *WW* 14; *P3A* 19

hy (*see* heo)

hy, hyes, hyen, hyeghte; hyede, etc *v* hasten, come; hurried *WW* 12, 453, 467; *P3A* 59, 60, 213, etc; *DL* 199, 386

hye *n* haste *CT* 265

hynde (*see* hende)

hyne, hynds *n* retainers, servants *WW* 212, 438; *DL* 279

hyrne *n* corner *WW* 238

i *prep* in *CJ* 167, 307

i-bet *v* relieved *JM* 188

icheon, ichone *pron* each one *WW* 6, 62

i-core *v* relieved *JM* 118, 172

i-diht *v* prepared, constructed *G* 3

i-fayned *v* imitated *CN* 74

i-fere, i-feere *adv* together, in company, simultaneously *TN* 9; *JM* 56, 74

i-kud *v* known *Als* 19

i-liche *adv* similarly *P3A* 113

ilke, ylk *a* each, same, that *Als* 551; *BW* 27; *DL* 262; *CNII* 39, 56; *JM* 73

i-loced *v* determined *G* 4

i-maked *v* created *TN* 35

i-meten *v* measured *G* 3

i-mynt *v* marked out *G* 2

interly *adv* entirely *BW* 84

i-pricked *v* clothed, adorned *Als* 24

i-schent *v* destroyed *TN* 169; *JM* 203

i-tinbred *v* constructed *G* 7

i-wend *v* transformed *TN* 170

i-wenestou *v* + *pron* do you think *Als* 337

iwis, iwisse, i-wys(e) *adv* indeed, certainly *CN* 40, 127, 163, 179; *MR* 49; *CT* 15

iye *n* eyes *NK* 31 (*also see* eghne)

joitt *n* jolt *AW* 15

jyngland v jiggling, jingling *AW* 15

kaitiffe (*see* caytef)

kaple *n* pack horse *P3A* 189

kayre(n) (*see* cayre)

kelde *a* cold *F* 11

ken, kennest; kende *v* know, teach; informed *WW* 462, 479; *P3A* 553; *DL* 131; JM 95

kene *a* eager *In* 5

kepeþ, kepide *v* opposes; kept, detained *TN* 16; *P3A* 353

kere, kyreth; kered *v* go, move; went *DL* 47, 118

kerpede (*see* carpe)

kerue *v* carve *SI* 113

kest *v* cast, turned *P3A* 68

keuduart *n* rascal (?) *P3A* 68

kiluarde *a* treacherous *P3A* 516

kinde, kynde *n* inclination, nature *Als* 369; *MM* 74; *NK* 4

kirtle *n* gown *DL* 83, 89

knawe *n* knave, servant *MR* 20

kneuz *v* knew *CJ* 319

knoppe *n* nob, button *WW* 81

kweynte *a* skillful *Als* 19

kyd *a* renown *P3A* 441, 458, etc

kydde *v* known, reputed *WW* 315

kyreth (*see* kere)

kystes *n* chests *WW* 255

kyth(e) *n* country, land, people *WW* 124, 199, 416; *P3A* 466, 493; *DL* 47, 436

kythe *n* law, custom *WW* 134

kythe, kithen *v* make known *WW* 104, 218; *P3A* 168; *DL* 391

lache *v* catch, take *WW* 406; *P3A* 211, 239

laghe (*see* laye)

lake *v* disparage *CT* 132

lake *n* wicked custom *DL* 302

lande, launde *n* meadow, lawn *WW* 48, 54, 209; *P3A* 24, 199

laped *v* covered *WW* 111

lare *n* teaching, learning *CT* 47; *CJ* 110

large *a* generous *Als* 91

largeliche *adv* generously *Als* 60

larges *n* generosity *CN* 156

las *v* gathered, collected *Als* 380

laste *adv* least *P3A* 283

lastest *v* slander *TN* 107

lasyd *v* laced, fastened *PB* 79

lauȝt, laughte *v* took, seized *Als* 219; *WW* 286; *P3A* 52

law *a* low *CT* 170

lawe (*see* lowe)

lawryr *n* laurel *MN* 6

lawhe, lawth, lowe *v* laugh *CNII* 82; *MM* 36; *D* 23

lay(e) *n* law, faith *P3A* 198; *CJ* 16, 30, 263

layke *n* sport *P3A* 49

layke *v* amuse (himself) *P3A* 259

laythe *a* ugly, loathsome *P3A* 152

le *n* lie *CT* 222

leake *n* pleasure *DL* 249

leche *n* physician *Als* 470; *JM* 90; *TN* 151

lede, leed; ledis, ledys *n* man; men *WW* 88, 108; *P3A* 106, 152; *DL* 315

lede *n* language, speech *Als* 22

ledis *v* leads *WW* 148

leem *n* light *JM* 125

leer (*see* lere)

leeue (*see* leue)

lefe *v* leave *BW* 54

leid *v* put aside *Als* 468

lek *v* locked, closed *Als* 607

lele *a* splendid *P3A* 115

lelely, lelly *adv* loyally *WW* 430; *P3A* 274

lemede *v* shined *Als* 540

lemman *n* lover, paramour, sweet-heart *WW* 428; *P3A* 174; *TF* 20

lene *a* lean *TN* 159; *MM* 71

lengen, lenged *v* linger, tarry *P3A* 199, 655

leode *n* people *CJ* 133

leof, leoue *a* dear, valued *JM* 1, 146

leom *n* gleem *CJ* 238

lere (*see* lyre)

lere, lerre, leer; lered *v* teach, learn; taught *WW* 223; *CT* 184; *JM* 11, 52; *MR* 11; *Als* 202; *CJ* 196, 264

lergeness *n* generosity *MN* 84

les(e) *a* untruthful *TN* 67

lesyng, lesinge(s) *n* lie; falsehoods *TN* 130; *CNI* 44; *CN* 283; *CNII* 21, 40

let, lette, lettyn *v* hinder(ed) *JM* 125; *PB* 46, 47

iete *v* allowed *Als* 250

leþi *a* wicked *CN* 14

leuede *v* left, abandoned *WW* 286

leuedi, leuedy *n* lady *In* 92; *TN* 25

leue(n), leeue, leuest, levyst *v* believe (in) *Als* 600; *WW* 259; *CJ* 69, 304; *CNI* 27; *F* 25; *MR* 81

leuere *a* dearer, preferable *P3A* 199, 277

ley *v* lay *WW* 234

lewed(e) *a* foolish, ignorant *JM* 36; *MR* 3, 97

lidder *a* evil *DL* 249

lien *v* lie, recline *Als* 242

likame *n* body *P3A* 275

likne *v* liken, compare *MM* 57

linde *n* linden tree *Als* 242

list(e) *v* choose, wish *P3A* 168, 588; *MM* 44

lite *a* light, soft *Als* 181

liþe *a* terrible *In* 77

lo, loo *interj* behold *CJ* 34; *MM* 13

lod *n* load, burden *Als* 609

lodli, lodly *a* foul, loathsome *Als* 567; *DL* 162

lodli, lodly *adv* foully *Als* 247, 277

lofte *a* high, aloft *WW* 150, 163, 332

loge; lugede *v* lodge, dwell; sheltered *P3A* 542, 663

lokyng *n* glance *CNI* 71

lomes *n* equipment *WW* 234

longes *v* belongs *CT* 7

loppes *n* fleas (?) *BW* 165

lore *n* teaching, learning, knowledge *CN* 259; *JM* 36, 52, 77; *CJ* 264; *F* 25

lor(e)n *v* lost *Als* 7; *JM* 168; *CJ* 72, 110

lotes *n* lots *Als* 27

loþ *a* hateful, spiteful, disagreeable *F* 25; *TN* 50

lotheliche *a* loathsome *DL* 374

louely *adv* lowly, humbly *JM* 78

louerd *n* lord *In* 63

loute; loutted, lowted *v* bow; inclined, bent *Als* 295; *P3A* 52; *DL* 70, 116, 334

louue *a* low *In* 47

lowe, lawe *n* cave, mound, hill *Als* 567; *WW* 49

lowe *v* (*see* lawhe)

lure *n* loss, disaster *P3A* 323

lustne *v* listen *JM* 78

lustes *n* pleasures, delights *BW* 215

luþer *a* worthless *JM* 90

luþernes *n* wickedness *CJ* 287

lyame *n* leash *P3A* 38, 61

lympe *v* happen *WW* 369

lympes *v* is obliged *WW* 449

lumpis *v* pawn *WW* 284

lyre, lere *n* face, complexion *WW* 415; *DL* 170

lys *v* lies, belongs *MM* 39

lyte *a* little *BW* 45

lythe *n* people, vassals *P3A* 185, 207

lythe *v* listen *CT* 225

makande *v* making (building) *P3A* 278

make *n* make *WW* 446

malt *v* speak *CJ* 97

maner *n* manor house *CJ* 155

marche *n* region *P3A* 151

marlelyng *v* fertilizing with marl (lime) *P3A* 142

maseere *n* drinking bowl *CJ* 218

mauger *prep* inspite of *DL* 316

mawes *n* stomachs, mouths *WW* 355

mawkes *n* maggots (snails ?) *BW* 112

maȝne *n* might *WW* 166

meanye (*see* meyne)

mede, meede *n* reward, recompense *Als* 239; *BW* 63; *MM* 8; *TN* 64, 159

medlet *v* mingled, mixed *JM* 83

meete *a* fitted-out *CJ* 155

mefed *v* moved, incited, recited *BW* 4, 208, 213

mekill, mekyll (*see* michele)

mekyd *v* kneeled *BW* 13

mell, melleste *v* speak, tell *WW* 264; *BW* 158

mendys *n* amends *P3A* 359

mene *n* prayer *BW* 201

mene *n* a means *CT* 133

mene *a* mean, common, poor *MM* 10

menge *v* mix *P3A* 592

mensken *n* honor, courtesy *F* 22

menskfully *adv* gracefully *P3A* 114

mene(þ); ment *v* moan; complained *P3A* 160; *F* 20; *In* 8; *TN* 43

merke *a* dark *DL* 406

meruelid *v* marveled *NK* 64

mes *n* mass *CJ* 69

meten *v* measure *G* 6

mete(s) *n* food(s) *NK* 49; *MM* 55

meuyd *v* upset *CT* 158

meyne, meanye *n* company of retainers *Als* 416; *DL* 98, 121, 243

michel(e), mikel, mikle, mykel, mykil, mekill, muchelle *a* great, large *Als* 21, 416; *In* 14; *BW* 158; *P3A* 344, 479; *DL* 300; *TN* 158; *CN* 254; *CJ* 26

mid *prep* with *JM* 132

mikel *adv* greatly *In* 22

minde *a* mindful *Als* 371

minned *v* spoke *DL* 349

mis *a* wrong *CJ* 63

mod(e) *n* mind, thoughts, spirit, mood *Als* 230; *In* 3; *CNI* 12, 103

mody; modyere *a* proud, bold; bolder *Als* 5; *P3A* 295, 302, etc

mold(e) *n* earth *P3A* 295; *DL* 134, 163, 290; *CJ* 173; *G* 2, 6

momelide *v* mumbled *P3A* 160

mon(e) *v* must *MN* 68, 69

mone *n* moan, complaint *BW* 87; *CJ* 61

mones *n* man's *TN* 35

moni *a* many *In* 28

monyscyon *n* admonition *BW* 213

mot *n* castle *CJ* 173

mot *n* speck *Als* 155

moten *v* contended *P3A* 105

moten (*see* mow)

mow, mowen, mouwe, moten *v* may, might, be able *Als* 241; *TN* 12; *CJ* 1

mowdewarp *n* mole *BW* 109

muchel(e) (*see* michele)

munnnyng *v* remembering *F* 21

munte *v* think about *F* 21

murþes *n* pleasures, mirths *CJ* 156, 162

musters *n* maneuvers *DL* 277

myche-whate *n* many things *P3A* 105

mykil (*see* michele)

myne *v* remember *P3A* 530

myntid *v* aimed *P3A* 48

mysse *n* misdeeds, sins *P3A* 641; *MR* 30

myster *n* need *WW* 361

name (*see* nim)

nap *n* cup *Als* 150

naytly *adv* exactly, skillfully, fittingly *P3A* 108, 167, 457, 554

nayttede *v* practiced *P3A* 607

neore *v* + *neg* were not *JM* 32

nere *v* + *neg* were not *TN* 34

nese, nesse *n* nose *P3A* 45, 99

neuen; neuened *v* name; named *P3A* 108, 297, 580

neytes *n* nits, lice, eggs *BW* 131

nim; name, nome *v* take; seized *Als* 224, 418; *P3A* 86, 539

niþe *n* malice, hatred, envy *Als* 323; *In* 17

nocht *n* naught *MN* 44

noldest *v* + *neg* would not *MM* 72nome (*see* nim)

nome (*see* nim)

none *n* noon *CT* 65

nones *n* occasion *P3A* 118

nother *conj* neither *NK* 19

noweder *adv* nowhere *Als* 494

noyede *v* annoyed *P3A* 573

nyce, nys, nyse *a* foolish, ignorant *BW* 160; *MM* 34; *MN* 65

nylle *neg* + *v* will not *CNI* 32

o, oo, on *n* one *CN* 177, 209, 236; *CJ* 51; *MM* 7; *NK* 68

o *prep* on *JM* 271

oc *conj* but *Als* 353

ofþunche *v* displease *F* 47

on (*see* o)

onde *n* malice, spite *Als* 323

one *a* only, alone *P3A* 149

oonys *adv* once *MR* 111

or *adv* ere, before *WW* 43; *DL* 140

ore *n* mercy, grace *Als* 596, 618

ouer-brade *a* over-spread *WW* 342

oules *n* awls *Als* 550

oungod *a* un-good *In* 2

ow *pron* you (thou) *JM* 205

owdyr *conj* either *BW* 131

palefreis *n* riding horses *Als* 35; *In* 15

pales *n* palace *WW* 498

palle(s) *n* costly cloths, palls *Als* 30; *CJ* 166

palt *v* push *CJ* 99

pappe; pappis *n* breast(s) *P3A* 176; *DL* 381

parage *n* lofty self-esteem *In* 32

parde, perde *inter* by God (from *par Dieu*) *BW* 71, 72

passis *v* surpasses, overcomes *NK* 4, etc.

pay *n* liking *PB* 36

payes; payed *v* pleases; pleased *WW* 297, 433; *CJ* 291

paynymes *n* paynims (pagans) *P3A* 421

peces *n* pieces *Als* 557

pellour, peloure, pelure *n* fur *WW* 393; *CJ* 166; *D* 5

pelte *v* strike *CT* 10

perde (*see* parde)

peris *n* liking *CN* 277

pergett *v* plaster *WW* 301

perrie, perry(e) *n* jewlry *P3A* 129, 192; *DL* 88

pertly *adv* proudly *WW* 129

pervynke *n* periwinkle *P3A* 9

pike *v* pick, take *Als* 117

piliole *n* wild thyme *P3A* 9

pite *n* pit *Als* 206

playstere *n* healer *P3A* 176

pleid *n* debate *MN* 115

plett *v* embraced *AW* 39

pleyne(d) *v* complain(ed); sung a love-complaint *CN* 73; *PB* 74

plontes *n* plants *WW* 332

plunket *a* light blue *WW* 65

plyght *v* promise *CT* 2

polayle *n* poultry *P3A* 144

poles *n* pools *WW* 235

poo *n* peacock *P3A* 365

porueȝe *v* provide *Als* 391

pourpul, pourpre *n* purple cloths, silks *In* 15; *CJ* 166

poynte *n* deed *P3A* 380

praye *n* prey, booty *P3A* 341

preiȝe *n* prize *MM* 7; *JM* 147

preiȝe *v* pray *Als* 466

pres(s)e *n* throng; company of knights *P3A* 368, 612; *DL* 52, 203

prest (*see* priste)

preue *a* proud *BW* 164

pris *a* valuable, costly *In* 15

pris, prys *n* prize, price, value *TN* 142; *JM* 54; *CJ* 6, 23

priste, prest *a* eager, esteemed *Als* 536; *WW* 169; *P3A* 421, 618

pristly, prestlye *adv* eagerly *P3A* 241; *DL* 203, 306

prou, prowe *n* profit, benefit, advantage *JM* 21

pufilis *n* furs *P3A* 144

purfiled *v* edged, bordered *D* 5

pyne *n* pain *P3A* 555; *CJ* 80, 100

pyssemoure *n* ant *BW* 111

qnaue *n* knave *MR* 97

qued *n* sin, the Evil One, misfortune *Als* 218, 619

quelle *v* kill *MR* 71

quik *a* living *CJ* 191

quintfull *a* haughty *DL* 155

quite *a* free *Als* 183

quite *v* rewarded *Als* 208

quoynte *a* gay *Als* 412

racches (*see* ratches)

radde *n* fear *P3A* 429

radly(e) (*see* redely)

rafte *v* robbed *Als* 342

railinge (*see* rayling)

rakill *a* rash *P3A* 481

rank *a* profuse *MM* 2

rapes; rapt *v* moves quickly, alters; carried away *CJ* 285; *BW* 25

rassif *v* exchanges *MN* 76

ratches *n* hunting dogs *Als* 563

ratons *n* rats *WW* 254

raþe *adv* early, soon *JM* 40, 44; *CJ* 228

raught(en) *v* grasp; reached, extended *WW* 42; *P3A* 29, 75

rawnsede *v* ransomed (freed) *P3A* 414

rayled(e) *v* adorned, decorated *WW* 60, 343; *P3A* 119, 128

rayling, railinge *a* bright, decorative *DL* 24, 376

rech(e), rechen *v* care (about) *WW* 363; *TN* 191

reche *v* reach *JM* 24

red(e), reed *n* advice, counsel *Als* 224; *In* 13; *CNII* 53; *F* 29, 41

rede *v* advise, instruct, counsel *TN* 27; *CN* 163, 236; *CNII* 64, 86; *PB* 117; *JM* 44; *MM* 78; *MR* 13, 59; *CT* 59

redely, radly(e) *adv* readily, promptly *P3A* 107, 166, 556; *DL* 355; *CJ* 116, 150

redomyt *a* adorned, wreathed *MN* 77

reed (*see* rede)

refte *v* bereft of *P3A* 563

rehet *n* refreshment *CJ* 224

reken; rekened *v* count; recounted *P3A* 107, 141

reme *v* weep *WW* 258

renke(s) *n* man, men *WW* 23, 100, 270; *P3A* 137, 253

reowe (*see* rewen)

res *n* course *CJ* 285

reuliche *adv* roughly, rudely *Als* 504

reuly *a* sad *Als* 477

reuþfele *a* sorrowful *In* 3

rewe(n), reowe, rewed, rewyth *v* rew, regret, take pity, be merciful *Als* 622; *P3A* 562; *CNII* 56; *PB* 94; *F* 29; *D* 28

rewest *v* take away, deprive *TN* 154

rewlithe *v* rules *SI* 38

rewthe *n* pity *WW* 258

reykin *v* wander *Als* 359

reynand, reynawnde *a* reigning *BW* 3, 158

rial *a* royal *CJ* 224

rigge, rygge *n* backbone *P3A* 78, 87

rihtwys *a* rightful, just *CJ* 16

rise *n* rose bush (?), trellice (?) *DL* 66

ritt(e) *v* cut, rip *P3A* 73, 75

ro *n* repose, rest *Als* 311, 316; *CJ* 95; *F* 30

rode, rood(e) *n* cross, rood *WW* 343; *P3A* 555; *DL* 377; *CT* 36; *CJ* 90, 227

rosett *n* russet *P3A* 261

rothelede *v* spoke (?) *P3A* 261

roue *a* rough, hairy *Als* 505

roune *n* song *TN* 2

roungen *v* rang *WW* 39

rout (*see* rowte)

rouʒtest *v* cared *Als* 67

rowmly *adv* roomily, amply *P3A* 137

rowte, rout *n* company *WW* 202, 270; *DL* 146, 200, 251

rudd *n* face *DL* 66

ryall *a* royal *SI* 84

ryally *adv* royally *NK* 49

ryfe *a* rife, numbers *WW* 258

rygalte *n* rule *P3A* 598

ryk *n* realm CJ 307

ryme *v* clear away *WW* 289

sade, sadde *a* heavy, sober, solid *WW* 146, 193; *P3A* 333

sadlye *adv* quietly *DL* 322

sale *n* hall *CJ* 172

salust *v* salute *MN* 18

samen *adv* together *WW* 360

sandisman *n* messenger, envoy *WW* 204

sare *adv* sorrowfully *MR* 12

sawe(s) *n* saying(s), proverb(s), speech *WW*
11, 67; *P3A* 602; *TN* 95; *JM* 2; *MR* 29; *CT* 169

sawter *n* psalter *BW* 140

say(e)d *v* slumbered *DL* 36, 454

schake *v* rush *WW* 403

schalkes *n* men, warriors *WW* 317, 432

schap *n* creature *Als* 580

schawe(s), shawe *n* woods, grove *WW* 53, 403; *P3A* 4; *TN* 124, 179

schenchipe *n* ignominy *WW* 432

schene *a* beautiful, bright *CNI* 16; *CJ* 156, 210; *MN* 113; *PB* 66

schent *v* destroyed *WW* 317

schewere *n* mirror *P3A* 291

schille *a* shrill *CJ* 181

schiltrons *n* squadrons *WW* 53

schire *a* bright, clear *CJ* 210

schirle *adv* completely *P3A* 646

schone *n* shoes *CT* 3, 66

schone, schonn *v* shun *Als* 346; *WW* 432

schop(e) *v* shaped, created, made *Als* 185, 581; *CJ* 54, 283

schrew *v* curse *CT* 215

schreyf (*see* schriue)

schride *v* clothe *Als* 413

schrides *n* lace *D* 6

schriue, schreyf *v* shrive, confess *CJ* 313; *MR* 15

schunte *v* avoid, shun *P3A* 291

scripcion *n* description *BW* 209

sectours, sektours *n* executors *Als* 113; *WW* 302, 443

see *n* seat *JM* 7, 184

see *n* sea *CJ* 3

seere, sere *a* many *WW* 3; *P3A* 162, 254, 489

sege *n* seat *WW* 483; *P3A* 470

segge(s) *n* man, men *WW* 89, 137, 192, etc; *P3A* 135, 126, 471

seiss *v* cease *MN* 33

sekatours (*see* sectours)

sekire *a* certain *P3A* 635

selcouth *a* wondrous *DL* 96

selco(u)thes n marvels, strange happenings *WW* 3; *P3A* 501; *DL* 181

seled *v* sealed *WW* 146

selly *a* strange, marvelous *Als* 3; *WW* 99

semede *v* cared for *TN* 116

semely, semeli *a* pleasing, impressive *CJ* 58; *MR* 120

semet *v* seems, appears *Als* 199

sendell *n* silk *WW* 180

senke *v* poured out *Als* 516

seo *v* see *JM* 145

ser *a* sad *Als* 475

serely *adv* separately *P3A* 218, 225, 322

serfulli *adv* sorrowfully *Als* 12

seþþe(n) (*see* sith)

seu *v* said? saw? *In* 63

sewes *n* sauces *WW* 381

sewet *v* pursued, followed *P3A* 34, 45

sewte *n* pursuit *P3A* 63

shawe (*see* schawe)

shede *v* distribute *MM* 62

shende, shent *v* ruin, destroy, put to shame *DL* 370; *TN* 11; *CNI* 99

shene *a* bright, beautiful *D* 1

shone *n* shame *TN* 48

side *a* wide, thick *DL* 167

sidre *n* cedar *PB* 19

siker *a* certain *In* 24

sith(e), siþ, seþþen, siþin, sythen *adv* since, after, then, because *Als* 195; *WW* 1, 276; *P3A* 335, 460; *DL* 127, 365; *CJ* 42, 66, 100, 247

siþes *n* times *MR* 118

skathill *a* wicked *WW* 443

skaþe *n* injury, harm *TN* 15

skayled *v* dispersed *P3A* 385

skere *v* keep pure, shield *TN* 15

skille, skylle *n* reason *JM* 47; *CT* 14

skyftede *v* divided *P3A* 383

slome *a* heavy *P3A* 101

slomery *a* slumbery *BW* 206

smoþer *n* dense smoke *Als* 572

snelle *a* quick, active *Als* 41

sodayn *a* sudden *BW* 193

soget *v* subjected *BW* 163

somers *n* sumpter horses *Als* 26

sonde *n* sand *CJ* 19

sonde *n* messenger *CJ* 293

sonde *n* ordinance, command *P3A* 442

soppe *n* sop *P3A* 438

sort *n* lot, chance *PB* 62

sot, sottes *n* fool, fools *P3A* 266; *D* 21

sote *a* sweet, pleasant *PB* 9

soth(e), soþe *n* truth *BW* 188; *WW* 221; *CN* 161; *CJ* 4; *JM* 198

sothely, soþeli *adv* truly *P3A* 568; *BW* 180; *JM* 2, 75

sotted *v* dulled *P3A* 286

sottes *n* fools *P3A* 266

sowpped *v* supped, drank *WW* 215

sownnede *a* sound, safe *P3A* 434

sowre *n* soar (male deer) *P3A* 34, 45

soyle *v* absolve *CJ* 313

spaclyche *adv* especially *F* 29

sparthe *n* halberd *WW* 238

spede *v* succeed, prosper *CT* 174

spedfully *adv* thriftily *WW* 224

spedles *a* worthless *WW* 325

spele *v* spare *Als* 590

spere *v* fasten *Als* 533

spille, spyll, spillest, spilleth *v* kills, wastes *BW* 120; *DL* 208; *TN* 134; *JM* 19

spytterd *n* spider *BW* 112

stalled *v* enstalled *JM* 16

stede *n* place *P3A* 21

steden *n* steeds *In* 15

stelkett *v* moved quickly *P3A* 51

sterue *v* die *MM* 87

steuen *n* voice *DL* 408

stih, stiʒ *n* path *CJ* 149, 153

stintest, stynt(e), styntt; stinted *v* stop; ceased *Als* 123; *WW* 107, 195, 229; *P3A* 268; *DL* 177; *MN* 29; *TF* 36

stirkes *n* heifers *P3A* 147, 190

stotayde *v* paused *P3A* 51

stounde, stownde *n* a while, a period of time *CNII* 56; *CJ* 142; *CT* 21; *BW* 115, 178; *JM* 45

stourre *n* battle *P3A* 272

stre *n* straw *MM* 26

streite *adv* closely, narrowly *Als* 534

strende *n* progeny, offspring *CJ* 74

strif *n* debate, dispute *In* 25; *TN* 7

stroyʒe *v* destroy *MM* 60

stude *n* place, stead *In* 1

sturte *n* stirrings *WW* 265

stynt(e) (*see* stintest)

sueir *a* lazy *MN* 85

suere *v* swear *CT* 36, 206

suerte *n* certainty *SI* 16

sufferayne *n* sovereign *BW* 153

sugge(n) *v* say, tell *TN* 122, 184, 188

sunnes *n* sins *In* 17, 55

swa *adv* so *CJ* 126

swaynes *n* swains, peasants *DL* 54

sweeres *n* swearers (sworn-men) *DL* 54

swerue *v* move, leap *MM* 82

swelt *v* killed *DL* 337

sweuen, sweuynn *n* dream *WW* 46; *P3A* 102

swikel(e) *a* treacherous, deceitful *TN* 38; *In* 21, 23

swire *n* neck *DL* 337

swith, swythe, swiþe *adv* quickly, at once *WW* 46, 320; *P3A* 369, 502; *JM* 77, 87; *CJ* 205

swow *n* swoon *CN* 87, 89

swylk *adv* such *BW* 155

swythe (*see* swith)

swyuyd *v* had sexual intercourse *CNII* 2

syde *a* ample *F* 16

syth(e)n (*see* sith)

tacches *n* habits *CN* 192

tachede *v* attached *P3A* 67

talents *n* talon, claws *DL* 174

tartaryne *n* silken fabric (from Tartary) *P3A* 132

tast *v* test *D* 22

tauȝt *v* directed to *CJ* 78

taysede *v* aimed *P3A* 44

tayttely *adv* swiftly *P3A* 219

te *v* go *TN* 190

teeles, telys *n* teals (small ducks) *WW* 352; *P3A* 219

teenfull *a* sharp *DL* 174

telys (*see* teeles)

teme *v* instruct *Als* 225

tene *n* sorrow *PB* 71

tene, tenys, tenyn; teneden, teened *v* grieve, feel pain; troubled *WW* 247, 341; *P3A* 242, 321; *DL* 391

tenefull *a* peevish

tent; tented *v* take heed, attend; attended *WW* 445; *CJ* 270, 299

ter *n* tear *Als* 477

the, thene, þhe *v* prosper, thrive *CT* 11, 16, 42, etc; *JM* 29

tholed(e) (*see* þolede)

threpe *n* strife, argument *P3A* 268

throw *n* period of time *CT* 195

threpen; threpden, threpid *v* clamor; bickered *WW* 37; *P3A* 14, 104, 262

thro *a* keen, vigorous *P3A* 104

throly *adv* vigorously *WW* 37; *P3A* 14, 133

thrynges *v* moves *P3A* 368

tighte *v* set up, drew *P3A* 44, 79, 361

tiht *a* firm, tight *CJ* 27

tille *prep* to *CJ* 299

titly *adv* quickly *P3A* 613

to *prep* till *WW* 245

to-borste *v* burst asunder *Als* 453

tode *n* toad *Als* 555

ton . . . toþer *pron* the one . . . the other *CJ* 17, 25

tone *v* taken *MN* 102

tope *n* head *CT* 188

tord *n* turd *CT* 110

to-rent *v* torn *Als* 550

tortoys *n* tortoise *BW* 108

toþer (*see* ton)

touch *n* quality, characteristic *NK* 11

tounen *v* tune (i.e. play a tune) *WW* 358

tounnes *n* tuns, casks *WW* 189

towrenche *v* tear apart *Als* 446

toyled *v* pulled *Als* 504

to-ȝain *adv* against *Als* 173

travall *n* labor *MN* 116

triste *a* trustworthy *P3A* 564, 624

tristly *adv* valiantly *P3A* 326

troches *n* points of the antlers *P3A* 67

trompers *n* trumpet-players *WW* 358

trone *n* throne *CJ* 53

trouwe, trow(es), trowys(t); trowede *v* believe, think, trust; believed *P3A* 604; *CJ* 53, 62, 124; *CT* 105, 108, 124; *BW* 70; *MM* 86; *MR* 58, 97

trynes *v* hurries *WW* 122

tulke *n* man *P3A* 313

tuly *a* red *WW* 82

turnes *n* tricks *DL* 249

tushes *n* tusks, fangs *DL* 168

tuttynge *a* flaring *WW* 82

twey *num* two *CT* 58; *CJ* 7

tyde *n* time *CJ* 193

tylere *n* stock *P3A* 44

tyne, tynt *v* lose, lost *CJ* 112; *MN* 31

tynen *v* harrow *WW* 288

þei(h) *adv* though *In* 42; *JM* 51

þester *a* dark *In* 1

þey *conj* although *TN* 21

þhe (*see* the)

þider *adv* thither *CJ* 176

þo *adv* when, then *In* 3

þoled(e), tholed(e) *v* suffered, endured *Als* 335, 460, 617; *P3A* 403; *DL* 1

þral *n* slave *Als* 340
þraste *v* thrust *Als* 519
þreten *v* threaten *In* 31
þriuen *v* thriving *Als* 309
þro *a* strong *Als* 309
þulke *a* that *CJ* 30
þunne *a* thin, weak *Als* 366

vayle *v* avail *JM* 182
vchon *pron* each one *JM* 210
vestueris *n* clothing *SI* 22
vmbe *a* around *P3A* 657
vmbestounde *adv* sometimes *WW* 100
vmbtourne *a* around *WW* 412
vmbycaste *v* wander around *P3A* 61
vmbygon(e) *v* encircle(d) *WW* 62, 118
vndernomen *v* undertaken *Als* 357
vndire-ȝode *v* undermined *P3A* 283
vnhap *n* misfortune *Als* 146
vnheh, vnheȝe *a* un-high, low *G* 8, 9
vnlust *n* sloth *Als* 325
vnneþe *adv* scarcely *Als* 84
vnrid(e) *a* cruel *Als* 63; *DL* 171
vnsele *n* misfortune *P3A* 438
vntid, vntiȝt, vntiȝth *n* vice, sin, evil *Als* 135, 222, 349
vnwrest *a* weak *Als* 318
vp-braid *v* criticize *WW* 426
vp-brayde *v* raised, taken up *WW* 149, 208
vtteraunce *n* (the) beginning *BW* 88
vttire *adv* farther; entirely; out *WW* 468; *P3A* 66, 381
vysment *n* counsel *CT* 25

walawo, weilavei *interj* woe, alas *Als* 13; *In* 105
wale *a* pleasant, short, swift *WW* 34, 396, 460
walt *v* wielded *WW* 420
waltered *v* tossed *WW* 248
wane *v* diminished *MM* 61
war *v* aware *CJ* 227
wardone *n* recompense *BW* 56
warnestorede *v* provisioned *P3A* 412
warrant *v* preserve *DL* 206
waryed (*see* weryed)
warysowne *n* payment *BW* 127
wast *v* wasted *TF* 46
wayn *n* wain, wagon *Als* 467
wayt; waytted *v* guard; watched *WW* 213; *P3A* 99, 657; *DL* 48

waytten *v* know *WW* 257
webbe *n* banner *WW* 64
wed *n* compact, pledge *CJ* 266
wede(s), wedis, weddis, weeds *n* clothing *Als* 33, 529; *WW* 284, 420, 426; *DL* 185; *MM* 54
weder, wedres *n* weather *P3A* 2; *MM* 57
weder *conj* whether *TN* 191
wedres (*see* weder)
weene (*see* wene)
weile *interj* woe, alas *Als* 13
weilavei (*see* welawo)
wele *n* wealth, possessions, goods; happiness *Als* 588; *WW* 236, 268, etc; *P3A* 149, 175, 637; *TN* 8, 47
wemles *a* spotless *CJ* 41
wend(en), wendes *v* change, turn, go *Als* 230, 418; *WW* 104, 198; *P3A* 3, 37, etc; *TN* 81; *CNI* 68; *CJ* 77
wend(e) *v* think, expect *In* 20; *MR* 50, 130
wene, weene *v* know, expect, think *WW* 186; *DL* 344; *CNII* 26, 58; *CJ* 211
wenestouȝ *v* + *pron* do you think *Als* 205
werdes *n* chances *P3A* 3
werped(e) *v* woven, filled *WW* 64, 250
werre *n* war *WW* 497
weryed, waryed *a* accursed *WW* 242; *P3A* 336
wet(e), wette, wiete *v* know *WW* 200, 366; *CNI* 95; *MR* 4; *NK* 38
whilom, whylome *adv* once, formerly *In* 3, 33; *WW* 20
whyne *adv* whence *BW* 166
widdis *n* woods *MN* 19
wiete (*see* wete)
wight *a* quick *DL* 217
wightly *adv* quickly *WW* 104
wijs (*see* wys)
wikkedehed *n* wickedness *Als* 76, 362
wil *n* resolve *D* 22
wilnes *v* desires *WW* 216
wilsom *a* remote (?) *BW* 8
winlye *a* lovely, blissful, happy *DL* 45, 75, 80, 428
winn(e) *a* blissful, joyful *DL* 5, 129, 293
winne, wynne *n* possessions, pleasure, joy *Als* 76, 362; *CNI* 62; *F* 14
wise *n* manner, respect *Als* 419
wisse, wistist; wist(e) *v* know; knew *Als* 188, 345, 369, 399; *WW* 47, 120; *P3A* 507

wit *n* wisdom, reason *JM* 24, 81, 82; *CJ* 62

wit *n* blame *Als* 259

wite(n), witt, wyte, witeþ *v* teach, know *DL* 120, 130; *TN* 123; *JM* 110, 121, 153; *MR* 4; *CT* 27

witerli, wittirly *adv* certainly, precisely, full well *In* 96; *WW* 200, 389

wod, woed *a* crazy, mad, wild *Als* 16; *TN* 73, 181; *WW* 373

wodwales *n* woodpeckers *WW* 351

wodwyse *n* wild man of the forest *WW* 71

wolde *v* would *JM* 110

wold(e) *n* power; realm *Als* 360; *CJ* 64

wolle *n* wool *WW* 250

won, wones *n* dwelling; buildings *Als* 171, 569; *CJ* 202

wond *n* reed *Als* 367

wonde, wondes *v* cease; hesitates *JM* 5; *P3A* 611, 632

wone *v* won, defeated *CJ* 62

wone *n* custom, habit *Als* 326, 352

woned *v* accustomed *Als* 17, 563

won(n)es, wonie, wonynge; wonnede *v* dwell(s), dwelling; lived *Als* 496; *WW* 245, 280, 385; *P3A* 193, 603; *CT* 43; *CJ* 307

woning *n* dwelling *Als* 167, 169

wordly *adv* worthily *Als* 339

worschype, worship *n* repute *CT* 214; *NK* 3

worth, worthe(s), worthen *v* becomes, turns (to) *WW* 130, 253; *P3A* 461, 485, 496, etc; *DL* 9, 248

worttes *n* vegetables *WW* 346

wost, woost, wot(e) *v* know *Als* 264; *CN* 40; *CNI* 14; *MR* 45, 153; *CT* 96

wothe *n* danger *P3A* 37

wouȝ *a* evil *Als* 438

wowe *n* wall(s) *In* 51; *TN* 57

wrac, wrake, wreche *n* vengeance, punishment, harm *Als* 472, 512; *WW* 198; *JM* 5, 20, 101

wre *v* embrace *TN* 58

wreche (*see* wrac)

wrethyn *a* twisted *WW* 71

wriche *n* wretch *WW* 309, 424

wriþinde *v* wavering *Als* 367

wrocht, wroghte *v* wrought, created, made *WW* 25, 296; *MN* 44

wrothely *adv* angrily *WW* 324

wroþe *a* wroth, angry *F* 39

wryeth *v* deceives, conceals *WW* 6

wryghede *v* discovered *P3A* 97

wurdli *a* valuable *Als* 33

wusten *v* knew *JM* 210

wy; wyes *n* man; men *WW* 8, 56, 120, etc; *P3A* 193

wyde-whare *adv* far and wide *WW* 257, 326

wyl *n* wile *Als* 446

wynne (*see* winne)

wynne *v* go *NK* 43

wys, wijs, wysses *v* guide(s) *WW* 226; *MR* 126, 190

wyse *n* manner, fashion *WW* 75, 110; *DL* 110; *BW* 65

wyte (*see* wite)

yerne *a* iron *DL* 185

y-mint *v* intended *Als* 92

ynewe *a* enough *WW* 280, 405

yorne *adv* eagerly *DL* 250

y-spilt *v* killed, destroyed *Als* 175

y-stint *v* ended, stopped *Als* 94

ythand *a* steady, constant *MN* 115

ȝape; ȝapest *a* skillful, vigorous; liveliest *WW* 75, 119; *P3A* 134, 171, 270

ȝare *adv* readily *CJ* 273

ȝare *adv* yore, long ago *TN* 42; *CJ* 45

ȝarked *v* made *WW* 75

ȝeem *n* care, heed *JM* 129

ȝeme *v* care for, protect, guard *Als* 195; *WW* 114, 152, 376, 419

ȝenede *v* yawned *Als* 539

ȝeply *adv* vigorously *CJ* 320

ȝernd *v* yearned for *Als* 459

ȝerne *n* yarn *CT* 207

ȝerne *adv* earnestly, readily, vigorously *Als* 614; *P3A* 34, 104, 227, etc

ȝett *v* granted, surrendered *P3A* 398, 535, 575

ȝeue *v* give *CJ* 103

ȝing *a* young *JM* 51, 96

ȝode *v* walked, went *CJ* 226

ȝol *n* Yule *CJ* 45

ȝolden *v* yielded *P3A* 398

ȝonde *a* yonder *CJ* 34

ȝonge *v* go *In* 84

ȝore *a* long *Als* 598

ȝoten *v* poured *Als* 514

ȝwilene *adv* for a time, once *Als* 16